Francis Bowen

A Treatise on Logic or the Laws of Pure Thought

Compromising both the Aristotelic and Hamiltonian Analyses of Logical Forms...

Francis Bowen

A Treatise on Logic or the Laws of Pure Thought
Compromising both the Aristotelic and Hamiltonian Analyses of Logical Forms...

ISBN/EAN: 9783337228484

Printed in Europe, USA, Canada, Australia, Japan

Cover: Foto ©Thomas Meinert / pixelio.de

More available books at **www.hansebooks.com**

A TREATISE ON

LOGIC,

OR,

THE LAWS OF PURE THOUGHT;

COMPRISING BOTH

THE ARISTOTELIC AND HAMILTONIAN
ANALYSES OF LOGICAL FORMS,

AND SOME CHAPTERS OF

APPLIED LOGIC.

BY FRANCIS BOWEN,
ALFORD PROFESSOR OF MORAL PHILOSOPHY IN HARVARD COLLEGE.

"Nam neque decipitur ratio, nec decipit uuquam."
MANILIUS.

CAMBRIDGE:
SEVER AND FRANCIS,
BOOKSELLERS TO THE UNIVERSITY.
1865.

PREFACE.

THE revival of the study of Logic, at least in England and America, as an important element of a University education, dates only from the publication of Dr. Whately's treatise on the subject, little over thirty years ago. Yet so much has been accomplished for the advancement of the science during this short period, that this treatise, with all its excellences, must be admitted to be now as far behind the times as were the compilation by Aldrich, and the meagre compendium by Dr. Watts, the use of which it superseded. Dr. Whately lived long enough to be able to appropriate to himself the epigrammatic boast, that he had labored so effectually as to render his own work useless. Without the interest which was awakened in the study of the science by the publication of his book and the discussions which it excited, it is not too much to say that many of the valuable works upon Logic, which have appeared during the last thirty years, either would not have been written, or would have lacked some of their most interesting and important features. Sir William Hamilton's own labors in this department, by which he certainly accomplished more for the science than has been done by any one man since Aristotle, began with an elaborate article on Dr. Whately's treatise in the Edinburg Review, a paper which, as he has himself declared, contains the germs of all his subsequent discoveries. Besides what Hamilton has accomplished, the publications within this period of Professor Mansel, Dr. Thomson, Mr. De Morgan, Mr. Boole, Mr. J. S. Mill, and a host of others, have given an entirely new aspect to the science. Among recent American works upon Logic, honorable mention ought to be made of those by Mr. Tappan, and by Dr. W. D. Wilson of Geneva.

The only hope that this volume may be found to be of some use consists in the fact, that, as I was the last to enter the field, I have been able to profit by the labors of my predecessors. Certainly it could not have been written without their aid, and one of the chief objects held in view in the preparation of it has been to gather together, and digest into system, their several improvements and elucidations of the science. At the same time, the work would not have been carried on in the same spirit in which they began it, if I had not ventured respectfully to dissent from some of their doctrines, and even to present some opinions which will very likely be found to have no other merit than that of originality. As Le Clerc remarks, in introducing his own lucid and thoughtful compendium of the science to the reader's notice, " *si, in haece Logica, nihil esse novi, aut pleraque nova dixerim, lectorem perinde fefellero.*"

When Dr. Whately wrote, it was not so frequent a practice as it has since become for English scholars to profit by the labors of their German brethren, and hence some of the greatest deficiencies of his book. It cannot be said that the study of Logic ever declined in the schools of Germany, as it did in those of France, England, and this country. Upheld for a time by the genius of Leibnitz and the indefatigable industry of Wolff, it was at last reduced to rigorous system, its boundaries were fixed, and its relations to Psychology and Metaphysics accurately determined, by the master mind of Kant. Though this great Metaphysician prepared no distinct work upon the subject, the volume relating to it which passes under his name being a mere compilation from his loose notes by Jasche, the science has profited more by his labors than by those of any other Continental writer of modern times. Indeed, the publication of his "Criticism of Pure Reason" formed hardly less an era in the history of Logic than in that of Metaphysics. In one respect, it is true, it had an injurious influence, as it established the practice, which has since become wellnigh universal in Germany, of modifying the doctrines of this science in order to furnish a basis on which might be erected any peculiar scheme of speculative Philosophy. Since Kant's time, a multitude of treatises upon Logic have been published by German writers, about half of them having no other purpose than that of preparing the way, and furnishing the materials, for some extravagant speculations in Metaphysics. This mode of treatment was carried to an outrageous extent by Hegel, who labored to break down altogether the boundary that had been established by Kant, and whose elaborate work, bearing the name of Logic, is a mere perversion and caricature of that science, as it is metaphysical from beginning to end. Even Trendelenburg, who has contributed more than any other person to the rapid decline of Hegelianism in Germany, is not free from blame in this respect, his very able work, *Logische Untersuchungen*, being devoted in great part to building up a philosophical system of his own.

But the very prevalence of this abuse in Germany furnishes an additional motive for the study of the subject. A key to German Metaphysics can be obtained only by a thorough mastery of the principles and the terminology of Logic. To some persons, perhaps, this consideration may not have much weight, as they will object, that it is of little use to be able to open the door, if the room contains little more than rubbish. Still I cannot but believe — and the opinion is founded on considerable experience as an instructor in both departments — that a fair knowledge of Logic is a natural, and even an indispensable, preparation for the successful pursuit of Psychology and Metaphysics; — may I not add, of any philosophical speculations whatever? It appears certain, that the University lectures of Kant, Fichte, Schelling, and Hegel could not have been made even intelligible, much less instructive, to hearers who had not previously acquired at least the elements of Logical science. Hence the multitude of manuals and text-books upon this subject, which have appeared in Germany during the last three quarters of a century, many of them having passed through numerous editions, and each betraying very plainly the particular system of Philosophy to which it was intended to serve as an introduction. Some familiarity with the principles of Logic appears essential for a thorough comprehension even of the metaphysical doctrines of Sir William Hamilton, which, both in their philosophical and theological bearings, seem likely to exert a considerable influence over English and American minds for many years to come.

PREFACE.

Hamilton's "Lectures on Logic" are marked with the inevitable defects of a posthumous publication, the larger portion of which was probably never intended by the author to be given to the public; and though very ably edited by Professor Mansel and Mr. Veitch, they present a mass of crude material from which a knowledge of the peculiar doctrines of the writer cannot be extracted but with considerable difficulty. Indeed, the "Lectures," which form the body of the book, were evidently prepared in great haste, when the author's appointment to the Professorship in this department, in 1836, obliged him to collect at short notice the materials for an extended course of instruction. He appears to have met this sudden call by hurriedly translating a series of extracts from the most approved German text-books, especially those of Krug, Esser, and Bachmann, merely interpolating here and there some of the comments, corrections, and additions which could not fail to occur to so rich a mind as his, while traversing so broad and familiar a field. These Lectures, containing only a glimpse of one feature of the peculiar system which has since become identified with his name, he seems to have repeated from year to year, during his whole period of office, with no material enlargement or alteration of the manuscript, though doubtless inserting, from year to year, many extemporaneous expositions of his corrections of the leading doctrines of Logical science, as these occurred to him at successive periods. The whole transaction seems to me to afford an instructive comment on the futility of what is called the Professorial mode of teaching, which has always prevailed in the University of Edinburgh, and which consists in getting up very hastily a course of lectures during the teacher's first year of office, and repeating them, parrot-like, from year to year, without any regular use of a text-book or manual of instruction. If such lectures contain anything really valuable, in addition to what is already before the world, they are apt very soon to find their way to the press; if they are of little worth, they are almost sure to be repeated, with little alteration, to one class after another, and with as little profit to the hearer as exercise to the reader. It may be doubted whether the most fertile and best-trained minds, at least in the speculative sciences, are capable of preparing every year an entirely new course of lectures, without either filling them with crudities and truisms, or lapsing into paradox and extravagance, such as have too frequently characterized the productions of German Professors.

With all his amazing activity of mind and prodigious erudition, Hamilton appears to have been either too indolent, or too critical of his own labors, to be able, without great delays, to digest his materials into a shape fit for publication. He was not an adept in the very low, but very necessary, art of book-making. But for his controversy with Mr. De Morgan, I doubt whether he would ever have worked up into form as much as he did of his "New Analytic of Logical Forms," the publication of which was promised as far back as 1846. Stimulated by opposition, however, though impeded by ill-health during the later years of his life, he appears to have labored strenuously, after the last-mentioned date, to fulfil this promise. Death surprised him long before he had completed his preparations; and out of the mass of fragmentary materials which were found among his papers, with some aid from the few critical and controversial articles that he had already printed, his editors pieced together, with great difficulty, the imperfect view of his improved system of Logic, which appears as a long Appendix to the volume of his Lectures. The manuscripts which they selected and arranged were judiciously printed just as he left them, and with very little editorial comment. The reader must gather from them as best he may, always keeping in view the date attached to each fragment, a connected view of Sir William Hamilton's latest doctrines upon the subject. This posthumous work has at least one odd characteristic, as the body of the work and the Appendix flatly contradict each other, by giving opposite views of the science to which they relate.

These are the sources whence I have endeavored to collect the materials for a general survey of the science of Logic in its present state, embracing what is common to all systems, and a review of most of the questions relating to it which are still open to discussion. Among English authors, after Sir William Hamilton, I have been chiefly indebted to Professor Mansel; for without the aid afforded by his *Prolegomena Logica*, and the notes and supplementary matter appended to his edition of Aldrich, of which Hamilton justly remarks that *la sauce vaut mieux que le poisson*, this book would have cost me much more labor, and yet would have wanted what are now its best claims to notice. I have also derived much help from the excellent "Outline of the Laws of Thought," by Dr. Thomson, the present Archbishop of York. Among the German writers, besides all whose names have been already mentioned, I have made profitable use of Kiesewetter,

Fries, Beneke, Dressler, and Drobisch, besides consulting a host of others. Of the earlier logicians, it seems to me that Burgersdyck, with the annotations of Heereboord, gives the clearest account of the science as it was taught in the schools before the influence of Descartes and Locke began to be felt; and that the Port Royal "Art of Thinking," of which an admirable translation, with Notes and an Appendix, by Mr. Baynes, has recently been published, is far the best of the treatises on the subject which were in use during the eighteenth century. Throughout the work, I have kept constantly in view the wants of learners, much of it having been first suggested while attempting to expound the science in my own classroom. My highest ambition will be satisfied if it should be found to be of use to other teachers.

CAMBRIDGE, March, 1864.

CONTENTS.

CHAPTER I.

	PAGE
PSYCHOLOGICAL INTRODUCTION	1
Intuitions distinguished from Concepts	1
The Nature of Thought	10
Relations of Thought to Language	16
Mental Characteristics of Brutes	18
The Formation of Concepts	19
Language aids Thought	21
And is often substituted for it	24

CHAPTER II.

DEFINITION OF LOGIC	30
The Form distinguished from the Matter of Thought	31
Universal distinguished from Special Logic	34
Divisions of the Science	36
Utility of the Study of Logic	38

CHAPTER III.

THE PRIMARY AXIOMS OF PURE THOUGHT	47
These Axioms reduced to one Principle	48
This Principle explicated into three Axioms	49
Analytic distinguished from Synthetic Thought	52
The Principle of Synthetic Thought explicated	53
Hamilton's Postulate of Logic	56

CHAPTER IV.

THE DOCTRINE OF CONCEPTS 59
    The Elements of a Concept 62
    The twofold Quantity of Concepts 66
    First and Second Intentions 70
    The Relation of the two Quantities to each other . . . 72
    Infinitated Concepts 75
    The Quality of Concepts 77
    The Standards of Nominal and Real Definition . . . 84
    The Relations of Concepts 86
    The Laws of Homogeneity and Heterogeneity . . . 90
    Definition and Division 93

CHAPTER V.

THE DOCTRINE OF JUDGMENTS 105
    The Nature of the Copula 109
    The Predicables and the Categories 112
    The Quantity of Judgments, Aristotelic Doctrine . . . 120
    The Quality of Judgments, " " . . . 123
    Quantity as affected by Quality, " " . . . 125
    The Relation of Judgments 127
    Conditional Judgments 128
    The Hamiltonian Doctrine of Judgments 132
    Explication of Propositions into Judgments 141

CHAPTER VI.

THE DOCTRINE OF IMMEDIATE INFERENCE 148
    Æquipollence or Infinitation 152
    Conversion 156
    Hamilton's Doctrine of Conversion 160
    Opposition and Integration 162
    Conspectus of Judgments and Immediate Inference, Aristotelic
        Doctrine 166
    Hamilton's Doctrine of Opposition and Integration . . 168

CHAPTER VII.

THE DOCTRINE OF MEDIATE INFERENCE: THE ARISTOTELIC ANAL-
YSIS OF SYLLOGISMS 174
The Canon of Categorical Syllogisms 175
This Canon explicated into Six Rules 180
Dictum de omni et nullo 187
Figure and Mood 190
Reduction to the First Figure 194
The Mood of a Syllogism 197
The Technicalities of Reduction exemplified . . . 202
Conditional Syllogisms 207
Disjunctive Syllogisms 212
Dilemmas or Hypothetico-Disjunctives 215
Defective and Complex Syllogisms 219
Sorites 222
Conspectus of the Aristotelic Doctrine of Syllogisms . . 226

CHAPTER VIII.

THE HAMILTONIAN DOCTRINE OF SYLLOGISMS 228
Analytic and Synthetic Order of Enouncement . . . 228
Reasoning in the two Quantities 234
The Doctrine of the Figures 239
The Unfigured Syllogism 244
Hamilton's System of Notation or Symbolization . . . 246
The Number of Moods increased by Quantifying the Predicate . 251
The worse Relation of Subject and Predicate . . . 253
Hamiltonian Table of Moods 256
Falsity of the Special Rules demonstrated 259
Applicability of the different Figures to Deduction and Induction 261
Conditional Syllogisms reduced to Immediate Inferences . . 264

CHAPTER IX.

OF FALLACIES 267
Fallacies *in dictione* improperly so called 269
Division of Formal and Material Fallacies 271
Syllogisms of more than Three Terms; Ambiguous Middle . 272

Undistributed Middle; Composite and Divisive sense . . 278
Illicit Process of the Major and Minor Terms . . . 281
The Sophism of Eubulides, the Liar 288
Sophisms respecting the Quality of the Reasoning . . 290
Violation of the Canons of Hypothetical Reasoning . . . 293
Material Fallacies; *petitio principii* 294
Fallacy of the Impossibility of Motion 296
Ignoratio elenchi 298
Argumentum ad ignorantiam 300
Non Causa pro Causa; post hoc, ergo propter hoc . . . 306
Ignava Ratio 309
Achilles and the Tortoise 312

CHAPTER X.

APPLIED LOGIC 314
Science formed by Analysis and Synthesis 317
Classification in Science 322
The Relation of Cause and Effect 324
Necessary Cognitions *à priori* 328
These Cognitions not mere Laws of Thought . . . 330
Elements of our Concepts of Individual Objects . . . 334
The preliminary Classifications of Science 340
Science advances through the improvement of Classifications . 343
Failure of the attempts made to classify the Sciences . . 346

CHAPTER XI.

DEMONSTRATIVE REASONING AND DEDUCTIVE EVIDENCE . . 351
Demonstration applicable to mere Concepts, not to Real Things 352
Why Mathematical reasoning is demonstrative . . . 353
Mathematical evidence not a mere perception of identity . . 359
Distinction between Pure and Applied Mathematics . . 361
The Conclusion not deduced from the Major Premise . . 362
The only New Truth is that enounced in the Subsumption . 364
Particular facts not learned, but proved, by Reasoning . . 367
Different classes of Major Premises 371
Technical terms used in the Construction of Science . . . 374

CHAPTER XII.

INDUCTION AND ANALOGY	376
Want of Universality in the Sumption fatal to strict Reasoning	376
Induction and Analogy are means for discovering Truth . .	380
Difference between them illustrated	381
Analogy is Aristotle's Reasoning from Example . . .	382
Analogy leads only to Probable Conclusions . . .	383
Induction presupposes the correctness of previous Classifications	385
Uniformity of Nature the basis of Induction . . .	388
This Maxim not an Ultimate Fact	389
And not first obtained by Induction	391
But derived from the Principle of Causality . . .	395
What is Physical Necessity	400
All Induction proceeds by simple enumeration	401
A universal Logic of Induction cannot be established . .	403
A General Fact, a Law of Nature, and a Cause distinguished .	405
How a Law of Nature is discovered	409
Physical Causes proved by the Laws of Nature subsumed under them	414
Induction discovers, the Law of Causality proves . . .	416

CHAPTER XIII.

THE SOURCES OF EVIDENCE AND THE CAUSES OF ERROR . .	419
Intuition the basis of all Certainty	419
Intuition of external objects as external	421
Memory as a Source of Evidence	423
The art of Writing an auxiliary to Memory . . .	426
The experience of others a necessary aid	427
Testimony distinguished from Authority	428
And Veracity from Competency	430
Hume's Argument against Miracles examined	432
The Criticism of Tradition and Ancient Writings . .	433
The Theory of Probabilities	437
Moral Causes of Error	445

LOGIC.

CHAPTER I.

PSYCHOLOGICAL INTRODUCTION.

Intuitions distinguished from Concepts. — Mental Characteristics of Brutes. — Relations of Thought to Language.

THE beginning of all knowledge is in single acts of the Perceptive or Acquisitive faculty, each of which relates immediately to an individual object or event. Such acts are called Intuitions or Presentations; the former is the more generally received appellation. Each Intuition gives us a knowledge of its object so far only as this object is perceived *now* and *here*, and also as it is *one*, or undivided, though not necessarily indivisible. To *recognize*, or know over again, the object as similar to another thing perceived on a former occasion or in a different place, or to analyze it into its parts or attributes, or to refer it to a class of things previously known, and thereby to give it a common name, requires the aid of a different and higher power of the mind. In receiving Intuitions, the mind exerts no *conscious* activity whatever; it is passively receptive of any impressions that may be made upon it, and does not in any way consciously react upon or modify those impressions. It is like a mirror reflecting the objects that are held up before it, perhaps giving distorted or unfaithful images of them on account of the imperfections of its own surface, but having no power to change or in any way affect them by its own will.

The impression made upon my mind by the portrait of a friend which I am now looking at, as it hangs before me, or by the sounds to which I am listening as they are struck upon a violin; the image now present to my memory of the relative whom I have recently lost; the picture of a waterfall in a wood which my imagination at this instant forms; the consciousness which I have of the present state of my own mind; — all these are Intuitions, as each one of them relates to a single object, and each is *immediate*, — that is, it does not come through the intervention of any other state of mind. But what is denoted by the word *man*, *sound*, or *waterfall*, is not an Intuition, for it does not refer to one object only, but to many. *Man*, for instance, includes under it John, Thomas, William, and many others; and it does not convey a complete image of any one of these persons, but only a partial representation equally applicable to any of them. John, when considered simply *as man*, is not regarded as he really is, that is, as possessing all his individual attributes and peculiarities, but only as having those attributes which he possesses in common with all other men; he is not viewed *immediately*, but only through the medium of what is called a *Concept*, or a *Thought* of what is common to many. These words, therefore, *man*, *sound*, *waterfall*, and all other common names, do not denote Intuitions, but Thoughts.

The Perceptive or Acquisitive faculty, through which we receive Intuitions, as it is a merely passive power, or a capacity of being affected in a certain way, constitutes what may be called the *receptivity* of the mind. The Thinking or Elaborative faculty, — i. e. the Understanding, — as it has no Intuitions of its own, but voluntarily reacts upon and modifies those received from the Perceptive faculty, comparing them with each other, and thereby combining them into one Thought, or disjoining them as dissimilar or incompatible, belongs to the *spontaneity*, or self-activity, of the intellect.

In the ordinary exercise of our faculties, Intuitions are so intermingled with Thoughts, so quickly pass into them, and are so closely connected with them, that it is difficult to illustrate the distinction between the two by giving an example of an Intuition so isolated and peculiar that there will be no danger of confounding it with any portion of a voluntary and more complex process of mind. But a good illustration may perhaps be found in the case, so frequently referred to, of a person born entirely blind, and subsequently enabled by a surgical operation, for the first time, to see. Suppose that the first visual sensation given to such a person were that of a flash of red light. This sensation, it is evident, would be to him entirely peculiar or *sui generis*. He could not, at first, refer it to any class of things with which he was formerly acquainted; he could not give it a name; he could not analyze it into parts or attributes. He did not will to produce or to modify it; it comes to him, so to speak, of its own accord. He could *know* it, but not *recognize* it, as the presentation of an entirely new object, by which his mind was involuntarily affected in a new and surprising manner. Such, we may suppose, are the Intuitions of brutes; and the faculty of Intuitions, as the Perceptive or Acquisitive faculty may be called, — a mere *receptivity*, unmodified by any voluntary act of the patient, — is probably the most prominent of the few mental powers which brutes possess in common with man. In respect only to Intuitions produced in him by external causes, man has no advantage over the lower animals.

But although all our knowledge begins in Intuitions, it does not end with them. In man, the mere receptivity of mind is so soon modified by its spontaneity, — the mere Intuition so quickly passes into voluntary or consciously active

Thought properly so called, — that we can hardly tell where the one ends and the other begins. To recur to the case just mentioned; the moment the person who has now first received his sight begins to consider or reflect upon the new presentation that has thus been made to him, he probably, in a certain sense, *recognizes* it as *a new sensation*, — that is, he *refers it to a class* of feelings with which he was formerly acquainted, as coming to him through the other senses, and which, as similar in some respects, though different in others, he has ranked together and called by one name, " sensations " or " feelings." Such recognition is an act of *Thought* properly so called. It includes *comparison* of this Intuition with others, and a conscious *discrimination* of those respects in which it is similar to others from those in which it is unlike them. The Perceptive faculty gives us Intuitions of single objects, each of which is to us a distinct unit, having no connection or relation with anything else; the Understanding, a higher faculty, gives us Thoughts, or enables us to analyze each thing into its parts or attributes, and thus to recognize its various points of resemblance and difference, and so to form classes of things. The former power furnishes the rude material — " the Matter," as it is technically called — of our knowledge; the latter supplies " the Form," elaborating and disposing this rude material in a systematic way, or according to regular laws, by throwing it into groups, so as to render it conceivable to Thought. Hence the Understanding has been called the *unifying* faculty, by which the many is reduced to unity.

If we look out of a window for the first time upon a landscape that is entirely new to us, the momentary glance gives us only an Intuition of the scene, or a confused knowledge of it as one whole, without any distinction of parts, and without recognition of any of these parts as former objects of knowledge. This is because the Understanding requires time to do its work. But if we dwell long enough upon the scene, first, we *recognize* (or know over again) one familiar set of objects, and call them *trees ;* then, other classes of objects previously known, and call them respectively *buildings, rocks, hills,* &c. Lastly, we consider the relations of these objects and classes of objects to each other and to similar objects formerly known, in respect to distance, magnitude, color, &c., and are thus enabled *to think* the landscape as a whole. This Thought contains a far more perfect knowledge than the Intuition, which was all that the senses gave us at the first momentary glance.

Now, how much is implied in the successive *recognition* of the component parts of this knowledge as objects previously known, and therefore appropriately designated by a familiar name? Of course, as the landscape is supposed to be now seen for the first time, we do not recognize any individual tree, building, or hill in it as precisely *the same* object that we have formerly seen. We mean only that we recognize it as *similar* to some former objects of knowledge; that is, having seen many objects which agreed with each other as similar in many of their parts, — as possessing trunks, branches, and leaves, — we have formed them into one class, and called them *trees.* The object in the new landscape is then recognized, not as familiar in itself, but as belonging to a familiar class of things; we do not *recognize* it as an Intuition, but as a Concept, — not as *this* tree, but as *a* tree. Conception is that act of the Understanding or Thinking faculty whereby we unite similar objects into one class by overlooking their points of difference and forming their common attributes into one Concept or Thought, the name of which thus becomes the *common name* of all the individuals included in the class. Here, again, the *unifying* office of the Understanding appears; the Concept reduces the many to unity, — brings together many objects into one Thought or many attributes into one subject. Thus we are properly said to *know* many objects which we have never seen; for, through hearing or reading descriptions of them, we have formed a right Concept of what they are, and thus are enabled to *recognize*—i. e. know them over again—and call them by their appropriate name, when we do see them. But this evidently is only *mediate* knowledge, and is more or less imperfect and inadequate, depending on the scantiness or fulness of the Concept. As Mr. Mansel remarks, a Concept "is not the adequate and actual representative of any single object, but an inadequate and potential representative of many." And again, "it is not the sensible image of one object, but an intelligible relation between many."

Concepts can never come to us from without, for the external world has no Concepts. It has not even Intuitions or Percepts, but only real objects,—that is, persons and things, and their marks or attributes. Every real object has an indefinite or countless number of such attributes; for, however long and carefully we may observe it, we can never be sure that we have ascertained *all* its elements and qualities. Carry the chemical analysis of it one step further than before, or place it in new relations with other real objects, and it will manifest new properties or activities, the existence of which was formerly unsuspected. Observation, which proceeds by a series of Intuitions, can make known to us an indefinite number of these attributes, but can never exhaust them. Hence the knowledge which we can acquire by Intuition, though constantly increasing in fulness and complexity, can never become complete, and is always attended with some uncertainty; as any conclusions that we form respecting the object may be vitiated by the presence of a quality or element of whose existence we were ignorant. Moreover, the limited compass and finite powers of the human mind cannot take in at once all even of those attributes whose presence is perfectly known. The image or representation of the object in our minds immediately

becomes confused, when we attempt to make it grasp too
much, or to comprehend, in truth, more than a very few of
the known attributes. Giving up the attempt at completeness, then, we form a Concept of the object embracing
comparatively few of its ascertained qualities, but selecting
those which are most distinctive and essential, in order
thereby more readily to discriminate it from other objects
of a different class. Such a Concept is certainly incomplete,
but it is clear in proportion to the narrowness of its dimensions. We can more easily grasp it in thought, and contemplate it at once in its entireness, because it has so little
complexity. On the other hand, the lack of fulness is apt
to render the boundaries of the Concept somewhat less distinct. Consequently, any object, so far as it is known only
mediately, or *through* such a Concept, is known only in a
few of its leading attributes; and it may even be doubtful
whether another object, which resembles it in these attributes, but departs very widely from it in others, ought to be
ranked in the same class with it, and called by the same
name, or not. If my Concept of *tree*, for instance, is limited to these few particulars, — *a vegetable organism possessing a main trunk, branches, and leaves,* — it will be doubtful
whether many small plants ought to be called *trees* or *shrubs*.
But if I attempt to enlarge the Concept by introducing
more attributes, so as to distinguish *tree* fully from all other
plants, the idea becomes cumbrous and confused; we cannot so easily embrace it in a single act of thought.

While the Percept or Intuition belongs only to the particular attribute or object — this one color, house, tree, or
stone — which has impressed it upon the mind, the Concept refers to all the things whose common or similar attributes or traits it *conceives* (*con-capio*), or *grasps together*
into one class and one act of mind. Thus, for example,
the Concept *red color* includes all similar red colors of any
object whatever; the Concept *tree* refers to all trees, the

Concept *house* to all houses, &c. And naturally enough; for though the *red* or the *white* of this object is not the identical red or white of that object, — is at least numerically different from it, and separated from it by the accidents of place and time, the one being perceived *here* and the other *there*, the one being seen *now* and the other *formerly*, — yet as the two produce exactly the same impression upon the mind, or create the same sensation, they are regarded as virtually the same color for all the purposes of thought. Thus, also, though any one tree differs from every other tree in many other respects besides the accidents of place and time, yet it is common to all trees to have a root, a trunk, branches, and twigs. Now as the Concept *tree* is discriminated from all other Concepts only by possessing these four Marks or attributes, it must necessarily apply to all trees, which are regarded as the same for all the purposes of thought. And so it is with all Concepts. Hence they are also called *Universals*, or *General Ideas*.

As Esser remarks, "A Concept is the representation of an object through its distinctive Marks; — that is, not through those Marks which distinguish it from other objects in general, but from those which come the nearest to it. The distinctive Marks of an object are evidently those which make it to be this object, and not some other one; i. e. they are its *peculiar* and *essential* Marks. The common and unessential Marks, therefore, do not necessarily belong to the Concept; if they were added to it, they would not only overburden and complicate the Concept, but would lessen its applicability to other objects of the same kind. Hence it is self-evident how the Concept is related to the sensible Intuition. Namely, the Concept is the Intuition stripped of its contingent or unessential (individual) attributes or Marks; and the Intuition is the Concept clothed with the contingent or unessential (individual) Marks."

A Concept may be derived from one object as well as from many similar ones; that is, it may not represent an actual, but only a possible, class or plurality of things. This may be illustrated by the description which a zoölogist would give of a newly discovered animal, that was too unlike those formerly known to be included in the same species with any of them. Many slight peculiarities of such an animal would be passed over altogether, as unessential either to the class to which it belonged, or to any other. And of the more important Marks, which might be presumed to be specific and not individual in character, those only would be selected for careful description which would serve to distinguish the new object from those which, through their similarity in other respects, might be presumed to belong to the nearest species, or those most akin to the strange specimen. The description thus formed, containing possibly not more than two or three Marks, would be at once a brief and clear Concept actually drawn from an individual, but potentially applicable to a whole class, should other specimens of it be subsequently discovered. In a similar manner, the mind may *think* any individual object under a Concept consisting of a few well-chosen Marks, instead of knowing it simply by an Intuition as a confused aggregate of many parts and elements, as brutes would do. We *perceive* only *single things*, for such only are *presented* to us; we *think* only actual or possible *classes of things*, for Nature does not give us *classes*, though she furnishes us the *resemblances* of things, through which we proceed to classify them. All classification is an act of the mind, and is more or less arbitrary, depending on our selection of the attributes or relations in reference to which we classify them.

It is evident that Concepts must be much clearer representations of things than the confused aggregate of Percepts or Intuitions on which they are founded. With their light they irradiate and make clearly intelligible everything to which they are referred, or with which they come together into consciousness; and thus to explicate and make clear through Concepts the perceived or represented objects is, says Dressler, what it is, in the strict logical acceptation of the word, *to think*. In this sense, therefore, *to think* is to make clear through Concepts something already otherwise represented or known to consciousness.

Esser says, "To think is to designate an object through a Mark or attribute, or, what is the same thing, to determine a subject through a predicate." According to Sir William Hamilton, "Thought is the comprehension of a thing under a general notion (Concept) or attribute"; and again, "All thought is a comparison, a recognition of similarity or difference, a conjunction or disjunction;—in other words, a synthesis or analysis of its objects. In Conception, that is, in the formation of Concepts (or general notions), it compares, disjoins, or conjoins attributes; in an act of Judgment, it compares, disjoins, or conjoins Concepts; in Reasoning, it compares, disjoins, or conjoins Judgments. In each step of this process, there is one essential element; to think, to compare, to conjoin, or disjoin, it is necessary to recognize one thing through or under another; and therefore, in defining Thought proper, we may either define it as an act of comparison, or as a recognition of one notion as in or under another." According to other logicians, Thought is the reduction of complexity and plurality to unity, or the bringing together of what is confused, various, and manifold or multitudinous in our Intuitions into the clear unity of consciousness.

All these definitions evidently point to one thing, or indicate what is substantially the same process. Comparison is the means through which we unite what is similar, and separate what is unlike or opposed; for only through comparison do we recognize likeness or unlikeness, agreement or opposition. Now we analyze, divide, and distinguish only in order subsequently to bring together and combine. We discriminate the various elements or attributes of objects through comparison of them with each other, and then unite them with other objects and attributes according to their similarities as ascertained by a fresh act of comparison; and this union of many things in one class, this reduction of a plurality of Intuitions under one Concept or general notion, is the means through which the infinite variety and multitude of natural objects are reduced to the limited compass of the human understanding, and made intelligible. A new individual object is to us an isolated and incomprehensible thing, until we have recognized its similarity with something else, and thereby assigned it to a class, or comprehended it under a Concept, and given it a common name.

According to some etymologists, *think* comes from the same root as *thick*,* and originally signified *thickening*, or pressing together of many into one; and this exactly describes the special function of the understanding. As we have already remarked, while a Percept or Intuition is a *single* representation, limited to this one thing which excited it or impressed it upon the mind, a Concept is a *collective* (general or universal) representation of a whole class of things. To make a formal definition, we may say that *a Concept is a representation made up from several particular Percepts, through the union of their similar elements.* It is through Concepts that we *think*, — that is, clearly *understand*, *comprehend*, or *conceive* something; for these words mean precisely the same thing, namely, to represent with *clearer* consciousness what was already represented in our minds.

Besides the Percept and the Concept, the later German philosophers distinguish the so-called *Idea*, as the pattern-

* The *n* in *think* is casual, and does not appear in the participle *thought*. So in German, *dick*, *denken*, *gedacht*.

representation, ideal Concept, or *beau-ideal*, by which we understand such a representation as surpasses or goes beyond the perceived and the conformed to experience. The Idea is that whereby we think an object in its highest possible perfection, and consequently unlike anything which we have actually witnessed. Hence it does not refer, like the Intuition, to a single thing, nor, like the Concept, to a whole class of things; but it wholly surpasses in completeness or perfection the object to which it is referred. Such are the Ideas of the artist, moral and religious Ideas, &c.

The Kantians use *Representations* to designate the genus which includes, as its several species, Percepts, Concepts, and Ideas. The aggregate of the Percepts which any one has had may be said to constitute his experience.

Intuitions afford the only sure means of first creating, and of subsequently rectifying and enlarging, our Concepts. Thus, I may have some scanty knowledge, obtained by reading perhaps, of a species of plant or flower that I have never seen. The Concept thus formed may err both by excess and defect; by excess, because it may include some parts or attributes which are not peculiar to this species, but are common to it with many others; by defect, because it may not comprise enough of the attributes common to all the plants in this class, and peculiar to them or not belonging to any other plants, to enable me to recognize and distinguish an individual of this species when I see it. It is only intuitive knowledge, or that gained by direct observation, which can enable me to correct these errors.

Intuitions, then, are the only test of the *reality* of Concepts; for they alone can determine whether the Concepts properly correspond to the actual objects in nature which they are meant to describe. In this sense, Intuitions are not only the beginning, but the basis and the source, of all our knowledge. All Concepts, however, are not meant to represent actual objects; they may be imaginary or fanciful. I can conceive a centaur or a griffin, though no such animal ever lived. Yet even in this case, though the Concept, *as a whole*, is unreal or imaginary, it must be made up only of real *parts* or attributes, — that is, of such as have been embraced in some preceding Intuition. I have never seen a centaur; but I have seen the head of a man and the body of a horse, and I can unite, in Thought, these real parts into an unreal whole. So, again, I can think or conceive any combination, however fantastic, of colors that I have previously seen; but I cannot introduce into the painting, even in Thought, any color that I have never seen. A person born blind, and remaining so, cannot conceive any color whatever; just as one who has never had the sense of hearing can form no Concept of sound. Intuitions, then, are the basis, not only of all Knowledge, but of all Thought.

The perception which gives us a new Intuition may take place either through the external senses, or exclusively through that internal source of knowledge, sometimes called an internal sense, but more properly denominated Consciousness, by which we are made aware of the existence of our own sensations, thoughts, and feelings.

Consciousness, indeed, is the universal witness which testifies to the reality, not only of sensation and feeling, but of the external perceptions which come to us through the outer senses. I see a bright red color, I hear a particular sound, only so far as I am conscious of that act of seeing or hearing; if I were not conscious of it, it would be to me as if it were non-existent. For *to know*, and *to know that I know*, are phrases that designate one indivisible act of mind; and *to know that I know* is a phrase which means the same thing as *to be conscious*. Hence, though it is an act of sense whereby I perceive the red color or hear the sound, it is at the same time an act of consciousness; as, otherwise, I should have no knowledge either of the act of perception, or of the outward phenomenon to the existence of which it testifies.

I am conscious also of *internal* perceptions, of hunger, pain, fear, joy, etc. Still further, I am conscious of *myself*, as the one being that perceives, fears, or rejoices. Every act of consciousness is twofold, testifying to the existence both of *the subject*, — that is, of the being or person who is conscious, — and of *the object*, — that is, of the feeling, perception, or other phenomenon of which he is conscious. The very language which I am compelled to use in making known the fact to another person testifies to this duality of the act. Any phrase used for this purpose must contain at least two terms, one expressive of *the subject*, and the other of *the object*, of consciousness. Thus, in the proposition "I feel hunger," the pronoun "I" denotes the person who feels, and "hunger" the phenomenon which is felt. In some languages, the whole may be expressed in a single word, as in the Latin "esurio"; but the expression here is elliptical, the "ego," or the subject of consciousness, being always understood. The two elements can only be known together, simultaneously, and in their relation to each other. One is not known through the other, or in consequence of the other, or after the other; but they are known together, in one act of mind. I cannot be conscious of *hunger* without, at the same moment and in the same act, being conscious of *myself* as feeling the hunger.

All the phenomena, then, both of the external and internal world, are presented to the mind each in its distinctive or peculiar Intuition. In other words, any Intuition differs from every other Intuition, at least in the relations of time and space. Thus, two successive Intuitions by the same person, of the same thing, are distinguishable at least in this respect, that the one preceded the other, or took place at an earlier time. In like manner, — to borrow an example from Mr. Mansel, — "I see lying on the table before me a number of shillings of the same coinage. Examined severally, the image and superscription of each is undistinguishable from that of its fellow; but in viewing them side by side, *space* is a necessary condition of my perception; and the difference of locality is sufficient to make them distinct, though similar, individuals." As already remarked, each Intuition is of a distinct thing as perceived *now* and *here*, — that is, in its own peculiar relations both to time and space. On the other hand, a Concept is freed from these relations of space and time; I can *think* what is denoted by the word *tree*, without identifying it with this or that particular tree, standing on a particular spot, and seen at a particular time.

As already remarked, it is the capacity of Thought properly so called which constitutes the immeasurable superiority of the human over the brute mind; but it is also true, that the necessity of Thought arises from the immeasurable inferiority of man's intellect to that of his Creator. If the human mind were omniscient and of infinite compass, it would behold all things intuitively, and would not be confused and overburdened by the multitude of these single cognitions. But it is far otherwise; the mind is limited and imperfect, and can grasp at once but few objects, — according to the common opinion, only five or six. It can permanently retain in memory, so as to reproduce at will, it can accurately represent in imagination, only a few of its primary Intuitions. We must have recourse to the artifice of Thought; we must discard all individual attributes and peculiarities, in order, through meagre Concepts, to rise to a larger and clearer, though consciously imperfect, comprehension of a multitude of things. As will be shown hereafter, it is precisely the scantiness of the general notion in respect to its import, which renders it more comprehensive in respect to the number of things which it embraces; in other words, if we would know more objects, we must know each of them less perfectly. Unable to master the vastness and complexity of Nature by taking in detail the objects which she offers to us, each in its separate Intuition, we throw them, through discarding their differences, into groups and classes. The mind can then grasp at once six or seven of these groups, instead of being limited, as before, to six or seven individuals. Then, by forming successively groups of groups, or classes of a higher order of generalization, our mental horizon is enlarged till we can take in, or comprehend (*con-prehendo*), all the objects that we have ever known. But this is like ascending a very high mountain, whence, though we obtain a broader view, the outlines and colors of objects below are but faintly seen, and many are wholly lost in the distance.

The nature of Language illustrates this process of the formation of Thought. In fact, taken in its strictest sense, Language is the expression of Thought only; it has to do, not with Intuitions, but with Concepts. Intuitions, from their very nature, can be designated only by Proper Names; and *words* properly so called are Common Names. Every word has a meaning, and is therefore susceptible of definition, or at least of explanation. But a Proper Name, strictly speaking, has no meaning; as Mr. J. S. Mill remarks, it is a sign which *denotes* this one thing, but which *connotes* nothing. Like a pointing of the finger, it designates the individual who is meant; but it says nothing as to the nature or character of that individual. In so far, indeed, as usage has limited one class of names to males, and another to females, in so far the names connote *sex;* and precisely to this extent they cease to be Proper, and become Common, Names. If, to a person who does not know James, I say, " James did this," the effect is precisely the same as if I had said, " A man or boy did it." If a word is to express an Intuition, it must be accompanied by other words, or at least be marked by emphasis or a significant gesture, so as to restrict its meaning to a determinate single thing; and these limiting words can be dispensed with only when the context, or the custom of speech, supplies the necessary limitations. For example: "this house now before us," "that house on the hill," "the house in Cambridge which I showed you yesterday," are phrases wherein the *general* meaning of the word *house* is narrowed down to this or that *particular* building, which may be known through an Intuition. In other cases, the context or emphasis suffices to limit the signification of such phrases as "his house," "John's house," "*the* house," etc., to the one thing which was intended.

Dr. Reid puzzles himself in attempting to explain how it comes to pass, that, whilst all the objects and events which we perceive are individual or singular, all the words in a language are general. But the reasons are obvious. First, we cannot have countless words for the innumerable single objects which we perceive, as no memory could retain them : — think, for a moment, of the myriads of leaves, blades of grass, insects, and other classes of things, which we are constantly beholding. Secondly, these very instances show, that, at least as far as our perceptions are concerned, the similarity of objects is often as great as their diversity, and even greater. Thirdly, one main purpose of language being the communication of Thought to others, what we need to know or to communicate is not so often a particular fact respecting this single object, as it is a general truth respecting a whole class of objects; we do not so often need to say, Avoid or seek this one thing, as, Avoid or seek *all* of which this is a specimen. We are more frequently concerned, *in our mental operations*, with classes than with individuals, though the latter alone furnish employment for our hands. Fourthly, many things are usually massed together even to our perception, as individual trees in a forest, and therefore can never be exhaustively designated by one expression. By the law of 'parsimony, therefore, language makes up its millions of names or designations out of comparatively few words, just as its thousands of words are constructed out of some twenty or thirty elementary sounds or letters.

Language, then, deals only with groups or classes of things; and the process of classification necessarily precedes the formation of language. This theory explains at once the most striking deficiency of the lower animals, — their incapacity of using language. As they have only Intuitions, the only names which they can apply or understand are Proper Names, — the appellations of this or that particular thing. These they *can* understand. A dog can easily be taught to know the name of his master, even when pronounced by another person. They can even be taught to know the names of particular places and buildings, so that they can understand and obey, when they are told to go to *the barn, the river,* or *the house.** But it is always *the particular barn,* or other object, with which they have been taught to associate this sound or significant gesture as its Proper Name. Carry the animal to a distant place, near which may be a set of corresponding objects, and then tell him to go to *the barn* or *the river,* and he will not understand the order as applying to the new set of objects, but will set off immediately for the old building or place, with whose Proper Name alone he is familiar. As Kant remarks, a dog knows (*kennt*) his master, but does not *recognize him through his peculiar Marks or Attributes* (*erkennt*), and thereby properly *discriminate* him from other persons.

These Intuitions, which are common to man and the

---

* In Mr. Lockhart's amusing account of Sir Walter Scott's first favorite dog, "Camp," he says: "As the servant was laying the cloth for dinner, he would address the dog lying on his mat by the fire, and say, 'Camp, my good fellow, the Sheriff's coming home *by the ford* [or *by the hill*],' and the sick animal would immediately bestir himself to welcome his master, *going out at the back door or the front door, according to the direction given,* and advancing as far as he was able."

brute, and which are mere *impressions* passively received by the mind, may be stored up in the memory, but out of consciousness, as fruits of experience; they may be subsequently recalled to consciousness, or *reproduced*, either by casual association or voluntary reminiscence; and, when so recalled, they may be *re-presented*, or pictured forth to the mind, by an act of that faculty which we usually call Imagination. Brutes, as well as men, are capable of all these acts of Memory, Reproduction, and Imagination, *when exercised upon Intuitions alone;* for they are all implied in dreaming, and a dog asleep upon a rug before the fire often shows, by his barking and growling, that he has vivid dreams. Man can remember and reproduce Concepts or Thoughts, as well as Intuitions. Imagination, whether in man or the brute, is concerned only with Intuitions, as it pictures forth nothing but definite images of this or that particular object or event. Thoughts properly so called are *conceived* or *understood*, but cannot be *imagined*.*

Agreeably to what has been said, the mental process of forming Concepts may be reduced to three steps, viz. : —

1. *Comparison*, whereby, among many attributes or objects, we determine which are similar and which are different or unlike.

2. *Combination* or *Reduction to Unity*, whereby, for instance, this, that, and the other color are recognized and identified as what is usually called "one and the same" shade or hue of *red ;* or several quadrupeds are recognized as all belonging to one class called *horse*.

3. *Abstraction*,† whereby we separate and throw aside

---

* If this simple distinction had been made, the old dispute between the Nominalists and the Realists could never have arisen. The former clearly perceived that Concepts could not be *imagined;* the Realists knew very well that, in thinking, our thoughts were concerned with something more than mere words. Both were right.

† This word, according to its etymology (*abs-traho*, to draw off from), is

— i. e. put out of Thought — the dissimilar or incongruous attributes which, if retained, would prevent the other elements from flowing together into unity.

Each of these steps evidently involves an act of *Judgment*, — that is, of that function of the Understanding or Thinking Faculty whereby we affirm or deny one Intuition or Concept of another. Hence, we may either consider Judgments as the elements of Concepts, or Concepts as the elements of Judgments. Logicians generally have treated of the functions of Conception or Simple Apprehension first, and those of Judgment afterwards; and, as this arrangement is in some respects more convenient, I shall follow their example, though strict method would perhaps require this order to be reversed.

All men are capable of comparison, and of discerning those similarities on which the formation of Concepts depends. But it does not so readily appear how many different persons are naturally led to form the same Concepts, according as circumstances render them familiar with similar classes of things. This is well explained by Dressler. Before the elements which are common to the constituent Intuitions can be really united into Concepts, they must be excited in consciousness simultaneously, or in immediate succession; if they arose only separately, and at intervals, like disjoined fragments, there would be no mutual attraction to draw them together. But when thus brought before the mind at the same time, the synthesis of their common elements into one Concept is a perfectly natural process, in which we need no guidance, " as they flow together by a sort of spontaneous attraction for each other,

---

properly applied to the dissimilar elements which are put aside or abandoned, though, until recently, logicians used it to designate the process of retaining and combining the similar elements. Sir W. Hamilton would say that we *prescind* the similar which is retained, and *abstract* the different which is thrown off.

each of them being the object of a livelier and clearer consciousness than any of the dissimilar elements. For example; if I see at once, or in quick succession, six different trees, I perceive their similar properties — i. e. root, trunk, branches, etc. — *six times* over, being once for each tree, and thus have a livelier or stronger consciousness of them than I have of those which, as dissimilar or peculiar to one tree, I perceive only once. Moreover, for the very reason that these common elements are *similar* — that is, as they have fewer points of divergence or contrast — they more easily coalesce and melt into one Concept." As Hamilton remarks, " the qualities which by comparison are judged similar are already, by this process, identified in consciousness; for they are only judged similar inasmuch as they produce in us indiscernible effects."

But this is not all. " The Concept thus formed by an abstraction of the resembling from the non-resembling qualities of objects would again fall back into the confusion and infinitude from which it has been called out, were it not rendered permanent for consciousness by being fixed and ratified in a verbal sign." Hence, Language is necessary, not only that we may communicate our Thoughts to others, but that we may permanently retain and readily use these Thoughts for our own purposes. Concepts are factitious units, and the particular attributes which constitute them are somewhat arbitrarily selected, being more or less numerous, and having greater or less resemblance, according to circumstances. A Concept, as we have already remarked, cannot be pictured in Imagination; and the presence of one of the real objects included under it does not necessarily suggest the particular attributes out of which it was formed, to the exclusion of others perhaps equally prominent to the eye. Hence, a Name must be given to it, which will be, of course, a Common Name for all the individuals contained under it; or the factitious aggregate will be dissolved and lost to memory almost as soon as formed. The name preserves the unity of the aggregate just as it was originally constituted, precisely as a cord holds a bundle of things together, and enables us to handle many objects as if they were but one. The Memory is then burdened with the retention only of one word, which, when recalled, by the law of association will suggest its meaning, instead of being urged to remember a considerable number of attributes, which can neither be separately or collectively pictured in the Imagination. An Intuition, on the other hand, needs not to be designated by a Name, as the presence of the object immediately excites it anew in its original perfection, and Imagination can *re*-present it almost as adequately and vividly as the reality. But the Concept can neither be retained in mind, nor, so to speak, readily manipulated in Thought, without the aid of a verbal sign.

This mutual dependence of Thought and Language, each bearing all the imperfections and perfections of the other, has been admirably illustrated by Hamilton.

"Though, in general, we must hold that language, as the product and correlative of thought, must be viewed as posterior to the act of thinking itself, — on the other hand, it must be admitted, that we could never have risen above the very lowest degrees in the scale of thought without the aid of signs. A sign is necessary to give stability to our intellectual progress, — to establish each step in our advance as a new starting-point for our advance to another beyond.

"A country may be overrun by an armed host, but it is only conquered by the establishment of fortresses. Words are the fortresses of thought. They enable us to realize our dominion over what we have already overrun in thought, — to make every intellectual conquest the basis of operations for others still beyond. Or another illustration: You have all heard of the process of tunnelling, of tunnelling through a sand-bank. In this operation it is impossible to succeed unless every foot — nay, almost every inch — in our progress be secured by an arch of masonry, before we attempt the excavation of another. Now, language is to the mind precisely what the arch is to the tunnel. The power of thinking and the power of excavation are not dependent on the word in the one case, on the mason-work in the other; but without these subsidiaries, neither process could be carried on beyond its rudimentary commencement. Though, therefore, we allow that every movement forward in language must be determined by an antecedent movement forward in thought, still, unless thought be accompanied at each point of its evolution by a corresponding evolution of language, its further development is arrested. Thus it is that the higher exertions of the higher faculty of Understanding — the classification of the objects presented and re-presented by the subsidiary powers in the formation of a hierarchy of notions; the connection of these notions into judgments; the inference of one judgment from another; and, in general, all our consciousness of the relations of the universal to the particular, consequently all science strictly so denominated, and every inductive knowledge of the past and future from the laws of nature: not only these, but all ascent from the sphere of sense to the sphere of moral and religious intelligence — are, as experience proves, if not altogether impossible without a language, at least possible to a very low degree.

"Admitting even that the mind is capable of certain elementary Concepts without the fixation and signature of language, still these are but sparks which would twinkle only to expire; and it requires words to give them prominence, and, by enabling us to collect and elaborate them into new Concepts, to raise, out of what would otherwise be only scattered and transitory scintillations, a vivid and enduring light."

But Words are not only signs and preservatives, they are also substitutes, for Thoughts; and this peculiarity of Language is an excellence or defect in it, according as it is or is not judiciously used. As Bishop Berkeley remarks, "It is not necessary, even in the strictest reasonings, that significant names which stand for ideas should, every time they are used, excite in the understanding the ideas they are made to stand for. In reading and discoursing, names are for the most part used as letters are in algebra, in which, though a particular quantity be marked by each letter, yet, to proceed right, it is not requisite that, in every step, each letter should suggest to your thoughts that particular quantity it was appointed to stand for." Having once satisfied ourselves, by spreading out in thought all the attributes which are combined in any Concept, — or, to be still more careful, by having once called up in Imagination a picture of some one individual possessing all these attributes, and therefore contained in the class, — that the meaning of the word, which is the Sign of that Concept and the Common Name of that class, is within our power, we proceed to use that word *symbolically*, — that is, as a mere sign, and therefore with much more ease and rapidity than if it were necessary to stop, each time it recurs, and repeat the process of verifying its meaning. Hence it may be said that the use of language gives us the power of thinking in short-hand; words are stenographic thoughts. Moreover, this abbreviated expression of thought is a great help to the memory. Having once ascertained by reflection the relation of various Concepts to each other, — that is, having formed judgments and reasonings, and expressed them in propositions, — it is a far easier and shorter method to remember the few words which constitute such a proposition, than to recall successively each of the mental processes which are now embodied in it, and through which it was first obtained. Language is the great repository of thought, not only in books, but in our own minds. The algebraist easily recalls to mind a few brief formulas, which enable him to perform almost mechanically long numerical computations, which the mere arithmetician must slowly and painfully think out step by step. Even when the meaning of the words is not sufficiently familiar to enable us to perform the whole process symbolically, or by the use of words alone, we can often do so in part; — that is, we need only to explicate, or spread out in our minds, that particular portion of their meaning which happens to be all that is necessary for the special purpose which we now have in view. Thus I may not know the full meaning of a technical term in some science, or of a certain verb in the Greek language, and still be enabled to use it without error in that one of its numerous applications with which use may have made me familiar. This *symbolic* knowledge, as it was termed by Leibnitz, bears about the same relation to the full thought, of which it is the abbreviated expression, that our ordinary cursive handwriting does to an ideographic system, or to the picture-writing of the Mexicans.

On the other hand, it should be remembered that there is peculiar danger in this use of words as a temporary substitute for thought. Dr. Campbell mentions it as the reason why many persons, even among the judicious and the well-informed, are sometimes led both to talk and write nonsense without knowing it. When the use of words is not checked by a frequent recurrence in thought to the precise limitations of their meaning, even the best of us are occasionally betrayed into applications of them which a moment's reflection would prove to be incongruous and absurd. The ordinary safeguard against such blunders is, that, having become familiar by use with certain words in their ordinary relations and connections with other words, anything new or peculiar in the combinations in which they are sometimes found, or in which we may ourselves be tempted to place them, at once attracts our notice, and puts us upon the lookout to detect a possible absurdity. Take, for instance, the following stanza, which occurs in the "Song by a Person of Quality," written by Pope to ridicule this very class of blunders, as frequently committed by people of fashion in their attempts to string together in verse the mere commonplaces of poetical expression: —

> "Gloomy Pluto, king of terrors,
> Armed in adamantine chains,
> Lead me to the crystal mirrors
> Watering soft Elysian plains."

As *chains* usually *bind* and *mirrors reflect*, not even the smoothness of the measure can here cause us to slide over the absurdity of supposing Pluto to be *armed* by the former, or plains *watered* by the latter.

To avoid such blunders, it is not enough to be able merely to explicate in thought the meaning of each word taken by itself, or separately, but the *combination of words* must express a possible *union in thought* of what is expressed by them. Whether this can be done can be ascertained only through the process of what Mr. Mansel calls "individualizing our Concepts,"— that is, of calling up in imagination a picture of some particular thing denoted by the words *taken together*, because possessing together all the attributes contained in such a union of Concepts. It is only by the failure of the attempt to form such a mental image, that we are led to perceive the absurdity of such expressions as a *bilinear figure*, an *iron-gold* mountain, or a *watering mirror*. Hence it appears, that what is perfectly intelligible in language, when the words are taken separately, may be absolutely inconceivable in thought. I know what each of the words *bilinear figure* means; but such a figure is inconceivable, and therefore the union of the two words is absurd.

It was remarked by Burke, in his Essay on the Sublime

and Beautiful, that words are not only used as substitutes for thoughts, but, through the laws of association, they also serve to call up the same emotions which are naturally produced by the presence or imagination of the real objects which they denote. Thus, there are many words which have feelings of awe, sorrow, or affright so firmly associated with them, by long habit, that the mere utterance of them in a sermon is enough to solemnize the minds of the congregation, even before the hearers have time to think of what they mean.

The doctrine of the Nominalists, then, is true to this extent, — that very often, in the use of language, there is nothing before the minds either of the speakers or the hearers but mere words; and yet these words are significantly and correctly used, and they answer their purpose of exciting emotion and imparting knowledge. But it is also often true, that, in the use of words, all the powers of the Understanding, or Thinking Faculty, are in active exercise; — that we compare, combine, discriminate, judge, and discern new relations before unthought of, the subsidiary powers of the Memory and Imagination, all the while, furnishing their aid whenever needed; and it is only by such concomitant activity of the Thinking power, that we can have full assurance that the words in question are correctly used, and the boundaries of our knowledge are enlarged. Thus, in the thoughtful use of words, we are continually spreading out in our minds the attributes of which the Concepts are made up, individualizing them, comparing them with each other, discovering new relations between them, and carrying them up into higher orders of generalization, or extending them to more objects.

A few remarks may be necessary in explanation of the nomenclature which has been here employed. The English words *thinking*, *thought*, are commonly used, in a very vague and comprehensive sense, to denote any cognitive act or object of the mind. But, as applied in Logic, they are strictly limited to one well-defined class of our cognitive functions. After the illustrations that have now been given, the peculiar characteristics of Thought properly so called are perhaps sufficiently understood.

Hamilton justly observes, that most of the words which signify operations of the mind have a triple ambiguity, for they may denote either, 1. the *faculty;* or, 2. the *act;* or, 3. the *product* of the act. To avoid this uncertainty, the *Understanding* is here used exclusively to denote the Faculty of Thinking in the narrower sense, or what Hamilton calls the "Elaborative Faculty," because it elaborates, or works up into Thought, the raw material which is furnished to it by the Perceptive powers. Like any other faculty, the Understanding at any particular time may, or may not, be in exercise. Its function or peculiar office is *to think;* hence, thinking denotes the *act,* while Thought signifies the *product,* of this faculty. As will be shown hereafter, Thought is the generic term, for there are three species of it; viz. Concepts, Judgments, and Reasonings or Inferences. The old logicians referred the origin of these three species of Thought to as many distinct faculties, which they denominated respectively Simple Apprehension, Judgment, and the Discursive Faculty. Of these, Simple Apprehension corresponds very nearly to that sort of Thinking which we now call Conception, its products being denominated Concepts. In like manner, the products of the Perceptive or Acquisitive Faculty, hitherto called Intuitions, might more conveniently be termed Percepts, as we should then have an English verb, *perceive,* to express the *act* of that Faculty of which these are *products.* If it were allowable to coin an English verb to express the act of intuition, answering to the German *anschauen,* analogy would direct us to say *intuit.* The Discursive Faculty (from *discurrere,* to run to and fro) was so called because, in Reasoning or drawing Inferences, the mind *runs over* from one Judgment, as the Ground or Reason, to another, as the Consequence or Conclusion. But the whole Understanding is more properly called by this name; for, in forming Concepts, the mind *runs over* the Percepts or Intuitions from which they are derived, in order to separate the similar elements from the unlike, and consciously to unite the former into one product of Thought.

CHAPTER II.

DEFINITION OF LOGIC.

Divisions of the Science. — Utility of the Study.

LOGIC is the Science of the Necessary Laws of Pure Thought.

The Greek word, λόγος, from which Logic is derived, signifies both the inward *thought*, and the *word* or outward form in which this thought is expressed; and thus includes both the *ratio* and the *oratio* of the Latins. This fact, and the intimate connection which, as we have already seen, exists between Thought and Language, has caused some writers, especially those who adopt the Nominalist theory to its full extent, to maintain that "Logic is entirely conversant about Language." But it is not so; for Logic is primarily and essentially conversant with Thought, and only secondarily and accidentally with Language; that is, it treats of Language so far only as this is the vehicle of Thought. Just the reverse is true of the science of Grammar, which treats primarily of Language, and only secondarily of Thought. Logic might be called the Grammar of Thought.

Others have held that "the process or operation of *reasoning* is *alone* the appropriate province of Logic." But this is putting the part for the whole, and is as inadequate as it would be to restrict Geometry to the measurement of spherical bodies, to the exclusion of lines, angles, plane surfaces, and rectilinear solids. There are three classes of the products of Thought, namely, Concepts, Judgments, and

Inferences or Reasonings, with each of which Logic is immediately concerned, as, indeed, no one of them can be adequately discussed without consideration of both the others. If, on the one hand, it can be said that conception and judgment are both subsidiary to the process of reasoning, so, on the other, judgment is the primary and essential operation, of which conception and inference are only special forms or complex results.

Pure, or, as it is sometimes termed, Formal Thought, is *the mere process of thinking, irrespective of what we are thinking about.* It has already been said that the Acquisitive or Perceptive Faculty furnishes " the Matter," while the Understanding supplies " the Form," of our knowledge. This distinction between Matter and Form is one of considerable importance in the history of philosophy. The former is the crude material or the stuff of which anything consists, or out of which it is made; while the latter is the peculiar shape or modification given to it by the artist, whereby it has become this particular thing which it is, and not something else which might have been fashioned out of the same substance. Thus, *wood* is the Matter of the desk on which I am writing, whilst the Form is that which entitles it to be called a desk, rather than a table or a chair. Vocal sound is the Matter of speech, and articulation is its Form. It is evident that these are two correlative notions, each of which implies the other: Matter cannot exist except under some Form, and there cannot be any Form except of some given Matter. But though the two cannot actually be separated, the mind can consider each separately through that process, called *abstraction,* whereby the attention is wholly given to the one to the exclusion of the other. We may think separately of the attributes which are common to a whole class of Forms, disregarding altogether, for the moment, the Matter of which each of them really consists. Borrowing algebraic symbols, the Matter in each case may be designated by a letter of the alphabet, the peculiar significance of which is, that it stands for any Matter whatever, and not for any one in particular. Thus, *A is B*, is the Form of an affirmative judgment, wherein A and B stand for any two Concepts whatever. Hence, whatever is true of the general formula, *A is B*, will be true also of any such particular instances, as *Iron is malleable*, *Trees are plants*, &c., wherein the Form is associated with some particular Matter. In saying, then, that Logic is concerned only with the Forms of Thought, or Pure Thought, or Thought in the abstract, — for all these expressions signify the same thing, — we mean only, that what is Material in Thought is extralogical, and, as logicians, we have nothing to do with it; just as the geometer has nothing to do with the particular diagram on the paper before him, except so far as it is a symbol, or universal Form, of all possible figures of the same general character. As Hamilton remarks : " The objects (the Matter) of thought are infinite; no one science can embrace them all, and therefore to suppose Logic conversant about the Matter of thought in general, is to say that Logic is another name for the encyclopædia — the *omne scibile* — of human knowledge. The absurdity of this supposition is apparent. But if it be impossible for Logic to treat of *all* the objects of thought, it cannot be supposed that it treats of *any;* for no reason can be given why it should limit its consideration to some, to the exclusion of others. As Logic cannot, therefore, possibly include all objects, and as it cannot possibly be shown why it should include only some, it follows that it must exclude from its domain the consideration of the Matter of thought altogether; and as, apart from the Matter of thought, there only remains the Form, it follows that Logic, as a special science of thought, must be viewed as conversant exclusively about the Form of thought."

Again, the definition of Logic assumes that the process

of Thinking, like every other operation in nature, does not take place at random, but according to certain fixed Laws or invariable modes of procedure. There could be no communication of Thought from one mind to another, if the process of Thinking in all minds were not subject to the same general rules. We follow these laws for the most part unconsciously, as a distinct recognition of them is not by any means necessary for correct thinking; just so, many persons speak and write correctly without any knowledge of the grammarian's rules. But they can be discovered through analysis of their results, and the business of the logician is to search them out and arrange them in order, just as the grammarian's duty is to set forth those secondary laws of Thought which control the formation and the use of Language. Logic, says Dr. Thomson, "like philosophy, of which it is a part, arises from a reflection of the mind upon its own processes; a logician is not one who thinks, but one who can declare *how* he thinks."

But here a distinction is to be made, for Logic takes cognizance not of the contingent, but only of the necessary and universal, laws of Thought. Psychology, as the science of the mental phenomena in general, includes, of course, the procedures of Pure Thought; but it includes them only in their contingent and phenomenal character, as actually existing now and then, but not as necessarily existing at all times. Logic does not consider the subsidiary processes, such as Perception, Memory, and Imagination, through which we collect the *materials* for thinking. The operations of the Thinking Faculty are also contingently modified by the coexistence of other powers and affections of the mind; they are obstructed by indolence, and warped by prejudice and passion. Logic does not regard these accidental perversions of the Understanding, but takes into view only those fundamental and absolute principles, to which all Thought is necessarily subject, and which shine by their own light, as they cannot be transgressed except by the idiot or the madman. A violation of one of these Laws is not so much an error in Thinking, as a negation of Thought. They are axiomatic in character; that is, they cannot be proved or deduced from higher principles, for such proof or deduction would be itself an act of Thought, and therefore would presuppose the validity of the very principles which it was intended to guarantee. These Laws cannot be proved, but they can be enunciated and explained; when understood, their truth is self-evident, for they rest upon the immediate testimony of consciousness. As necessary and universally known, they are never consciously broken; but we may be betrayed into an apparent transgression of one or more of them, through an incautious yoking together of certain words or formulas of expression, without sufficiently *thinking* of what they denote. Some Hibernicisms, as they are termed, are of this character. The judge, who, when puzzled by the ingenuity of two lawyers who were pleading a cause before him, exclaimed in a pet, "I believe you are both right," really violated that universal Law of Pure Thought, called the Principle of Excluded Middle, which declares that, of two contradictory propositions, one must be true, and the other false. Logic, as it proceeds from axiomatic principles, and derives none of its materials from experience, but considers only those laws which underlie all experience and first render it possible, is a purely demonstrative science, like algebra or geometry. It treats of those arguments only which are certain and irrefutable; or if it indirectly considers some of those forms which come short of perfect demonstration, such as Analogy, Imperfect Induction, and Example, it is only for the purpose of testing them by a reference to the standard forms the validity of which they presuppose, and which they endeavor, as it were, to approximate.

Universal Logic considers the Laws of Thought in their

application, not to this or that special class of objects, but to all objects whatsoever. This is the *Logica docens* of the Schoolmen, and contains the abstract theory of the science in its widest sense, without any of the limitations that arise from any special purpose or study which the thinker may have in view. It corresponds to the science of Universal Grammar, which treats only of those principles which belong to language *as such*, and therefore are exemplified in all languages, putting aside altogether the peculiarities of Hebrew, Greek, German, or any other particular tongue. On the other hand, *Special* Logic, or the *Logica utens* of the Schools, is the Logic of Mathematics, or the Logic of History, or of any other particular science; consequently, it involves a consideration of the Laws of Thought so far only as they are exemplified or involved in the processes of this one science. Herein Logic becomes subsidiary to the objects of the special inquiry which it is intended to promote or regulate. It presupposes a knowledge of those objects, and it forms an introduction to that inquiry. Hence, it is no longer Logic considered for its own sake, but it is Geometry, History, or some other science, considered in a logical point of view. The discussion of it is therefore relegated to treatises on that science of which it forms a part, and for which it is a special preparatory study. Legal Logic is a part of the science of Law. Mathematical Logic is an introduction or an appendage to pure Mathematics. But, in what now lies before us, it is evident that we have to do only with Universal Logic, which is one, while Special Logic is multiform; which is independent, while that requires an acquaintance with other objects of study and other modes of investigation; which is a part of the Philosophy of Mind, or of Philosophy itself in its wider sense, while that is a portion of a comparatively narrow science.

There are certain other portions of what has usually

been called Logic, which, though they do not properly belong to the science itself, yet, as they are generally discussed, often at great length, in most treatises upon it, may properly be defined and explained here, while a full consideration of them may be regarded as an appendix to the body of the work. Properly speaking, Pure Logic terminates with the consideration of the three classes of products — namely, Concepts, Judgments, and Reasonings — which are the elements into which all Thought is resolved. But Thought itself is subsidiary to the attainment of knowledge, — that is, to Science. The question remains, then, after we have fully treated of Concepts, Judgments, and Reasonings, taken separately or considered in themselves alone, what use is to be made of them, taken together, in the construction of Science. A full answer to this question, as it would involve a study of the *objects* of Science, — that is, of the matter of the special sciences, — evidently falls outside of the province of Logic. But a partial answer to it, regarding Science in its relation, not to the objects known, but to the knowing mind, may be considered as a natural appendage to Logic, as it embraces the conditions not merely of possible, but of perfect, Thought. Such an answer is usually called the Doctrine of Method, or Logical Methodology. Pure Logic considers only the Necessary Laws to which all Thought *must* conform ; the Doctrine of Method regards those rules and principles to which all Thought *ought* to conform in order to obtain its end, which is the advancement of Science. Pure Logic treats merely of the elements of Thought, while Logical Methodology regards the proper arrangement of these elements into an harmonious whole. All Method is a well-defined progress towards some end ; and the end in this case is the attainment of truth. Practically speaking, the Doctrine of Method is a body of rules or precepts looking to the proper regulation of the Thinking Faculty in the pursuit of knowledge; and, as such, it necessarily lacks the precision and the demonstrative certainty which are characteristic of the principles of Pure Logic. The Laws of Pure Thought are absolute; the merits of Perfect Thought are various, and attainable in different degrees, according to circumstances.

Another distinction has been taken, in this science, between Pure and Applied Logic, or, as Sir William Hamilton prefers to call the latter, Modified Logic. The former, as we have seen, considers the Thinking Faculty alone, as if it constituted the whole of the human mind, and therefore as if its Laws and Products were unaffected by any collateral and disturbing influences, but were manifested in precisely the same manner by different persons. It takes no account of the defects and hinderances which obstruct the normal action of the understanding. Modified Logic, on the other hand, considers Thought as it is, and not merely as it ought to be. It regards " the Causes of Error and the Impediments to Truth by which man is beset in the employment of his Faculties, and what are the means of their removal." And yet it is a *universal* science, — as much so as Pure Logic; — for it does not consider the Matter of Thought. The obstacles and imperfections which it points out are not those which arise from the objects of inquiry, but from the inquiring mind. They are subjective or psychological causes of error. Lord Bacon is probably the first philosopher who attempted a systematic enumeration of the causes of error. He made a quaint classification of them, under the significant name of *Idols*, into the four genera of Idols of the Tribe, or the necessary faults and imperfections of the human intellect itself; Idols of the Den, which arise from the special constitution, education, and habits of each individual man; Idols of the Forum, proceeding from the defects of the language which we are obliged to employ as an instrument of Thought and a means of communication; and Idols of the Theatre, or the various dogmas of ill-founded systems of philosophy which have found their way into men's minds through tradition, negligence, and credulity.

But Modified Logic is not properly called Logic, as it is a branch of Psychology, which treats of the phenomena of mind in general, and not merely of the normal action and necessary laws of one special faculty, the Understanding. As Modified Logic, however, is nearly allied in purpose with the Doctrine of Method, both looking to the same general end, — the attainment of truth through the proper regulation of the Thinking Faculty, — the two may well be considered together, under the general name of *Applied Logic*, as a kind of supplement to the science properly so called. Moreover, the connection between Thought and Language being so intimate, as we have seen, that neither can exist without the other, it would be an injurious, and, in fact, an impossible refinement, in a Treatise on Logic, to try to avoid frequent reference to those mistakes in thinking which proceed from an incautious use of words.

The utility of the study of Logic — at least, of *Formal Logic* — has been, perhaps, more generally doubted or denied, during the last two or three centuries, than that of any other recognized science. In England especially, ever since Bacon's time, but more particularly since that of John Locke, the study has been as unreasonably decried as it was, during an earlier period, unduly exalted. The popular voice has been against it, and, till within the last thirty years, it steadily lost ground even in the Universities, where the popular voice is not often heard or respected. This unjust depreciation of the study was due in great part to the extravagant pretensions formerly put forward in its favor. An age which acknowledged Bacon and Descartes to be its intellectual leaders was likely to scrutinize with extreme jealousy the claims of a science long held forth by its votaries as the science or art "of the right use of reason," or "of forming instruments for the direction of the mind"; as "the head and culminating point of philosophy," "the art of thinking," "the medicine of the mind," "the lighthouse of the intellect," "*ars artium et scientia scientiarum, qua aperta, omnes aliæ aperiuntur, et qua clausa, omnes aliæ clauduntur.*" Especially was this the case, as a dark shade had already been cast upon this boastful study by the rapid decline and visibly approaching extinction of those systems of philosophy, theology, and physical science which acknowledged the same parentage, and had long been associated with it in asserted pre-eminence and exclusiveness.

Logic fared not much better in the hands of those, its later disciples, who abated the extravagance of its pretensions, indeed, and, by throwing aside many of its technicalities and nice distinctions, rendered its aspect less abstruse and forbidding. But, still adhering to the opinion that its main purpose was to furnish practical rules for the guidance of the understanding in the search after truth, they destroyed its unity, broke down the boundaries which separate it from Psychology, Grammar, and Metaphysics, and encumbered it with a mass of disciplinary precepts which would be out of place anywhere but in treatises on practical education. The authors of the excellent "Art of Thinking," which commonly passes under the name of the "Port-Royal Logic," deemed it necessary to apologize even for the limited space which they had devoted to the special doctrines of this science, on the ground that "custom has introduced a sort of necessity of having at least a slight knowledge of Logic"; and they remarked, that, as the heads of chapters sufficiently indicated the topics considered in them, those of exclusively logical import might be omitted in the perusal without serious injury to what remained. "When we thought any matter might be of service in forming the judgment," they added, "we never scrupled to insert it, to whatever science it might belong"; and, accordingly, "in this Treatise, the reader will find many things relating to Physics and Ethics, [still more, they should have added, belonging to Grammar,] and almost as much Metaphysics as it is necessary to know." This is equivalent to denying that Logic has any claims to be considered as a distinct science, or that a thorough and systematic evolution of its principles would be of any practical benefit.

The ground of these misapprehensions is entirely removed by the view which has here been given of the province and the purpose of Logic. Its boundaries are clearly defined, its pretensions are moderate, and it accomplishes all that it is intended to perform. As a Formal Science, it takes no account of the Matter of Thought, which is all derived from processes of observation or intuition that lie beyond its province. It is not concerned with the something that is known, but only with the manner of knowing it. It is not an *organon* of discovery, then, or a means to be used for the extension of any science. It analyzes the Laws of Thought; but, as these Laws are necessary and universal, — that is, as they exist in full force even in the humblest and least-instructed intellect, — it does not profess to teach anything absolutely new, but only to bring out into distinct consciousness and scientific arrangement what exists or takes place implicitly in every mind. These Laws of Thought exist there in a latent or involved form; and we follow their guidance unconsciously, just as a person who has learned to speak and write only by moving in good society, and following the example of others, uses language in strict conformity with grammatical laws, though he is unacquainted with these laws even by name. The test of the validity of any doctrine in logical science is, that those to whom it is now for the first time communicated immediately recognize it as nothing new, except in the form of statement, but as a principle to which they have always conformed ever since they began to *think*. The purpose of Logic, then, is only to teach us how we always *have* thought, and not any new mode of thinking, or new precautions, through which we may avoid the errors to which we were formerly liable, or by which we may discover truths that were formerly unattainable. It has no counsels to give, except to urge careful and uniform compliance with Laws which every one admits to be authoritative and universal, and to which he has always intended to conform. As Mr. Mansel remarks, the science advises only the better performance of existing obligations, and does not attempt the imposition of new ones. "A treatise on Logic is not designed primarily to give men facility in the practice of reasoning, any more than a treatise on Optics is intended to improve their sight; and it would be as correct for a writer on the mathematical principles of Optics to entitle his work 'Optics, or the Art of improving defective Vision,' as it is for a writer on the principles of Logic to adopt for his title, 'Logic, or the Art of Reasoning.'"*

Indirectly, indeed, the science may be regarded as a medicine of the mind. As it brings out into clearer consciousness the laws to which all just thinking must conform, the indistinctness and confusion of thought to which we are all liable are dissipated, and the errors which often follow the symbolic use of language, or the substitution of words for thought, are exposed and eliminated. In these respects, we think rightly as soon as we have learned to think clearly; for the necessary forms of the understanding govern without dispute, when their applicability to the case in hand has become manifest. "The progress of the sciences," says Hamilton, "consists, not merely in the accumulation of new matter, but likewise in the detection of the relations

* Introduction to Aldrich's *Logic*, third edition, p. lvii

subsisting among the materials accumulated; and the reflective abstraction by which this is effected must not only follow the laws of Logic, but is most powerfully cultivated by the habits of logical study." As we spread out Concepts into their constituent Intuitions, or individualize them in particular Imaginations, their true relations to each are intuitively perceived, and inconsequence or contradiction in uniting them becomes impossible. All this, however, is but the elimination of Formal error; the Matter of thought comes from other sources; and for the mistakes which arise from limited observation, or imperfect induction, Logic has no remedy to offer. It guarantees the correctness neither of the premises nor of the conclusion, but only the validity of the inference from the former to the latter. Hence, what is formally correct may be materially false; I may reason rightly from wrong premises to a false conclusion. On the other hand, as an error in the Form necessarily vitiates the whole process of Thought, it may certainly be said that Logic furnishes us with a negative criterion between truth and falsehood. The blunders which it exposes are vital, but they are not those which are most insidious, or even of the most frequent occurrence.

Truth is the agreement of a cognition with the object which it is intended to represent. Now Logic, as it takes no cognizance of the object, which is the Matter of Thought, is evidently incompetent to determine whether such agreement exists or not. But there is a preliminary question to be settled before we come to a consideration of the object; we inquire whether the cognition agrees with itself, — that is, whether it is Formally correct. And this question Logic is competent to determine with absolute certainty. The Formal correctness of a cognition does not by any means insure its Material truth; but as Kant remarks, it is to be regarded as a *conditio sine qua non* of such truth.

The high place which Logic once held among the proper

studies of a University, and which within a few years it has wellnigh reclaimed, is vindicated by the great value of the effort which is necessary to master it, considered simply as a vigorous exercise of the understanding. Indeed, its chief function is disciplinary, for the effort to acquire it may be said to equal or surpass in value the subsequent use to be made of the acquisition. It is not of so much importance to know, as it is to have strengthened and developed all the faculties in learning to know. No other study taxes so severely the power of abstract thought, and hence no one furnishes better preparatory training for the pursuit of all the sciences which do not consist mainly in accumulating facts and registering the materials thus obtained.

Little needs to be said of the intrinsic dignity of the subject. "Admitting," says Heinrich Richter, as translated by Hamilton, "that this science teaches nothing new, that it neither extends the boundaries of knowledge, nor unfolds the mysteries which lie beyond the compass of our reflective intellect, and that it only investigates the immutable laws to which the mind in thinking is subjected, still, inasmuch as it develops the application of these laws, it bestows on us, to a certain extent, a dominion over our thoughts themselves. And is it nothing to watch the secret workshop in which nature fabricates cognitions and thoughts, and to penetrate into the sanctuary of self-consciousness, to the end that, having learnt to know ourselves, we may be qualified rightly to understand all else? Is it nothing to seize the helm of thought, and to be able to turn it at our will? For through a research into the laws of thinking, Logic gives us, in a certain sense, a possession of the thoughts themselves. It is true, indeed, that the mind of man is, like the universe of matter, governed by eternal laws, and follows, even without consciousness, the invariable canons of its nature. But to know and understand itself, and out of the boundless chaos of phenomena presented to the senses to form Concepts, through Concepts to reduce that chaos to harmony and arrangement, and thus to establish the dominion of intelligence over the universe of existence, — it is this alone which constitutes man's grand and distinctive pre-eminence." " Our whole dignity," says Pascal, " consists in thought."

It is also argued by Sir William Hamilton, with great force, that " Logic is further useful as affording a Nomenclature of the laws by which legitimate thinking is governed, and of the violation of these laws, through which thought becomes vicious or null.

" It is said, in Hudibras, —

> ' That all a Rhetorician's rules,
> Serve only but to name his tools ';

and it may be safely confessed that this is one of the principal utilities of Rhetoric. A mere knowledge of the rules of Rhetoric can no more enable us to compose well, than a mere knowledge of the rules of Logic can enable us to think well. There is required from nature, in both, the faculty; but this faculty must, in both departments, be cultivated by an assiduous and also a well-directed exercise; that is, in the one, the powers of Comparison must be exercised according to the rules of a sound Rhetoric, in the other, according to the rules of a sound Logic. In so far, therefore, the utility of either science is something more than a mere naming of their tools. But the naming of their tools, though in itself of little value, is valuable as the condition of an important function, which, without this, could not be performed. Words do not give thoughts; but without words, thoughts could not be fixed, limited, and expressed. They are, therefore, in general, the essential condition of all thinking worthy of the name. Now, what is true of human thought in general, is true of Logic and Rhetoric in particular. The nomenclature in these sciences is the nomenclature of certain general analyses and distinctions, which express to the initiated, in a single word, what the uninitiated could (supposing — what is not probable — that he could perform the relative processes) neither understand nor express without a tedious and vague periphrasis; while, in his hands, it would assume only the appearance of a particular observation, instead of a particular instance of a general and acknowledged rule. To take a very simple example: — there is in Logic a certain sophism, or act of illegal inference, by which two things are, perhaps in a very concealed and circuitous manner, made to prove each other. Now, the man unacquainted with Logic may perhaps detect and be convinced of the fallacy; but how will he expose it? He must enter upon a long statement and explanation, and, after much labor to himself and others, he probably does not make his objection clear and demonstrative after all. But between those acquainted with Logic, the whole matter would be settled in two words. It would be enough to say and show, that the inference in question involved a *circulus in concludendo*, and the refutation is at once understood and admitted. It is in like manner that one lawyer will express to another the *ratio decidendi* of a case in a single technical expression; while their clients will only perplex themselves and others in their attempts to set forth the merits of their cause. Now, if Logic did nothing more than establish a certain number of decided and decisive rules in reasoning, and afford us brief and precise expressions by which to bring particular cases under these general rules, it would confer on all who in any way employ their intellect — that is, on the cultivators of every human science — the most important obligation. For it is only in the possession of such established rules, and of such a technical nomenclature, that we can accomplish, with facility, and to an adequate extent, a criticism of any work of reasoning. Logical language is thus, to the general reasoner, what the notation of Arithmetic, and still more of Algebra, is to the mathematician. Both enable us to comprehend and express, in a few significant symbols, what would otherwise overpower us by their complexity; and thus it is, that nothing would contribute more to facilitate and extend the faculty of reasoning, than a general acquaintance with the rules and language of Logic, — an advantage extending indeed to every department of knowledge, but more especially of importance to those professions which are occupied in inference, and conversant with abstract matter, such as Theology and Law."

CHAPTER III.

THE PRIMARY AXIOMS OF PURE THOUGHT.

HAVING defined Logic to be the Science of the Necessary Laws of Pure Thought, our first object must be to ascertain what are the Fundamental and Universal Laws, here called Primary Axioms, to which all Thought, as such, is subject. In the separate consideration, which will come afterwards, of the three classes of Thoughts, — namely, Concepts, Judgments, and Reasonings, — we may expect to find Special Laws or Rules which are applicable only to one or two of these divisions. Such Special Rules may or may not be derivative in character; — that is, they may be either immediate inferences from the Primary Axioms which govern all the products of the Thinking Faculty, or they may be independent, as resting upon their own evidence. Of this hereafter. But our first inquiry must be, whether there are any Axioms of universal applicability, which underlie and govern *every* act and product of the human Understanding; and, if there are such, to determine their character and significance.

If there are such Axioms, they must be few, meagre in import, not susceptible of proof, and recognizable by all as familiar truisms, which have always implicitly directed their thoughts, though perhaps, on account of their very obviousness, they have never been explicitly stated or drawn out into distinct consciousness. They must have these characteristics, because they concern only the Forms of Thought, or the manner of thinking irrespective of what we are thinking about; and as these Forms themselves are necessarily limited in number and narrow in significance, the Axioms which underlie them all, and constitute their common features, must be still fewer and poorer in import. They cannot admit of proof, as their truth is presupposed in every act of reasoning, and therefore no argument or proof is possible unless their veracity is taken for granted. They must be recognized by all as mere truisms, because they are thus self-evident, and because their truth has been acknowledged and acted upon in every Form of Thought which we have ever experienced. The First Principles of all the sciences are avowedly thus few and meagre, as is seen to be the case with the introductory axioms of Geometry and Physics. With still more reason do we expect the First Principles of all Thought to possess this character, as they stand in the same relation to the axioms of the special sciences, that these axioms do to the most advanced theorems which have been built upon them, or which have been constructed by taking them for granted.

After this explanation, we need not be surprised to find that all the Primary Axioms of Pure Thought are perhaps reducible to this single principle: — *All Thought must be consistent with itself.* If it be inconsistent, — if, directly or indirectly, it contradicts itself, — it is self-destructive, and the Thought is null. Thus stated, the principle is coincident with that which is usually called the Law of Contradiction, though, as Hamilton remarks, it ought rather to be termed the Law of Non-Contradiction. Practically speaking, every Thought which must be rejected as formally invalid — that is, which is radically vicious in Form, whatever be its Matter — offends against this principle. By logicians generally, however, this principle has been explicated into three general Axioms, called the Law of Identity, the Law of Contradiction, and the Law of Excluded Middle. The ground of this explication may be thus set forth.

The primary element of all Thought is a Judgment, which arises from a Comparison. Hence, all Thought must proceed either by affirmation or denial, as these are the only two possible forms of Judgment. Having compared any two Concepts with each other, we either perceive their identity, similarity, congruence, or some other relation whereby we affirm their union in one act of Thought; or we perceive the opposite relation between them, such as difference, unlikeness, or incompatibility, whereby we deny one of the other. As any Concept can be compared with any other, and as the Judgment which follows such comparison must either *affirm or deny* one of the other, there being no *third* form of Judgment conceivable, we have the Axiom which is usually called the Law of Excluded Third or Excluded Middle, — *Lex Exclusi Tertii aut Medii*. Either A is B, or A is not B: if we make any Judgment, — that is, if we *think* at all, — one of these two must be true; for no third form is conceivable. It has been enounced in various forms: — Of two contradictory judgments, one must be true; Every predicate may be affirmed or denied of every subject; Every conceivable thing is either A or not-A. Of course, A and not-A, taken together, include the universe, — the universe not only of all that is actual, but of all that is conceivable; for as not-A excludes A only and nothing else, it includes the universe excepting A only.

Still further: — Not only are affirmation and negation the only conceivable forms of Judgment, but, as contradictory opposites, they are absolutely incompatible or mutually destructive. The admission of one is tantamount to a rejection of the other. If taken together, they destroy each other, and the Thought is rendered null. We cannot affirm both A and not-A of the same thing. Here we have the well-known Law of Contradiction, more properly of Non-Contradiction, of which the formula is, A *is not not*-A.

Evidently this Law is the principle of all logical negation and discrimination. It has been variously expressed:— Contradictory attributes cannot be affirmed of the same subject; What is contradictory is inconceivable. It is less correctly expressed in the adage, "It is impossible for the same thing to be and not to be." This is a maxim which concerns the Matter of Thought, and therefore we must add to it the material limitations, *in the same place, at the same time, in the same respect,* &c. It is a mistake, then, to maintain that the Axiom, "Contradictory attributes cannot be affirmed of the same subject," is not universally true, because we can form such assertions as this: *A man can be both young and not-young, though not at the same time.* In Logic, where we consider only the *Form* of the Thought, a Judgment must be expressed by the present tense of the verb *to be;* for what we affirm is not the past or future union of two real phenomena, but the present coexistence and agreement of two Concepts in the mind. Hence, the logical Judgment, *this man* IS NOT *young*, is absolutely incompatible with the assertion, *this man* IS *young*, though it is compatible with the very different assertion, *this man* HAS BEEN *young*.

Once more: The formula, *A is not not-A*, proves, on reduction, to be the exact equivalent or consequence of this, *A is A.* Here we have the principle of affirmation and agreement, as the former was that of negation and difference. If an object cannot be thought under contradictory attributes, it is because it has a definite character of its own, excluding one of the contradictories through including the other. "The universe of conceivable objects," to adopt Mr. Mansel's language, "embraces both *A* and *not-A;* it is only when definitely conceived as the one, that an object cannot be conceived as the other. Every object of thought, as such, is thus conceived by limitation and difference; as having definite characteristics by which it is marked off and distinguished from all others; as being, in short, *itself*, and nothing else." Here, then, we have a third Primary Axiom, expressed as the Law of Identity: *Every A is A;* Every object of thought is conceived as itself; Every thing is equal to itself or agrees with itself; Every whole is the sum of all its parts.

Thus we have three Primary Axioms of Pure Thought, — the Law of Identity, the Law of Contradiction, and the Law of Excluded Middle, — all of which may be regarded as explications of the single rule, that *all Thought must be consistent with itself*, or as corollaries from this one principle, that Judgment, which is the basis of all Thought, proceeds only by affirmation and denial. The mutual dependence and correlation of these three Axioms may be further illustrated thus.

I can think any object only by placing it under a Concept, or Class-notion expressed by a General Term; and I can do this only by recognizing that it possesses the attributes which belong to this Concept and are common to all the members of this Class (Law of Identity, affirmation of similarity or agreement); by discriminating it from other objects which have different attributes (Law of Contradiction, negation of agreement); and both this affirmation and denial proceed by the Law of Excluded Middle, which declares, for each given attribute, that the one or the other is absolutely necessary. Either it does, or does not, belong to the object, and the object does or does not belong to the Class. In respect to the Laws of Identity and Contradiction, says Sir William Hamilton, "each infers the other, but only through the principle of Excluded Middle; and the principle of Excluded Middle only exists through the supposition of the two others. Thus, the principles of Identity and Contradiction cannot move, — cannot be applied, — except through supposing the principle of Excluded Middle; and this last cannot be conceived existent except through the supposition of the two former. They are thus coördinate, but inseparable. Begin with any one, the other two follow as corollaries."

Hence he symbolizes the three Axioms by a Triangle, thus: —

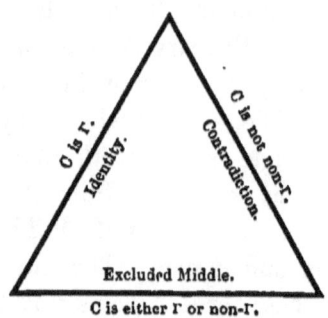

These three Axioms are sufficient for all purposes of *analytic* Thought. There is, however, another large class of Judgments, which are dependent in part upon a fourth Axiom; and, as a preliminary to the consideration of it, we must explain the difference between analytic and synthetic Thought. Kant was the first to bring this distinction into notice as one of great importance in philosophy.

In an analytic Judgment, the Predicate affirms nothing which was not already, though implicitly, contained in the Concept which forms the Subject. We analyze a Concept into the Marks or attributes of which it consists, and then predicate of it one or more of these Marks. Of course, no other knowledge is requisite for forming such a Judgment than is already contained in the Subject itself, as the Predicate affirms nothing more than what is so contained. Thus, if I say, *Body is extended, A circle is round, An equilateral triangle has three equal sides,* I merely repeat, or state explicitly, what is already implied in the very notion of a *body,* a *circle,* and an *equilateral triangle.* But in the propositions, *Body is heavy, A circle is a particular section of a cone, A triangle is a figure the three angles of which are equal to two right angles,* the Predicate adds something that was not previously known and included in the notion of the Subject. There must be some *reason* for such addition; otherwise, all Thought which is not merely analytical in character would be arbitrary and inconsequent. Pure Thought, which deals only with the Form, and not with the Matter, of Thinking, does not ask what this *reason* is, and seeks not in any way to determine its character. It only demands that there should be *some* reason,— that the connections of Thought, or those reductions to unity in which all Thinking consists, should not be merely casual or capricious; in which case, there would be no proper connection at all.

Besides the first postulate of the Understanding, that *all Thought should be consistent with itself*, we have, then, this second demand, in reference at least to synthetic Judgments, that *all Thought should be consequent;* that is, that it should never affirm or deny a union of two Concepts without any ground for such affirmation or denial. The sufficiency of this ground or reason is a *material* question, with which the logician, as such, has nothing to do. Leibnitz was wrong, then, in denominating this principle that of " the Sufficient Reason." The limitation is superfluous, for the only reason required is one that will make the union of the predicate with the subject *conceivable*,—not an *actual* union of real things; and the reason which is insufficient for *this* end is no reason at all. This axiom, which is properly called that of Reason and Consequent, or the Condition and the Conditioned, is expressed in the formula, *affirm nothing without a ground or reason;* or, *every affirmation must have a ground or reason why it is affirmed.*

As the former postulate was evolved into three Axioms, so this one may be explicated into two, such explication being, in fact, only a statement of the meaning of the words employed. The first of these derivative Axioms is, that *to affirm the Reason or the Condition is also to affirm the Consequent or the Conditioned;* for the Reason would not be the Reason unless the Consequent followed it. The second Axiom is, that *to deny the Consequent is also to deny the Reason;* for, again, if the Consequent does not follow, the Reason cannot exist, since the Reason means only that which necessitates the Consequent. The two Axioms are thus pithily stated by the old Logicians: *Positâ conditione ponitur conditionatum, sublato conditionato tollitur conditio;* or thus: *A ratione ad rationatum, a negatione rationati ad negationem rationis, valet consequentia.*

Observe, however, that the converse of these two Axioms does not hold good. To affirm the Consequent is not to affirm any given Reason, since the Consequent may have followed from some other Reason; and the same consideration shows that it is not competent, from a denial of any given Reason, to infer a denial of the Consequent. The primary Axiom asserts only the necessity of some Reason or other, not of any one Reason. The explication may be thus summed up in a tabular form:—

There must be a Ground or Reason for every affirmation.
Affirming the Reason   affirms also the Consequent.
Denying the Reason,   nothing follows.
Affirming the Consequent, nothing follows.
Denying the Consequent denies also the Reason.

Strictly speaking, this Axiom is applicable to all analytic, as well as to all synthetic Judgments, and therefore, like each of the other three Axioms, it is a Universal Law of Thought. But in the case of analytic Judgments this Axiom does not need to be separately considered or enounced, for the *ground* or *reason* to which it refers is contained in the Judgment itself; we cannot *think* the latter without the former. Thus, we cannot think of *body* without *extension;* and therefore, when we affirm that *body is extended,* the Judgment carries its own reason or justification along with it. But in synthetic Thought, as when we say that *matter is compressible,* we see no reason in the Thought itself why the attribute of *compressibility* should be affirmed of it, any more than *incompressibility.* The Axiom of Excluded Middle tells us that one or the other *must* be so predicated, — that matter must be either compressible or incompressible. Another necessary Law of Thought — that of Reason and Consequent — forbids us to predicate either of these contradictories to the necessary exclusion of the other, without a ground for such preference; and the reason in this case must be derived from some source exterior to the Judgment itself, as no analysis of the latter will afford any such reason. We may, indeed, predicate neither; we may leave the Thought, so far as this pair of contradictories is concerned, wholly indeterminate. But if we affirm anything of it, beyond what is already contained in it, there must be a reason, express or implied, for such affirmation.

With obvious propriety, analytic Judgments are also called *explicative,* as they merely unfold, and thereby bring into clearer consciousness, what we already possess. By them our knowledge is cleared up and rendered explicit, but is not at all enlarged. Synthetic Judgments, on the other hand, are properly called *ampliative,* as by them our sum of knowledge is increased. Each of these requires a reason, as otherwise its result would not be the enlargement of knowledge, but the caprice of ignorance.

It is rightly observed by Krug, that the relation of Reason and Consequent is something different from that of Cause and Effect. It is true that Cause and Effect, *so far as they are conceived in thought,* stand to each other as Reason and Consequent. But the converse is not true; all Reasons are not Causes, and all Consequents are not Effects. The two relations may be distinguished from each other as being respectively what the old logicians called the *ratio cognoscendi* and the *ratio essendi*. Thus, to take an example, *the ground being wet* is the Reason why I know that *it has rained;* this is the *ratio cognoscendi*, and it is evidently a relation of one *thought* to another *thought;* though the wetness of the ground is certainly not the Cause of the rain, yet, because I *know* that the ground is wet, I am justified in *thinking* that the rain has fallen. On the other hand, the falling of the rain is the Cause of the ground being wet; this is the *ratio essendi*, and it is the relation of one *real thing*, or actual occurrence, to another; and, as such, it is independent of any thought, as the one thing would still cause the other, though there were no mind to observe their connection. Hence, the relation of Reason and Consequent is a mere synthesis of thoughts; the thought of wetness of the ground suggests, and, so to speak, justifies the thought of rain. But Cause and Effect expresses an actual union of physical events, the real existence of the one compelling or necessitating the existence of the other.

This seems the proper place to introduce what is called "the postulate of Logic," — a precept which Logicians have always assumed, and acted upon in part, but which, before Sir William Hamilton's time, they never distinctly enounced, or carried out consistently in all its consequences. To adopt his language, —

"The only postulate of Logic which requires an articulate enouncement is the demand, that, before dealing with a judgment or reasoning expressed in language, the import of its terms should be fully understood; in other words, Logic postulates to be allowed to state explicitly in language what is implicitly contained in the Thought."

This assumption is grounded upon the two fundamental

propositions already stated and explained, namely, that Logic deals only with the Form, and not with the Matter, of Thought; and that it is concerned primarily with the Thought, and only secondarily with the accident of its expression. The science claims, therefore, to fill up the gaps and elisions of ordinary discourse, wherein much is sacrificed to brevity of speech, and to pare down the complexity and redundance of rhetorical expression into logical simplicity and precision. For ordinary purposes, and for the Rhetorician's use, language is a vehicle for the rapid and effective communication both of Thought and feeling; consequently, it deals much in hints and abbreviated forms of speech, taking for granted all that the reader's and hearer's mind will readily supply, and aiming only to bring his faculties of reasoning, imagination, and emotion into play in the right direction. The Logician, on the other hand, seeks to express nothing but Thought; and he aims to make language a perfect representative of the Thought in its simplicity and entireness. His proper function is to point out those minute but frequently recurrent elements of Thought, which, precisely because frequently recurrent, are elided or passed over in ordinary discourse. Of course, the expressions which he thus finds occasion to use will often appear awkward and redundant, tediously minute, and even tautological. But he is not responsible for their rhetorical demerits; the only question for him is, whether they fully and correctly express ALL that is actually passing in Thought. Thus, the common form of argumentation is the Enthymeme, which consists of but two propositions; but its Logical form is the Syllogism, consisting of three. No one but a silly pedant ever speaks or writes Syllogisms, except in a treatise on Logic. But the only question is, whether everybody does not *think* Syllogisms whenever he speaks or writes Enthymemes. To take another instance, Hamilton's doctrine of the thoroughgoing quantification of the predicate has been objected to for this reason, among others, that the propositions which it vindicates are so awkward and unnatural, that they seem "got up for the purpose of seeing what one can do." Perhaps so; and yet the objection is an idle one. For if there are occasions when we must *think* affirmative Judgments with universal predicates, and negative Judgments with particular ones, the Logician's first duty is to express this fact, however awkward and even ludicrous such expression may seem.

CHAPTER IV.

THE DOCTRINE OF CONCEPTS.

1. Their Quantity; 2. Their Quality; 3. Their Relation; 4. Their Definition and Division.

A CONCEPT is a combination, or a reduction to unity in Thought, of those elements and qualities of the objects which we are thinking of, whereby they are distinguished from all other objects, and especially from those which, in other respects, are most similar to them.* These distinguishing attributes, which are the elements of the Concept, are called its Marks; for through them the objects of Thought are *determined*, or known to be what they are, and discriminated from what they are not. The word, or General Term, which is the appellation of the Concept, is, consequently, the Common Name of all the objects that are included under it. It is a convenient use of language, (though the words are sometimes applied in a different manner,) to say that the word or Name *connotes*

---

* The words *Concept* and *Notion*, often used as synonymes, are perhaps best distinguished etymologically; — Concept (*con-capere*) as the grasping up together of a plurality of attributes into one Thought; Notion (*noscere notis*, to know an object by its Marks), as the taking note of the several Marks or characteristics of an object. The meaning of Notion might, perhaps, be conveniently limited to the *apprehension* of any single Mark (*nota*), while Concept signifies the *comprehension* of all the attributes which are characteristic of a certain class of things. Thus, I have a Notion of each of the Marks, *cold-blooded, vertebrated, animal, breathing by means of gills*, and *living in the water*, taken singly; and I have a Concept of them taken together, as the characteristic Marks of a *Fish*, or of the whole class of Fishes. As thus limited, Nótions are a subordinate class of Concepts.

the attributes or Marks which make up its signification,* and *denotes* the individual things contained under it which possess those attributes. Thus, the name *Man* connotes *biped, two-handed, rational, animal,* and denotes all individual men and classes of men.

It has already been explained, that a Concept is not necessarily the Thought of an actual, but only of a possible, class of objects; that is, its name may actually denote only one thing, as, for example, the one animal, just discovered, of a species hitherto unknown. Hence, Esser was led to define a Concept as "the representation of an (one) object through its distinguishing Marks." But even in this case, the representation, in order to be a Concept, must be a *partial* representation; that is, it must represent, not all the Marks, but only the distinguishing Marks. Thus it becomes the representative of a possible class or plurality of things; if other specimens should be subsequently discovered possessing these distinguishing Marks, the Concept would include them also. It is only when the object is immediately *presented* before us either by the Senses or the Imagination, so that we have a *Presentation* or Intuition of it, as one whole, with *all* its

---

* "As these qualities or modes are only identified with the thing by a mental attribution, they are called *attributes;* as it is only in and through them that we say or enounce aught of a thing, they are called *predicates, predicables,* and *predicaments,* or *categories* (these words being here used in their more extensive signification); as it is only in and through them that we recognize a thing for what it is, they are called *notes, signs, marks, characters;* finally, as it is only in and through them that we become aware that a thing is possessed of a peculiar and determinate existence, they are called *properties, differences, determinations.* As consequent on, or resulting from the existence of a thing, they have likewise obtained the name of *consequents.* What in reality has no qualities has no existence in thought, — it is a logical nonentity; hence *e converso,* the scholastic aphorism, *non-entis nulla sunt predicata.* What, again, has no qualities attributed to it, though attributable, is said to be *indetermined;* it is only a possible object of thought."
— HAMILTON, *Lectures on Logic,* Am. ed., p. 55:

attributes, that its Name is a Proper Name strictly so called; for if it is present only in Thought, our representation of it is necessarily partial, as not including all its Marks, and its Name is then virtually Common, as the designation of a possible plurality of things. Thus, if I am contrasting in Thought two historical characters, as Cesar and Pompey, these two names *to my conception* become General Terms, as several individuals may each possess the few Marks which, for the purposes of this contrast, I attribute to those two old Romans. Gray's affecting lines may be attributed to any churchyard:—

> "Some mute inglorious Milton there may rest,
> Some Cromwell, guiltless of his country's blood."

Still further; not merely may a Concept actually denote only one thing, it may actually connote only one Mark. But here, as before, there is a possible plurality in actual unity. Thus, in the present state of my knowledge, my Notion or Concept of *red color* may be absolutely simple,— that is, it may have but this one Mark of *redness*. But additional acquaintance with the science of Optics would teach me that this red color is *an element of white light*, and that it has *a certain degree of refrangibility*, by virtue of which *its position in the solar spectrum is at one end of the scale*. Here are three additional Marks of *red color*. In like manner, every Concept, though actually simple, must be regarded as containing a possible plurality of Marks. I say, it *must* be so regarded; for every Concept must *denote* some existing object,— existing, that is, either really or potentially; and no such object can be conceived of except as possessing a possible plurality of Marks. For every object can be conceived to be what it is, only by discriminating it from several things which it is not; and such discrimination is possible only through a plurality of attributes.

This will be more evident, if we consider for a moment the various kinds of Marks by which one Concept may be distinguished from another. The following enumeration of them, which might be much enlarged, is taken in great part from Esser.

Marks are divided,—1. Into *affirmative* and *negative*, according as we know through them either what the object is, or what it is not; thus, *rational* is an Affirmative, *imperfect* a Negative, Mark of Man. 2. Into *internal* and *external*, according as the Mark is attributed to the object either in and for itself, or on the ground of the relation in which it stands to some other object; thus, *biped* is an Internal, *Father* or *Son* an External, Mark of Man. 3. Into *permanent* and *transitory*, according as they are always, or only sometimes, found in the object; thus, *metallic* is a Permanent, *hot* is a Transitory, Mark of Iron. 4. Into *peculiar* and *common*, according as they belong to these only, or also to other objects; thus, *right-angled* is a Peculiar, *plane-figure* is a Common, Mark of a Square. 5. Into *essential* or *necessary*, and *accidental* or *contingent*, according as they can, or cannot, be separated from the object; thus, *rational* is an Essential, *learned* an Accidental, Mark of Man. 6. Into *original* or *immediate*, and *derivative* or *mediate*, according as they are either Marks of the thing itself, or only Marks of other Marks of it; thus, *free-willed* is an Original, *able to compute by numbers* a Derivative, Mark of Man, the latter being only a consequent or Mark of *rationality*.

We gain another view of the elements of a Concept by dividing them into,—1. Kinds of Existence; 2. Qualities, or Modes of Existence; and 3. Relations, or Forms of Intermediate Existence.

First, in order to conceive, we must conceive *something*,—i. e. some *being* or *existence*,—which, as an object of Thought, may be distinguished from other things, and to which qualities can be attributed. If there is no such *entity*, at the bottom of the Concept, to give it unity, the Thought is null; *non-entis nulla sunt predicata.* There are but two kinds of Being or Existence, one of which is thus necessarily presupposed in Thought; namely, Real and Imaginary or Potential. One or the other must enter into every Concept, not as attributed to it, but as presupposed in forming it. In other words, every *Thought* must be of some real or imaginary *thing.*

Secondly, whatever exists must exist in some determinate mode; that is to say, it must have one or more qualities. Being or existence, as defined above, includes *all* things, both real and possible; hence, in order to think any particular thing, we must discriminate it from other things; and we can do this only by attributing to it Qualities, or particular modes of existence. By presupposing existence, then, we have a *thing*, or object of *possible* Thought; by giving to it qualities, we have a definite thing, or object of *actual* Thought. The thing exists in itself, *per se;* the quality exists only in the thing, — that is, in something different from itself, *per aliud*, or, as the logicians say, *per accidens.*

Thirdly, a Relation exists neither in itself, *per se*, nor in the thing as different from itself, *per aliud*, but *between* the thing and some other thing with which it is compared. This intermediate state of existence is the only characteristic feature of Relations, whereby they are distinguished from other Qualities. The Relation does not merely *result* from a comparison and discrimination, for this is true of all Qualities; but it only *exists* as between one thing and another, thereby necessitating a Thought of both. Thus, the Relation of Husband and Wife exists in neither of them, but between them, and can be apprehended only by thinking of the two together.

"Every object," says Drobisch, "is thought as a *deter-*

minate object only through the Marks appertaining to it, by means of which it is comparable, in respect to its nature, with other things, and is distinguishable from them. Without these Marks, it is only an *indeterminate something*, a thing or being without further determination; just as, on the other hand, these Marks have no independent being in and for themselves, but they can be separated only in Thought from the object in which they exist. In the Concept of the object, then, there is the Thought of an independent but indeterminate *something*, united with determinate, but (in themselves considered) dependent, Marks; the Concept of the object is *the union* of the two. (Thus, my Concept of Man is a *living, rational, organic* SOMETHING, *having a mortal body and an immortal soul.*) The Marks are the manifold, the plurality, and the *indeterminate something* is that which gives unity to these Marks, in the Concept of an object. The Concept is complex, therefore, and admits of separation into its elements; and this separation is called Analysis."

It is obvious enough, that the distinction between Concept and Marks is not absolute, but relative; they may be used interchangeably. Any Concept may become the Mark of some other Concept; and every Notion, which may appear in one Thought as a Mark, becomes in another an independent Concept. Thus, the Concept *animal* is a Mark of *man;* and *metal*, which is a Mark of *iron*, is itself a Concept, including under it *iron, tin, lead,* &c. The only distinction consists in the two different uses which are made of them in Thought. If a Concept is used only as a means of determining some other Concept, and so without direct reference to the objects or things which it denotes, it is a Mark; but if used as a Class-notion of certain objects, and with only secondary reference to the attributes or qualities involved in it, it is a Concept in the stricter sense. In other words, if used connotatively, it is called a Mark; if used denotatively, it is called a Concept.

The only law of *pure* Thought applicable to the formation of Concepts is the Axiom of Non-contradiction. A Concept must not have contradictory Marks, as these destroy each other, and the Thought so far becomes void or null. Thus, looking only to the Form of Thought, to the Concept A may be attributed the Marks B, C, D, and so on without limitation; but B and not-B cannot be so attributed.

Looking to the Matter of the Thought, however, a further limitation arises. Considered in relation to each other, Marks are either Congruent or Repugnant; the former can, and the latter cannot, be attributed to the same Concept. Thus, *sweet* and *red* are Congruent, as the same apple may have both Marks; but *sweet* and *bitter* are Repugnant, since they cannot be united in the same object. If the tyro should object, that one part of it may be sweet, and another part bitter, the answer is, that the two parts are two different objects. Marks are said to be Contradictory, when the one is a simple or direct negation of the other; as *sweet* and *not-sweet*, *B* and *not-B*. They are Repugnant or Contrary, when the negation is indirect, as when the one is denied, not directly, but by putting in its place, or in the same Concept, another Mark with which it is incompatible. The mere Form of the Marks tells me whether they are Contradictory or not; but to know whether they are Congruent or Repugnant, I must know the Matter of the Thought,—that is, I must have recourse to experience.

Again, if considered as mere Marks, or with reference to their connotation only, the attributes which are united in the same object are *disparate Notions*, for they are different without any similarity. This holds true of Congruent, as well as of Repugnant, Marks; thus, *sweet* and *red* are Disparate, for the quality of sweetness has no resemblance whatever with that of redness. On the other hand, if considered as Concepts, or with reference to what they denote, they are properly called *disjunct* or *discrete Notions*, for they are only relatively different; they have at least so much in common, that they can be co-ordinated under some higher Concept. Thus, *sweet apples* and *red apples* are so far similar, that they both belong under the Class-notion *apples* or *fruits*. It is only stating the same distinction in other words to say, that Disparate Notions are Congruent, for they can be united in the same Concept; but they do not denote any objects. On the other hand, the Disjunct do denote Objects, but they are not Congruent, for they cannot be united *in*, but are only contained *under*, the same Concept.

To apprehend still further the nature of Concepts, they must be viewed in three aspects. First, if considered in themselves alone, they have Quantity; secondly, if considered in reference to the mind or thinking subject in which they are conceived, they have Quality; thirdly, if considered in reference to each other, they have Relation.

1. The Quantity of Concepts.

It follows from the definition which has been given, that a Concept is a magnitude or Quantity, and that this Quantity is twofold. First, it has a number of Marks, which are reduced to unity in Thought, because they are all conceived as inhering in one object or thing. This is its Quantity of Intension. Secondly, it denotes a number of objects, which are reduced to unity in Thought as one class or species, because each of them possesses all these Marks. This is its Quantity of Extension. Thus, the Intension of *bird* is a *winged, feathered, vertebrated, biped, animal;* in its Extension are contained all individual birds and classes of birds, as *eagles, vultures, hawks, pigeons,* &c. The plurality of objects which are denoted by the Concept are said to constitute a Logical whole, or the whole of Extension; the plurality of Marks connoted by the Concept form a Metaphysical whole, or the whole of Intension.

This distinction of Quantity has been expressed by Logicians in various ways, which are here enumerated for convenience of reference, though the forms of expression already given will be adhered to in the present work.

A Logical or Universal whole   A Metaphysical or Formal whole *
   has Extension,   has Intension,
   Breadth,   Depth,
   Sphere;   Comprehension;
   contains under it,   contains in it,
   denotes,   connotes,
   Objects,   Marks,
   Things.   Attributes.

This twofold Quantity of Concepts enables us to understand the seemingly opposite assertions, that the Subject of a proposition is in the Predicate, and yet that the Predicate is in the Subject. With reference to the Quantity

---

* Besides the Logical and the Metaphysical, three other sorts of wholes have been distinguished by Logicians.

1. The Essential or Physical whole is that which consists of Matter and Form, or substance and accident, as its essential parts. The characteristic of this whole is, that, as its parts do not exist out of each other, they cannot be separated except in Thought. As Burgersdyck says, "the Form permeates the Matter, and *informs* all its parts," so that Form and Matter are inseparable.

2. The Mathematical or Integral whole, on the other hand, has parts which are external to each other, so that they can be divided asunder. This is the case with geometrical figures, as the *triangle,* the *parallelogram,* and with the *human body* and the *limbs.* These have *partes extra partes.*

3. A Collective whole, or whole of Aggregation, has its parts separate and accidentally thrown together; as, *an army,* a *heap of stones.*

of Intension, the Predicate is in the Subject, inasmuch as it is but one of several Marks which make up our Notion of the Subject. Thus, *man is animal; animal* may be regarded as a part of *man*, because it is a part of the meaning of the word; and, when taken in connection with the other parts, *living, two-handed, rational*, makes up the whole Intension of the Concept *man*. But in respect to the Quantity of Extension, *man* is contained under *animal*, — the Subject in the Predicate, — since he is but one out of many kinds, all denoted by this one General Term, or contained under this one Concept, *animal*.

"We find two expressions in Aristotle, both of which are sometimes rendered by 'being in,' — *inesse*. 1. ὑπάρχειν, by which the Predicate is said to be in the Subject. This is equivalent to κατηγορεῖσθαι. Τὸ A ὑπάρχει παντὶ τῷ B = τὸ A κατηγορεῖται κατὰ παντὸς τοῦ B = *A inest omni B* (= *A is predicated of every B* = *All B is A*). 2. εἶναι ἐν, by which the Subject is said to be in the Predicate. A ἐστιν ἐν ὅλῳ τῷ B = *Omne A est B* (*All A is B*). This is exactly the reverse of κατηγορεῖται. The English language is defective in not having, like the Greek and Latin, a proper Copula to express the relation of Intension as well as that of Extension. Thus the relation expressed by ὑπάρχει and *inest* can only be strictly rendered into English by a circumlocution, 'A is a quality belonging to B.' With the ordinary Copula, both must be translated into the language of Extension." *

Besides the Concepts which are formed from individual things, by abstracting their differences and uniting their common or similar elements, we can, by a perfectly similar process, form Concepts of Concepts; and then, again repeating this process, we obtain Concepts of *these* Concepts, and so on indefinitely. In this way, we have in each case

---

* MANSEL, *Notes to Aldrich*, p. 45.

a hierarchy of Concepts, of which only the lowest in order directly denotes individuals, while all the others directly denote other Concepts or classes, and only indirectly denote the individuals contained in those classes. Thus, *spaniel, terrier, hound, mastiff*, &c. are Concepts of the first or lowest order, each of them directly denoting certain individual animals, whose common attributes have become, in Thought, the Marks of their class. Then, abstracting the differences of these classes, we have *dog* as a Concept of the second order, directly denoting *spaniel, terrier*, &c., and indirectly denoting the same individuals as before. Having formed in a similar manner secondary Concepts of *cat, wolf, fox, bear*, &c., by comparing all of these with *dog*, abstracting the differences and combining the similarities, we obtain the tertiary Concept *carnivora*. Again, comparing *carnivora* with *rodents, marsupials, ruminants*, &c., we have a Concept of the next higher order, *mammal*, of which the Marks, forming the Intension, are *vertebrate, viviparous, warm-blooded, animal, suckling its young*. It is evident that we can go on in this manner, rising through Concepts successively broader and broader in generalization, till we reach the limit of human Thought in the Concept *thing, entity*, or *object of Thought*, which connotes nothing but *existence* (real or potential), and denotes *everything*.

I have here intentionally taken an illustration of the logical process of generalization from Natural History, as the science in which classification is most extensive and precise, though with the disadvantage of introducing here a number of technical names peculiar to that science, and with which, as belonging to the Matter of Thought, Logic has nothing to do. But every word in our language, or in any language, perfectly corresponds to one of these zoölogical technicalities, in that it occupies a definite place in some one of the countless hierarchies of Concepts which the human mind, for various purposes, has been led to form. The greater part of our mental life is spent in generalizing by successive steps, — that is, in forming Concepts of Concepts; — but always, except in the science of Logic, with special reference to the particular things denoted by these Concepts. Logic, which deals only with the Form, and not the Matter, of Thought, needs a set of technicalities of its own, to describe these steps of generalization, and all other processes of *pure* Thought, with reference, not to the things which they denote, but to each other and to the thinking mind. This is precisely the distinction, so famous in the Scholastic philosophy, between *first* and *second intentions*, — a distinction which has been ignorantly ridiculed by those who did not understand it, but which in itself is perfectly intelligible, and is as necessary as other technical distinctions in science, all of which, before they can be understood, require a knowledge of the elements of the special science in which they are taken. The burlesque question, *utrum chimæra bombinans in vacuo posset comedere secundas intentiones*, is a good specimen of the fun which for a long time was heaped on the study of Scholastic Logic.

A *first intention* or *notion* is a Concept, whether of a low or a high order, which denotes things. Thus, in the illustration just given, *spaniel, dog, carnivor, mammal*, — each and all denote certain animals; they are First Intentions. On the other hand, a *second intention* or *notion* is a Concept which denotes *first intentions* — i. e. the former Concepts — in their relation, not to the things denoted, but to each other. Thus, if the three lower steps in every hierarchy of Concepts are denominated respectively, Variety, Species, Genus, then these three names, applicable not only to *spaniel, dog, carnivor*, but to every other corresponding set of three successive steps of generalization, express *second intentions*. "First Intentions," says Mr. Mansel, "as conceptions of things, are predicable of the individuals conceived under them. Thus we may say, 'Socrates is man, animal, &c.'

Second Intentions are not so predicable; we cannot say, 'Socrates is species, genus, &c.' So, when Genus is said to be predicable of Species, it is not meant that we can predicate the one Second Intention of the other, so as to say, 'Species is Genus'; but that the First Intention *animal* is predicable of the First Intention *man*, the relation of the one to the other being expressed by the Second Intentions *genus* and *species*. For this reason, Logic was said to treat of *second intentions applied to first*."*

It is obvious that Second Intentions are the peculiar technicalities of the abstract sciences of Logic and Grammar. In the physical sciences, we have to deal only with Concepts of things; but Logic and Grammar need Concepts of our modes of thinking and speaking of things, so far as these modes are related to each other. Thus, we need the technical terms Genus and Species to express the relations in which the several Concepts, that form any one hierarchy or series, stand to each other. These relations are indicated in the following table.

* *Notes to Aldrich*, p. 20.

72   THE DOCTRINE OF CONCEPTS.

Second Intentions, or Concepts of Concepts, as thought relatively to each other.	First Intentions, or Concepts of things.	Intension, or Marks connoted.	Extension, or Objects denoted.
Summum Genus.	*Thing* or *Entity*.	Existing.	Everything.
Species or subaltern Genus.	*Animal.*	Existing, organized, sentient.	Every Vertebrate, Mollusk, Articulate, and Radiate.
Species or subaltern Genus.	*Mammal.*	Existing, organized, sentient, suckling their young.	Every vertebrated animal which suckles its young.
Species or subaltern Genus.	*Carnivor.*	Existing, organized, sentient, suckling their young, eating flesh.	Bears, wolves, foxes, lions, tigers, &c.
Species or subaltern Genus.	*Dog.*	Existing, organized, sentient, suckling their young, eating flesh, digitigrade quadruped, &c.	Mastiffs, spaniels, hounds, terriers, &c.
Infima Species.	*Spaniel.*	Silky-haired, water-dog, having all the preceding Marks.	All individual spaniels.

Put any other, an entirely different, series of First Intentions in the place of those given in the table,—take, for instance, the series *Man, European, Frenchman, Parisian,*—and it is evident that the relations of these Concepts also to each other will be correctly indicated by the same Second Intentions as before. *Man* is now the Summum Genus, *Parisian* is the Infima Species, and the intermediate Concepts are the Subaltern Genera or Species.

A mere inspection of the table also brings to light the one law of Thought which determines the Quantity of Concepts. It is, that *Intension and Extension, the two Quantities of every Concept, are always in inverse ratio to each other.* They must both be present; there must be at least a minimum of each; for a Concept must always connote something and always denote something. But if we take a great number of objects, we can find but few attributes or Marks which are common to them all, while a few objects may have many common attributes. Looking at the table, we see that, in the Summum Genus, the Intension is least: in the case there given, only one Mark — *existing* — is connoted; while the Extension is greatest, for the same Concept denotes *everything*. Descending from the Highest Genus, we see that the Intension steadily increases through the Subaltern Genera, while the Extension regularly diminishes. In the Lowest Species, the Intension is at its maximum, as *Spaniel* connotes all the Marks of the higher Genera and one or two additional Marks, and the Extension is at its minimum, as there are fewer *Spaniels* than *Dogs*, still fewer than *Carnivora*, &c. It is only stating the same law in other words to say, with reference to any one hierarchy or series of Concepts, that any increase of the Intension produces, *ipso facto*, a diminution of the Extension, and any diminution of the former an increase of the latter. Observe, however, that it is only the *original and essential* Marks of which we speak, when we say that the number of Marks is inversely proportional to the number of objects denoted. The Original Marks carry their Derivatives along with them by necessary implication; and therefore we do not really increase the Intension, but only render it more explicit, when we annex certain Derivative attributes which were not formerly expressed — perhaps not even thought — as belonging to it. Thus, the Intension of *triangle*, as a *plane figure having only three sides and three angles*, is not at all enlarged by adding this Mark, *the sum of these three angles being equal to two right angles*, even though I now for the first time learn that this is their sum. Though I did not, therefore, previously *think* this Mark of the Concept, it did nevertheless belong to it implicitly, or by necessary inference; and hence its express recognition does not alter either Quantity. In like manner, it is only the Essential Marks which determine the boundaries of a Concept; we do not enlarge the Intension of *man* as a *rational animal*, by adding this Accidental Mark, *sometimes learned*. As for the Mark *capable of learning*, that is a Derivative from *rational*.

The metaphysical meaning of *essence* is, *that internal constitution of a thing which makes it what it is*, — which is not only the source of its attributes, but is necessary to its existence. In this sense, of course, no finite mind can attain to a knowledge of the Essence of any real thing whatever. Passing by the disputes on this head as beyond our province, it is enough to say that Logic (which has nothing to do with "real things," as they belong to the Matter of Thought) considers the Essence of a Concept to be *the aggregate of its Marks*, or, in other words, *the sum of the attributes which it connotes*. Still further: — Formal Logic cannot inquire into the nature of these attributes, but designates them indifferently by letters of the alphabet, as being all of the same kind. It necessarily presupposes, as above stated, that only Original and Essential attributes are used as Marks of a Concept; and hence it looks only to their number, and not to their quality. Therefore, the law is universal and absolute, — add or subtract a single Mark, and the Extension, or number of objects denoted, is thereby diminished or increased. *Essential* means *inseparable* or *necessary*; take away an Essential attribute, and the Concept ceases to be what it was, and becomes another Concept with a wider Extension. Thus, from *man* as a *rational animal*, remove the Mark of *rationality*, which is Essential to him, and the remaining Concept is *animal*, which denotes all men and brutes also.

Generification, usually called *Generalization*, is the process of rising, through the successive abstraction of Marks, from lower to higher Concepts. It is so called because the lower Concept is relatively a Species, and the higher one, to which we proceed, is relatively a Genus, having a wider Extension. Thus, we proceed from the lower Concept *Mammal*, which is in this relation a Species, to the higher Concept *Animal*, which is in the same relation a Genus, by throwing out the Mark *suckling their young*. The name of this process, therefore, correctly indicates the act of *becoming a Genus*.

The contrary process, of descending from higher to lower Concepts through the successive assumption of Marks, is called *Determination*, — more properly *Specification*, as it expresses the act of *becoming a Species*. It has been well said, that it is the process of "thinking *out* objects by thinking *in* attributes." Thus, we descend from the Genus *Mammalia* to the Species *Carnivora*, by throwing out all herbivorous animals, through bringing in the Mark, *eating flesh*.

It has already been observed, in treating of the Axiom of Excluded Middle and its applications, that every pair of Contradictory attributes, *A* and *not-A*, divide the universe between them, as one or the other must belong to *everything*. Because a given attribute, *A*, can be affirmed only of a certain number of objects, it must be denied of *all other* objects; and we may express such denial by saying, all these others are *Not-A*. Hence we have a peculiar class of Concepts, called Negative or Privative, more properly Infinitated, of which the characteristic is, that they denote almost everything, and connote 'next to nothing,' — that is, nothing positive. Thus they afford a curious illustration of the law, that the two quantities of a Concept exist only in an inverse proportion to each other. Logically considered, the Extension of the Concept *Not-A* is infinite, embracing the universe of existence both real and potential; for the subtraction of a finite quantity, A, does not diminish infinity. Consequently, its Intension is zero; for it does not connote any Mark, but only the absence of the Mark, A.

Practically considered, however, or with reference to the Matter of the Thought, "the universe" in such cases is not thought absolutely, but relatively; it means only *the totality* of that class of objects which we are thinking of, and to which A belongs. Thus, the two Concepts *Frenchman* and *not-Frenchman* are not thought to include all *things*, (which, if taken strictly, they would do,) but only all *men*. In like manner, *not-male*, which, if rigidly construed, would denote every stock and stone, besides many animals, is actually thought merely as a synonyme for *female*, and so denotes only about one half of the animal kingdom. Sometimes, the *name* is seemingly positive, but the Concept or *thought* is truly negative. Thus, *parallels* are lines that do *not* meet; therefore, as two negatives destroy each other, *not-parallel* are lines that *do* meet,—a really positive Concept under a Privative or Infinitated form. For this reason, some writers have argued that *infinite*, i. e. *not-finite*, is not thought negatively, but positively; for *finite*, meaning *limited* or *bounded*, is a restriction or negation of the magnitude which *infinity* asserts positively. On the other hand, it is maintained that the essence of Thought, as such, consists in limitation or restriction; for we cannot think any object except by distinguishing it, through its peculiar Marks, from other objects; consequently, to deny *this* restriction or negation, is to deny that the object in question has any peculiar Marks, or that it is distinguished from other objects in any manner whatever, and thereby to reduce the Thought of it to zero.

2. The Quality of Concepts.

When considered in relation to the mind or thinking subject in which they are conceived, Concepts may be said to have Quality, according as they more or less perfectly represent to this mind the objects which they denote, and the Marks or attributes by which those objects are distinguished. The three virtues of Clearness, Distinctness, and Adequacy constitute the perfection of Thought. The corresponding vices, of course, which render Thought imperfect, are Obscurity, Indistinctness, and Inadequacy. The Quality of a Concept depends on the degree in which it possesses each of these merits or faults.

It is evident, from this account, that the Quality of Concepts, depending on the characteristics not merely of possible, but of *perfect*, Thought, properly belongs either to the Doctrine of Method, or to what Hamilton calls Modified Logic, rather than to Pure Universal Logic. As the subsidiary processes of Definition and Division, however, by which the Qualities of Clearness, Distinctness, and Adequacy are obtained, are applicable to all Concepts, and, in a certain degree, regulate their formation and use in all minds, there is sufficient reason for considering the subject here, instead of regarding it as a mere appendage to the science, to be treated only at the close. It is sometimes convenient to depart a little from a rigorously systematic arrangement, more being gained than lost by the sacrifice. For this reason, and even as a matter of necessity, several matters properly appertaining to the Relation of Concepts have been partially considered in the preceding section, under the head of their Quantity. The filiation and interdependence of the parts of a science are often such, that it is impossible to give a proper explanation of any one of them without presupposing some knowledge of the others.

A Concept, being the reduction of a plurality both of Marks and Objects to unity, supposes the power of thinking *one* and *many* both separately, and in their relation to each other, or together. We think the Concept *clearly* as a unity, when we can clearly distinguish it as one whole from other unities, — that is, from other Concepts regarded as wholes. We think it *distinctly* as a plurality, when we can distinguish both the Marks and the Objects which constitute it from each other. The Clearness of my Concept of a given metal — *iron*, for instance — depends on the fulness and precision with which I distinguish it as one whole from other Concepts, especially of those substances which, like the other metals, *tin, copper, platinum*, as nearest or most similar, would be most likely to be confounded with it. The opposite of this merit is Obscurity. On the other hand, the Distinctness of a Concept depends on the fulness and precision whereby I apprehend it as a plurality, — that is, as connoting many attributes or Marks, which I clearly distinguish from each other, and as denoting many Objects, which also I can clearly distinguish from each other. The former, or the distinct apprehension of the several Marks, is its Internal Distinctness; the latter, the distinct apprehension of the several Objects contained under it, is its External Distinctness. The opposite of this merit is Indistinctness.

It is evident that these qualities of a perfect Concept may exist in an indefinite number of degrees; and it is also evident, that a Concept may be quite Clear, while it is but very imperfectly Distinct. A young child may have a very Clear notion of a *clock*, as distinguished from the other objects in the room, and still have but a very Indistinct apprehension of its parts, properties, and uses, or of the various kinds of horological instruments all denoted by this name. On the other hand, Distinctness necessarily involves Clearness; I cannot have a Distinct apprehension of all the Marks of a Concept, without being thereby enabled clearly to distinguish it as one whole from other Concepts. The fact, that we may be able very clearly to discriminate a whole from other wholes, or a Concept from other Concepts, though we can but indistinctly separate in thought the parts or the Marks which constitute that whole or that Concept, is thus illustrated by Hamilton, from the analogy of our Perceptive and Representative Faculties.

"We are all acquainted with many, say a thousand, individuals; that is, we recognize such and such a countenance as the countenance of John, and as not the countenance of James, Thomas, Richard, or any of the other 999. This we do with a clear and certain knowledge. But the countenances which we thus distinguish from each other are, each of them, a complement made up of a great number of separate traits or features; and it might, at first view, be supposed that, as a whole is only the sum of its parts, a clear cognition of a whole countenance can only be realized through a distinct knowledge of each of its constituent features. But the slightest consideration will prove that this is not the case. For how few of us are able to say of any, the most familiar face, what are the particular traits which go to form the general result: and yet, on that account, we hesitate neither in regard to our own knowledge of an individual, nor in regard to the knowledge possessed by others. Suppose a witness be adduced in a court of justice to prove the identity or non-identity of a certain individual with the perpetrator of a certain crime, the commission of which he had chanced to see;— would the counsel be allowed to invalidate the credibility of the witness by, first of all, requiring him to specify the various elements of which the total likeness of the accused was compounded, and then by showing that, as the witness either could not specify the several traits, or specified what did not agree with the features of the accused, he was therefore incompetent to prove the identity or non-identity required? This would not be allowed. For the court would hold that a man might have a clear perception and a clear representation of a face and figure, of which, however, he had not separately considered, and could not separately image to himself, the constituent elements. Thus, even the judicial determination of life and death supposes, as real, the difference between a clear and a distinct knowledge: for a distinct knowledge lies in the knowledge of the constituent parts; while a clear knowledge is only of the constituted whole.

"Continuing our illustrations from the human countenance; we all have a clear knowledge of any face which we have seen, but few of us have distinct knowledge even of those with which we are familiar; but the painter, who, having looked upon a countenance, can retire and reproduce its likeness in detail, has necessarily both a clear and a distinct knowledge of it. Now, what is thus the case with perceptions and representations, is equally the case with notions. We may be able clearly to discriminate one concept from another, although the degree of consciousness does not enable us distinctly to discriminate the various component characters of either concept from each other."

Clearness and Distinctness, with their opposites, were first regarded as qualities of *vision* merely, being applied only to objects *as seen*, their signification being afterwards extended by analogy to the other senses, and finally to Thought. The distinction between them, first fully pointed out by Leibnitz, was admirably illustrated by Krug, in a passage which is thus paraphrased by Hamilton.

"In darkness — the complete obscurity of night — we see nothing, — there is no perception, — no discrimination of objects. As the light dawns, the obscurity diminishes, the deep and uniform sensation of darkness is modified, —

we are conscious of a change, — we see something, but are still unable to distinguish its features, — we know not what it is. As the light increases, the outlines of wholes begin to appear, but still not with a distinctness sufficient to allow us to perceive them completely; but when this is rendered possible, by the rising intensity of the light, we are then said to see clearly. We then recognize mountains, plains, houses, trees, animals, etc., that is, we discriminate these objects as wholes, as unities, from each other. But their parts, — the manifold of which these unities are the sum, — their parts still lose themselves in each other; they are still but indistinctly visible. At length, when the daylight has fully sprung, we are enabled likewise to discriminate their parts; we now see distinctly what lies around us. But still we see as yet only the wholes which lie proximately around us, and of these, only the parts which possess a certain size. The more distant wholes, and the smaller parts of nearer wholes, are still seen by us only in their conjoint result, only as they concur in making up that whole which is for us a visible minimum. Thus it is, that in the distant forest, or on the distant hill, we perceive a green surface; but we see not the several leaves, which in the one, nor the several blades of grass, which in the other, each contributes its effect to produce that amount of impression which our consciousness requires. . . . . Clearness and distinctness are thus only relative. For between the extreme of obscurity and the extreme of distinctness there are in vision an infinity of intermediate degrees. Now, the same thing occurs in thought. For we may either be conscious only of the concept in general, or we may also be conscious of its various constituent attributes, or both the concept and its parts may be lost in themselves to consciousness, and only recognized to exist by effects which indirectly evidence their existence."

82 THE DOCTRINE OF CONCEPTS.

The Adequacy of a Concept depends on the number and the relative importance of the Marks which constitute it, considered as more or less perfectly representing the objects which it denotes. A Concept may be perfectly Clear and perfectly Distinct, and still be a very Inadequate representation of the class of things for which it stands; for it may connote but two or three out of the many attributes which they possess, and even these two or three may be relatively insignificant, or of trifling import as compared with several of those which are omitted. The old Concept of *man*, happily ridiculed by Aristotle, which described him as a *two-legged animal without feathers*, is Clear, for it enables us easily to distinguish *man* from all other animals; and it is Distinct, for its three Marks are easily distinguishable from each other; but it is very Inadequate, as it omits man's crowning and peculiar attribute as a *rational* being. We may have a very Clear and Distinct Concept of an *elephant*, as a *quadruped that drinks through its nostrils;* obviously, however, this is a very Inadequate representation of that sagacious and gigantic brute.

The difference between the artificial system of Botany invented by Linnæus and the Natural System of Jussieu illustrates very well the importance of making a proper selection, and taking a sufficient number, of attributes wherewith to determine the classes of things which we think. Every plant may be perfectly distinguished from all other plants, and easily referred to its proper class, in a system founded, like that of Linnæus, exclusively upon the number, situation, and connection of its stamens and pistils. Such a system furnishes an easy mode of ascertaining the names of plants, just as the alphabetical arrangement of words in a dictionary is the easiest way of enabling one to find any word that he wants. But the arrangement is artificial and arbitrary, the number and relative situation of the stamens and pistils in a plant no more determining its leading and essential characteristics, than the significance and mutual relations of words depend upon the position which their initial letters happen to occupy in the alphabet. In the Natural System, these prominent and essential attributes of plants are made to mark out the classes into which they are divided, and thus the relations which actually exist between the things themselves stand out with the same relative prominence in the thoughts wherein they are represented to consciousness. The Concepts here not only *denote* their objects, but *represent* them in a manner which approximates, though distantly, the fulness of Intuition.

The three merits of Clearness, Distinctness, and Adequacy, which constitute the Quality of a Concept, presuppose a reference to some standard, which, for the very reason that it is a *standard*, must be independent of our Thought, — that is, not subject to arbitrary change in Thought. Strictly speaking, every Concept considered merely as such, or as an individual Thought in consciousness, must have its own degree of each of these merits, and cannot change this degree without becoming a different Concept from what it was. Whatever faults may be imputed to it when it is compared with some standard, it may still be said of it, even in its present state, that it connotes something and denotes something, and thus has all the essential characteristics which enter into our definition of a Concept. Any change to which it may be subjected is not an improvement of *this* Concept, but the substitution of another in its place, having different Marks, and therefore denoting not the same objects as before. Such a change or substitution can be required only through a reference in Thought to some standard, to which this Concept, or the Concept as it now stands, does not conform, but to which it was previously implied that it ought to conform.

There are two standards, one of *the name* and the other of *the thing*, to one or the other of which every Concept which the mind can form is, at least tacitly, referred. Words, which are the names of Concepts, are the means of communicating our Thought to others; and they cannot perform this office unless they have the same signification to the hearer as to the speaker; that is, each name must call up the *same* Concept in the minds of both. A Concept may be faulty, then, *not as a Concept*, (for in this respect, or in reference to the mere Form of Thought, one Concept is as good as another,) but because it has a wrong name, whereby it improperly assumes to be the same Thought which is designated by that name in the minds of other persons generally. Thus it is that language, among its other offices, has an important influence in the regulation and fixation of Thought. We do not classify things and form Concepts of them arbitrarily, each one according to his own preferences; but the necessity of maintaining intercourse with other minds imposes on us a constant effort to approximate our Thoughts to theirs, — that is, to the Thoughts which they have fixed and established for general use through stamping upon them certain names. The Thoughts which I attach to the words *church, state, government*, for instance, may be as correct and proper, *in themselves considered*, as the connotation which you attach to them; but it is a decisive objection to my mode of thinking, if I attach these old and familiar names to peculiar combinations of Thought which they never before designated, and to which people generally do not now give these appellations. Owing to the symbolic use of language, in which, as already explained, words are employed as temporary substitutes for Thoughts, we are continually learning and using words *before* we have fully learned their meaning. Gradually, by a process of induction, we accommodate our use of these words to their established usage; and it is while thus learning, that our Thoughts are said to be wanting in Clearness, Distinctness, and Adequacy. In truth, it is not our Thoughts which are thus faulty, but our apprehension of *other people's* Thoughts, or, what is the same thing, of the meaning which they attach to certain words. My own Concepts of *church*, *state*, &c. are Clear and Distinct enough, unless indeed I now hear these words for the first time; but I cannot clearly distinguish what I imperfectly understand to be *your* Concepts of them from certain other kindred or nearly allied Thoughts; or I have but an Indistinct knowledge of the several Marks which are connoted in the Concepts which you and other men have of them; or my connotation of these Marks is Inadequate, — that is to say, not so full as other people's.

The second standard to which our Concepts are referred, when they are said to be deficient in Quality, is the class of *things* which they denote, and which they consequently ought to represent as perfectly as possible. Thus, every artisan, through long use, has a more Adequate, Clear, and Distinct Concept of each of the tools of his trade, each of the objects which he works upon, and each of the processes to which these objects are subjected, than it is possible for other persons to possess who have no special familiarity with the business. The Concepts which these other persons have may be perfect enough for the correct use of language; that is, they may apply the technical names rightly. But when compared with the full and accurate Notions which have been acquired by experts, they appear to be, as they are, very imperfect representations of *the things* themselves.

The difference between these two standards to which all Concepts, in respect to their Quality or degree of perfection, are referred, enables us to understand the distinction which logicians long ago established between *nominal* and *real* Definitions. This distinction has been very imperfectly apprehended by many, especially by those who, unable to find any other mode of distinguishing the two sorts of definition, have held that a Nominal one consisted only in explaining the meaning of the word by synonymes, or by unfolding its etymology. Such a process would be Grammatical rather than Logical; rightly considered, it is no definition at all. A Nominal Definition is *the distinct explication of all the Marks which are connoted in the name of the Concept by general consent, as evinced in the use of language.* But language is imperfect, and words in common use often signify much less than exact science requires. A Real Definition is *a distinct explication of all those Marks, and those only, which a careful examination of the class of things denoted by the word proves to be both Original and Essential.* It is obvious that the Nominal and the Real Definition of a Concept will often coincide. This is usually the case with the technical terms in every science, especially those of recent origin, whose connotations are usually determined with great care before their names are invented. In other cases, as already explained, the two definitions may differ very widely from each other.

The further consideration of Definition, and of Division also, as the subsidiary processes by which the Quality of Concepts may be improved, must be postponed till after we have treated of

3. The Relations of Concepts.

The *Relation* of Concepts, as already remarked, is a technical phrase, which is understood to mean their Relations *to each other only*, and not to the other forms of Thought, which will be considered hereafter.

A series or hierarchy of Concepts, formed by successive steps of Generification, like the one given in the table on page 72, represents a succession of Concepts as *subordinated* to each other in their two Quantities of Extension and Intension. But the names of the Second Intentions, which express the Relations of these Concepts or classes to each other, are given with primary reference to the Extension only. Unless express notice is given to the contrary, therefore, we shall always speak only of their Relation in Extension. Of any two Concepts in such a series, that one is called the *Superior*, *Higher*, or *Broader*, which has the greater Extension, — that is, which denotes the larger number of individual objects; it may also be called the *Superordinate*. The other, having less Extension, or denoting fewer Individuals, is called *Inferior*, *Lower*, *Narrower*, or *Subordinate*. Thus, referring to the table again, *animal* is Superior or Superordinate to *mammal*, which, as included under it, or denoting fewer individuals, is called Inferior or Subordinate. The Superior, also as the more *general* notion, and as obtained by the process of Generification or throwing out Marks, is called the *Genus;* while the Inferior, as more *specific*, and obtained by the process of Specification, or thinking in Marks, is called the *Species*. These names being merely relative, it is evident that the same Concept is, at the same time, a Genus to any lower Concept, and a Species to any higher one.

The Highest or Broadest Concept in such a series, denoting most individuals and connoting fewest Marks, is called the Summum Genus; hence, it is defined by logicians to be *a Genus which cannot become a Species*. On the other hand, the lowest Concept in the series, as denoting the least and connoting the most, is called an Infima Species. In fact, it denotes individuals only, and not any classes or Species of individuals; therefore it is defined to be *a Species which cannot become a Genus*. Each intermediate Concept, as we have just said, is a Species to those above it, and a Genus to those below it. Its next Higher neighbor is called its *proximate* Genus; and its next lower one might be termed a *proximate* Species, though this term is not in frequent use.

When the name of any Higher Concept is applied as the name of a Lower one, or of an individual, it is called its *abstract* name, or its *denomination in the abstract;* the peculiar or proper appellation of this lower Concept or individual is called its *concrete* name. Thus, *animal* is an Abstract, and *man* the Concrete, name of *a rational animal;* and again, relatively, *man* is the Abstract, and *John* the Concrete, appellation of the individual, *this man whom we are speaking of*. These names obviously have reference to the Intension of the Concept, the Abstract name being obtained by Abstraction, that is, by throwing out Marks, and the Concrete signifying all the Marks taken together (*con-cresco, grown together*), or the whole Intension.

According to another and more frequent use of language, an "Abstract name" has a narrower signification than the one here indicated, being applicable only to one peculiar Species of Higher Concept, instead of denoting the Abstract use of any Higher Concept whatever. What appears only as a Mark of the Concept in its Lower or Concrete use, is itself a Higher Concept; and if its *denotation* is then altered, — that is, if it no longer denotes *things* as before, but only various kinds and degrees of that *attribute* which the Concrete term connotes, — it is then, and then only, commonly called an Abstract term. Thus, to recur to the instance already given, *man* connoting *rational animal*, we may take *rational* instead of *animal* as the Higher Concept; and then, altering its denotation, we may understand it to mean, not *rational beings*, but various kinds and degrees of *rationality*. Hence, such terms as *rationality, redness, whiteness, humanity*, &c. are called Abstract names. According to this use, an Abstract term is one which *denotes* that which, in its Concrete application, it *connoted;* it is a Mark or *attribute* considered as a *thing.*

The Relations thus far explained, as arising from the higher or lower position of a Concept in the series or hierarchy to which it belongs, are all denominated Relations of *Subordination.* They may be aptly symbolized by a series of concentric circles, thus: —

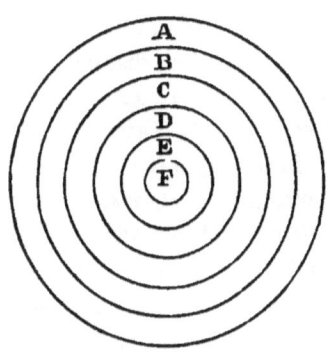

Here, A, having the greatest extent, and so containing all the others under it, represents the Summum Genus; while F, as least extended, and denoting only individuals, not classes, represents the Infima Species. Any intermediate circle, C, is a subaltern Genus or Species, being Genus to D and Species to B.

If we were to use the same diagram to symbolize the Relations of Intension, since the two Quantities are in inverse ratio to each other, the order of the letters would be reversed. F, as connoting the most Marks or having the largest Intension, would be the outermost circle, and A, having the least Intension, would be the innermost or smallest.

In general, and for practical purposes, the terms Summum Genus and Infima Species are applied not in an absolute, but only in a relative sense; — relative, that is, not to the totality or the smallest class of *all conceivable things*, but to the totality or the smallest *convenient* class of *those things only which we are now thinking of;* say, all the objects of some particular science. Thus, in Zoölogy, *animal* is considered as the Summum Genus, no notice being taken of vegetables and minerals; and what is usually termed a "Variety" or "Sub-Variety" — King Charles Spaniel, for instance — is an Infima Species.

Absolutely speaking, logicians maintain that Summum Genus and Infima Species are both unattainable, — that they are limits of classification in Thought, which we can approximate, but never reach. They express this impossibility under the form of two Laws of Thought. The first of these, called the Law of Homogeneity, affirms that things the most dissimilar must, in some respects, be similar or homogeneous; and consequently, any two Concepts, how unlike soever, may still both be subordinated under some higher Concept. Thus, *animals* and *vegetables*, distinct as they are from each other, are both contained under the higher Concept *organized natural objects*. And even from this connotation, if we subtract the Mark *organized*, the remainder will be a still higher Concept, *natural objects*, which will include *minerals*, as well as *animals* and *vegetables*.

On this ground, Mr. Mansel and other logicians maintain that *thing* or *entity*, connoting but *one* attribute, *existence* (real or imaginary), which would seem to be an absolute Summum Genus, is not thinkable. They deny that it is a possible object of Thought, on the ground seemingly that it does not contain a *plurality* of attributes. But as reasons have already been assigned (page 61) why a Concept, as actually thought by us, may have only one attribute or distinguishing Mark, I cannot see why *ens* is not thinkable, as distinguished from *nihil*, which has not even this one attribute of (real or imaginary) *existence*, and is therefore certainly not conceivable. That it is a very vague and indefinite Thought, is admitted; this is a consequence of its connotation being reduced to a minimum. But to say, that "distinguishable from *nothing*" is tantamount to affirming that it is *not distinguishable at all*, seems to me in this connection, or for the purposes of pure Thought, a mere quibble. I can certainly think a difference — that is, a relation — between *being* and *no-being*, though only one term of the relation is positive, and the other is merely *negative*. The algebraist finds a very distinct relation between *plus a* and *minus a*, as the presence of one in place of the other affects the results of his calculation very sensibly; and both these expressions are clearly distinguishable from *zero*. It is too much of a paradox to affirm that there is no difference in Thought between *something* and *nothing*.

About the second principle, called the Law of Heterogeneity, there is no dispute. According to this Law, things the most similar must, in some respects, be dissimilar or heterogeneous; and consequently, any Concept, however large its Intension may be, may still have that Intension increased, without thereby descending to individuals. What is relatively an Infima Species, or considered as such for the purposes of some particular science, may be again subdivided into two or more, and so on indefinitely. Thus, King Charles Spaniel may be subdivided into such Spaniels *one year old*, and those of *two years or older;* into those *born in Europe*, and those *born in America;* into those *above*, and those *below, three pounds in weight*, &c. Though, as Mr. Mansel remarks, " as far as the Laws of Thought are concerned, it is permitted to unite in an act of conception all attributes which are not contradictory of each other, it is impossible in practice to go beyond a very limited number. The number of attributes in the universe not logically repugnant to each other is infinite; and the mind can therefore find no absolute limits to its downward progress in the formation of subordinate notions." *

The Relation of Co-ordination exists between different Species which have the same Proximate Genus; two or more Species are thus said to be Co-ordinate when each excludes the other from its own Extension, but both or all are included under the Extension of the same nearest Higher Concept. For instance, *dog, wolf, cat, lion, bear,*

* *Prolegomena Logica*, p. 169.

&c. are Co-ordinate Species under the same Genus, *Carnivora;* each excludes the other, — what is *wolf* is not *cat*, — but all alike are *Carnivora*. As the two Quantities of a Concept are in inverse ratio, and as, in reference to Extension, the Species is contained under the Genus, so, in reference to Intension, the Genus is contained in the Species. Thus, the Intension of every Species contains the Genus, — that is, the aggregate of Marks which characterize the Genus, — and the Specific Difference, — that is, the aggregate of Marks by which this Species is distinguished both from the Genus to which it is Subordinate, and from the other Species with which it is Co-ordinate. *Man is a rational animal:* — here, *animal* expresses the Genus to which *man* belongs, and *rational* is the Specific Difference whereby *man* is distinguished from other Species of animals.

Two things may be said to be *generically different*, when they belong to different Genera; *specifically different*, when they belong to different Species; *individually or numerically different*, when they do not constitute one and the same reality. But as every member of the hierarchy, except the highest and the lowest, may be viewed indifferently as either Genus or Species, *generic difference* and *specific difference* are only various expressions for the same thing.

"Individual existences," as Krug remarks, "can only be perfectly discriminated by external or internal Perception, and their numerical differences are endless; for of all possible Contradictory attributes, the one or the other must, on the principles of Contradiction and Excluded Middle, be considered as belonging to each individual thing. On the other hand, Species and Genera may be perfectly discriminated by one or few characters. For example, *triangle* is distinguished from every Genus or Species of *geometrical figures* by the single character of *trilaterality.* It is, therefore, far easier adequately to describe a Genus or Species than an Individual; as, in the latter case, we must select, out of the infinite multitude of characters which an Individual comprises, a few of the most prominent, or those by which the thing may most easily be recognized." We may *describe,* but cannot *define,* an Individual, as there would be no end to the enumeration of its peculiar attributes. In such case, the only adequate definition is a view — an Intuition — of the thing itself. *Omnis intuitiva notitia est definitio.*

The other Relations of Concepts to each other may be very briefly indicated. Concepts are said to *intersect,* when the Extension of one coincides in part, and only in part, with the Extension of the other. Thus, *Frenchman* and *Protestant* are Intersecting Concepts, for some Frenchmen are Protestants and some are not, some Protestants are Frenchmen and some are not. These may be symbolized by two circles whose circumferences cut or intersect each other. *Exclusive* Concepts — *animal* and *vegetable,* for instance — do not coincide in any part of their Extension, and may therefore by symbolized by two circles which lie wholly apart the one from the other. *Reciprocating, Convertible,* or *Coextensive* Concepts are those which have precisely the same Extension, as *living being* and *organized being,* since everything which lives is organized. Two circles of the same diameter, and laid one upon the other so as to coincide throughout, would aptly represent Convertible Concepts.

4. Definition and Division.

It has already been said, that a Concept is *internally* Distinct when we can fully enumerate and clearly distinguish from each other all its original and essential Marks. The process through which this is accomplished is called

Definition. Again, a Concept is *externally* Distinct when we can fully enumerate all its subordinate Genera and Species. This process is called the Division of the Concept. Both processes have reference to one or the other of the two standards, — the *name* and the *thing*, — by which it is determined whether the Concept in our minds is, what it purports to be, a faithful copy or representation of what is generally designated by that name, or a full enumeration of the original and essential attributes of the class of things so designated. We will first consider Definition of *names* only, Division relating only to classes of *things*, the object of both processes being not to determine and render distinct the Concepts which we already possess, but to substitute others for them which shall more perfectly answer our purposes. The Concept to be defined should be called the *definiendum*, the Definition itself being the *definientia*.

A Definition consists primarily of two parts, the Proximate Genus and the Specific Difference of the Concept defined; for these two elements, as we have just seen, make up the whole Intension of every class. Thus, *carnivor is a flesh-eating mammal;* the word *mammal* here denotes the Proximate Genus, and *flesh-eating* the Specific Difference which distinguishes *carnivora* from other mammals. Such a Definition, however, is incomplete, as it is further necessary to define the Genus which makes a part of it; and this can be done only by considering this Genus (*mammal*) as a Species, and assigning to it its own Proximate Genus (the next higher one in the hierarchy), *animal*, and its Specific Difference, *suckling its young*. We proceed in this manner till we have reached the Summum Genus, each Specific Difference successively taken up being the Mark which was abstracted in the original process of Generification, and the sum of these Differences being, therefore, the aggregate of all the Marks which make up the Intension of the Concept first proposed to be defined. What may be called the secondary or proper Definition, then, as before stated, is the distinct explication of all the Marks which are connoted in the name of the Concept. Thus, having successively defined *dog* as *carnivor*, *carnivor* as *mammal*, *mammal* as *animal*, and *animal* as *thing*, annexing in each case the corresponding Specific Difference, we then sum up all these Specific Differences, and thus form the proper Definition consisting solely of these Differences, — that is, of all the Marks which the *definiendum* connotes. Hence it appears, that though the defining analysis is of the Intension only, yet it is regulated by the Extension, as the Extension determines the order in which the Intension is resolved into the Marks which are its elements.

It is obvious also, that Definition by Genus and Specific Difference in all its successive steps supposes a previous knowledge of the whole hierarchy of Concepts through which it ascends, and therefore it only explicitly enumerates the Marks which were already implicitly known. The Classification here precedes, and is the means through which we form, the Definition. Usually, however, we proceed in the inverse order of this process: we seek first for the Definition, — that is, for a knowledge of all the original and essential attributes of a class of things, — as a preliminary step towards determining the Classification, or assigning the class to its proper place in a hierarchy of Concepts. Here, the Definition is primarily of the *thing*, and only secondarily of the *name*, the problem being how to determine the sum of the original and essential characteristics of this class of things. The following are the Rules usually given by Logicians for the solution of this problem, — that is, for the proper formation of Definitions.

1. A Definition must be adequate; that is, it must have

precisely the same Extension as the thing defined. If not, if the Predicate defining denotes more objects than the Subject defined, the Definition is too Wide; if it denotes fewer objects, it is too Narrow. Thus, when a triangle is defined "a figure having three rectilinear sides," the Definition is too Narrow, as there are spherical triangles to which it will not apply. If we say, "water is a compound of oxygen and hydrogen," the Definition is too Wide, as it includes not only water, but something else, — a deutoxide of hydrogen. When this rule is complied with, the Definition and the thing defined are Reciprocating or Convertible Concepts; consequently, everything to which the Definition applies, and nothing to which it does not apply, is the thing defined. When this is the case, our Concept of this class of things has become perfectly Clear, or distinguishable from all other Concepts.

2. The Definition must not be tautological; that is, it must not contain the name of the thing defined, as this is precisely the word which we are bound to explain. It is equally a violation of this rule to allow any of the derivatives of this name, or any of its correlative notions, either one of which can be explained only through the other, to constitute a part of the definition. This fault is called "defining in a circle." Lexicographers often fall into it unawares, as when they define a *board* to be "a thin plank," and then a *plank* to be "a thick board"; or when they say that *life* is "vitality, the state of being alive, the opposite of death."

3. A Definition ought not to proceed by Negative or Disjunctive attributes, when it is possible to avoid both. You cannot teach me what a notion is, by merely declaring what it is not, or that it is one of several things without indicating which one is intended. It is no real Definition to say of *parallels*, that they are "lines which do not meet," or of *oxygen*, that it is "one of the gases

fit for respiration." But convenience often requires what Logicians call division by *dichotomy*, in which a Genus is divided into two Species having Contradictory Marks; that is, one of these Species has, and the other has not, certain well-defined characteristics, the latter, of course, being capable only of Definition by negation. Thus Cuvier, having determined with great precision the attributes of Vertebrated animals, found it convenient to regard all other animals as Invertebrates, that is, as *not* possessing these attributes.

4. A Definition must be precise, — that is, it must contain nothing unessential or superfluous. Thus, all Derivative Marks should be excluded as superfluous, after their Originals have been enumerated; for they are virtually contained in those Marks from which they are deducible by the necessary Laws of Thought, so that the mention of them only cumbers the Definition without really enlarging it. That a triangle is *half of a parallelogram*, is no proper part of the Definition of a triangle, inasmuch as it is a necessary consequence of this figure having three sides and three angles. Unessential attributes are also superfluous; that man is a *featherless* biped is an accident, not an essential trait, of his humanity. Give him a coat of feathers, and he is still *man;* but deprive him of *rationality*, and he is no longer human.

5. A Definition must be perspicuous; for we define only in order to make more clear, and obscure or figurative expressions do not conduce to this end, but only increase the difficulty. "Tropes and figures," says Krug, "are logical hieroglyphics: they do not indicate the thing itself, but only something similar." But many expressions, originally metaphorical, have ceased to be so through long use in their secondary meaning. Their original signification has become obsolete, and no longer recurs to perplex us. This is the case with nearly all the words which

now denote mind and its operations, though they were first applied only to what is material.

Dr. Thomson takes a wider view of Definition, as including any Predicate which may be "useful to *mark out* for us more clearly the limits of the subject defined, and is therefore capable of being employed as a Definition for some thinker or other." "Any of the Predicates we propose to include," he continues, "though not the *absolute* Definition, not the Genus and Difference, may be employed as a Definition by some particular person, and may to him fulfil the purpose of the best logical Definition which can be given, "and therefore ought, if possible, to be comprehended under the same head." In conformity with this view, he enumerates the following six sources from which convenient Definitions may arise.

"i. From Resolution, when the Marks of the definitum are made its definition; as in 'a pension is an allowance for past services.' It is not necessary that the Marks should be completely enumerated, — that the conception should be strictly adequate, — but only that the Marks should suffice for the identification of the Subject, as belonging to it all and to it alone; so that Aristotle's Property would be included in it. ii. From Composition, the reverse of the last method, in which the definitum, a conception of which the component Marks are enumerated, stands Subject to a Definition implicitly containing those Marks; as, 'those who encroach upon the property of others are dishonest.' iii. From Division, where we define the Subject by enumerating its Dividing Members; as, 'Britons are those who dwell in England, Scotland, or Wales.' All the judgments called disjunctives are under this head. iv. From Colligation, the exact reverse of the last; where the Dividing Members of a conception are enumerated in the Subject, and the divided conception itself added to define them; as, 'historical, philosophical, and mathematical sciences are the sum (i. e. *are all*, or *equal*) of human knowledge.' This is the form which Inductive Judgments naturally assume. v. From change of Symbol, where both Subject and Predicate are symbolic conceptions, the latter being given as a substitute for the former on a principle of expedience only; as, 'probity is honesty.' This is the nominal definition of some logic-books. vi. From Casual Substitution, where one representation is put for another on a principle of expedience only, as serving to recall the Marks, which both possess in common, more readily to the hearer's mind; as, 'the science of politics is the best road to success in life; pleasure is the opposite of pain.'

"Table of Definition."

A Conception is defined	By its Intension (or Marks)	being unfolded,	= i.	Resolution, or Definition proper.
		being reunited,	= ii.	Composition.
	By its Extension (or Sphere)	being divided,	= iii.	Division.
		being reunited,	= iv.	Colligation.
	By Accidental Coincidence	of a Symbol,	= v.	Nominal Definition.
		of Notation,	= vi.	Accidental Definition."

As *absolute* Definition resolves the Intension of a Concept into its constituent Marks, so Division resolves the Extension into its constituent Genera and Species. In its most general acceptation, *division* is the separation of any whole into its parts. But Logical Division, with which alone we are here concerned, is such a separation of a Logical Whole only, — that is, of a class containing under it other classes, which are regarded as its parts. An *individual* is so called (*in-divido*) because it cannot be (logically) divided; the process of cutting it apart is properly called Partition, not Division. The Mathematical or Integral whole is such an individual, and can be sundered into its parts only by Partition. The parts of an Essential or Physical whole, as they interpenetrate and *inform* each other, cannot be separated at all except in Thought. But a Logical whole is itself a creation of Thought, formed out of lesser wholes of the same kind, into which it can be resolved by mental analysis.

By Partition, *triangle* may be resolved into smaller triangles, or into angles and sides; the former Partition may be actual, while the latter can only be ideal,—that is, it is possible only in Thought. By Division, on the other hand, *triangle* is resolved into *rectilinear* and *curvilinear* triangles, or into *equilateral*, *isosceles*, and *scalene* triangles, as these are Species comprehended under one Genus.

The Genus to be divided is called the *divisum*, and the constituent Species into which it is resolved are the *dividing members* (*membra dividentia*). Agreeably to the nature of a hierarchy of Concepts, the parts which result from such a Division are in themselves wholes containing other parts under them, and the dividing process repeated upon these is called a Subdivision. The same Concept may likewise be differently divided from different points of view, each separate analysis proceeding on what is technically termed its own *fundamentum divisionis*, or peculiar Ground of Division. Thus, *man* may be divided geographically into *European*, *Asiatic*, *American*, &c.; or, in reference to color, into *white*, *red*, and *black* men; or, in reference to religion, into *Christians*, *Mohammedans*, and *Pagans;*—local position, color, and religion being here the successive *fundamenta divisionis*. So the books in a library may be arranged either according to size, as folios, quartos, octavos, &c.; or according to the languages in which they are written, as Latin, French, English, &c.; or according to the subjects of which they treat, as theological, scientific, historical, &c. Perhaps the most important point in the philosophy of the Classificatory

Sciences is the right selection of a *fundamentum divisionis*, or Ground of Division.

If a Division has only two parts or members, it is called a *dichotomy;* and if such a Dichotomy is exhaustive, as it should be, these two members are evidently Contradictories of each other; for whatever is contained in one is thereby excluded from the other, and the two, taken together, constitute the whole. Accordingly, these two Dividing Members can always be expressed under the formula B and *not-B*. Thus, in dividing *triangle*, instead of calling the two members *rectilinear* and *curvilinear*, it is better to denominate them *rectilinear* and *non-rectilinear*. A Division into three members may be called a *trichotomy;* into many, a *polytomy*.

Logicians have commonly given the following Rules for the proper Division of a Concept.

1. Each Division should have but one *fundamentum divisionis*, by which every part of the process is regulated. The intervention of more than one Ground of Division in the same process is the Logical fault which is called a Cross Division. Thus, a Division of *man* into *European, American, Negro,* and *Pagan* is faulty, because the Ground of Division for the first two Dividing Members is *local position;* for the third, it is *color;* and for the fourth, it is *religion*. The consequence of this blunder is, that the same individual might be contained in each of the last three Members;— for he may be at once American, Negro, and Pagan. Whatever we may select as a Ground of Division, it must evidently be a Mark or attribute of the Divisum, and the number of distinct forms or varieties, under which this attribute appears in the class of things to be divided, will determine the number of Dividing Members. One of the Dividing Members, however, and but one, may be marked only by the absence of this attribute.

2. The Mark selected as the Ground of Division should be an Essential attribute of the Divisum, and one which has as many Derivatives, or which determines as many of its other attributes, as possible; otherwise, the Division will be complex and purposeless. Thus, the color of the hair is an unessential attribute of man; mankind might be divided into a large number of classes in this respect, but as very few of his physical, and none of the intellectual or moral, qualities of a man can be inferred from the fact that he has red, brown, or black hair, the Division would be useless. On the other hand, a classification of men according to their nationality or race, their geographical position, or their religion, is found to be an eminently fruitful one, as many of their other attributes are found in invariable connection with these leading characteristics, so as to be readily determined by them. The purpose for which a Division is made often determines the selection of its Ground. Thus, *soldiers* may be conveniently divided into *cavalry* and *infantry*, as this distinction is one of great moment in military affairs; but to divide men in general into *foot* and *horsemen* would be absurd.

3. No Dividing Member must by itself exhaust the Divisum; and the Dividing Members, taken together, must exhaust, and no more than exhaust, the Divisum. As the Genus and the Co-ordinate Species into which it is divided stand to each other in the relation of a whole to its parts, the propriety of this rule is manifest. *Man* cannot be divided into *rational* and *irrational*, for the one class of rational beings includes all men, so that neither of the Dividing Members is *a part*, or the result of a Division, properly so called. Again, as *all* the parts are required to constitute a whole, if the Co-ordinate Species, taken together, do not exhaust the Genus, the Division is obviously imperfect; one or more members remain to be supplied. If, on the other hand, they overlap the Genus,

there is somewhere an excess, which ought to be subtracted and referred to another class. *Government* cannot be divided into *monarchical, aristocratic*, and *democratic;* as there is a fourth class, the *mixed*. The old Division of the science of *language* into Grammar, Logic, and Rhetoric is redundant, as Logic is concerned with the laws of thought rather than of utterance, and therefore properly belongs to the science of mind.

4. The Co-ordinate Species into which a Genus is divided must be reciprocally exclusive; that is, no one of them must, in whole or in part, contain any other. In order to ascertain whether this rule, the propriety of which is obvious, has been complied with, Logicians apply the test of Dichotomy, to which any other Division, however complex, may be reduced. Thus, all the Co-ordinate Species, B, C, D, E, &c., of any Genus, A, may be represented under any one of the formulas, B and *not-B ; C* and *not-C ; D* and *not-D,* &c. If the Dividing Members are mutually exclusive, C, D, and E will each be found under *not-B ;* B, D, and E, under *not-C ;* B, C, and E, under *not-D ;* and so on. This rule is violated in a Cross Division, where, as we have already seen, the same individuals may appear under two or more of the Dividing Members: and also when a Member of a Subdivision is improperly co-ordinated with the Members of a primary Division. This last fault, however, is properly ranked under the next following rule. The ten Categories of Aristotle are now generally condemned as a faulty Division, because the last six of them are only subdivisions of the fourth, *Relation*. "For the Category *where* is the relation of a thing to other things in space; the category *when* is the relation of a thing to other things in time; *action* and *passion* constitute a single relation, — that of agent and patient"; &c.

5. A Division must proceed step by step, in regular

order, from proximate to remote differences, not overleaping any step which is properly intermediate. In other words, each Species, as it appears among the Dividing Members, must emerge directly from the Division of its own Proximate Genus. *Divisio ne fiat per saltum vel hiatum.* Even the ordinary Division of all natural objects into *animals, vegetables,* and *minerals* is faulty in this respect, its three Species not being properly co-ordinate, as one step has been omitted. The primary Division should be by Dichotomy into *organic* and *inorganic* things, *animals* and *vegetables* appearing subsequently as a subdivision of the *organic.*

CHAPTER V.

THE DOCTRINE OF JUDGMENTS.

1. The Predicables and the Categories. — 2. The Quantity, Quality, and Relation of Judgments according to the Aristotelical Doctrine. — 3. The Hamiltonian Doctrine of Judgments. — 4. The Explication of Propositions into Judgments.

JUDGMENT is that act of mind whereby the relation of one Concept to another, or of an individual thing to a Concept, is determined, and, as a consequence of such determination, that two Concepts, or the individual thing and the Concept, are reduced to unity in Thought. A Judgment expressed in words is a Proposition, the two terms of the Judgment being called the Subject and Predicate of the Proposition. The assertions, *iron is malleable*, *John is brave*, determine a relation of agreement between the two terms involved in each, whereby these two are conceived as one, and thus expressed, *malleable iron*, *brave John*. On the other hand, the Judgment, *quadrupeds are not rational*, determines the relation of disagreement between the two Terms, so that one is now denied to be a Mark of the other, or, what is the same thing, the negative Mark, *irrational*, is now attached to the Concept, *quadruped*.

As we have already defined a Concept to be a representation of one or more objects through their distinctive Marks, it is evident that Judgment is the process through which Concepts are formed. In fact, to judge is to recognize a particular Mark or attribute as belonging, or not belonging, to a certain object or class of objects. The Judgment is not, strictly speaking, a comparison, but it is the mental act of conjoining or disjoining two things which results from a previous comparison of them with each other, and a consequent recognition of their agreement or disagreement. Hence, as Hamilton remarks, "every Concept is a Judgment fixed and ratified in a sign"; and, again, "a Concept may be viewed as an implicit or undeveloped Judgment; a Judgment as an explicit and developed Concept." Thus, the Concept *man*, which has the four Marks *biped, two-handed, rational, animal*, is the combined result of four separate Judgments which affirmed each of these attributes to be characteristic of *man*. Aristotle, the Father of Logic, seems to have regarded Judgments as the primary elements, out of which Concepts are formed; for his whole system is based upon an analysis of Judgments. Modern writers have preferred, as more convenient, and at least equally correct, the view which has here been taken, that Concepts are the elements of Judgments. In truth, each presupposes the other. If it be asked which, in the order of the mind's development, comes first, the answer is, neither; but a partial and confused apprehension of a thing, which is a young child's substitute for a Concept, and which is first cleared up by a succession of Judgments producing Concepts properly so called. Judgment is not arbitrary or dependent upon the will; I *must, in Thought,* affirm the union or the separation of the two Terms, according as the relation of agreement or disagreement is perceived to exist between them. Hence, the Judgment is always, at least subjectively, true; the Proposition, which is only the verbal affirmation, may be either true or false, according as it does, or does not, agree with the mental Judgment.

The mere succession or coexistence of two Thoughts in the mind does not constitute a Judgment. I may think first of *man*, and then of *animal;* but no Judgment takes place until I affirm in Thought a perceived relation between them, — until I think *man* IS *animal*. Such a relation cannot be perceived between them unless one is regarded as an attribute or determination of the other; — that is, one must be regarded as determining, and the other as determined. For if both were viewed as determining, there would be nothing determined; and both cannot be determined, unless there is something determining them. Hence there are three necessary parts of a Judgment; — first, the Concept or thing determined, which is called the *Subject;* secondly, the determining or attributive notion, which is called the *Predicate;* and, thirdly, that which expresses the relation of determination between the Subject and the Predicate is called the *Copula*. The Subject and Predicate are called the *Terms* (*termini*) or Extremes of the Judgment; and the Copula may therefore be symbolized as a straight line connecting the two points which are its Terms or ends.

Though a Judgment necessarily consists of two Terms, it is nevertheless a *single* act of mind. There is a separate act of mind, whereby I perceive or conceive each of the two Terms taken separately; but it is only one act by which I perceive and affirm the relation between these two Terms, and thereby unite them into one process of Thought.

When the mental Judgment comes to be expressed in words as a Proposition, each of its three parts does not necessarily appear as a distinct word. The idiom of language often requires or enables us to express two, or even all three, of them by a single word; but, in accordance with the general Postulate of Logic, that we must be allowed to express all that is implicitly thought, we cannot deal logically with the Proposition until its form is so modified as to allow all the three elements to appear separately. Moreover, as has been already remarked, the Copula of a

Judgment, since it expresses the *present* union of two thoughts now before the mind, must always appear as the *present tense* of a verb, — usually of the verb *to be :* IS or IS NOT is commonly regarded as the only distinctive expression of the logical Copula. Thus the Propositions, *the sun shines ; pluit ; cogito, ergo sum ; he came yesterday ; John will arrive ;* if reduced to their logical form as Judgments, must be thus expressed: *the sun is shining; the rain is falling; I am thinking, therefore I am existing ; he is the person who came yesterday ; John is he who will arrive.* In each of these cases, all that precedes the Copula, *is* or *am*, is the Subject, and all that follows the Copula is the Predicate.* The substantive verb, when used as a Copula,

---

* Hence we perceive how unfounded is the objection which has been made to the science of Formal Logic, on the ground that it does not expound the whole theory of reasoning, because it furnishes no explanation of an inference so obvious as this : —

A is greater than B ;
therefore, B is less than A.

But here the Predicate is not B or A, but "greater than B" and "less than A"; the meaning of these two expressions, therefore, belongs to the *Matter* of Thought, with which, as a logician, I have nothing more to do than with the meaning of A or B taken alone. That these two expressions have a correlative meaning, is a fact which belongs to the science of language rather than to that of Thought. Instead of regarding one of them as an inference from the other, it would be more correct to say that the two are equivalent statements of the same fact ; they express one relation between two Concepts. That *two lines converge from A to B* is only another way of saying that the same *two lines diverge from B to A* ; there is but one thing to be said, though there are two modes of saying it. In like manner, we may say, but we do not argue, that

Socrates is the husband of Xantippe ;
therefore, Xantippe is the wife of Socrates.
God alone is omnipotent ;
therefore, no one is omnipotent but God.

In such cases, the second proposition is an interpretation of the preceding one, not an inference from it. We learn from a dictionary, not from a treatise on Logic, what different phrases are equivalent statements of one and the same Thought.

never means *exists;* but the idea of *existence,* when it is intended to be conveyed, forms the Predicate. *He is,* in the sense of *he exists,* is logically interpreted, *he is existing. Fuit Ilium;* Troy is that which has been, — is that which exists no longer.

Logicians generally maintain that the Copula is precisely equivalent to the mathematical sign of equality. In many cases, this is undoubtedly true. If the Predicate is simply a definition of the Subject, or if the Proposition in any manner expresses the entire equivalence of its two Terms, it can then be expressed in the manner of an equation. Thus, *Saltpetre* = *nitrate of Potash; Alexander* = *the son of Philip.* But the two Terms of a Judgment are not always convertible or equivalent. What is thought and expressed is always a relation between the two Terms, but is not always a relation of equivalence or identity. Sometimes, as in a negative Judgment, it is a relation of disagreement; sometimes the Predicate expresses merely one attribute of the Subject, and then the relation is that of a whole to its part, since only a portion of the Subject's Intension is affirmed of the Subject. When we say, *the apple is red,* we do not mean *apple* = *red,* but only that a red color is one out of many attributes of the apple, — is a part of its Intension. In this case, the Copula signifies rather possession, *to have,* than equality, *to be.* The form of the Judgment as thought is, *the apple has a red color* as one of its many attributes.

It is evident, then, that there are two classes of Judgments, properly distinguished by Dr. Thomson as Substitutive and Attributive. In Substitutive Judgments, the sign of equality may be used as the Copula; the Predicate is properly identified with the Subject, or made convertible with it, and therefore every attribute of the one may also be affirmed of the other. If $A = B$, then every x of A is also x of B; all that is true of "Alexander" is also true of "the son of Philip." But if the Judgment is only Attributive, the sign of equality cannot be used; the two Terms are not convertible, and consequently it cannot be inferred that they possess the same attributes. Sweetness or sourness is a quality of the apple, but not of the red color which belongs to the apple.

The distinction here explained is a valid and important one in respect to Judgments considered simply as such, or as mere phenomena of Thought, irrespective of any use to be subsequently made of them in reasoning or other mental processes. In Attributive Judgments, the Predicate is actually thought only connotatively, as a Mark or attribute of the Subject, and not denotatively, as the name of a class of things. And hence Mr. Mill is led to maintain, that such Judgments never express truths of classification, and, therefore, that the generally received doctrine of Predication, that it consists in placing something in a class or excluding something from a class, is entirely unfounded. " When I say that *snow is white*," he argues, " I may and ought to be thinking of *snow* as a class; but I am certainly not thinking of *white* objects as a class; I am thinking of no *white* object whatever except *snow*, but only of that, and of the sensation of *white* which it gives me."

All this is granted. *At the moment of forming the Judgment, white* is not consciously before the mind as the name of a class of things. We *then* think of it only connotatively, — only as a Mark. But it is still true that we originally learned the meaning of the word *white* not only as a Mark connoting a quality, but also as a Concept denoting a class of things, — namely, white objects; otherwise, it would not be, what it certainly is, a Common Name of snow, milk, chalk, and many other things. And though this its denotative meaning — its Extension — is not consciously before the mind when it is used as a Mark or as a Predicate, it is still there potentially, and must be brought out or expressed when we attempt to found an inference upon this Judgment, or to employ it as one of the premises in a syllogism. To borrow Mr. Mill's own instance, — if I am in doubt whether Chimborazo is snow-covered, I may reason thus: —

All mountains of a certain altitude, and whose summits are perpetually white, are snow-covered.

But Chimborazo's lofty summit is always white, — that is, it is one of this class of mountains.

Therefore, Chimborazo is snow-covered.

As already observed (p. 64), "the distinction between Concepts and Marks is not absolute, but relative; they may be used interchangeably." That a Concept or Common Name is sometimes used only as a Mark, or with no *conscious* reference at the moment to its denotation, is surely no proof that it is always so used, or even that the denotative meaning, or Extension, is not potentially present in this very case, so that it may be revived, if need be, and an inference founded upon it. Because words are sometimes used symbolically, or without spreading out in Thought all their signification, it does not follow that they are always so used, or that such use of them may not be checked, and kept from falling into error, by occasionally bringing up into consciousness what they always potentially signify in Thought. It follows, then, that although a Judgment, *as actually thought,* may not be a truth of classification, and therefore that the Copula may not be equivalent to the mathematical sign of equality, yet it may always be reduced to the form of such a truth, and then this mathematical sign fully expresses its proper form; and in reasoning, such a reduction is generally necessary. Though it is not true that *apple = red*, it is true that *apples = some red objects;* or, as it is more commonly expressed by Conversion, *some red objects are apples.*

1. THE PREDICABLES AND THE CATEGORIES.

In his analysis of Judgments, Aristotle was led to consider how many kinds of Predicates there are, when viewed relatively to their Subjects;—in other words, to determine the Second Intentions of Predicates considered in relation to Subjects. Thus was formed his celebrated doctrine of the Predicables,—a doctrine which was considerably modified, but not improved, by his followers, Porphyry and the Schoolmen. According to Aristotle, every Judgment affirms or denies one of four relations of a Predicate to its Subject. It expresses either,—1. the *Genus*, i. e. the class under which it is included, as when we say, *man is an animal;* or, 2. the *Definition*, which, as we have seen, is the Genus and the Specific Difference taken together, and may be reduced to an enumeration of all the *essential* Marks of the Subject, as, *a Carnivor is a flesh-eating Mammal;* or, 3. a *Property*, that is, some *peculiar* attribute of the Subject, belonging to it universally, belonging to nothing else, and yet not regarded as essential to it, for we could conceive of the thing without it,—as *polarity* is a Property (*proprium*) of the *magnet*, and *risibility* of *man;* or, 4. an Accident, which is an attribute that happens to belong to the Subject, but, as unessential, is separable from it, as *man is learned*.

Two of these Predicables, namely, the Definition and the Property, are convertible with the Subject, or may change places with it; and of these two, the former expresses the whole Essence (all the essential qualities), while the latter, strictly speaking, is no part of the Essence; for we can conceive of man as not having the attribute of *risibility*, but we cannot conceive of him as deprived of *rationality*.. So, the magnet can be conceived of without *polarity*, as its magnetic or attractive power was known long before its property of pointing to the north was discovered; but its magnetic or attractive quality is essential to our conception of it. Of the two other Predicables, Genus and Accident, neither is convertible with the Subject; and, again, the former expresses a part of the Essence, and the latter does not. Thus we have the following scheme of the Predicables:—

Definition	expressing the whole Essence	} convertible with the Subject.
Property	expressing no part of the Essence	
Genus	expressing a part of the Essence	} inconvertible with the Subject.
Accident	expressing no part of the Essence	

Porphyry and the Schoolmen modified this analysis, but did not improve it, in their attempt to make it conform to their philosophical doctrine of Realism. The Realists maintained, that Universals or Species are not mere classes of things arbitrarily formed by the mind, but are real existences, with perfectly well-defined limits, existing in things, and yet independently of them and of our conceptions of them. Each Universal is the common and essential element — the Essence — of all the individual things which are included under it and denoted by its Name. Whatever other attributes these individuals possess do not belong to their Essence, but are considered as their Properties or Accidents. According to this view, Species has a determinate and fixed meaning, corresponding very nearly to what we have termed the Infima Species; it was absolutely the lowest class to which anything can be referred, and not merely the lowest relatively, as we have defined it. Every Specific Difference, moreover, signifies absolutely *the* attribute whereby a given Species is distinguished from every other Species of the same Genus. Both Species and Genus are thus supposed to be absolutely determined, following the patterns or archetypes of them which exist in the Divine Mind, and which presided over their creation, instead of being mere creatures of our Thought, and springing from arbitrary classifications, according to which the same individual may be referred to any one of several different Species, and again the same Species to one Genus or another, according as it suits our purpose. The Realists maintained that the hierarchy of classification is not fluctuating and arbitrary, formed by man for his own convenience, and therefore always changing to suit his ever-varying purposes; but they held that it resulted from the real nature of things, as determined by the Creator, and therefore is a perfect and immutable copy of the Divine Thought. To adopt Mr. Mill's language, "they did not admit every class which could be divided into other classes to be a Genus, or every class which could be included in a larger class to be a Species. *Animal* was by them considered a *Genus;* and *man* and *brute*, co-ordinate Species under that Genus: *biped* would not have been admitted to be a Genus with reference to *man*, but a *proprium* or *accidens* only. It was requisite, according to their theory, that Genus and Species should be of the *Essence* of the Subject. *Animal* was of the Essence of *man; biped* was not. And in every classification, they considered some one class as the lowest or Infima Species; *man*, for instance, was a lowest Species. Any other divisions into which the class might be capable of being further broken down, as *man* into *white, black*, and *red* man, or into *priest* and *layman*, they did not admit to be Species." They wrongly assumed, — 1. that the Divine Mind classifies at all (see p. 15); 2. that it would be possible for man to follow the thought of the Creator so far as to copy without error such classification, even if it existed; 3. that there is no occasion, even for purposes of human science and convenience, to distribute the same individual things into different systems of classification, assuming various Grounds of Division, according to the special ends in view.

Adopting the Realist hypothesis, the Schoolmen distinguished these five Predicables, — Genus, Species, Difference, Property, and Accident. Comparing this list with that of Aristotle, we perceive that Definition is omitted, — being resolved into its two elements, Genus and Specific Difference, both of which are admitted into this scheme, — and that Species also is added. The Species here intended is the Infima Species, or proximate class, and is usually defined as being the whole Essence of the individuals of which it is predicated. Difference is also taken absolutely, being regarded as predicable of this class and of none other, — that is, as serving to distinguish this Species, not merely from the other Species in the same Genus, but from all others whatever. Aristotle omitted Difference from his list, because, as he says, it is "of the nature of Genus," or, as we should say, it is interchangeable with Genus. In truth, each of the two elements of a Definition is a Genus; they are two communicant or overlapping Genera. But it is more convenient to regard one as determined, and the other as determining, — that is, one as Genus and the other as Difference. Thus, *man is a rational animal;* here are two Genera, *rational beings* and *animal beings*, which partially include, and partially exclude, each other. As there are some *rational beings* which are not *animal* (*angels*, for instance), so there are some *animals* (*brutes*) which are not *rational;* but *man* is both *animal* and *rational*, — that is, he is the common part of the two overlapping Genera. He is, therefore, a *rational animal* being, or, what is precisely the same thing, he is an *animalized rational* being. In the former case, *animal* is the Genus and *rational* is the Specific Difference; in the latter case, this is reversed, *rational* being the Genus and *animal* the Difference. Thus: —

Let A = animal;
     B = rational;
then, C = rational animal.

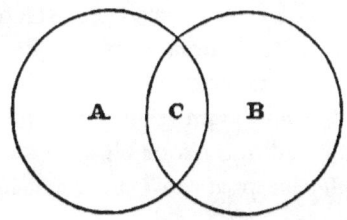

Aristotle evidently perceived, what his followers did not, that there is no real distinction between Genus and Difference; that both of them are, in truth, Genera; and hence that Difference, being of the nature of Genus, cannot be admitted into the list of distinct Predicables.

Having ascertained the Second Intentions of Predicates, which are the Predicables, Aristotle attempted to carry the analysis of Judgments one step farther, by determining their First Intentions, and was thus led to form his celebrated list of the ten Categories or Predicaments. In other words, having determined *how many sorts of Predicates* there are in relation to their Subjects, he next inquired *how many and what particular things* may be predicated of any Subject. Considering every Judgment as the answer to a question, he sought to ascertain how many and what different questions may be asked concerning a Subject, — what are the several determinations of which it is capable. The inquiry evidently concerns the Matter, and not the Form, of Thought, and therefore does not properly fall within the province of Logic, which is exclusively occupied with Second Intentions. But the Categories may be regarded as a curiosity in the history of the science, and as a monument of the genius of its founder for abstract thought and comprehensive generalization. Great ingenuity has been wasted upon the discussion of them by his followers. For many centuries, during which the boundaries of the science were not so strictly defined as they now are, the doctrine of the Categories occupied a prominent place in every treatise upon Logic. A very brief explanation of it will answer our present wants.

The Greek verb from which *category* is derived properly signifies *to accuse*, or *to affirm something of any one*, and hence, *to predicate*. But the noun has been diverted by logicians from signifying *affirmation* or *predication*, and applied to *a list* or *class of things of the same kind which may be predicated of any Subject*. Aristotle affirms that there are ten Categories, or classes of things that may be so predicated,—namely, 1. Substance; 2. Quantity; 3. Quality; 4. Relation; 5. Place; 6. Time; 7. Posture; 8. Possession; 9. Action; 10. Passion. According to a fashion very common among the Scholastic logicians, of manufacturing Latin verses as aids to the memory in retaining the technicalities of the science, the several Categories are indicated in the two following lines, though in a somewhat different order from that given above, as shown by the numerals prefixed.

$$\overset{1}{\text{Arbor}}\ \overset{2}{\text{sex}}\ \overset{3}{\text{servos}}\ \overset{4}{\text{fervore}}\ \overset{9}{\text{refrigerat}}\ \overset{10}{\text{ustos}};$$
$$\overset{5}{\text{Ruri}}\ \overset{6}{\text{cras}}\ \overset{7}{\text{stabo}},\ \overset{8}{\text{nec tunicatus ero}}.$$

The four Predicables, argues Aristotle,—"the Accident, the Genus, the Property, and the Definition,—will always be in one of these Categories [or classes]; since, through these, all propositions signify either *what* the Subject is, or *how much* it is, or *what sort of a thing* it is, or some one of the other Categories"; as, *what relation it bears* to some other thing, or its *place*, its *time*, its *posture*, what it *has*, or *does*, or *suffers*. Adopting Aristotle's own examples of predication under each of these classes, we may, for instance, affirm of anything,—1. under the Category of Substance, that it is *a man, a horse*, or the like; 2. under that of Quantity, that it is *two cubits long, three cubits*, &c.; 3. under that of Quality, that it is *white, grammatical*, &c.; 4. under that of Relation, that it is *double, half as large, greater*, &c.; 5. under that of Place, *in the Lyceum, in the Forum*, &c.; 6. under that of Time, *yesterday, last year*, &c.; 7. under Posture, *standing, seated*, &c.;* 8. under Possession, *having shoes* or *armor*, &c.;

---

* Many writers have interpreted Aristotle's seventh Category, κεῖσθαι, as *Situation*. But, as *Situation* is identical with *Place*, this interpretation makes the seventh redundant and unnecessary. Besides, the examples here selected prove that Aristotle here understands κεῖσθαι to signify *Posture*.

9. under Action, *it cuts, burns,* &c.; 10. under Passion, *it is cut, is burned,* &c.

The purpose of Aristotle in framing his scheme of the Categories, and the nature of the Categories themselves, have been very differently understood by different writers, who, in commenting upon them, seem to have had much more reference to their own systems of metaphysical philosophy than to a fair interpretation of the text of their author. Thus, Kant assumes that Aristotle's intention was to form a complete list of the *a priori* conceptions of the intellect, or of the forms which the mind imposes upon things by its own mode of thinking them. Under this interpretation, he asserts very truly, that the analysis is not formed upon any one principle; that the enumeration is incomplete; that empirical notions are intruded among the pure, and derivative among those which are original.

Mr. Mill supposes that the Categories are "an enumeration of all things capable of being named, — an enumeration by the *summa genera;* that is, the most extensive classes into which things could be distributed; which, therefore, were so many highest Predicates, one or other of which was supposed capable of being affirmed with truth of every namable thing whatsoever." Taken in this light, he finds, of course, that the list is both redundant and defective; that Relation includes Action, Passion, and several others; and that "mental states," which, in Mr. Mill's opinion, are neither substances nor attributes, are omitted entirely.

Sir William Hamilton's interpretation of the Categories agrees very nearly with that of Mr. Mill. He finds that they are an enumeration of the highest genera of Being or Existence, — that is, of all things whatsoever; and, under this view, justly objects that Being ought first to be divided by dichotomy, into *absolute* and *relative* Being, the first of which coincides with Aristotle's first Category, that of Substance, while the second includes the other nine; and that the last six may all be reduced to the fourth, that of Relation.

Trendelenburg, who is followed by Mr. Mansel, maintains that the Categories are, to adopt the language of the latter, "an enumeration of the different modes of naming things, classified primarily according to the grammatical distinctions of speech, and gained, not from the observation of objects, but from the analysis of assertions." This doctrine seems to be correct; but it is obviously irrelevant, for it explains only the genesis, not the nature, of the Categories. To show the source of the classification, or how Aristotle was led to make it, is very different from explaining the nature of the things classified, and the real distinctions between the several classes.

And the ground for the other criticisms falls away when it is considered, that the distinction between the Form and the Matter of Thought — that is, between Logic and Metaphysics — is but very imperfectly preserved by Aristotle. But although much of what properly belongs to Metaphysics is intruded into his treatises upon Logic, and *vice versa*, it is never considered there primarily in its metaphysical nature, but only in its logical relations. The doctrine of the Categories, as conceived by him, is not an attempt to enumerate the highest classes into which *things in general* can be distributed; for this would be a purely metaphysical speculation, and, as such, open to criticism on metaphysical grounds. But it is a classification of things *in so far only as these things are predicates*, — that is, of things considered merely in one of their logical aspects. To such a classification, metaphysical objections, like those of Kant, Mill, and Hamilton, are evidently irrelevant. For instance: — metaphysically, Place is included under Relation, for it is the relation of a subject to a fixed point in space. But, logically, these two Categories are distinct, for it is one thing to assign a Subject to a fixed point in space; a second, to assign its relation to another thing in quantity or quality; and a third and fourth, to assign its quantity and quality absolutely. Aristotle's scheme or general conception of the Categories may be censured, as depending on a mixture of two incongruous aspects of Thought, the logical and the metaphysical; but for all that appears, it is as well executed as such a hybrid scheme can be.

2. THE QUANTITY, QUALITY, AND RELATION OF JUDGMENTS, ACCORDING TO THE ARISTOTELIC DOCTRINE.

The question now arises, how many things can be determined about a Judgment considered merely as such, — that is, by considering its mere Form, without reference to the Matter of the Concepts which are its Terms. In the first place, we may inquire concerning the number of objects about which we judge, and thus determine the *Quantity*, or Extension, of the Judgment. Secondly, we may ask what sort of a Judgment we form respecting the two Terms, — that is, whether we affirm a relation of agreement or of disagreement between them; we thus ascertain the *Quality* of the Judgment, or whether it is affirmative or negative. Thirdly, we may inquire respecting the different modes in which a relation of agreement or difference between the two terms may be affirmed, and thus determine what is called the *Relation* of a Judgment. In this manner are answered the three questions which may be asked concerning any Judgment or Proposition whatsoever, — *Quanta? qualis? quæ?*

A fourth question has generally been asked by logicians, as to the degree of certainty with which a Judgment is affirmed. This was called the *Modality* of the Judgment, being the mode or measure in which we hold it to be true.

Several degrees of it were usually distinguished, according to the following formulas:—

Judgments are either

Pure	A *is* B.	Assertorical.
or Modal	{ A *may be* B.	Contingent or Problematic.
	A *must be* B.	Necessary. ⎫
	A *cannot be* B.	Impossible. ⎬ Demonstrative.
	A *can be* B.	Possible. ⎭

But the whole doctrine of Modality is now rightfully banished from Pure Logic, as it evidently belongs not to the Form, but to the Matter, of Thought. Any number of Modal Propositions may be framed, all of which would have as good a claim to consideration as those just specified. Thus, A is *rightfully* B, A is *justly* B, A is *maliciously* B, are as good Modals as A is *possibly* B, or A is *certainly* B. In truth, since the Copula in Logic is only a sign of equality, or the present tense of the verb *to be*, the qualifying word must be logically regarded as a portion of the Predicate; thus, A is a *possible*, or a *necessary* B. Hence it is manifest that the signs of Modality belong to the Matter of the Thought, with which here we have no concern.

In respect to Quantity, according to the Aristotelic logicians, Judgments are either *Universal* or *Particular*. A Universal Judgment is one in which the Predicate is affirmed of the whole Subject taken distributively. Thus, *All men* (i. e. *each* and *every* man) *are mortal; No quadruped* (i. e. *not any one out of all* quadrupeds) *is rational;* are Universal Judgments.

A Particular Judgment is one in which the Predicate is affirmed only of a part — an indefinite part — of the Subject. For example: *Some men* (i. e. *some at least, some — I know not how many*) *are learned; Some trees are not deciduous.*

On the other hand, *all* taken collectively (as, *All the Greeks* — i. e. *the Greek nation — conquered the Persians*), is the sign of a *Singular* or *Individual* Judgment, in which a Predicate is affirmed of one thing, or of a class of things taken as one whole. But as here also the Predicate is affirmed of the *whole* Subject, Singular Judgments, for all logical purposes, are considered as Universals.

In like manner, *some certain — some, a definite part —* embracing these very cases which I am thinking of and no other — is the sign, not of a Particular, but of a Singular Judgment, and is therefore properly ranked with Universals.

"Individual names," says Mr. Mansel, "are distinguished as *individua signata*, expressed by a proper name, as *Socrates; individua demonstrativa*, by a demonstrative pronoun, *hic homo; individua vaga*, by an indefinite pronoun, *aliquis homo, quidam homo.*" But he properly objects that this last class, the indefinites, ought to be considered as Particulars rather than as Singulars. "If we say *quidam conscionatur, quidam legit*, there is no evidence that the same person is spoken of in the two propositions; while *Socrates*, except by a mere quibble, will always designate the same person. There may, indeed, be two persons of the same name; but, in this case, the name fails to accomplish the intended distinction, and we must specify, — *Socrates the son of Sophroniscus.*"

The logicians formerly distinguished another class of Judgments as *Indefinite*, meaning those in which the Subject, having no sign or predesignation of Quantity affixed to it, is not expressly declared to be either Universal, Singular, or Particular. Thus, *Elephants are sagacious animals; — Learned men are to be found at Oxford.* But this omission of the predesignation of Quantity is merely an accident of expression, and therefore belongs only to Propositions, and not to Judgments, which are always *thought* as having some one of the three specified kinds of Quantity. According to the Postulate of Logic, which requires us to state explicitly all that is implicitly thought, the two examples just given are logically stated thus: *All elephants are sagacious;* — *Some learned men are found at Oxford.*

An improved classification or nomenclature of Judgments in respect to Quantity is proposed by Sir William Hamilton. Since both Universals and Singulars have a determinate or known Quantity, — namely, the whole either of a class or of a unit, — he would call them *Definite* Judgments; while Particulars, expressing an indeterminate or unknown part of a whole, should be called *Indefinite*. But as confusion might arise from abandoning technical terms which have been so long in use, we shall continue to distinguish Judgments in respect to Quantity as either Universal or Particular, Singular being ranked with the former, and the latter expressing an indefinite part.

In respect to Quality, Judgments are distinguished as either *Affirmative* or *Negative*, according as they affirm a union or a disjunction of their two Terms. In every real Negative Judgment, the negative particle, wherever in the sentence it may appear, belongs only to the Copula; since the question always is, whether a union of the Subject and Predicate *is*, or *is not*, affirmed. Hence the presence of a negative particle in the proposition is not a sure sign that it is a Negative Judgment, for this particle may belong in thought to one of the two Terms. Thus,

"Nil admirari prope res est una, Numici";—
"Not to admire is all the art I know";—
"Æneas potuit — non vincere Turnum";—

are Affirmative Judgments. This, also, is an affirmation:—

"Una salus victis — nullam sperare salutem."
"The only chance of preservation for the vanquished is, not to hope for preservation."

Hence, by an easy artifice, a Negative Judgment may be changed, *in Form*, to an Affirmative one of equivalent meaning, by taking off the negation from the Copula, and affixing it to the Predicate. Thus, X *is not* Y, is the same as, X *is* not-Y; for if the universe is divided into only two parts, *Y* and *not-Y*, the exclusion of X from one of these parts is necessarily an inclusion of it in the other. And as two negatives cancel each other, an Affirmative may be made to take the Form of a Negative Judgment, by negativing *both* the Copula and the Predicate. X *is* Y, may be changed into, X *is not* not-Y. "The soul *is* indivisible," is equivalent to " The soul *is not* divisible "; and " All the righteous *are* happy," is the same as " *Not* any of the righteous *are* unhappy." We shall soon see what use can be made of this artifice in the doctrine of Immediate Inference.

By combining the Quantity and Quality, as there are two kinds of each, we have four distinct forms of Judgments, which are designated by the four vowels **A, E, I, O**. To aid the memory, these distinctions have been expressed in this Latin distich:—

> Asserit **A**, negat **E**, sed universaliter ambæ,
> Asserit **I**, negat **O**, sed particulariter ambo.

These lines have been thus translated into English doggerel:—

> **A**, it affirms of *this, these, all,*
> Whilst **E** denies of *any;*
> **I**, it affirms, whilst **O** denies,
> Of *some* (or few or many).*

Examples of these Propositional Forms, as they are called, are given in the following table:—

Symbols.	Examples.	Quality.	Quantity.
A.	*All animals are sentient.*	Affirmative.	Universal.
E.	*No plant is sentient.*	Negative.	
I.	*Some men are honest.*	Affirmative.	Particular.
O.	*Some trees are not maples.*	Negative.	

* It is suggested by Hamilton, with great plausibility, that these four letters were selected because A and I are the first two vowels in *affirmo*, E and O the two vowels in *nego*.

Observe, however, that though the predesignation *all* is the sign of **A**, a Universal Affirmative, *not all* is not the sign of **E**, a Universal Negative, but is always Particular, and leaves the Quality ambiguous, as it may be either Affirmative or Negative. *Not all* denies universality, and is a direct assertion that *some are not*, and an implied assertion that *some are*. Thus, *Not all is gold that glitters*, asserts directly that *some glittering things are not gold*, and, by implication, that *some glittering things are gold*. "Not every one who says unto me, Lord! Lord! shall enter into the kingdom of Heaven"; — i. e. *some* who say this shall *not* enter.

The predesignation *some* is likewise ambiguous. It may mean *some at least*, — i. e. *some, perhaps all;* or it may mean *some at most*, — i. e. *some, not all*. Thus, a chemist might say, *Some metals are dissolved by acids*, meaning " *Perhaps all metals are thus soluble*, but at any rate, *some are.*" On the other hand, he may say, *Some metals are malleable*, meaning, *some — excluding all*, for he knows that *some* metals are *not* malleable. In a Negative Judgment, if we consider *some* to mean *perhaps all*, it is evident that "Some X is not Y" may be construed " Perhaps *no* X is Y "; but if *some* signifies *not all*, then *some is not* excludes, or is inconsistent with, *none — not one*. The wholly indefinite meaning, *some, perhaps all*, is the one generally received in Logic; the other meaning is called by Sir W. Hamilton *semi-definite*, because, by excluding *all*, it is so far definite. Though this latter meaning has been generally neglected by logicians, it leads, as we shall see hereafter, to some important additional inferences, and modifies, to a considerable extent, the old doctrines concerning Opposition.

Hitherto we have considered the Quantity of the Judgment only, and we have now to consider the Quantity of the two Terms as affected by the Judgment in which they stand. A Term is said to be *distributed* when it is taken distributively, or in the whole of its Extension,—that is, when it is affected, or should be affected, by the predesignations *all, each, none,* &c.; it is *not distributed* when it is taken only in an indefinite part of its Extension,—as usually signified by the predesignations *some, not all,* &c. The received or Aristotelic doctrine upon this matter is, that the distribution of the *Subject* depends upon the *Quantity* of the Judgment, thus;—in Universal Judgments, the Subject is distributed, but in Particular Judgments, it is not distributed. *No unjust action is expedient;*—this is a Universal Proposition, and its Subject is evidently distributed, as the meaning is, *not any one out of all unjust actions is expedient.* But in the Particular Proposition, *Some men are learned,* it is obvious that the Subject, *men,* is not distributed.

On the other hand, the distribution of the *Predicate* depends upon the *Quality* of the Judgment, thus;—in Negative Judgments, the Predicate is distributed, but in Affirmatives, it is not distributed. This rule is evidently founded upon the doctrine that all predication is classification; and consequently, that when we affirm, we thereby include the Subject in the class denoted by the Predicate, not meaning that the Subject constitutes *the whole* of that class, but only *a part* of it; and that, when we deny, we thereby exclude the Subject *wholly,* or from *any part* of the class. Thus, when we say, "Men are animals," we mean, "Men are *some* animals," since it is not true that *all* animals are men. On the other hand, when we say, "No man is immortal," we mean to exclude *man* from *every part* of the class of "immortal beings," so that no immortal whatever can be human. And even in the case of Particular Negatives, as, "Some Frenchmen are not Parisians," we still mean absolute or total exclusion,— that not any Parisian whatever is one of the "Some Frenchmen"—say, inhabitants of Lyons—whom we were speaking of.

According to this doctrine, the four fundamental Judgments, if the statements are intended to convey the whole Thought which is implied in them, must be thus expressed:—

A. All X are *some* Y.   All animals are *some* sentient beings.
E. No X is *any* Y.   No plant is *any* sentient being.
I. Some X are *some* Y.   Some men are *some* honest persons.
O. Some X are not *any* Y.   Some trees are not *any* maples.

Hence the rule for the distribution of the two Terms in a Judgment may be thus briefly expressed:—In **A**, only the Subject is distributed; in **O**, only the Predicate; in **I**, neither; in **E**, both.

Those who maintain this doctrine are perfectly aware, of course, that the Predicate is sometimes taken universally in Affirmative Judgments, as when we predicate either Definition or Property; but they assert that this results from considering the Matter, not the Form, of the Judgment, and therefore is not entitled to notice in Pure Logic. And they further maintain, that the Predicate is *never* quantified particularly in a Negative Judgment. Sir W. Hamilton, however, as we shall see, has denied both portions of the doctrine, and, by substituting for it his own theory of "the thoroughgoing quantification of the Predicate," has revolutionized the whole science of Logic.

In respect to the Relation of the Predicate to the Subject, Judgments are divided into *simple* or *absolute*, and *conditional*. In the former, which are technically called *Categorical*, the Predicate is conceived as a Mark, and is therefore absolutely affirmed or denied of the Subject, there being no other ground or reason for the attribution or denial than what is contained in the Subject itself. All

Categorical Judgments are included under these two formulas, *A is B, A is not B.* *Conditional* Judgments are those in which the Predicate is affirmed or denied of the Subject, not absolutely, but only under some condition or prerequisite. This condition may be conceived as primarily affecting the Subject, or the Predicate, or both; and hence we have three forms of Conditional Judgments, distinguished as Hypothetical, Disjunctive, and Dilemmatic or Hypothetico-Disjunctive. Thus, in respect to Relation, we have four kinds of Judgments, as distinguished in the following table.

Categorical.   A is B, or, A is not B.

Conditional. ⎧ *Hypothetical.*   If A is B, A is C.
               ⎨ *Disjunctive.*   A is either B or C.
               ⎩ *Dilemmatic,* or
                  Hypothetico-Disjunctive.   If A is B, then C is either D or E.

In a Categorical Judgment, *Man is mortal,* there is evidently no ground or reason for the attribution but an internal one; the Mark of *mortality* is conceived as an essential attribute of *man* under all circumstances or conditions whatsoever. But in each of the other forms, the attribution is conditional. In the Hypothetical Judgment, *If death is a transition to a happier life, then it is desirable,* we do not affirm absolutely that *death is desirable,* but affirm it only under a condition affecting the Subject, *death.* In a Disjunctive, as, *Every deliberate action is either good or evil,* the condition evidently affects the Predicate, as neither of its two forms is affirmed absolutely, but either is affirmed only on condition that the other is denied. The Dilemmatic, as it has two conditions, the one affecting the Subject and the other the Predicate, is obviously a combination of the two preceding forms, and is therefore properly called the Hypothetico-Disjunctive. All Hypothetical Judgments obviously consist of two parts, the first of which is called the *Condition* or *Antecedent,* and the second, the *Consequent;* and the assertion or

Judgment is, that *if* the Condition exists, the Consequent follows.

A Conditional Judgment, though seemingly complex, is really simple, and expresses only a single act of Thought; it contains but one assertion. Thus, in the Hypothetical just cited, we do not assert that *death is a transition*, or that *death is desirable;* but only, *if* it is a transition, *then* it is desirable. Hence the affirmation is evidently single, and the particles *if* and *then* form the Copula of this Judgment, as they connect its two parts together. In a Disjunctive, *either is* and *or is* form the Copula, which reduces an apparently complex Judgment to a simple one. Sometimes *where* and *there* take the place of *if* and *then* in a Conditional Judgment; as, *where fire is, there is heat; where light is, there is shadow.*

In Hypotheticals, the Consequence, or tie which binds together the Antecedent and the Consequent, may be either *mediate* or *immediate*. It is Mediate, only when there is nothing in the Terms of either of the two parts which binds them together; as when we say,

If A is B, C is D.
If the air is still and cloudless, the dew will fall.
If God is just, sinners will be punished.

In such cases, the Consequence may be valid, but it is not Immediate; for, as there are four distinct Terms, the two Parts have no common Term, and are therefore connected only by some unknown cause, or by what is in the mind, but is not expressed. The unexpressed medium, which binds the two Parts together in the last case, is our knowledge that *God governs the world*, and that *justice consists in rewarding the good and punishing sinners;* therefore, if God is just, sinners will be punished.

The Consequence is Immediate, when there are only three Terms in the two Parts, so that, since one of these

Terms is necessarily repeated, it forms an immediate connection of the Parts with each other. In order that there may be this repetition of one of the Terms, either the two Parts must have the same Subject, or the same Predicate, or the Predicate of the first must be the Subject of the second, or the Subject of the first must be the Predicate of the second. In other words, the Hypothetical must appear under one of the four following formulas.

If A is B, A is C.	*If men do wrong, they deserve punishment.*
If A is B, C is B.	*If metals are fusible, gold is fusible.*
If A is B, B is C.	*If patience be a virtue, virtue may be painful.*
If A is B, C is A.	*If happiness is mere freedom from pain, insensibility is happiness.*

In each of these cases, the Consequence is Immediate, because it results from a general rule, which is presupposed in the Proposition that is before us, and may be evolved from it without any further appeal to experience. Because "all C is A," we can immediately infer that, "if A is B, C is B"; or conversely, because the latter Proposition is universally true, the former can be deduced from it by necessary implication. *If the earth is immovable, and is lighted in all parts by the sun, the sun revolves round it;* — this is true so far as concerns the dependence of the one Proposition upon the other, though either Proposition, taken separately, is false. Hence, we do not deny a Hypothetical Judgment by denying either or both of its parts, but only by denying the Consequence of one from the other. This is usually done, in Latin, by placing the negation at the beginning.

Non si miserum fortuna Sinonem
Finxit, vanum etiam mendacemque improba finget.

In English, we may deny a Hypothetical by substituting *although*, or some equivalent, for *if* in the Reason, and then negativing the Consequent.

If you eat of the forbidden fruit, you shall die.
Although you eat, &c., you shall not die.

Or the Proposition may be thus denied.

It is not true that if you eat, &c.

Disjunctives are denied in the same manner.

Conditional Judgments can be reduced to Categoricals, though, for logical purposes, it is more convenient to retain them in the Conditional form. The Condition is equivalent to a limitation, and therefore can always be expressed by a limiting adjective (see page 143). In the formula, *If A is B, then A is C*, it is not asserted that *all* A is C, but only those A which are B. Let d represent such A; then the equivalent Categorical formula is, dA are C. To take a concrete instance: — *If the iron is magnetic, it has the attribute of polarity;* this is equivalent to the Categorical Judgment, *magnetic iron is polar.* Conversely, if any Categorical Judgment has its Subject limited by a qualifying word, the limitation can be resolved into a condition, and the Judgment thus becomes Conditional. Thus, *Virtuous men are happy*, is equivalent to *If men are virtuous, they are happy.*

Disjunctives are reduced in a similar manner to as many Categoricals as there are disjunct members of the Predicate. Thus, —

A is either B or C = $\begin{cases} \text{All those A which are not B are C,} \\ \text{and} \\ \text{All those A which are not C are B;} \end{cases}$

and if d represents the former and f the latter, we have dA are C, and fA are B. Even then, the Thought is not complete until we add, $dA + fA =$ all A. It amounts to the same thing to say, that a Disjunctive may be first resolved into as many Hypotheticals as it has disjunct members; and each of these may, then be reduced, as before, to a Categorical. Thus, *If A is not B, it is C;* and, *If A is not C, it is B.* Evidently, then, Disjunctives are only *complex* Hypotheticals.

3. The Hamiltonian Doctrine of Judgments.

According to the Aristotelic doctrine, as we have seen, in all Affirmative Judgments, the Predicate is Particular, while in all Negative Judgments it is Universal. Thus we have but four fundamental Judgments or Propositional Forms, which have been designated by the four vowels **A, E, I,** and **O**. According to Sir William Hamilton's doctrine of "the thorough-going quantification of the Predicate," in both Affirmative and Negative Judgments, the Predicate may be distributed or undistributed, — that is, may be either Universal or Particular. This doctrine gives us eight Propositional Forms, which are thus indicated: — *A* signifies that the Term to which it corresponds, whether Subject or Predicate, is *universal*, whilst *I* signifies that it is *particular*; *f*,* standing in the place of the Copula, signifies that the Judgment is *affirmative*, whilst *n** signifies that it is *negative*. Thus we have the following table of Hamilton's eight fundamental Judgments, those of them which are recognized under the Aristotelic doctrine being also indicated, as before, by the four vowels.

Affirmatives.

	Afa.	All X are all Y.	e. g. All copperas is *all* sulphate of iron.	(1.)
(A.)	Afi.	All X are some Y.	" All whales are *some* mammals.	(2.)
	Ifa.	Some X are all Y.	" Some men are *all* logicians.	(3.)
(I.)	Ifi.	Some X are some Y.	" Some quadrupeds are *some* amphibious.	(4.)

* These two letters are selected because they are the two first consonants of *affirmo* and *nego.*

Negatives.

(**E.**) Ana.	Not any X is any Y.	e. g. Not any fish is *any* warm-blooded.	(5.)
Ani.	Not any X is some Y.	" Not any Englishman is *some* Briton (Scotch).	(6.)
(**O.**) Ina.	Some X are not any Y.	" Some Frenchmen are not *any* Parisians.	(7.)
Ini.	Some X are not some Y.	" Some trees (oaks) are not *some* trees (maples).	(8.)

The question is, whether these four Forms, viz. Afa, Ifa, Ani, and Ini, which have been added to the list by Sir W. Hamilton, are legitimate and natural Forms of Thought, — whether we do not have frequent occasion to *think* them as Judgments, though we seldom or never express them as Propositions. It is admitted that the predesignations of quantity, *some*, *all*, *any*, here italicized as belonging to the Predicate, are usually elided in expression. This is the case even with the old Forms, **A**, **E**, **I**, and **O**; for language aims always at brevity, and therefore usually omits all that is so obvious as to be easily understood, since its expression would only cumber and lengthen the sentence unnecessarily. Thus, we usually say, *Men are animals;* but nearly all logicians acknowledge that the *Thought*, of which this is an abbreviated expression, is, *All men are some animals*. But the peculiar function of Logic is to analyze, not language, but Thought; it deals, not with Propositions, but with Judgments. Hence its necessary postulate, that we must be allowed to express logically all that is contained in what we think. The question is, whether we are not often obliged to think Judgments under the Forms, *All are all*, *Some are all*, *Not any is some*, and *Some are not some*.

Now the evidence in favor of the first two of these Forms, the affirmatives Afa and Ifa, is so strong, that the only wonder is, how they could have been almost universally rejected by logicians for over two thousand years, down to the time of Sir W. Hamilton. In the first place, any process of inductive reasoning can be properly reduced to logical Form only in this manner: —

X, Y, Z, &c. are B.

But X, Y, Z, &c. are (or represent) *all* A.

Therefore, all A are B.

Here the second premise is *materially* false; but with this fault, as logicians, we have nothing to do. Logic does not guarantee the truth of the premises, but only the validity of the inference from the premises to the conclusion. And that this inference is valid in the preceding formula may be seen by taking an instance in which neither of the premises is faulty. If I am playing chess, and my king is in fatal check, I must reason thus: —

I can neither move my king, nor interpose a man, nor capture the attacking piece.

But these three are *all* the modes of obviating check.

Then I am checkmated.

Here the Predicate of the second premise is quantified universally; and men reason in this manner every day, when they are reduced to a choice among a few only possible modes of action, and each of these modes is fatal. The following example shows how we reason inductively: —

Copper, tin, lead, iron, &c. are fusible.

But copper, tin, lead, &c. are (or represent) *all* metals.

Then all metals are fusible.

As already hinted, every adequate Definition — that is, every one in which the Definiendum and the Definition are convertible terms — has its Predicate universally quantified in Thought. To take the instance already given, *All copperas is sulphate of iron*, or, conversely, *All sulphate of iron is all copperas*. So, also, every exhaustive Division must be thought as a Judgment with a universal Predicate. Thus, the geometer, having demonstrated a certain proposition successively of equilateral, isosceles, and scalene triangles, adds in Thought, But *these are all triangles;* therefore, the theorem holds good of all triangles.

"In fact," says Hamilton, "ordinary language quantifies the Predicate so often as this determination becomes of the smallest import. This it does directly, by adding *all, some,* or their equivalent predesignations, to the Predicate; or it accomplishes the same end indirectly, in an exceptive or limitative form.

"ᵃ) Directly,—as, *Peter, John, James, etc. are all the Apostles;—Mercury, Venus, etc. are all the planets.*

"ᵇ) But this is more frequently accomplished indirectly, by the equipollent forms of *Limitation* or *Inclusion,* and *Exception.**

"For example, by the limitative designations, *alone* or *only,* we say, *God alone is good,* which is equivalent to saying, *God is all good,* that is, *God is all that is good; Virtue is the only nobility,* that is, *Virtue is all noble,* that is, *all that is noble.* The symbols of the Catholic and Protestant divisions of Christianity may afford us a logical illustration of the point. The Catholics say, *Faith, Hope, and Charity alone justify;* that is, *the three heavenly virtues together are all-justifying,* that is, *all that justifies; omne justificans, justum faciens.* The Protestants say, *Faith alone justifies;* that is, *Faith,* which they hold to comprise the other two virtues, *is all-justifying,* that is, *all that justifies; omne justificans.* In either case, if we translate the watchwords into logical simplicity, the predicate appears predesignated.

"*Of animals man alone is rational;* that is, *Man is all rational animal. What is rational is alone or only risible;* that is, *All rational is all risible,* etc.

"I now pass on to the Exceptive Form. To take the motto overhead,—'On earth there is nothing great but man.' What does this mean? It means, *Man — is — all*

---

* The English Exclusive particles are, *one, only, alone, exclusively, precisely, just, sole, solely, nothing, but,* &c. These particles annexed to the Subject predesignate the Predicate universally, or to its whole extent.

earthly great. (*Homo — est — omne magnum terrestre.*)
And the second clause — 'In man there is nothing great
but mind' — in like manner gives, as its logical equipollent,
Mind — is — all humanly great, that is, *all that is great in
man.* (*Mens est omne magnum humanum.*)"

The case may not seem so clear in respect to the two
negative Forms, Ani and Ini, in which the Predicate is
Particular; for the expression of them in language is so
awkward and unnatural as to have provoked the remark,
that they seem to be got up as if for the purpose of showing what one could do. It would certainly be accounted a
forced and uncouth assertion, to say that *not any iron is
some metal*, — i. e. is not lead; or that *some men* (Englishmen) *are not some men* (Frenchmen). Dr. Thomson admits that they are *conceivable,* but denies that they are
actual, cases of negative predication. He argues that
" such a Judgment is never actually made, because it has
the semblance only, and not the power, of a denial. True
though it is, it does not prevent our making another Judgment of the affirmative kind from the same Terms." It
would be more correct to say that we can make "another
Proposition," instead of "another Judgment," from the
same Terms; for the "some metal" in the Predicate of the
negative Judgment is not *thought* as the *same* "some metal"
in the Predicate of the affirmative. The two assertions
are incompatible in Thought, though they happen to be
identical in expression. Thus, —

Iron *is not* some metal, — i. e. is not lead.
Iron *is* some metal, — i. e. is iron.
Englishmen *are not* some men, — not *French*men.
Englishmen *are* some men, — *English*men.

In fact, the law of Division, that the Dividing Members
must exclude each other, compels us to think *some are not
some,* — *these are not those,* — *these are different from those.*
As already shown, negation is only the affirmation of dif-

ference or exclusion; 'A *is not* B,' is equivalent to 'A *is not*-B.' Now we never have occasion to affirm difference or exclusion except for the purpose of distinguishing co-ordinate Species from each other; for if the two classes were not recognized as belonging to the same Genus, — that is, as similar in some respects, — it would not be necessary to think or to say that they differ in certain other respects. We never say, *Fishes are not stars*, since the two things are so unlike that there is no danger of confounding them. But we think and say, *Oaks are not maples, Spaniels are not terriers*, as the classes are here *thought* as belonging to the same proximate Genera, *trees* and *dogs*. In Thought, therefore, these two Judgments are explicated thus: *Some trees are not some trees; Some dogs are not some dogs.*

Even the Aristotelic doctrine admits that *Unskilful are some physicians* is a legitimate Judgment, for it is the simple converse of *Some physicians are unskilful*. But it amounts to precisely the same thing whether we say, *Unskilful are*, &c., or *Not* (any) *skilful are some physicians*. Considered as Propositions, one of these may be condemned as faulty in expression; but as Judgments, one cannot be admitted and the other rejected, for they are one and the same Judgment.

Again, whenever we predicate a Genus of a Species, the Predicate is obviously quantified as Particular; and *some*, which is the predesignation of particularity, must then be thought in its semi-definite sense, as *some, excluding all*. In this sense, we cannot think that *some are*, unless we also think that *some are not*. Then, every such Judgment carries with it by necessary inference, or as a part of itself, another Judgment, negative in Form and with a Particular Predicate. Thus the Judgment, *Men are some animals* (rational bipeds), is incomplete and even impossible in Thought, unless we also think, *Men are not some* (other) *animals* (brutes). Either of these two assertions thus carrying the other along with it by necessary implication, it is more natural to adopt in words the affirmative form, as the more frequent and familiar one, even when the negative meaning is more prominent in Thought. As Hamilton remarks, "men naturally preferred to attribute positively a part of one notion to another, than to deny a part."

It has already been argued, (page 110,) that although the Predicate in any Judgment may be actually thought only *connotatively*, or as a Mark, it is still potentially a Concept, and as such, it *denotes* a class, or has Extension. To predicate, therefore, is virtually to classify, or to assign a Subject to its proper place in a class, thereby attributing to it all the Marks of that class. Now it is argued by Mr. Baynes, with great force, " that when we bring an object under a notion, that is, when we predicate of it that it belongs to such a class, we must know that it occupies a certain place in that class. For if we were uncertain what place the individual object occupied in the class, or whether it occupied any place at all, we should not know the class, and could not therefore bring any object under it; — *e. g.* if I do not know whether *rose* comes under the Concept *flower*, — whether it is equal to some part, or the whole, or superior to it, — I cannot, of course, predicate *flower* of *rose*, since I do not know what the Concept means, what it contains, and what it does not. If, therefore, we understand the object at all, we must fix, in Thought, the sphere which it occupies under the class to which, in predication, we have assigned it. In other words, if we comprehend what we utter, *every notion holding the place of predicate in a proposition must have a determinate quantity in thought.*" * We cannot, for instance, predicate *bird* successfully of *pigeons*, of *winged and feathered bipeds*, and of *animals*, unless we know at least so much of the characteristics of the class *bird* as to be able to think that

---

* Baynes's *New Analytic of Logical Forms*, pp. 9, 10.

"all pigeons are *some* birds," "all winged and feathered bipeds are *all* birds," and "some animals are *all* birds." In like manner, we cannot exclude a Subject from a given Concept or class, — as when we say, *Whales are not fish*, unless we either think *fish* as *cold-blooded, vertebrated animals, living in the water and breathing by gills*, in which case we think " whales are not *any* fish " ; or accept the vulgar notion of *fish* as *finned animals living in the water*, and then think " whales are not *some* fish," — viz. not cold-blooded fish. This leads us to remark, that, in fact, any limitation of the predicated class by a limiting adjective is equivalent to quantifying that Predicate particularly ; — e. g. *Pines are not deciduous trees* = Pines are not *some* trees.

These reasons, and others which will be mentioned when we come to treat of Conversion, seem conclusive in favor of Sir W. Hamilton's doctrine, that, potentially at least, the Predicate is always quantified either universally or particularly, both in affirmative and negative Judgments.

But if each of the two Terms of a Judgment has its own quantity assigned to it in Thought, then, for still stronger reasons than those which have already (pp. 64, 110) been assigned, the distinction between Subject and Predicate ceases to be of any moment. In fact, every Judgment comes from an act of comparing two *quantified* Terms with each other; and as the result of such comparison, we have an equation, or non-equation, established between these Terms, and it is completely indifferent which of them is placed first. Thus, having compared two Concepts, A and B, I find either that they agree, or do not agree, with each other. This agreement or difference may be expressed equally well in either of the following formulas : —

A is B.	A is not B.
B is A.	B is not A.
A and B are equal.	A and B are not equal.
Convertible or equal are A and B.	Unconvertible are A and B.

In these last two formulas, the two compared notions do not stand to each other as Subject and Predicate, but are, in the same proposition, either both Subjects or both Predicates.

In common language, if the two Terms are both quantified universally in Thought, it is admitted to be of no consequence which is placed first; usually, that which is prior or pre-eminent in Thought appears as the Subject. Thus, we say either, *Electricity is not the nervous fluid*, or, *The nervous fluid is not electricity; Common salt is chloride of sodium*, or, *Chloride of sodium is common salt*.

But if the two Terms differ in Quantity, the convenience of language requires, in most cases (not in all*), that the one which has the wider Extension should appear as the Predicate, and that its Quantity, though present in Thought, should be silently passed over in expression. It is more convenient that the Term which has the less Extension, as it is more definite or limited in meaning, and therefore can be more easily grasped in Thought, should be placed first; and then, the Quantity of the Predicate, as it is known to be greater than that of the Subject, (and it matters not how much greater it is,) may be omitted in expression for the sake of brevity. *Metals are fusible substances* is a shorter and more natural expression than *Some fusible substances are metals*, though the two propositions convey precisely

---

* Such propositions as these, for instance, are common: —
It is disgraceful to be a slave to passion.
Turpe est obsequi libidini.
Happy is he who is able to know the causes of things.
Felix qui potuit rerum cognoscere causas.
It is rain which has fallen.
It is foolish to listen to flatterers.
If the Term of the wider Extension must be the Predicate, we should say, — *To be a slave to passion is disgraceful; He who can discover the causes of things is happy; That which has fallen is rain; To listen to flatterers is folly.*

the same meaning. Hence the old logicians, having more regard to Language than to Thought, maintained that the former order was the only legitimate one; they analyzed this order only, and based upon it their whole system. "Natural, or regular, or direct predication they held to be that in which the genus is predicated of the species, the species of the individual, the attribute of its subject, and, in general, the extensive whole of its part; and in which, therefore, the Subject notion was always of less extent than the Predicate notion. Unnatural, indirect, or irregular predication was the reverse of this, — that, to wit, in which the species was predicated of the genus, the subject of its attribute, and, in general, the extensive part of its whole."*

But when it is acknowledged that Logic has to do primarily with Thought, and only secondarily with Language; that each of the two Terms has its own Quantity assigned to it in Thought; and that the purport of the Judgment is merely to affirm the agreement or non-agreement of these two quantified Terms, — it becomes evident that every proposition is logically reduced to an equation, or non-equation, of two Terms, the relative position of which is of no importance whatever. *All metals are some fusible things*, and *Some fusible things are all metals*, are two statements of precisely the same import. And in like manner with negatives; — *Some Frenchmen are not any Parisians*, is the same Judgment as, *Not any Parisians are some Frenchmen.*

4. The Explication of Propositions into Judgments.

Strictly speaking, as we have seen, Pure Logic deals only with Judgments, and refers to the science of Language for the doctrine of Propositions, or the proper expression of Judgments in words. But the claims of Logic

* Baynes's *Analytic*, p. 12.

to be regarded as a universal science, and its doctrine that all Thought can be reduced to distinct Judgments, so that the logical theory of Judgments is applicable to every mental product into which Thought enters, cannot be defended, or even properly understood, until it is clearly shown how all Propositions, even the most complex in character, may be reduced to simple Judgments. We shall therefore consider the explication of Propositions here, though the subject properly belongs to Applied Logic.

Every pure Judgment corresponds to one of these two forms, — *A is B*, or *A is not B;* and if thus expressed in words, it is called a *Simple* Proposition. In this case, neither Subject nor Predicate necessarily consists of a single word; either or both may be described in many words, provided that the union of these words expresses but one Judgment or a single act of Thought. Thus, *Well organized and skilfully administered governments are productive of happiness to their subjects*, is a Simple Proposition, as well as *John is sick*. On the other hand, several acts of Thought combined in one statement constitute a *Compound* Proposition, the plurality of which may reside either in the Subject, or in the Predicate, or in both. Thus, *James and William are young and healthy*, is a *Compound* Proposition, which may be resolved into these four Simple ones: — *James is young; James is healthy; William is young; William is healthy*. A distinct Judgment is evidently necessary for each of these affirmations, whether they are expressed separately, or united into one *Compound* Proposition. Such a Proposition obviously may be partly true and partly false, according as all, or only some, of the Predicates are truly affirmed of all, or only some, of the Subjects.

But as a Simple Proposition contains only one Subject and one Predicate, it would seem that it must be either wholly true or wholly false. And so it would be, but that there are many Propositions, seemingly Compound, but really Simple, whose Subject or Predicate is a *Complex* term, containing by implication other Judgments, that may be called *incidental*. In these, the incidental Judgment may be false, while the main Proposition may be true. In those which are properly called Complex Propositions, the incidental or implied Judgment may appear, either as a part of the Subject or of the Predicate, with which it is joined by a relative pronoun, whose office it is to combine several Propositions into one, or only as a limiting or defining adjective, or participle, or adjective clause. Thus, it is the same thing to say, *God, who is invisible, created the world, which is visible;* or, *The invisible God created the visible world.* It is justly remarked by the Port Royal Logicians, that these incidental Judgments are to be regarded not so much as Propositions which we *now* make, but as Judgments *formerly* made, the Predicate of which is now regarded as a simple Mark or attribute of one of the Terms in our present main Proposition. Hence it is still true, that the Complex Proposition is Simple, because it expresses but one Judgment made at the moment.

The incidental Judgment expressed in an additional word or clause may be either *explicative* or *limitative*. It is Explicative, when it is of the nature of a complete or partial definition, and therefore belongs to the Term to which it is annexed in the whole of its Extension. Thus, *Man, who is born of woman, is of few days and full of trouble;* — here, the adjunct clause, *born of woman*, is to be understood as a definition applicable to *all* men. But in such a Proposition as this, *Men who are avaricious are unhappy*, the relative clause restricts or limits the predication of unhappiness to *some* men, — to those only who are avaricious. It is only these Complex Limitative Propositions which are equivalent to Hypotheticals: — thus, *All iron which is mag-*

netic is polar, has the same meaning as, *If iron is magnetic, it is polar*. It depends upon the Matter of the Thought, and can usually be determined by the context or the nature of the subject, whether the adjunct word or clause is to be considered as Explicative or Limitative.

With regard to Explicatives, it should be observed, that the falsehood of the incidental does not affect the truth of the principal Proposition. Thus, in the Proposition, *Harmodius and Aristogeiton killed Hipparchus, who was a tyrant*, or, *killed the tyrant Hipparchus*, the main assertion would still be true, even though Hipparchus was *not* a tyrant. If, however, there is an implied Inference or argument, that the principal Proposition is true *because* the incidental one is a correct definition, then the falsity of the latter becomes a reason for doubting, not for denying, the truth of the former. Thus, the Proposition, *The soul, which is an extended substance, must occupy space*, becomes doubtful when the incidental affirmation, that it is extended, is disproved; but it may still be true, for other reasons, that the soul must have some position in space.

In respect to Limitatives, no question can arise concerning the truth or falsity of the incidental Proposition; for its Predicate is not affirmed of the Subject to which the relative refers, nor is the existence of any such Subject affirmed. If I say, *Judges who never do anything by request or favor are worthy of praise*, the only assertion is a Hypothetical one. I do not affirm, that Judges never do anything by request or favor, or that there are any such Judges; but only, that *if* there are any such, *then* they deserve praise. The most orthodox believer in the atoning virtue of the death of Christ may still admit, that *a man who has never sinned, and is not sinful by nature, stands in no need of an atonement*. So far, indeed, as such a statement contains any implication that such a human being ever lived, it is false; but if construed strictly, it implies nothing of the kind.

Compound Propositions are divided into those which obviously contain a plurality of Judgments, and therefore do not need analysis and exposition; and those in which the plurality is concealed, so that it is apt to escape notice. The latter are called Exponibles, because they need to be analyzed and explained. These are divided into Exclusives, Exceptives, and Restrictives.

Exclusive Propositions limit the Predicate to this one Subject, thereby excluding it from every other Subject. Hence, every Exclusive contains two Propositions, one of which affirms the Predicate of *A*, and the other denies it of all *not-A*. Thus,

$$\textit{Only A is B} = \begin{cases} \textit{A is B.} \\ \textit{No not-A is B.} \end{cases}$$

$$\textit{God alone is to be worshipped} = \begin{cases} \textit{God is to be worshipped.} \\ \textit{No other being is to be worshipped.} \end{cases}$$

Hamilton, as we have seen, reduces these Compounds to Simple Propositions, by showing that the Exclusive particle annexed to the Subject quantifies the Predicate universally; thus: —

Only A is B = A is all B;

whence we infer immediately, by Infinitation, that

No not-A is B.

Sometimes the Exclusive particles *only, one, sole,* &c., are annexed adjectively to the Predicate, and then have the same meaning as *all.* Thus, *God is the sole object to be worshipped;* — i. e. God is *all* that should be worshipped.

Annexed adverbially to the Copula and Predicate taken together, the Exclusive particle limits the Subject to this one Predicate, thereby excluding it from every other Predicate.

Peter only plays; i. e. *he plays,* and *he does nothing else.*

James is only a lawyer; i. e. *he is a lawyer, and nothing else.*

But, *James is the only lawyer* = *he is all the lawyer* that you can find.

Exceptive Propositions state the Subject universally, yet with a specified exception, to which it is implied that the Predicate is not attributed. These also are equivalent to two Judgments, and these two, as in the case of Exclusives also, differ in Quality.

All but one have disappeared = $\begin{cases} \text{(Nearly)}\ \textit{all have disappeared;} \\ \text{but}\ \textit{one has not disappeared.} \end{cases}$

In respect to Quantity, Exceptives are to be considered as Universals. For although a part is excluded from the whole of the Subject, so that the Predicate is referred only to the remainder, yet this remainder constitutes a whole in itself, of which the Predicate is affirmed or denied.

It is obvious that an Exclusive and an Exceptive are only two modes of expressing the same thing, as it is easy to change them reciprocally from the one to the other; but the direct affirmation in one becomes the implied assertion in the other. A fool thinks that *no method except his own is right;* in other words, that *his own is the only right method.*

Restrictive Propositions are of two kinds, both of which are Limitative in meaning. The first sort restricts the assertion by a special clause, which determines more narrowly the signification of the Subject or the Predicate. *Ethics, considered merely as a doctrine of the expedient, is no longer a science of morality:* — this is equivalent to the two Judgments, *Ethics is a science of morality,* but *a mere doctrine of expediency is not such a science.* Here the Subject is the restricted Term; but in the following example, it is the Predicate. *A good magistrate is merciful to offenders, as far as the demands of justice will permit.*

EXPLICATION OF PROPOSITIONS INTO JUDGMENTS. 147

The second sort of Restriction is called Reduplicative, as it consists in a repetition of the restricted Term. *A judge, as judge, ought never to receive presents;* — that is, he may receive them, like other men, on ordinary occasions, but never in connection with the performance of his official duties. Here, also, the two Judgments into which the Proposition is explicated differ in Quality.

CHAPTER VI.

THE DOCTRINE OF IMMEDIATE INFERENCE.

1. Æquipollence or Infinitation. — 2. Conversion. — 3. Opposition and Integration.

INFERENCE or Reasoning is that act of Pure Thought whereby one Judgment is derived from another, or from two others. The Judgment from which another is deduced is called the Premise; and that which is derived is called the Conclusion. If the Conclusion is drawn directly from one Premise only, without the aid either of an Intuition or another Judgment, it is said to be an Immediate Inference. Thus, from the Premise that *No quadruped is rational*, I know at once, or by Immediate Inference, — that is, by an act of Pure Thought, — that *Every quadruped is irrational*, and that *No rational thing is a quadruped*. If the Conclusion can be drawn only through the intervention of a third Judgment, — in other words, if two Premises are necessary, — the result is a Mediate Inference, or Syllogism.

But in either case, the act of Reasoning or Inference, whether Mediate or Immediate, is simple, being one indivisible act of mind. The Premises are considered as given, and their truth is taken for granted; the Inference is the act of deduction, or drawing out the Conclusion from the Premises, and this act is necessarily simple. If it is performed in accordance with the Laws of Pure Thought, it is apodeictic or absolutely certain, as any opposite Conclusion would be Contradictory and absurd. In respect to their *Matter*, both the Premises and the Conclusion may be false; and yet the *Form* of Inference, or the transition from one to the other, may be intuitively true. Thus, the Mediate Inference,

Everything material is mortal;
The Soul is material;
Therefore the Soul is mortal; —

is false in each of its three Judgments. Yet its Conclusion is as correctly drawn, and the Syllogism is therefore just as valid, as in the following instance, where each of the three Judgments is true.

Everything material is divisible;
Gold is material;
Therefore Gold is divisible.

Hence, the *material* truth of the Conclusion depends upon the *material* truth of the Premises; its *formal* validity is the correctness of the process whereby it was deduced from the Premises. Pure Logic has to do only with the latter. Every correct step of Reasoning, considered simply as such, or in reference to its *Form*, is as indisputable as one of those Primary Axioms of Pure Thought on which it is based, or of which it is an application. The uncertainty or disputable character of much of what is improperly called Reasoning lies altogether in the Premises, and is referable to imperfect observation, to an improper use of words where language has become a substitute for Thought, or to over-hasty generalization. But the mere process of Reasoning, irrespective of the data about which we reason, is the same in the moral and physical, as in the purely mathematical, sciences; it is equally demonstrative in all, for it is conditioned by the absolute laws of Pure Thought. The longest chain of argument is but a series or repetition of Inferences, whether Mediate or Immediate, in which the formal validity of each step, taken by itself, is intuitively perceived.

150 THE DOCTRINE OF IMMEDIATE INFERENCE.

Logic, as Hamilton remarks, "is exclusively conversant about Thought strictly so denominated; and Thought proper, we have seen, is the cognition of one object of thought by another, in or under which it is mentally included; — in other words, Thought is the knowledge of a thing through a Concept or General Notion, or of one Notion through another. In Thought, all that we think about is considered either as something containing, or as something contained; — in other words, every process of Thought is only a cognition of the necessary relations of our Concepts. This being the case, it need not move our wonder that Logic, within its proper sphere, is of such irrefragable certainty, that, in the midst of all the revolutions of philosophical doctrines, it has stood, not only unshattered, but unshaken. In this respect, Logic and Mathematics stand alone among the sciences, and their peculiar certainty flows from the same source. Both are conversant about the relations of certain *a priori* forms of intelligence; — Mathematics about the necessary forms of Imagination; Logic about the necessary forms of Understanding; — Mathematics about the relations of our representations of objects, as out of each other in space and time; Logic about the relations of our Concepts of objects, as in or under each other, that is, as in different relations respectively containing and contained. Both are thus demonstrative, or absolutely certain, sciences, only as each develops what is given, — what is given as necessary, in the mind itself. The laws of Logic are grounded on the mere possibility of a knowledge through the Concepts of the Understanding, and, through these, we know only by comprehending the many under the one. Concerning the nature of the objects delivered by the Subsidiary Faculties to the Elaborative, Logic pronounces nothing, but restricts its consideration to the laws according to which their agreement or disagreement is affirmed."

"It is of itself manifest that every science must obey the laws of Logic. If it does not, such pretended science is not founded on reflection, and is only an irrational absurdity. All Inference, evolution, concatenation, is conducted on logical principles, — principles which are ever valid, ever imperative, ever the same. But an extension of any science through Logic is absolutely impossible; for by conforming to logical canons, we acquire no knowledge, receive nothing new, but are only enabled to render what is already obtained more intelligible, by analysis and arrangement. Logic is only the negative condition of truth. To attempt by a mere logical knowledge to amplify a science, is an absurdity as great as if we should attempt, by a knowledge of the grammatical laws of a language, to discover what is written in this language, without a perusal of the several writings themselves. But though Logic cannot extend, cannot amplify, a science by the discovery of new facts, it is not to be supposed that it does not contribute to the progress of science. The progress of the sciences consists not merely in the accumulation of new matter, but likewise in the detection of the relations subsisting among the materials accumulated; and the reflective abstraction by which this is effected must not only follow the laws of Logic, but is most powerfully cultivated by the habits of logical study."

Aristotle has defined Inference as "a thought or proposition in which, from something laid down and admitted, something distinct from what we have laid down follows of necessity." But this definition, though it describes the Syllogism accurately, seems at first to be inapplicable to Immediate Inference, in which, as there is only one premise, and as the act of Pure Thought through which we reason cannot add any new Matter (that is, any new Intuition or Concept), it would appear that the Conclusion cannot contain anything distinct from what has already been laid down.

And this is true; it cannot contain any new Matter, but it may represent this Matter under a new Form, so that the Conclusion and the Premise will be perfectly distinct Judgments. Thus, in the instance just given, "quadruped" and "rational" are the only Terms that appear in either of the two Conclusions, "irrational" being only the equivalent of "non-rational"; and both of these are contained in the Premise. And yet the Inference is not a mere repetition, but the Judgments which it involves are new and distinct from what was previously laid down; for one of them is affirmative, while the Premise is negative; and the other denies a certain Mark of any "rational thing," while the Premise denies a certain other Mark of any "quadruped." If it be argued further, that such Conclusions are *virtually* contained in the Premise, inasmuch as they become evident to any one who fully apprehends it, the answer is, that this is true of all Reasoning, even of Syllogisms and Inductions. That a certain step is obvious and easily taken, is surely no proof that it is no step at all, or that we can get along without taking it.

1. ÆQUIPOLLENCE OR INFINITATION.

The first sort of Immediate Inference which we have to consider is that which the Greek logicians called ἰσοδυναμία, and the Latins, *Æquipollence;* its more appropriate name is *Infinitation*. It has already been said, that every pair of Concepts, such as A and *not-A*, of which one is merely the Contradictory or the privative of the other, divide the universe between them. According to the axiom of Excluded Middle, either A, or its Infinitated correlative, *not-A*, must belong to everything, and must include everything; and according to the axiom of Non-Contradiction, the presence of one in any given case insures the exclusion of the other. Hence arise a number of Immediate Inferences, some of which are of frequent occurrence in our ordinary processes of thought. As already remarked, a negative Judgment can always be changed in Form to an affirmative, or an affirmative to a negative, simply by Infinitating one of its Terms, or by dropping its Infinitation; and the result is a new Judgment, the truth of which is an Immediate Inference from the truth of the antecedent Judgment whence it was derived. Here the Inference is only an application of the well-known grammatical rule, that two negatives cancel each other, and thus become equivalent to an affirmative. But the idiom of every language sanctions a greater or smaller number of exceptions to this general rule, none of which, however, are admissible in Logic, where every negation must be construed rigorously.

The following *memoriter* lines, which I copy from Burgersdyck, enumerate the more frequent forms of æquipollence and of the idiomatic force of negative expressions; but of course, all of them do not hold good in this meaning in any other language than the Latin.

Non omnis = quidam non; omnis non *quasi* nullus.
Non nullus = quidam; *sed* nullus non *valet* omnis.
Non aliquis = nullus; non quidam non *valet* omnis.
Non alter = neuter; neuter non *præstat* uterque.

In all cases of Immediate Inference by Infinitation, the dependence of the Conclusion upon the Premise is so obvious, and so directly governed by the Primary Axioms of Pure Thought, that no mistake is likely to arise, except from a momentary doubt as to the position or the proper force of the negative particle. The two following rules comprehend at least all the more important cases, and they hold true, I believe, without exception, for the four Propositional Forms which are recognized in the Aristotelic system.

Rule I. To change the Infinitation of the Predicate (either by Infinitating it, or by dropping its Infinitation), change the Quality of the Judgment;—the Quantity of the Judgment then remains unaltered.

RULE II. To change the Infinitation of the Subject, *convert* the Judgment (i. e. make the Subject and the Predicate change places with each other), and then either change the Quality, or change the Infinitation of the (old) Predicate also;—here, also, the Quantity of the Judgment remains unchanged.

The following are instances, both in the abstract and the concrete, of the application of these two Rules to all four of the fundamental Judgments, **A**, **E**, **I**, and **O**, and also to their Infinitated forms, here designated as **A′**, **E′**, **I′**, and **O′**. This enumeration was first made out by Mr. DeMorgan. It will be seen that it contains no instance of mere Conversion, as the cases under that head will be afterwards separately considered. To avoid a confusing repetition of the negative particle *not*, words compounded with the negative prefixes *un* and *in* have been adopted whenever it was practicable. For the same reason, *right* is used for *not-wrong; brutes* for *not-men; pitiless* for *not-compassionate;* &c.

PREMISES.	CONCLUSIONS.	
	By Rule I.	By Rule II.
A. Every X is Y.	= No X is not-Y.	= Every not-Y is not-X.
All metals are fusible.	= No metal is infusible.	= All infusible things are unmetallic.
O. Some X are not Y.	= Some X are not-Y.	= Some not-Y are not not-X.
Some men are not compassionate.	= Some men are pitiless.*	= Some pitiless beings are not *mere brutes* (not-men).
E. No X is Y.	= Every X is not-Y.	= Every Y is not-X.
No avaricious man is happy.	= Every avaricious man is unhappy.	= Every happy man is free from avarice.

* Strictly speaking, or according to the rules of Logic, "not-compassionate" has the same meaning as "pitiless," for it is the contradictory of "compassionate." But in common parlance, there is a slight difference in the meaning of the two words; "not-compassionate," like most other epithets compounded with a negative particle, means, not entire privation of the quality, but only the existence of it in a very low degree.

I. Some X are Y. = Some X are not not-Y. = Some Y are not not-X.
  Some wrong acts are excusable. = Some wrong acts are not inexcusable. = Some excusable acts are not right acts.

A′. Every not-X is not-Y. = No not-X is Y. = Every Y is X.
  Every unjust act is inexpedient. = No unjust act is expedient. = Every (truly) expedient act is just.*

O′. Some not-X are not not-Y. = Some not-X are Y. = Some Y are not X.
  Some invisible things are not intangible. = Some invisible things are tangible. = Some tangible things are not visible.

E′. No not-X is not-Y. = Every not-X is Y. = Every not-Y is X.
  No mortal who-is-not-a-brute is incapable of sin. = Every mortal who-is-not-a-brute is capable of sin. = Every mortal who-is-incapable-of-sin is a brute.

I′. Some not-X are not-Y. Some not-X are not Y. = Some not-Y are not X.
  Some invertebrates are wingless. = Some invertebrates are not winged. = Some wingless animals are not vertebrates.

The Infinitation of the four additional Judgments first considered by Sir W. Hamilton cannot with equal facility be reduced to rule. As either Afa or Afa′ is a perfect expression of the absolute identity of what the two Terms denote, either may be deduced by Infinitation from the other, and, by the same means, several other less perfect expressions of the same identity may be obtained. But of these less perfect expressions some may more properly be regarded as inferences by Subalternation. Thus, —

Afa. All X are all Y =
Afa′. All not-X are all not-Y
  = { No X is not-Y
      No Y is not-X
      Every not-X is not-Y } = { Every not-Y is not-X.
      All X are Y.
      All Y are X.

All extended are all divisible = All unextended are all indivisible.

On the other hand, as Ini and Ini′ are indefinite expressions of the partial disagreement of the two Terms, they

---

* Some writers upon the theory of morals, who have strenuously maintained that "no unjust act is expedient," have yet been very unwilling to admit that "every expedient act is just." Yet the latter proposition is a necessary inference from the former.

yield no inferences by Infinitation properly so called; though, if *some* be taken in its semi-definite sense, they yield a number of unimportant inferences by what Sir W. Hamilton calls *Integration*.

The following are the more common inferences by Infinitation from the two remaining pairs of these four Judgments. In these it will be observed that the Quantity of the Conclusion often differs from that of the Premise.

Ifa. Some X are all Y.   = All not-X are not-Y.   = No Y is not-X.

Some curvilinears are all circulars. { = All rectilinears are not-circulars. { = No circular is rectilinear.

Ani. No X is some Y.   { = Some not-X are not not-Y. } = Some Y are not-X.

No tyrants are some kings. { = Some who are not tyrannical are not unroyal. } = Some kings are not-tyrannical.

Ifa'. Some not-X are all not-Y. } = No X is not-Y.   { = Some not-X are not Y.

Some unsentient are all inorganic. { = No sentient thing is inorganic. { = Some unsentient are not organic.

Ani'. Not any not-X is some not-Y. } = Some X are not Y.   = Some not-Y are X.

Not any dishonest is some imprudent. { = Some honest are not prudent. { = Some imprudent are honest.

2. CONVERSION.

A Judgment is said to be *converted* when its Subject and Predicate have been made to change places with each other. Before Conversion, the Judgment is called the *Convertend;* after Conversion, it is the *Converse*. The logical doctrine of Immediate Inference by Conversion shows us when and why the truth of the Converse is a necessary consequence of the truth of the Convertend. In other words, Logic takes notice only of what is called *illative* Conversion, in which the Convertend and the Converse must either both be true, or both be false, together. Thus, the Conversion of *No A is B*, into *No B is A*, is illative; we can say,

No carnivorous animal is ruminant;
therefore, No ruminant animal is carnivorous.

But the Conversion of *Some A are not B*, into *Some B are not A*, is not illative; because we can say, *Some men are not logicians*, it does not follow that *Some logicians are not men*.

In Conversion of Judgments, the learner must remember that *the whole* Predicate must change places with *the whole* Subject; — that is, whatever belongs to the Predicate must be transferred to the Subject's place, and whatever relates to the Subject to the Predicate's place. For example; — *Some temple is in the city*, is not converted into *Some city is in the temple*, but into *Something in the city is a temple*. Again, — the Predicate of *Every old man has been a boy*, is not *boy*, but *has been a boy*; therefore, it is not converted into *Some boy has been an old man*, but into *Some one who has been a boy is an old man*. To avoid mistakes of this sort, every proposition, before Conversion, — or, indeed, before it is subjected to any logical treatment whatever, — should be reduced to its simplest logical form, — that is, to the formula *A is B*, or *A is not B*. Then no error can arise, if we remember that *all* which precedes the Copula, *is* or *is not*, is the Subject, and that *all* which follows the Copula is Predicate.

In treating of Conversion, as well as in other portions of the subject, we first consider exclusively the doctrine of the Aristotelic system, which admits only of four fundamental Judgments, and reserve for subsequent treatment the Hamiltonian theory of eight Judgments.

There are three sorts of Conversion. The first is applicable to **E** and **I**, Universal Negatives and Particular Affirmatives, and is called *Simple Conversion*, because both the Quantity and the Quality of the Judgment remain unchanged; that is, **E** is converted into **E**, and **I** into **I**. If it is true that *No man is immortal*, it follows by Immediate Inference that *No immortal is man;* for if any one immortal were a man, it would not be true that *No man is immortal*. Likewise, if *Some men are just*, it follows immediately that *Some just beings are men;* because the assertion that *No just being is a man*, would contradict the Convertend. By Simple Conversion, then, a Universal Negative passes over into a Universal Negative, and a Particular Affirmative into a Particular Affirmative.

The second sort is *Conversion per accidens*, in which the Quantity is changed from Universal to Particular, but the Quality remains unaltered. This is applicable to **A**, and also may be applied to **E**, though the latter, as we have just seen, may also be converted simply. But **A** cannot be converted simply; because, though *all men are animals*, it does not follow that *all animals are men*. The Judgment in the Convertend is, that *men* are included under the class of *animals*, not that they constitute *all animals;* they are only *some* animals. Hence the Converse is, *Some animals are men.* We have already seen that **E** is converted simply into **E**; but **O** also is obtained by Immediate Inference from **E**; for, if *None are*, it follows that *Some are not*. Hence, the Convertend, *No man is immortal*, yields as its Converse, not only **E**, *No immortal is man*, but **O**, *Some immortals are not men.* Conversion *per accidens*, then, changes **A** into **I**, and **E** into **O**, the Quantity in both cases being diminished, but the Quality remaining unchanged.

The Judgment **O** remains, and this cannot be converted either simply or *per accidens*. From the Convertend, *Some men are not learned*, we cannot infer that *Some learned beings are not men.* Indeed, properly speaking, **O** cannot be converted at all on the Aristotelic system; but by an artifice which is called Contraposition, the third sort of Conversion, another Judgment can be inferred from it, which is called its Converse, though it is properly the Converse of its Æquipollent or Infinitated equivalent. In order to convert by Contraposition, then, first infinitate the Convertend by Rule First, and then convert simply. Thus,—

Convertend.   Some A are not B.   Some men are not learned.
Infinitated equivalent. Some A are not-B.   Some men are unlearned.
Converse of this.   Some not-B are A.   Some unlearned persons are men.

Hence **I** is the Converse by Contraposition of **O**; and in like manner, **A** by Contraposition yields **E**, the effect of this sort of Conversion being to change the Quality of the Convertend, while its Quantity remains unaltered. **A** is thus contraponed:—

Convertend.   All A is B.   All men are rational.
Infinitated equivalent. No A is not-B.   No man is irrational.
Converse of this.   No not-B is A.   No irrational being is a man.

No inference can be obtained from **I** by Contraposition; for if infinitated, **I** becomes **O**, which cannot be converted except by infinitating it back again. Logicians seem to have overlooked the fact that **E** can be contraponed into **I**, though the inferred Judgment in this case, because its Quantity is diminished, is weak and comparatively worthless. Thus,—

No A is B.   No fish is warm-blooded.
Every A is not-B.   Every fish is cold-blooded.
Some not-B are A.   Some cold-blooded animals are fishes.

The results of the three sorts of Conversion have been summed up in this (nonsense) mnemonic line, in which each dissyllable contains the vowel-symbol first of the Convertend and then of its Converse; and each pair of these dissyllables is followed by the (italicized) abbreviation of the kind of Conversion by which the two preceding inferences have been obtained; *simp.* = Simple; *Acc.* = per accidens; and *Cont.* = Contraposition.

Ecce tibi, *simp.*; armi-geros, *acc.*; ante boni, *Cont.*

The same thing is more briefly indicated in these two Latin words, *Hoc capessit*, in which *oc-ca* signifies that **O** and **A** are converted by *C*ontraposition; *ape*, **A** and **E** *per accidens*; *essi*, **E** and **I** *s*imply.

160   THE DOCTRINE OF IMMEDIATE INFERENCE.

The most striking merit of Sir W. Hamilton's system of the thorough-going quantification of the Predicate is, that it abolishes at once this whole cumbrous system of Conversion in three kinds, with its attendant rules, and substitutes for it the universal and self-evident process of Simple Conversion. As it has already been demonstrated, that each Term of every Judgment has its own Quantity in Thought, and consequently, that the distinction of Subject and Predicate may be, for most logical purposes, left entirely out of view, every Judgment being reduced to an equation, in which, of course, it makes no difference which of the equated quantities is placed first, Conversion becomes at once a simple, uniform, and self-evident process. As an old logician (Du Hamel, as quoted by Mr. Baynes), remarks, " omnes conversionum leges pendent a cohæsione, vel potius ab *identitate*, subjecti et attributi ; quod si enim subjectum conjungitur et *identificatur*, ut aiunt, cum attributo, necesse est pariter attributum *uniri* et *identificari* cum subjecto." Though it is hardly necessary even for the youngest learner, I give examples of the Hamiltonian mode of converting each of the eight Judgments.

	Converted.		*Converse.*
Afa.	All rational are all moral beings	= Afa.	All moral are all rational beings.
Afi (A).	All lilies are (some) fragrant	= Ifa.	Some fragrant things are all lilies.
Ifa.	Some plants are all trees	= Afi.	All trees are (some) plants.
Ifi (I).	Some vicious men are rich	= Ifi.	Some rich men are vicious.
Ana (E).	No matter can move itself	= Ana.	Nothing that can move itself is matter.
Ani.	Not (any) indistinct are some sounds	= Ina.	Some sounds are not indistinct.
Ina (O).	Some virtuous men are not happy	= Ani.	Not (any) happy are some virtuous men.
Ini.	Some singers are not some (good) musicians	= Ini.	Some musicians are not some singers.

Conversion *per accidens*, says Mr. Mansel, is so called

because it is not a Conversion of the Universal *per se*, but only of the Particular which happens to be included in the Universal. "Some B is A," is *primarily* the Converse of "*Some* A is B," and only *secondarily* of "*All* A is B," or because "All A" includes "Some A." Properly speaking, then, it is no Conversion at all, but only an Immediate Inference by Subalternation from the proper Converse. This is clearly seen in the case of the Universal Negative, **E**; *No A is B*, is first converted into **E**, *No B is A*, whence we obtain by Subalternation **O**, *Some B are not A*.

Moreover, it is evident that, by reconverting the Converse, we ought to regain the Convertend. But this cannot be done after converting *per accidens;* we first convert **A** into **I**, and then reconvert **I**, not into **A**, but into **I**. For example; — *All men are mortal*, yields by accidental Conversion, *Some mortals are men;* and this is reconverted simply into *Some men are mortals.*

It is further argued by Hamilton, that the Aristotelic doctrine applies Conversion to the naked Terms only, — to the Subject and Predicate of the Convertend without regard to the Quantity of either; it thus changes *all* to *some*, and, as we have just seen, it makes the total Quantity of the Converse inferior to that of the Convertend. But this is evidently wrong; for the quantified Terms are the Concepts which were compared in Thought in the Convertend, and these only ought to appear after Conversion, and appear unchanged. Contraposition, as we have already shown, is a mediate process, the Conversion being possible only through a previous Infinitation; for the original Judgment, on the Aristotelic doctrine, is not convertible at all. But as every Judgment is certainly the result of a comparison, to assert that it is inconvertible, is to maintain that A can be compared with B, while, at the same moment, B is not compared with A; — which is absurd. Comparison is necessarily bilateral.

3. Opposition and Integration.

Opposition is said to exist between Judgments which have the same Matter (i. e. the same naked or unquantified Subject and Predicate), but differ in Quantity, or in Quality, or in both. The logical doctrine of Opposition shows us what can be immediately inferred as to the truth or falsity of one Judgment, from positing or sublating (i. e. affirming or denying) one of its Opposites. Thus, from positing **E**, *No A is B*, I can immediately infer the truth of its Subaltern Opposite, **O**, *Some A are not B*, and the falsity of its Contradictory Opposite, **I**, *Some A are B;* but I cannot infer, from sublating **E**, the truth of its Contrary Opposite, **A**, *All A are B*.

But here the word *Opposition* must be taken in a technical and qualified sense. It was first applied only to the relations between two Contraries, or two Contradictories; and this is its proper or strict meaning, as any two such Judgments are *opposed* to each other, the one negativing the other, and it is impossible that the two should be true together. But as it was convenient for Logicians to consider the relations of Subalternation and Sub-Contrariety under the same head with the two former, the meaning of the word was extended so as to cover all the relations existing between two Judgments of the same Matter, but of different Form, although some of these are relations not of opposition, but of congruity.

There are four sorts of Opposition. The first and most perfect of these is that of *Contradiction*, which exists between two Judgments which differ from each other *both in Quantity and Quality;* that is, between **A** and **O**, and between **E** and **I**. This sort of Opposition is governed by the Axiom of Excluded Middle, which declares that of two Contradictories, — that is, of two Judgments between which there is no " Middle," no intermediate Judgment, —

one must be true; and then the Axiom of Non-Contradiction adds, that the other must be false. Now, **A** and **O** are two such Judgments, and likewise **E** and **I**; so also the two Singular Judgments, *Socrates is wise*, and *Socrates is not wise*. Between either of these pairs, no "third" or intermediate Judgment is conceivable. Hence the universal rule for this sort of Opposition, that *Contradictories cannot both be true, and cannot both be false*. Therefore, as both cannot be true, if I posit (affirm) one, I immediately infer that the other is sublated (denied); and as both cannot be false, if I sublate one, the other is posited. For example;— if **E** is not true, that *No quadruped is rational*, **I** must be true, that *Some quadrupeds are rational*.

Observe that two Judgments properly contradict each other only when that which is affirmed by the one is denied by the other,— 1. *in the same manner;* 2. *in the same respect;* 3. *in the same degree;* and 4. *at the same time*. Thus, to borrow some examples from Aldrich,— 1. A dead body is, and is not, a man; that is, it is a dead man, but not a living one. 2. Zoilus is, and is not, black; that is, black-haired, but red-faced. 3. Socrates is, and is not, long-haired; that is, he is so, if you compare him with Scipio, but is not so, if you compare him with Xenophon. 4. Nestor is, and is not, an old man, according as you speak of him when in childhood, or when he was at the siege of Troy.

The second sort of Opposition is that of *Contrariety*, which exists between two *Universal* Judgments, that *differ in Quality, but are alike in Quantity;* that is, between **A** and **E**. Here the Axiom of Excluded Middle does not apply; for between **A** and **E**, there is a "Middle" or intermediate Judgment, namely, **I**. Though it is not true, either that *all men are wise*, or that *no man is wise*, it is true that *some men are wise*. Hence both Contraries may be false, so that I cannot infer the truth of one from the falsity of the other. On the other hand, as one of these Contraries affirms what the other denies, the Axiom of Non-Contradiction applies; both Contraries cannot be true; and, therefore, from the truth of one I can immediately infer the falsity of the other. Accordingly, the rule is, *Contraries may be false together, but both cannot be true.* Therefore, from positing either **A** or **E**, I can immediately infer that the other is sublated; but from sublating either, I cannot infer that the other is posited.

The third sort of Opposition is that of *Sub-Contrariety*, which exists between two *Particular* Judgments, that *differ in Quality, but are alike in Quantity;* that is, between **I** and **O**. To these, the Axiom of Excluded Middle is applicable; for there is no third, or intermediate, Judgment conceivable between *Some are,* and *Some are not.* Accordingly, both cannot be false, but one must be true. On the other hand, if **I** and **O** are *considered as Propositions*, that is, if the Judgments are expressed in words, the Axiom of Non-Contradiction does not apply to them; for both may be true. Though *some men are learned*, it is also true that *some men are not learned.* But observe, that the "some men" in the latter case are *not the same* "some men" as in the former; though expressed by the same *words*, they are *thought* as different. To make the former Proposition true, "some men" may be thought to be "graduates of Oxford"; to make the latter true, "some men" may mean "American Indians." As Propositions, then, and possibly as Judgments, the two assertions do not contradict each other, but may both be true. Hence the rule, that *Sub-Contraries may be true together, but cannot both be false.* Therefore, by sublating either **I** or **O**, we immediately infer that the other is posited; but by positing either, we cannot infer that the other is sublated. Of course, Sub-Contraries can be called " opposites " only in a qualified and technical sense; they are actually congruent, or, to adopt one of Hamilton's newly-coined words, they are "compossible."

The fourth sort of Opposition is that of *Subalternation*, which exists between Judgments *alike in Quality, but different in Quantity;* that is, between **A** and **I**, and between **E** and **O**. Here, again, it is evident that the "Opposition" is merely technical, the two Judgments being not merely consistent, but so nearly allied that the Particular can be inferred from its Universal by the Axiom of Identity. Since *all* includes *some*, if we affirm **A**, *All A are B*, we thereby also affirm **I**, *Some A are B;* and in like manner, to posit **E** is also to posit **O**. The same Axiom compels us to think, that sublating **I** sublates **A** also, and sublating **O** sublates **E** also. In this sort of inference, the Universal may be called the *Subalternans*, and the Particular, the *Subalternate*. Hence we have this rule for inference by Subalternation, that *if the Subalternans is true, the Subalternate is true also; and if the Subalternate is false, the Subalternans is false also.*

Summing up, we have the following list of Immediate Inferences by Opposition.

{ If **A** is true, **O** is false, **E** false, and **I** true.
{ If **E** is true, **I** is false, **A** false, and **O** true.

{ If **I** is false, **E** is true, **O** true, and **A** false.
{ If **O** is false, **A** is true, **I** true, and **E** false.

If **A** is false, **O** is true, } the others unknown.
If **E** is false, **I** is true, }

If **I** is true, **E** is false, } the others unknown.
If **O** is true, **A** is false, }

Hence it appears, that from the *truth* of a Universal or the *falsehood* of a Particular, we may infer the character of all the opposed Judgments; but from the *falsehood* of a Universal or *truth* of a Particular, we can know the character only of the Contradictory.

JUDGMENTS, considered in reference to QUANTITY, are either *Universal* or *Particular;* to QUALITY, are either *Affirmative* or *Negative;* to QUANTITY and QUALITY, are of four sorts:—

Affirmative Predesignations of *Universal* Judgments.
All — Every — Each— This — That — These — Those — a Proper Name.

A. *Universal Affirmative.*
e. g. All X is Y.
All metals are lustrous.

IMMEDIATE INFERENCE proceeds

BY INFINITATION

of the Terms of a Judgment, or by dropping their Infinitation, the Judgments thus produced being, in certain cases, *æquipollent,* or equivalent to those from which they were derived.

BY OPPOSITION,

or the relation that exists between Judgments which have the same naked or unquantified Subject and Predicate, but differ in Quantity, or Quality, or both.

FOUR KINDS

1. CONTRADICTION exists between Judgments which differ both in Quantity and Quality.
Rule. — Contradictories cannot both be true and cannot both be false. Hence,
to posit **A** is to sublate **O**
" **E** " " **I**
to sublate **A** is to posit **O**
" **E** " " **I**
and conversely,
to posit **O** is to sublate **A**
&c.

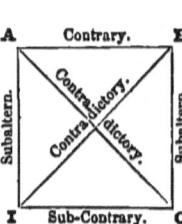

BY CONVERSION,

or causing the Subject and Predicate of a Judgment to change places with each other, but in such manner that if the Convertend is true, then the Converse will be true also.

THREE KINDS

1. SIMPLE, **E** & **I**,
without changing either the Quantity or the Quality. (*Ecce-tibi.*)
Convertend. No X is Y. **E** into
Converse. No Y is X. **E**.
Convertend. Some X are Y. **I** into
Converse. Some Y are X. **I**.

JUDGMENTS AND IMMEDIATE INFERENCE. 167

Negative Predesignations of *Universal* Judgments.

None — Not any — Not one — Not this — Not that — "Not" prefixed or suffixed to a Proper Name.

Predesignations of *Particular* Judgments, either Affirmative or Negative.

Some — Not all — or any indication of an *indefinite* part of a whole.

E. *Universal Negative.*
No X is Y.
No quadruped is rational.

I. *Particular Affirmative.*
Some X are Y.
Some swans are black.

O. *Particular Negative.*
Some X are not Y.
Some men are not famous.

Two Kinds of Infinitation.

Rule. — To change the Infinitation of the Predicate, either by infinitating it or by dropping its Infinitation, change the Quality of the Judgment; the Quantity of the Judgment remains unaltered.

Rule. — To change the Infinitation of the Subject, *convert* the Judgment, and then either change the Quality, or change the Infinitation of the (old) Predicate also. Here, also, the Quantity is unaltered.

Of Opposition.

2. Contrariety
exists between *Universal* Judgments that differ in Quality, but are alike in Quantity.
Rule.— Both Contraries may be false, but both cannot be true. Hence,
to posit **A** is to sublate **E**
"   **E** "   "   **A**

3. Sub-Contrariety
exists between *Particular* Judgments that differ in Quality, but are alike in Quantity.
Rule. — Sub-Contraries may both be true, but cannot both be false. Hence,
to sublate **I** is to posit **O**
"   "   **O** "   "   **I**

4. Subalternation
exists between Judgments alike in Quality, but different in Quantity.
Rule. — If the Subalternans (the Universal) is true, the Subalternate (the Particular) is also true; and if the Subalternate is false, the Subalternans is false also. Hence,
to posit **A** is to posit **I**
"   **E** "   "   **O**
to sublate **I** is to sublate **A**
"   **O** "   "   **E**

Of Conversion. (*Hoc capessit.*)

2. Per Accidens, A & E,
changing the Quantity, but not the Quality. (*Armi-geros.*)
Convertend. All X is Y.   **A** into
Converse. Some Y is X.   **I.**
Convertend. No X is Y.   **E** into
Converse. Some Y is not X.   **O.**

3. By Contraposition, A & O,
changing, not the Quantity, but the Quality, through infinitating the Predicate. (*Ante-boni.*)
Convertend. All men are mortal.   **A.**
Converse. No immortal is man.   **E.**
Convertend. Some men are not white.   **O.**
Converse. Some not-white are men.   **I.**

That the various points in the doctrine of this sort of Immediate Inference might be more easily remembered, the old logicians contrived, not some mnemonic verses, as on other occasions, but the accompanying ingenious diagram, which may be called the Square of Opposition. It is very easy to retain the whole theory in the memory, when we observe the proper position, upon this square, of the vowels which indicate the four species of Judgments. The upper line belongs to the Universals, **A** and **E**; the lower line to the Particulars, **I** and **O**; the left hand to the Affirmatives, **A** and **I**; and the right to the Negatives, **E** and **O**. Then it is easily remembered, that the two diagonals represent Contradiction, the upper line Contrariety, the lower one Sub-Contrariety, and each of the two sides Subalternation.

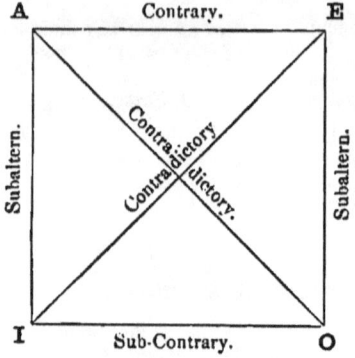

For the further convenience of learners, I have brought together in the preceding Conspectus the principal technicalities and rules in the Aristotelic doctrine of Judgments and Immediate Inference.

Hamilton has considerably enlarged and modified the doctrine of Immediate Inference by Opposition, by introducing, what the logicians had hitherto neglected, the semi-definite meaning of *some*,—that is, *some at most*,—*some* excluding *all* and *none*. In the Aristotelic doctrine, *some* was applied exclusively in its wholly indefinite meaning, as *some at least*,—*some*, *perhaps all;*—and in negatives, *some, perhaps none.* Yet, as Hamilton remarks, *some* is always thought as semi-definite when the other Term of the Judgment is Universal; and it is only when both

Terms are Particular, that the *some* of each is left wholly indefinite. Thus, when we say, *Some men are* (all) *black*, we mean to deny that *all* are black; *Some flowers are not* (any) *fragrant*, denies that *none* are fragrant.

But in the case of Subalternation, which Hamilton prefers to call *Restriction*, if we introduce this semi-definite meaning, and think *some* as *some only — not all*, instead of having an Inference from the Subalternans to the Subalternate, we find a true Opposition between them; to adopt the Hamiltonian word, the two Judgments are *Incompossible*. Thus, *Some* (only — not all) *men are yellow*, is really opposed to *All men are yellow*, instead of being an Inference from it; and in like manner, *Some* (not all) *bipeds are not men*, is opposed to *No bipeds are men*. This new sort of Opposition or Incompossibility, as it exists between two Judgments which are alike in Quality, either both Affirmatives or both Negatives, while the other two sorts, Contradiction and Contrariety, differ in Quality, is called *Inconsistency*. Of course, as two Inconsistents, like any other two Incompossibles or Opposites, cannot both be true, the true Inference is, that by positing either **A** or **I**, **E** or **O**, the other is sublated. To express the whole doctrine of Subalternation or Restriction in one rule; — If *some* means *some — perhaps all*, the Subalternate is a direct Inference from positing the Subalternans; but if *some* means *some — not all*, the Subalternans and Subalternate are Opposite or Incompossible, so that, by positing either, the other is sublated.

Again, it has already been shown that Sub-Contrariety is properly no Opposition at all, so that both Judgments may be true; though, as both cannot be false, sublating one enables us to posit the other. But if we introduce the semi-definite meaning of *some* here also, we have a new Inference from one to the other; — from the one *some*, which is a part, to the other *some*, which is the remaining part necessary to constitute the whole. This sort of Inference Hamilton would call *Integration*, as its effect is, after determining one part, to reconstitute the whole by bringing into view the remaining part. Thus, if I know that *Some* (not all) *men are white*, I can immediately infer that *Some* (other) *men are not white;* and if *Some poets are not philosophers*, it follows that *Some* (other) *poets are philosophers.* In such cases, though the two Judgments are different in Quality, they are not opposed, but congruent; and the Inference may be not only to *all* others *definitely*, but to *some* others *indefinitely*. It is valid, also, whether *some* appears in the Subject or Predicate. Thus, from *Men are some animals*, we immediately infer that *Men are not some* (other) *animals* (say, brutes). Here, the Inference concerns the Predicate, while in the preceding cases it concerned the Subject.

To apply the whole doctrine of Incompossibility and Integration, in both meanings of the word *some*, to the eight Hamiltonian Judgments, is evidently a long and complex process. The following table (page 172), in which the whole process is worked out, is borrowed from Sir William Hamilton, and placed here, not, of course, that it may be committed to memory, but because the examination of it will be a useful exercise for the learner. In explanation of it, observe that the Incompossibility, or the fact that the two Judgments cannot both be true, — and in some cases, the Restriction (Subalternation) and the Integration, — may be bilateral (here marked *bi*), as affecting both Subject and Predicate; thus,

All physical laws are *all* efficient causes.
Not any physical law is *any* efficient cause.

Or unilateral (*un*), as affecting either the Subject only· thus,

All men are all rational.
Some men are not (any) rational.

Or the Predicate only; thus, — *some* in the second Judgment being semi-definite, —

All dogs are *all* barking animals.
All dogs are *some* barking animals.

Or it may be *unilateral cross* (*un. cr.*), as reversing in the one Judgment the relation of Genus and Species — containing and contained — which exists between the Terms of the other Judgment; thus, *some* being semi-definite,

All whites are some civilized.
Some whites are all civilized.

Or *bilateral cross* (*bi. cr.*), as affecting both Terms, but in opposite relations, — as from Particular to Universal in the Subject, and from Universal to Particular in the Predicate; thus, *some* being semi-definite,

Some blacks are all Africans.
Not any black is some Africans.

Or *bilateral direct* (*bi. di.*), as affecting both Terms, and excluding any intermediate or third Judgment, both propositions remaining the same after conversion; thus,

Some men are (*some*) irrational.
Not *any* man is (*any*) irrational.

TABLE

OF THE MUTUAL RELATIONS OF THE EIGHT PROPOSITIONAL FORMS ON EITHER SYSTEM OF PARTICULARITY. (*For Generals only.*)

Numbered as on pp. 132, 133.	Value.	I. INCOMPOSSIBILITY of Propositions with Proposition, either as		II. INFERENCE from Proposition to Proposition, on the two Systems.		
Common to I. and II., in either of which all Propositions are related.		1. Wholly Indefinite. (*Some, perhaps all.*)	2. Semi-Definite. (*Some, not all.*)	To wit, from — to.	1. Wholly Indefinite. (*Some, perhaps all.*)	2. Semi-Definite. (*Some, not all.*)
Affirmat.						
1—2	Afa — Afi		Incons. un.	1—2	Restr. un.	Restr. bi.
1—3	Afa — Ifa		Incons. un.	1—3	Restr. un.	Restr. un.
1—4	Afa — Ifi		Incons. un. cr.	1—4	Restr. bi.	Restr. un.
2—3	Afi — Ifa					
2—4	Afi — Ifi		Incons. un.	2—4	Restr. un.	
3—4	Ifa — Ifi		Incons. un.	3—4	Restr. un.	
Negat.						
5—6	Ana — Ani			5—6	Restr. un.	
5—7	Ana — Ina			5—7	Restr. bi.	Restr. bi.
5—8	Ana — Ini	Doubtful, cr.	Doubtful, cr.	5—8	Restr. un.	
6—7	Ani — Ina	Contrar. bi.	Contrar. bi.	6—8	Restr. un.	Restr. un.
6—8	Ani — Ini	Contrar. un.	Contrar. un.	7—8	Restr. un.	Restr. un.
7—8	Ina — Ini	Contrar. un.	Contrar. un.			
Aff. Neg.						
1—5	Afa — Ana	Contrar. un.	Contrar. un.	1—8		Res. & Int. bi.
1—6	Afa — Ani	Contrar. un.	Contrar. bi. cr.			
1—7	Afa — Ina	Repugn. bi. cr.	Contrar. un.			
1—8	Afa — Ini	Contrar. un.	Contrar. bi. cr.	2—6		Integr. un.
2—5	Afi — Ana	Contrar. un.	Contrar. un.			
2—6	Afi — Ani	Contrar. un.	Contrar. bi. cr.			
2—7	Afi — Ina	Repugn. bi. cr.	Contrar. un.	2—8		Res. & Int. un.
2—8	Afi — Ini	Contrar. un.	Contrar. bi. cr.			
3—5	Ifa — Ana	Repugn. bi. cr.	Contrar. bi. di.			
3—6	Ifa — Ani			8—7		Integr. un.
3—7	Ifa — Ina			3—8		Res. & Int. un.
3—8	Ifa — Ini					
4—5	Ifi — Ana			4—6, 6—4		Res. & Int. un.
4—6	Ifi — Ani			4—7, 7—4		Res. & Int. un.
4—7	Ifi — Ina			4—8, 8—4		Integr. bi.
4—8	Ifi — Ini					

ABBREVIATIONS: Contrar. = *Contraries*; Incons. = *Inconsistents*; Int. or Integr. = *Integration*; Repugn. = *Repugnants, Contradictories*; Res. or Restr. = *Restriction, Subalternation*; Blanks, in I. = *Compossibles*; in II. = *No inference*.

This Table may not be quite accurate in details.

It appears from this Table, that *Afi* and *Ina* (**A** and **O**), which, on the Aristotelic doctrine, are Contradictories, become only Contraries when we admit the semi-definite meaning of *some;* for by sublating *Ina*, which denies only a part (*some only*), we know not whether to posit *Afi*, which affirms the whole, or *Ifi*, which affirms only some (other) part, or *Ana*, which denies the whole; since each of these three is incompossible with *Ina*. For the same reason, *Ifa* and *Ani*, which are only **A** and **O** converted, are merely Contraries on this system, though Contradictories on the other, wherein *some* means *perhaps all*. Indeed, there can be no Contradiction on this system, wherein *whole* and *part* negative each other, just as much as *affirmation* and *negation*. The only Contradictories are those in which the distinction of whole and part does not exist;—Judgments about Singulars or Individuals, for instance, and about Universals regarded as Singulars or as undivided wholes. Thus, *Common salt is chloride of sodium* contradicts *Common salt is not chloride of sodium;* for *Common salt*, though really a General Term, is here actually thought as undivided, so that the two Judgments contradict each other as directly as do these two Singulars,—*John is sick*, *John is not sick*. If either Judgment in one of these pairs is sublated, the other is necessarily posited.

"The propositional form *Ifi* is consistent with all the affirmatives; *Ini* is not only consistent with all the negatives, but is compossible with every other form in universals. It is useful only to divide a class, and is opposed only by the negation of divisibility."

The whole scheme of Opposition upon this system may be safely characterized as too complex to be of any practical use, though the learner may be profited by some study of its details.

CHAPTER VII.

THE DOCTRINE OF MEDIATE INFERENCE: THE ARISTOTELIC
ANALYSIS OF SYLLOGISMS.

1. Figure and Mood. — 2. Conditional Syllogisms. — 3. Defective and
Complex Syllogisms.

MEDIATE Inference is that act of Pure Thought, whereby the relation of the two Terms of a possible Judgment to each other is ascertained by comparing each of them separately with a third Term. Thus, if I cannot immediately determine whether A is, or is not, B, I can compare each with M. If, as the result of such comparison, it is found that *A is M* and *B is M*, then we infer *mediately* — that is, through this relation of each to a third — that *A is B*. But if this comparison shows that one of these Terms is, and the other is not, M, then we infer mediately that *A is not B*. The affirmative conclusion is evidently governed by the Axiom of Identity, which declares that *A is B*, if it is that (M) which is the equivalent of B; or to use language more consonant with the phraseology hitherto employed, and converting *B is M* into *M is B*, we say that B is a Mark of A, when it is a Mark of that (M) which is a Mark of A, — *nota notæ est nota rei ipsius*. The negative conclusion results from the Axiom of Non-Contradiction, which declares that *A is not B*, when it is equivalent to that (or has for a Mark that) (M), which is *not B;* or, what is the same thing, when it is *not* equivalent to that (M) which *is B*.

The fundamental principle of Mediate Inference or Syllogism is thus traced to those Axioms which, as we have already seen, must govern all the processes of Pure Thought; or rather, Mediate Inference itself is but one of the special applications of those Axioms. Instead of using these Primary Axioms themselves, logicians have usually, in order to demonstrate the processes of syllogistic reasoning, preferred to employ certain intermediate principles or maxims, one of which we have just mentioned, — that *the Mark of a Mark is a Mark of the thing itself*. But as these maxims can be directly deduced from the original Axioms, to which, indeed, they owe all their validity, it seems better to test the legitimacy of each step by a reference to the primary, rather than to any derivative, principle.

Thus far, A and B, in their comparison with M, have been regarded simply as undivided wholes; but it is evident that the same considerations will hold good if we substitute, for either or both of them, *all*, or any *indefinite part*, of a divided Universal. Thus, if we find that *Some A are M*, and *Some B are M*, we are compelled to conclude, by the Axiom of Identity, that *Some A are (some) B;* or, taking a negative instance, if *Some A are M*, and *Not any B is M*, then we infer that *Some A are not (any) B*. Hence we see the correctness of the derivative or intermediate principle which Sir W. Hamilton enounces as "the supreme Canon of Categorical Syllogisms," — IN SO FAR AS *two Notions* (Concepts or Individuals), *either both agree, or, one agreeing, the other does not agree, with a common third Notion,* IN SO FAR *these Notions do or do not agree with each other*. But if, by calling it "supreme," he means that it is the *ultimate* and *original* Canon, his position may be doubted; for it is evidently a compound statement, embracing, with an unimportant change of phraseology, the two Primary Axioms of Identity and Non-Contradiction, and guarding them with those limitations under which alone are they ever applicable.

We have seen that, though either or both of the two Terms be quantified Particularly, the Syllogism still holds good, — at least, to the extent to which the two Terms are quantified. But the third Term must be taken Universally at least once in comparing it with the other Notions; otherwise, we have no security that these others are compared with *the same,* or "a common," third Term. Though we know, for instance, that *A is some M,* and *B is some M,* still we cannot conclude that *A is B;* for the "some M" which is A may not be *the same* "some M" which is B. Though *Some learned men are pedants,* and *Some learned men are wise,* it does not follow that *Pedants are wise;* for two very different classes of learned persons are here spoken of. Hence we have this general rule for all Syllogisms, that *the Middle Term must be distributed* (i. e. taken Universally) *in at least one of the comparisons* which are instituted between it and the other two Terms. We say, "at least one" of the two comparisons; for the other may be quantified Particularly without injury to the reasoning. Thus, if *All men are mortal,* and *X, Y, and Z are* (some) *men,* we may legitimately conclude that *X, Y, and Z are mortals;* for to whatever class these "*some* men" belong, they are necessarily included under "*all* men," who are declared to be mortal.

A Syllogism evidently comprises three Judgments, one of which affirms the agreement or non-agreement of its two Terms with each other to be *the necessary consequence* of two other Judgments, in which a common third Term is affirmed to agree with both, or with one only, of these two Terms. The main Judgment is called the *Conclusion;* the two subsidiary Judgments, on which it depends, are termed the *Premises;* and the necessary connection between the Premises and the Conclusion — that which entitles us to infer the one from the other — is the *Consequence.* The essence of the Syllogism, and all that is actually affirmed in it, is this *necessary consequence* of the Conclusion from the Premises. Hence the Syllogism is really one, — a single and indivisible act of Thought. Though apparently complex — though, in a certain sense, including three Judgments — it does not affirm either one of them taken separately, but only the necessary dependence of one upon the two others. Thus, as we have seen, both Premises may be false, and the Conclusion may be false; and yet the Syllogism may be valid or correct in Form, for the latter may be legitimately deduced from the former. The following, for example, is a valid inference, though each of the Propositions is false.

All men are immortal,
All bipeds are men;
Therefore, all bipeds are immortal.

Hence, in order to dispute or deny a Syllogism *as such*, we do not need to deny either of its three Judgments, but only the Consequence, or the dependence of the Conclusion upon the Premises; in other words, a single negation denies all that the Syllogism, which is but one act of Thought, asserts. We say, *it does not follow* that A is B BECAUSE A is some M and B is some M; though possibly A is B for some other reason.

In explanation of the terms employed to denote the process of reasoning, the following passage is borrowed from Sir William Hamilton's Lectures on Logic : " *Reasoning* is a modification from the French *raisonner* (and this is a derivation from the Latin *ratio*) and corresponds to *ratiocinatio*, which has, indeed, been immediately transferred into our language under the form *ratiocination*. Ratiocination denotes properly the process, but improperly also the product, of reasoning ; *ratiocinium* marks exclusively the product. The original meaning of *ratio* was *computation*, and from the calculation of numbers it was transferred to the process of mediate comparison in general. *Discourse* (*discursus*, διάνοια) indicates the operation of comparison, the running backwards and forwards between the characters or notes of objects; this term may therefore be properly applied to the Elaborative Faculty in general [the Understanding]. The terms *discourse* and *discursus* are, however, often, nay generally, used for the reasoning process strictly considered, and *discursive* is even applied to denote Mediate, in opposition to Intuitive [or Immediate], judgment, as is done by Milton.

> ' Whence the soul
> Reason receives, and reason is her being,
> Discursive or intuitive; discourse
> Is oftest yours.'

The compound term, *discourse of reason*, unambiguously marks its employment in this sense.

> 'A beast that wants discourse of reason
> Would have mourned longer.'

Argumentation is derived from *argumentari*, which means *argumentis uti*. Argument again (*argumentum*) — what is assumed in order to argue something — is properly the middle notion in a reasoning, — that through which the Conclusion is established. It is often, however, applied as coextensive with *argumentation*. *Inference* or *illation* (from *infero*) indicates the carrying out into the last Proposition what was virtually contained in the antecedent Judgments. *To conclude* (*concludere*), again, signifies the act of connecting and shutting into the last Proposition the two notions which stood apart in the two first. A *conclusion* is usually taken, in its strict and proper signification, to mean the last Proposition of a reasoning; it is sometimes, however, used to express the product of the whole process. To *syllogize* means to form Syllogisms. *Syllogism* (συλλογισμός) seems originally, like *ratio*, to have denoted a *computation*, — an *adding up*, — and, like the greater part of the technical terms in Logic in general, was borrowed by Aristotle from the mathematicians. This primary meaning of these two words favors the theory of those philosophers who, like Hobbes and Leidenfrost, maintain that all Thought is, in fact, at bottom, only a calculation, a reckoning. Συλλογισμός may, however, be considered as expressing only what the composition of the word denotes, — a *collecting together;* for συλλογίζεσθαι comes from συλλέγειν, which signifies *to collect.* Finally, in Latin, a Syllogism is called *collectio,* and to reason, *colligere.* This refers to the act of collecting, in the Conclusion, the two notions scattered in the Premises."

Thus the *unifying* office of the Understanding, to which we have before adverted, is again brought to view. As a Judgment is an act whereby the two notions which are its Terms are brought together into one, so a Syllogism — Reasoning proper — Mediate Inference — is that act of Pure Thought whereby the two Judgments which are its Premises are collected and summed up into one in the Conclusion; or, what is the same thing expressed in relation to the Terms, whereby three notions are reduced to unity.

"Without the power of Reasoning," says Hamilton, "we should have been limited in our knowledge (if knowledge under such a limitation would deserve the name of *knowledge* at all) — I say, without Reasoning, we should have been limited to a knowledge of what is given by Immediate Intuition; we should have been unable to draw any inference from this knowledge, and have been shut out from the discovery of that countless multitude of truths, which, though of high, of paramount importance, are not self-evident. This faculty is likewise of peculiar utility, in order to protect us in our cogitations from error and falsehood, and to remove these, if they have already crept in. For every, even the most complex, web of thought may be reduced to simple Syllogisms; and when this is done, their truth or falsehood, at least in a logical relation, flashes into view." Hence, as Dr. Whately remarks, "the Syllogistic theory does not profess to furnish a peculiar method of reasoning, but only to set forth a method of analyzing that mental process which must invariably take place in all correct reasoning"; and again, "a Syllogism is evidently not a peculiar kind of argument, but only a peculiar form of expression in which every argument may be stated."

The power of reasoning, of drawing Mediate Inferences, like that of framing Concepts, is at once a proof of man's superiority over the brutes, and of his inferiority to his Creator. Brutes cannot reason, nor even form Judgments respecting classes of things, their knowledge being confined, as we have seen, to Intuitions, — to Singulars. On the other hand, the Infinite Mind knows immediately or intuitively the relation of one thing or class of things to another, without being compelled to ascertain indirectly their agreement or non-agreement through their relations to a third or Middle Term. The power of Mediate Inference is a help for an imperfect intellect; Omniscience needs no help.

The brief view which has now been given comprises all the essential principles of Mediate Inference, — that is, all the rules to which all Syllogisms, whatever may be their peculiarities in other respects, must conform. They may be summed up as follows: —

1. *A Syllogism must contain three Terms, and no more;* namely, the two whose agreement or disagreement we wish to ascertain, and the Third or Middle, with which each of these is separately compared. If there were four Terms, two of them must be intermediate, not appearing in the Conclusion; but then the Premises would have no *common* Term. If we know only that A is M and B is N, we have no means of ascertaining the relation of A and B to each other.

2. *A Syllogism must contain three Judgments, and no more;* namely, the two in which each of the Terms of the

Conclusion is compared with the Middle Term, and that in which these two are compared with each other.

3. *The Middle Term must be distributed (taken universally) in at least one of the Premises.* The necessity of this Rule arises, as we have seen, from the fact that the two Extremes, in order to be compared with each other, must have been separately compared with the *same common Middle*. If we consider no other kinds of Quantity than *all* and *some* (Universal and Particular), the Rule as here expressed is sufficient. But if we take into more definite view the Quantity of *some*, — namely, whether it does or does not exceed *one half*, — the Rule may be made seemingly less stringent. It is enough that the quantifications of the Middle Term in both Premises, added together, should exceed unity, — that is, exceed its possible totality or its distribution in any one; for the amount of such excess over unity then constitutes a *common* Middle Term. Something *more than all* the Middle Term has been mentioned in the Premises; and both Terms in the Conclusion must have this excess as a common element. If *A is three fourths of M*, and *B is one half of M*, then at least *one fourth of M* is common to *A* and *B*; and their agreement with *this* common term is enough to insure their agreement with each other. This is called by Hamilton the *ultra-total* quantification of the Middle Term. It deserves mention, but as it is of very infrequent use, the Rule as first enounced for the quantification of the Middle is practically sufficient.

4. *One Premise at least must be affirmative;* for if both Premises are negative, the Middle Term agrees with neither of the two others, and therefore affords no ground for any Inference as to their agreement or non-agreement with each other. Though we know that *A is not M* and *B is not M*, we do not *thereby* know whether *A* is or is not *B*. A good general is not a coward, and Pompey was not a coward; but these two assertions furnish no reason for believing that Pompey either was, or was not, a good general.

5. *If either Premise is negative, the Conclusion is negative;* for as one Premise, according to the preceding Rule, must be affirmative, if the other Premise is negative, there is a difference in the relation of the two principal Terms to the Middle Term, and hence a non-agreement between the two Terms themselves.

6. *Neither Term must be distributed in the Conclusion if it was not distributed in the Premise;* for if only *some* is premised, we cannot conclude *all.*

Logicians have usually added two other Rules, that *the Conclusion follows the weaker part*, a Negative being regarded as weaker than an Affirmative, and a Particular as weaker than a Universal; and that *no Conclusion can be drawn from two Particular Premises.* But both of these result only from a combination of Rules 5 and 6 with 3; hence they hardly need to be considered here, but I append a demonstration of them in the note.* No syllogism

---

* As the two additional Rules were constructed with special reference to the Aristotelic doctrine of Judgments, they can be conveniently demonstrated only by bearing in mind the following maxims, which have already been laid down in the exposition of that doctrine.

1. By Subalternation, Particular Judgments are included under their corresponding Universals; that is, if **A** is true, **I** is also true; and the same holds good of **E** and **O**.

2. The Subject of a Judgment, taken universally or particularly, is that which renders the Judgment itself Universal or Particular.

3. The Predicate of an Affirmative Judgment is always considered as Particular.

4. The Predicate of a Negative Judgment is always regarded as Universal, — that is, as distributed.

Now *there must always be in the Premises one more Term distributed than in the Conclusion;* for by Rule 3, the Middle Term (which does not appear in the Conclusion) must be distributed in at least one of the Premises; and by Rule 6, if any Term is distributed which does appear in the Conclusion, it must also be distributed in the Premises. Then it follows that *no Conclusion can be drawn from two Particular Premises.* For if these are **I** and **I**, as neither Subject nor Predicate of **I** is Universal, the Middle Term is not distributed. If they are **I** and **O**, then, by Rule 5, the Conclusion is

can be invalid which does not violate one or more of the six Rules first enounced.

After the usual manner of logicians, the foregoing Rules have been summed up in these mnemonic hexameters: —

> Distribuas medium, nec quartus terminus adsit;
> Utraque nec præmissa negans, nec particularis;
> Sectetur partem conclusio deteriorem,
> Et non distribuat nisi cum præmissa, negetve.

But the application of these rules may become a matter of considerable complexity, when it is considered that, from the same naked (unquantified) Terms, a great variety of different Syllogisms may be formed. Each of the three Terms may be either Particular or Universal; each of the three Judgments, either Affirmative or Negative; the Judgments may be placed in any order with respect to each

negative; then its Predicate is distributed; and Rule 6, taken in conjunction with what has just been stated respecting the number of distributed Terms in the Premises, requires one of these Premises to be Universal.

Again, *if either Premise is Particular, the Conclusion must be Particular.* For the Subject of a Universal Affirmative Conclusion must be Universal; therefore, in the Premise wherein this Subject appears, it must, by Rule 6, be Universal, and the Middle Term, which is therein joined with it, must consequently be Particular, since it must be the Predicate of an Affirmative Judgment. Then the Middle Term, in order to be once distributed, must be the Universal Subject of the other Premise. Hence, if the Conclusion is Universal *Affirmative*, both Premises must be Universal.

And if the Conclusion is Universal *Negative*, both Premises must also be Universal. For both Terms of the Conclusion are then distributed; and as the Middle Term must also be distributed, there must be at least three Terms distributed in the Premises. But this cannot be, unless both Premises are Universal, since both of them, by Rule 4, cannot be Negative. Hence, whether the Conclusion is Affirmative or Negative, if it be Universal, both Premises must be Universal. Then, if either Premise is Particular, the Conclusion must be Particular.

But according to Rule 5, if either Premise is Negative, the Conclusion is Negative. Then, *the Conclusion must follow the weaker part;* — that is, it must be Particular, if either Premise is Particular, and Negative, if either Premise is Negative. — Q. E. D.

other, and for three Judgments, six different orders of position are possible; and each of the three Terms may be either Subject or Predicate in either or both of the Premises, the two principal Terms also assuming either place in the Conclusion. The larger portion of the numerous Syllogisms thus formed, it is true, are invalid, as offending against one or more of the preceding Rules. We need some more succinct mode than that of severally applying to each Syllogism all these Rules, before we can be satisfied that it is impeccable. Many of these Syllogistic forms, moreover, are equivalents of each other; that is, the Reasoning may be changed from one form to another, without impairing its validity, or even changing its signification in any essential respect. But of these equivalent forms some are more natural and obvious than the others; the mind seeks for these by preference; and when the process of reasoning appears in one of these natural and preferred forms, its validity is determined with ease and in a moment. The application of the Rules to such cases is made with the quickness of instinct, and may be reduced almost to a mechanical process.

A highly ingenious, though artificial, system has been contrived of classifying these numerous Syllogistic forms under a few heads, throwing out at once all that are illegitimate, immediately recognizing the remainder, and then transmuting those which are valid in substance, but unnatural and obscure in form, into the easy and familiar types in which the mind quickly perceives their legitimacy. The study of this system, a ready use of which may be said to constitute the art of Syllogizing, is facilitated by a series of mnemonic contrivances, many of them of marvellous ingenuity and completeness. The notation and most of the operations are of an algebraic character; and attempts have not been wanting of late years to enlarge and perfect the system by a further introduction of mathematical signs and processes. The failure of such an undertaking is not to be wondered at, for it proceeds, as it seems to me, upon a mistaken opinion as to the relative position of the two sciences. Logic is not a department of mathematics. Rather the reverse is true. Mathematics is the science of pure *quantity*, — of reasoning about dimensions and numbers in the abstract, or as unmodified by any of the differences of *quality* by which all the objects of thought are actually distinguished; and it is, therefore, only a department, or a special application, of the far more comprehensive science which has for its object Reasoning itself and all its subsidiary processes, and thus covers the whole domain of Pure Thought. All computation is reasoning; but all reasoning is not computation, and therefore cannot be carried on by the processes, or be made subject to the special laws, of pure mathematics.

Syllogistic forms are classified with respect to *Mood* and *Figure*, the former having regard to the *value* of the three component Judgments, and the latter to the relative *position* of the three Terms in these Judgments. It will be convenient, then, to have a uniform mode of designating these three Terms. In future, S will stand for the Subject, and P for the Predicate, of the Conclusion, and M for the Middle Term. The *Consequence*, or what we usually express by the words *therefore, consequently*, &c., will be indicated by three dots placed thus $\therefore$. For example: —

M is P;
S is M;
$\therefore S$ is P.

To facilitate reference, the Logicians have given special names to these several Terms and Judgments. The Predicate of the Conclusion is called the *Major Term*, and its Subject the *Minor Term*. The Premise in which the Major is compared with the Middle Term is called the *Major Premise*, and that in which the Minor is compared with the Middle, is the *Minor Premise*. These names have reference to the Quantity of Extension only, and are founded upon the received doctrine, that the natural order of predication is that in which the Genus is predicated of the Species, the Species of the Individual, and, generally, the Extensive whole of its part. Then the more Extensive Term, the Major, usually occupies, at least in Affirmative Judgments, the Predicate's place. "This," says Dr. Thomson, "is the natural, though not invariable, order; and it is worthy of remark, that, even in Negative Judgments, where, from the negation, the two Terms cannot be set together to determine their respective Extension, if, apart from the Judgment, we know that the one is a small and the other a large class, — the one a clearly determined and the other a vague notion, — we naturally take the small and clearly determined Concept for the Subject. Thus, it is more natural to say that *the Apostles are not deceivers*, than that *No deceivers are Apostles*. So that, if our minds are not influenced by some previous thought to give greater prominence to the wider notion, and so make it the Subject," thus reversing the primary and natural order, the Term of *major* Extension will always be the Predicate, and that of *minor* Extension, the Subject.

As these names — Major, Middle, and Minor — thus correctly indicate the comparative Extension of the three Terms, an Affirmative Syllogism in which these Terms occupy their natural place is conveniently symbolized by three concentric circles, of which the outermost and largest indicates the Predicate of the Conclusion, or the Major Term; the innermost and smallest, the Subject of the Conclusion, or the Minor; and the intermediate one, the Middle Term. Thus: —

All mammals are viviparous;	All M are P.
All whales are mammals;	All S are M.
∴ All whales are viviparous.	∴ All S are P.

Here the reasoning is, that *S*, which is a part of *M*, must also be a part of *P*, since *M* is a part of *P*. We are thus led to another mode of enunciating the governing principle of all Syllogisms, that *a part of a part is a part of the whole;* or, as Leibnitz expresses it, *contentum contenti est contentum continentis*. This principle agrees in every essential respect with the famous *Dictum* of Aristotle, usually called the *Dictum de omni et nullo*, that *whatever is predicated* (affirmed or denied) *universally of any Class* (i. e. of any whole), *may be also predicated of any part of that Class*. Both principles have been already recognized and applied in the doctrine of Subalternation. The name of this *Dictum* is derived from the two forms which it assumes as applied either to affirmative or negative Conclusions; the *Dictum de omni* being thus expressed, *Quicquid de omni valet, valet etiam de quibusdam et singulis;* and the *Dictum de nullo* being, *Quicquid de nullo valet, nec de quibusdam nec de singulis valet.* Both of these principles are evidently of a secondary or derivative character, their affirmative and negative forms being grounded respectively upon the two Axioms of Identity and Non-Contradiction; for as a whole is identical with the sum of all its parts, whatever is affirmed or denied (distributively) of the whole is *thereby* affirmed or denied of each of its parts. Burgersdyck remarks, that, for the purpose of applying the Dictum to Syllogisms, it may more conveniently be thus expressed: *Whatever Predicate is universally affirmed or denied of any Middle Term or Part is also affirmed or denied of any Subject which is contained under that intermediate Term or Part.*

The mode of symbolizing the mutual relations of the three Terms of a Syllogism, which is applied above to a Universal Affirmative, may be extended to Negatives and Particulars. The total disagreement of two Terms with each other, which is expressed by a Negative Judgment, is properly indicated by two Circles which do not coincide in any part. Thus: —

No M is P;
All S is M;
∴ No S is P.

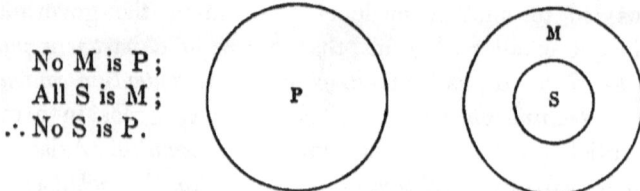

Both the partial agreement, and the partial disagreement, of two Terms, — as these are merely two aspects of one

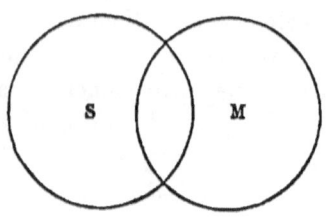

and the same Thought, — are properly indicated by the same symbol, namely, two circles which intersect. *Some S are M*, and *Some S are not M*, are both expressed by this symbol.

Excepting this ambiguity, all Syllogisms can be adequately symbolized by some combination of the preceding diagrams.

Hitherto we have regarded the Syllogism only as a means of evincing the relation of two Terms to each other through the relation of each to a common or Third Term. But the Dictum as expressed by Burgersdyck indicates another aspect of the Syllogism, equivalent indeed to the former one, but in certain respects more convenient for use. The Judgment in which "a Predicate is universally affirmed or denied of any Middle Term or Part" is a *General Rule;* the Judgment that a given "Subject is contained under that intermediate Term or part," is the *Subsumption* of this Subject under the condition of that Rule; and then the Conclusion following, that the given Subject is governed by that Rule, is a solution of the doubt with which we commenced, whether S is, or is not, P. Every Syllogism, then, must consist of three Judgments, one of which must be a *General Rule*, or, as Hamilton expresses it, a *Sumption;* another must be the *Subsumption* of a certain Subject under that Rule; and the third is the *Conclusion*, that this Subject is determined by the Rule. Thus: —

Sumption. No one who is content is miserable;
Subsumption. Some of the poor are content;
Conclusion. Some of the poor are not miserable.

It is not difficult to prove, say the Port Royal logicians, that all the Rules which we have given serve only to show that the Conclusion is contained under (or embraced in the Extension of) one of the Premises, which is a General Rule or Sumption, and that the other Premise, the Subsumption, shows this; and that arguments are vicious only when they fail to observe this method, and are always good when it is observed.

Kant expresses the general law of the Syllogism, as thus conceived, in the following formula: *Whatever stands under the condition of a Rule, that stands also under the Rule itself.* As the former view regards chiefly the three Terms, so this one has primary reference to the three Judgments, of which every Syllogism is composed. The former view does not contradict the latter; they are only two aspects of the same thing. But what we have hitherto termed the *Major Premise*, though it is usually the same Judgment that is here called the *Sumption*, is not always so. Thus, in the following Syllogism, (called by the Logicians *Disamis* of the Third Figure,) the first Judgment, as it contains the Predicate of the Conclusion, is the Major Premise; but the second Judgment is the Sumption.

Some wicked persons are men of high rank;
All the wicked are miserable.
∴ Some miserable persons are men of high rank.

As it has been demonstrated that *from two Particulars no Conclusion can be drawn*, every Syllogism must have for a

Premise at least one Universal Judgment; that is, one of
its Premises must be a Sumption or General Rule. In the
First Figure, which is the only natural and obvious form
of reasoning, and to which all the other forms can be reduced, the Sumption is always the Major Premise.

1. Figure and Mood.

The *Figure* of a Syllogism depends upon the relati·
position of its three Terms, and is determined by the po
tion of the Middle Term in the Premises. Now the M:
dle Term may be either the Subject of the Major Premise,
and the Predicate of the Minor, in which case we say the
Syllogism is of the First Figure; or it may be the Predicate of both, which is the Second Figure; or it may be the
Subject of both, thus constituting the Third Figure; or it
may be the Predicate of the Major and the Subject of the
Minor, thus converting the First, and giving rise to the
Fourth Figure. Accordingly, the four Figures are thus
indicated.

I.	II.	III.	IV.
M P	P M	M P	P M
S M	S M	M S	M S
∴ S P	∴ S P	∴ S P	∴ S P

They are also indicated in the following mnemonic
line: —

Sub præ; tum præ præ; tum sub sub; tum præ sub.

The line should be read thus: — The Middle Term is, first,
Subject, Predicate; then, *Predicate, Predicate*; then, *Subject, Subject*; lastly, *Predicate, Subject*.

The Fourth Figure is not recognized by Aristotle, but is
accepted, if at all, on the supposed authority of Galen.
Most modern logicians reject it, not as invalid, but as unnatural and unnecessary. As we have already said, the

natural order of predication is that in which the Genus is predicated of the Species, or the more Extensive of the less Extensive Term. Then it follows that the First is the only natural and obvious Figure, as it is the only one which observes this order throughout. Here, the Predicate of the Conclusion, which is the Term of widest Extension, appears as the Predicate of the Major Premise; and the Subject of the Conclusion, being the Term of least Extension, is the Subject of the Minor Premise, — the Middle Term appearing, as it ought, intermediate between the two, being of less Extension than P, and greater than S. Here also, as Dr. Thomson remarks, the Conclusion in no way disturbs the order of Terms which was first established in the Premises; for the Subject of the Conclusion appears also as a Subject in the Premises, and the Predicate as a Predicate; — that is, no Thought which was primary becomes secondary, nor any secondary primary. Take, for instance, the following Syllogism in the First Figure: —

1. No boaster deserves respect;
 Some heroes are (some) boasters;
 ∴ Some heroes do not deserve respect.

Here, everything is in its natural place; each Subject is of less Extension than its Predicate, and the Terms preserve the same relative places in the Conclusion which they occupied in the Premises.

But change this Syllogism into the Second Figure, by converting the Major Premise, thus: —

2. No person deserving respect is a boaster;
 Some heroes are (some) boasters;
 ∴ Some heroes do not deserve respect.

Here, the natural order is violated in one half of the reasoning; for the Subject of the Major is the Predicate of the Conclusion, and has wider Extension than its own Predicate.

Again, change the same Syllogism into the Third Figure, by converting the Minor Premise, thus: —

   3. No boaster deserves respect;
    Some boasters are (some) heroes;
   ∴ Some heroes do not deserve respect.

Here, the other half of the reasoning appears unnatural and forced. The Predicate of the Minor Premise becomes the Subject of the Conclusion, and is of less Extension than its own Subject.

To change this Syllogism into the Fourth Figure, we must convert *both* Premises, thus: —

   4. No person deserving respect is a boaster;
    Some boasters are (some) heroes;
   ∴ Some heroes do not deserve respect.

Here, both halves of the reasoning are contorted, so that it appears wholly unnatural. Not only is the Predicate of the Minor the Subject of the Conclusion and of less Extent than its own Subject, but the Subject of the Major is the Predicate of the Conclusion, and of greater Extent than its own Predicate. The mind revolts at this perversion; striving to preserve the same order in the Conclusion which it observed in the Premises, the Conclusion which it would naturally draw from these two Premises is this: —

   No person deserving respect is (some) hero.

Now, this Conclusion, which is natural and obvious, is the Converse of the former one, which was unnatural; and it reduces the Syllogism (changing the order of the Premises) from the Fourth to the First Figure. Hence it appears, that what is called the Fourth Figure is only the First with a converted Conclusion; that is, we do not actually reason in the Fourth, but only in the First, and then, if occasion requires, convert the Conclusion of the First. The reasoning is indirect, or Mediate in a double sense; the nominal Conclusion of the Fourth is actually, but indirectly, obtained by converting the Conclusion of the First. Hence, many Logicians exclude the Fourth altogether, and call those Syllogistic forms which would otherwise fall under it "indirect Moods of the First Figure." But we can also obtain, if we see fit, indirect Moods from the Second or Third Figure, by converting their Conclusions also. There is no reason, then, for giving a special class of these "indirect Moods" to the First Figure, any more than to the Second or Third; that is, there is no reason for considering the Moods of the so-called Fourth Figure at all. It is not only unnatural, but wholly unnecessary. We need only state, that, after obtaining the ordinary *mediate* Conclusions from either of the three Figures, we may, if occasion requires, obtain a second set of Conclusions *immediately*, by converting the former ones.

But we observe, secondly, that the natural but unexpressed Conclusion of the so-called Fourth, —
"No person deserving respect is (some) hero," —
is a shocking one for the Aristotelians, for it is a Negative with an undistributed Predicate. They will not allow that such a Judgment is possible; but here it appears as actual, — nay, as the only *natural* result of Premises to which, according to the Aristotelic doctrine, only a wholly *unnatural* Conclusion can be given by inventing a so-called Fourth Figure, otherwise not needed, and in every respect perverted and contrary to nature. Of course, Sir William Hamilton, whose system expressly recognizes these Negative Judgments (Ani) with undistributed Predicates, has taken advantage of this fact, and pressed it as an unanswerable argument against his opponents.

But to return to the Aristotelic doctrine. The reason ordinarily given for awarding a decided preference to the First over the other Figures is not either of the two here alleged, but one which immediately results from them, — namely, that the *Dictum de omni et nullo*, which is held to be a universal principle of all reasoning, is directly applicable only to the First Figure. This Dictum, which has respect exclusively to the Quantity of Extension, necessarily supposes that the order of Extension is strictly followed in the Syllogism; that is, that the Predicate in each of its three Judgments should be of wider Extension than the Subject. This is the case in the First Figure; but as we have seen, it is not so with the others. In the Second, the Subject of the Major, and in the Third, the Subject of the Minor Premise, has a wider Extension than the corresponding Predicate. In order to show that the Dictum is universally applicable, we must be able to reduce all Syllogisms, in whatever class they may at first be ranked, to the First Figure. Now, to judge from the instance just given, in which we have carried the same Syllogism successively through each of the four Figures, such a *Reduction* can be very easily accomplished. It is only necessary to convert one or both of the Premises. Recurring for a moment to the first mode of indicating the variations of Figure, —

I.	II.	III.	IV.
M P	P M	M P	P M
S M	S M	M S	M S
∴ S P	∴ S P	∴ S P	∴ S P

it is easy to see that the Second Figure is reduced to the First by converting its Major Premise; the Third, by converting its Minor; and the Fourth, by converting both. But as the order of the Premises may be transposed, as the Sumption and the Major Premise do not always coincide, and as the Judgment **O**, on the strict Aristotelic doctrine, is not convertible at all, it is not always easy to tell which Premise ought to be converted, and the process of Reduction practically becomes so complex and intricate, that, to facilitate it, an elaborate system and a whole set of mnemonics have been contrived. These will be explained hereafter.

The Aristotelic logicians appear to hesitate, or be in doubt, as to the motives for *reducing* the three lower Figures to the First. At times, they speak as if the only reason for such Reduction were the one already mentioned, — to reduce all Syllogistic forms to system by showing that they are all controlled by one governing principle, the *Dictum de omni et nullo*. The implication then is, that they are valid or competent forms of reasoning, even before such Reduction; and that they are reduced, therefore, only to render them more systematic and orderly in appearance. Then, again, they speak of *proving* them by this Reduction, as if otherwise they were weak and needed proof, even if they were not invalid. The truth is, the reasoning under either of these Figures is just as conclusive as under the First. In neither case can the Conclusion be denied without involving the denier in an absurdity, — that is, in a contradiction of one of the Primary Axioms of Pure Thought. Nay, more; in certain cases, it is, in one sense, more natural to make inferences by the Second or Third Figure, than by the First; that is, the particular object which we have in view in the general investigation or course of argument which we are pursuing, may more directly lead us to the former than to the latter. Thus, when we wish to *exclude* something from a class to which it had been wrongly assigned, or to *disprove* something which has been asserted, we are most frequently led to argue in the Second Figure, since any Conclusion in this Figure must be negative; for as the Middle Term is here Predicate in both Premises, it cannot be distributed unless one of the Premises is negative, and then, by Rule 5, the Conclusion is negative. " The arguments," says Whately, " used in the process called *Abscissio infiniti*, will, in general, be the most easily referred to this Figure. This phrase was applied by some logicians to a series of arguments used in any inquiry in which we go on *excluding*, one by one, certain suppo sitions, or certain classes of things, from that whose real nature we are seeking to ascertain."

Again, if our design is to establish *exceptions* to a pretended law or rule, — that is, if we would disprove the asserted *universality* of the Proposition, — the Third Figure will most commonly answer our purpose, for here all Conclusions must be Particular; we prove that *Some are*, or *Some are not*, and thus disprove the assertion that *All are not*, or *All are*. Conclusions in the Third Figure must be Particular, because both Terms of the Conclusion appear as Predicates in the two Premises; hence, if these Premises are both Affirmatives, their Predicates are Particular; and if one of them is Negative, the Conclusion can only be a Particular Negative, since a Universal Negative distributes both its Terms.

Because the two lower Figures are thus not only valid in themselves, but peculiarly appropriate for certain purposes, some logicians hold that it is unnecessary to reduce them to the First Figure. Each of the three, they maintain, has its own functions and its own governing principle. The principle which is assigned to the First, needs but to be slightly modified in order to be directly applicable to the Second or the Third; since all three are but various applications of the same Axioms of Thought. Thus, if the *Dictum de omni et nullo* be considered as the principle for the First Figure, for the Second we have the *Dictum de diverso*, — that *if one Term is contained in, and another excluded from, a third Term, then they are excluded from each other*. For the Third Figure, the principle is called the *Dictum de exemplo*, — that *two Terms which contain a common part partly agree; or, if one contains a part which the other does not, they partly differ*.

Reduction is not essential, therefore, but it is certainly convenient; the reasoning does not become more cogent by being reduced to the First Figure, but it is rendered more perspicuous, more simple and natural in expression, and any fallacies in it, which might otherwise escape notice, become at once so obvious that they cannot avoid detection. The whole theory of argumentation, moreover, is rendered more systematic and elegant, when its numerous modes are reduced to a very few fundamental forms, the validity of which is so manifest that they do not need to be tested by the application of previously determined rules.

The proper relative position of the three Judgments of a Syllogism appears so obvious, on the Aristotelic doctrine, that it has usually been taken for granted. If we reason only in order to instruct, to convince, or to refute, — and no other purpose seems to have been contemplated by the old logicians, — the natural order of Thought seems to be, that the Ground or Reason should precede the Consequence; that is, that the Premises, as their name imports, should precede, and, as it were, effectuate the Conclusion. And as regards the two Premises, if the reasoning is exclusively in the Quantity of Extension, the Major should be placed before the Minor, the Sumption or General Rule before the Subsumption.

The *Mood* of a Syllogism is the value of its three Judgments considered in respect to their Quantity and Quality. Since there are but four kinds of Judgments as thus viewed, indicated respectively by the four vowels **A, E, I**, and **O**, it is evident that three of these letters must express any possible Mood. When we have ascertained its Mood and Figure, the classified place and formal value of a Syllogism are determined. For instance, **E I O**, Fig. I., and **A A I**, Fig. III., are thus expressed: —

Fig. I.		Fig. III.	
No M is P;	**E**	All M are P;	**A**
Some S are M;	**I**	All M are S;	**A**
∴ Some S are not P.	**O**	∴ Some S are P.	**I**

As only four Judgments are possible, and three are necessary to constitute a Syllogism, the whole number of Moods can be numerically determined. Only *sixty-four* different arrangements can be made out of four letters taken three at a time; hence, sixty-four Moods are conceivable. But the greater number of these are invalid, as contradicting one or more of the General Rules which govern, as we have seen, all forms of Mediate Inference. The elimination of these invalid forms can be more easily effected, if we first reduce the expression of a Mood to its simplest form.

Strictly speaking, only the two letters which denote the Premises need to be taken into account; for the Quantity and Quality (and therefore the letter) of the Conclusion are determined by those of the Premises. Each Mood, then, being designated by only two letters, and only sixteen different arrangements being possible of four letters taken two at a time, all conceivable Moods are contained in the following list: —

1.)	A A	2.)	E A	3.)	I A	4.)	O A
	A E		E E		I E		O E
	A I		E I		I I		O I
	A O		E O		I O		O O

The Rule that *from two Negative Premises no Conclusion can be drawn*, excludes four from this list, namely, **E E**, **E O, O E**, and **O O**. The Rule that *no Conclusion can be drawn from two Particular Premises*, excludes three more, namely, **I I, I O**, and **O I**. Finally, **I E** is excluded because its Negative Conclusion distributes the Major Term, which is undistributed in **I**, the Major Premise; but according to Rule 6, *neither Term can be distributed in the Conclusion, if it was not distributed in the Premise*. We may here observe, that the violation of this last Rule, in respect to the *Major* Term, is called *illicit process of the*

Major; in respect to the *Minor* Term, it is called *illicit process of the Minor.*

These exclusions being effected, there remain but eight valid Moods, namely, **A A, A E, A I, A O, E A, E I, I A,** and **O A.** Not all, even of these eight, however, afford a valid Syllogism in each of the four Figures; for the altered position of the Middle Term may cause the greater number of them to offend against the Rules which forbid both an undistributed Middle and an Illicit Process whether of the Major or Minor Term. Special Rules have been enounced for each of the Figures, which will enable us to make the further exclusions that are requisite. It should be observed, that these Special Rules contain no new principle, but are immediately deducible from the General Rules, that have already been established for all Syllogisms; taking these General Rules in connection, however, with the two axioms by which the Aristotelians determine the implicit Quantity of the Predicate; namely, that, in all Affirmative Judgments, the Predicate is Particular, and that, in all Negative Judgments, the Predicate is Universal. This deduction may be left as an exercise for the learner. We will here consider the Special Rules under that theory which regards every Mediate Inference as proceeding from the Subsumption of a particular case under a General Rule or Sumption; little more than an alteration of phraseology will be needed to adapt them to the theory in which we speak only of Major and Minor Premises.

The Special Rules for the First Figure are, —
 1. The Sumption must be Universal;
 2. The Subsumption must be Affirmative.

These two Rules exclude **I A, O A, A E,** and **A O.** There remain **A A, E A, A I,** and **E I,** as the only valid Moods in this Figure; and these are named *Barbara, Celarent, Darii,* and *Ferio.* Observe that the three vowels in each of these names denote the Mood of the Syllogism to which it is applied; and the same is true of the technical names which will be given to the valid Moods in the other Figures.

The Special Rules for the Second Figure are,—
1. The Sumption must be Universal;
2. One of the Premises must be Negative, and therefore the Conclusion must be Negative.

These Rules exclude **I A**, **O A**, **A A**, and **A I**; ther there remain as valid in the Second Figure only the four Moods which have been named *Cesare, Camestres, Festino*, and *Baroko*.

The Special Rules for the Third Figure are,—
1. The Subsumption must be Affirmative;
2. The Conclusion must be Particular.

Throwing out **A E** and **A O** under these Rules, there remain for the Third Figure six Moods, named *Darapti. Disamis, Datisi, Felapton, Bokardo,* and *Ferison.*

The Special Rules for the Fourth Figure are,—
1. If the Sumption is Affirmative, the Subsumption must be Universal.
2. If either Premise is Negative, the Sumption must be Universal.
3. If the Subsumption is Affirmative, the Conclusion must be Particular.

Rejecting **A I**, **A O**, and **O A**, as offending against these Rules, there remain only five Moods, called *Bramantip, Camenes, Dimaris, Fesapo,* and *Fresison*, as valid in the Fourth Figure.

Taking the four Figures together, therefore, there are nineteen valid Moods; but as fifteen of these can be reduced to those of the First Figure, there are only four Moods which are at once valid, natural, and perspicuous. Regarding the last vowel in the names of these four (*Barbara, Celarent, Darii, Ferio*), we see that these are just sufficient to prove the four fundamental Judgments, **A**, **E**, **I**, and **O**.

If we exclude the Fourth Figure altogether, considering *Bramantip, Camenes,* &c. as indirect Moods of the First, there are but fourteen *direct* Moods. On the other hand, since from every Syllogism with a Universal Conclusion we can obtain, by Subalternation, a Particular Conclusion also, there are five other *indirect* Moods, which are anonymous, making twenty-four in all. Thus, **A A** in the First yields **I**, as well as **A**, for a Conclusion; and from **E A** in the Second, we may conclude not only **E**, but **O**. But these anonymous Moods, besides being indirect, are practically useless; since it is idle to infer *some* only, when the Premises warrant the inference of *all*.

Rejecting the Fourth Figure and the indirect Moods, it will be seen, from examining the last vowel in each of the names, that **A** is proved only in one Figure and one Mood; **E** in two Figures and three Moods; **I** in two Figures and four Moods; and **O** in three Figures and six Moods. "For this reason," says Mr. Mansel, "**A** is declared by Aristotle to be the most difficult proposition to establish, and the easiest to overthrow; **O**, the reverse. And, generally, Universals are most easily overthrown, Particulars more easily established."

The names of all the valid Moods have been put together into the following mnemonic hexameters, which deserve careful study, not only as a complete artificial system for the Reduction of all the Moods of the subordinate Figures to those of the First, (for which purpose the names were invented,) but as a literary curiosity. They have been in use in the Schools, as an aid to the memory, for over six centuries, their authorship being unknown. Mr. DeMorgan calls them "the magic words which are more full of meaning than any that ever were made." Sir William Hamilton says of them that "there are few human inventions which display a higher ingenuity."

>BARBARA, CELARENT, DARII, FERIOQUE prioris.
>CESARE, CAMESTRES, FESTINO, BAROKO secundæ.
>Tertia DARAPTI, DISAMIS, DATISI, FELAPTON,
>BOKARDO, FERISON habet. Quarta insuper addit
>BRAMANTIP, CAMENES, DIMARIS, FESAPO, FRESISON.

If, rejecting the Fourth Figure, we consider its contents as indirect Moods of the First, instead of the first line, the two following should be substituted: —

>BARBARA, CELARENT, DARII, FERIO, BARALIP-*ton*,
>CELANTES, DABITIS, FAPESMO, FRISESOM-*orum*,

the final syllables in italics being only euphonic.

As already mentioned, the three vowels in each of these names indicate the Quantity and Quality of the three Judgments which form the Syllogism. The consonants in the names belonging to the First Figure have no special meaning; but of those in the other Figures, every consonant (except T and N, which are merely euphonic) indicates some step to be taken in the process of *reducing* the Mood to a Mood of the First Figure.

The initial consonant, which is either B, C, D, or F, indicates that Mood of the First Figure (*B*arbara, *C*elarent, *D*arii, or *F*erio) to which the Reduction brings us. Thus, *Cesare* and *Camestres* are reduced to *Celarent;* *Festino*, *Felapton*, &c., to *Ferio*. The other consonants show how the Reduction is made. M indicates that the Premises are to be transposed; S and P, that the Judgment indicated by the vowel immediately preceding is to be *converted,* — s, that it is to be converted *simply,* while P signifies the conversion *per accidens*.

K, which occurs in the names of only two Moods, *Baroko* and *Bokardo*, denotes that the Judgment indicated by the preceding vowel is to be left out, another substituted for it, and the process to be then completed by a Reduction *per impossibile*, which will be explained hereafter.

A few examples will sufficiently illustrate the process. The name *Disamis* indicates the following Syllogism of the Third Figure, which is to be reduced to *Darii* of the First, by converting simply its Major Premise, transposing its Premises, and then converting its Conclusion.

DISAMIS	reduced to	DARII.
Some M are P;		All M are S;
All M are S;		Some P are M;
∴ Some S are P.		∴ Some P are S.
Some wars are justifiable;		All wars are inexpedient;
All wars are inexpedient;		Some justifiable acts are wars;
∴ Some inexpedient acts are justifiable.		∴ Some justifiable acts are inexpedient.

Festino of the Second is reduced to *Ferio* of the First Figure, by converting simply its Major Premise.

FESTINO	reduced to	FERIO.
No P is M;		No M is P;
Some S are M;		Some S are M;
∴ Some S are not P.		∴ Some S are not P.
No ruminant is solid-hoofed;		No solid-hoofed animal is ruminant;
Some herbivora are solid-hoofed;		Some herbivora are solid-hoofed;
∴ Some herbivora are not ruminant.		∴ Some herbivora are not ruminant.

Fesapo of the Fourth is reduced to *Ferio* of the First Figure, by converting both its Premises, the Major simply, and the Minor *per accidens*.

FESAPO	reduced to	FERIO.
No P is M;		No M is P;
All M are S;		Some S are M;
∴ Some S are not P.		∴ Some S are not P.

No Hindoo is white ;   No white is a Hindoo ;
All whites are civilized ;   Some civilized are whites ;
∴ Some civilized are not Hindoos.   ∴ Some civilized are not Hindoos.

Baroko and *Bokardo* have been stumbling-blocks to the logicians. In order to reduce either of them to the First Figure, the Premise which needs to be converted is O ; but according to the old doctrine, O is inconvertible. To overcome this difficulty, the logicians invented the awkward, roundabout, and operose process which they called Reduction *per Impossibile*. Through a Syllogism in *Barbara*, they proved, not directly that the Conclusion in *Baroko* and *Bokardo* is true, but that its Contradictory is false ; now, according to the Axiom of Excluded Middle (that two Contradictories cannot *both* be false), this is an indirect method of proving that the Conclusion is true. The process is as follows.

Of course, both Premises in every Syllogism are presumed to be true ; then, any Conclusion which contradicts either one of them must be false. Now, κ indicates, that, instead of the Premise signified by the vowel (**O**) immediately preceding, we are to substitute the Contradictory of the Conclusion ; and as this Conclusion is **O**, its Contradictory is **A**. But from the two Premises (**A A**) thus obtained, we have a Conclusion which contradicts the original Premise, **O**. Then the substituted Judgment in **A** (which is the Contradictory of the original Conclusion) must be false ; and therefore the original Conclusion itself is true. This is not exactly reducing the Syllogism to the First Figure, but it is indirectly proving, *through the First Figure*, that the Conclusion of the Syllogism must be true, because its Contradictory is false.

    BAROKO   reduced to   BARBARA.
All P are M ;   All P are M ;   [clusion.)
Some S are not M ;   All S are P ; (Contradictory of former Con-
∴ Some S are not P.   ∴ All S are M. (Contradicts former Minor Premise.)

FIGURE AND MOOD.   205

  BOKARDO reduced to BARBARA.
 Some M are not P ; All S are P ; (Contradictory of former
 All M are S ;   All M are S ; Conclusion).
∴ Some S are not P. ∴ All M are P. (Contradicts former Major
                 Premise.)

As this Conclusion in *Barbara* cannot be true, its Premise, which is the Contradictory of the former Conclusion, must be false; then the original Conclusion itself is true.

All this is awkward enough. Whately and others rightly remark, that these two difficult Syllogisms can be *reduced* in a much simpler and more elegant manner, through converting one of their Premises by Contraposition. Thus, let *Baroko* be now called *Fakoro*, and let *Bokardo* be named *Dokamok* (the substitution of these two names will not spoil the mnemonic hexameters); and let κ indicate Conversion by Contraposition.

  FAKORO reduced to FERIO.
 All P are M ;   No not-M is P ;
 Some S are not M ; Some S are not-M ;
∴ Some S are not P. ∴ Some S are not P.

All murders are intentional ; No unintentional act is a murder ;

Some homicides are not intentional ; Some homicides are unintentional ;

∴ Some homicides are not murders. ∴ Some homicides are not murders.

  DOKAMOK reduced to DARII.
 Some M are not P ; All M are S ;
 All M are S ;   Some not-P are M ;
∴ Some S are not P. ∴ Some not-P are S ; (or, convert
  by Contraposition,) ∴ Some S are not P.

Some imprudent acts are not vicious ; All imprudent acts are foolish ;

All imprudent acts are foolish ; Some not-vicious acts are imprudent ;

∴ Some foolish acts are not vicious.   ∴ Some not-vicious acts are foolish;
∴ Some foolish acts are not vicious.

These examples show that, after *Dokamok* has been reduced to *Darii*, the Conclusion must be contraponed back again, if we would have it in its original form.

Ingenious as this whole system of Reduction is, it is needlessly artificial and complex. The sole reason for reducing Syllogisms to the First Figure, we have said, is to exhibit the reasoning in its simplest and most natural form, and in that in which its validity, or invalidity, is most readily perceived. A few simple Rules may be given which will enable the learner to accomplish this object at once, in whatever Figure the argumentation may originally be propounded, and even without knowing what this Figure is.

1. Every process of reasoning must consist of a Judgment which is to be proved, and of one or two other Judgments alleged in its support; the former is the Conclusion, the latter are the Premises. The first step is to reduce each of these Judgments to its simplest logical form, — that is, to a Subject and Predicate connected by the present tense (affirmative or negative) of the verb *to be*. Care must be taken to determine accurately the Quantity and Quality of each of the Judgments.

2. The Middle Term is that which does not appear in the Conclusion. If no such Term is found in the Premises, the Inference is Immediate, and must be tried by the principles laid down in the preceding chapter, concerning Conversion, Opposition, &c. If there is a Middle Term, the Inference is Mediate; then the Major Premise is that Judgment in which this Middle Term appears connected with the Predicate of the Conclusion; the Minor Premise, that in which it is connected with the Subject of the

Conclusion. If only one Premise is given in the original statement, the other may be easily supplied by a moment's consideration, as its two naked Terms are known, and its Quantity and Quality may be inferred, through the General Rules already given for all Syllogisms, from the Quantity and Quality of the Conclusion and the given Premise.

3. The First Figure requires the Middle Term to be the Subject of the Major, and the Predicate of the Minor, Premise. If, in the Premises as determined, the Terms do not already appear in this order, one or both must be *converted*, either simply, or *per accidens*, or by Contraposition.

There can be no difficulty in the application of these Rules, which does not arise from some ambiguity in the language of the original statement; and to resolve such ambiguity is the business, not of the logician, but of the grammarian and the lexicographer. But a few cases will be incidentally resolved when we come to treat of Fallacies, a subject which cannot be fully considered without sometimes stepping out of the province of Pure Thought.

2. Conditional Syllogisms.

Thus far we have treated exclusively of the purely Categorical Syllogism, in which each of the component Judgments can be reduced to one or the other of the two Categorical formulas, *A is B*, or *A is not B*. The reasoning in this case, as we have seen, depends upon the two Axioms of Identity and Non-Contradiction. We come now to another class of Syllogisms, dependent upon the Axioms of Reason and Consequent, and Excluded Middle.

A *Conditional Syllogism is one of which the Major Premise, and only the Major Premise, is a Conditional Judgment*. There are three kinds of such Syllogisms, corresponding to the three classes into which Conditional Judgments are divided; namely, the *Hypothetical*, the *Disjunctive*, and the

Dilemmatic or *Hypothetico-Disjunctive*. The following are examples of each.

<table>
<tr><td>*Hypothetical.*</td><td>*Disjunctive.*</td></tr>
<tr><td>If A is B, C is D;</td><td>A is either B or C;</td></tr>
<tr><td>A is B;</td><td>A is B;</td></tr>
<tr><td>∴ C is D.</td><td>∴ A is not C.</td></tr>
</table>

Dilemmatic or *Hypothetico-Disjunctive.*
If A is B, C is either D or E;
C is neither D nor E;
∴ A is not B.

These Terms may be quantified in the Minor Premise, as in Categorical Syllogisms, and the Conclusion will still be valid, if its proper Quantity be assigned to it according to the Rules already given. Thus, if the Minor Premise of the preceding Hypothetical be "*All* A are B," we may conclude that "*All* C are D"; but if we know only that "*Some* A are B," we can only conclude that "*Some* C are D." We may likewise use the quantification of Singulars, and say, "*this* A," or "*in certain cases*, A is B"; then, "in this case," or "in the same cases," C is D.

Dr. Thomson seems to be wrong, therefore, when he gives the following as an instance of a Hypothetical Syllogism, Figure I. in which each of the three Judgments is Hypothetical.

In cases where M is N, C is D.
In cases where A is B, M is N.
In cases where A is B, C is D.

Here, the supposed Condition, "in cases where A is B," is only an awkward quantification of the Minor Premise and the Conclusion, equivalent to "*in certain cases*," or "*some* M is N"; therefore, *in these cases*, or *some*, C is D. The reasoning does not turn upon this phrase, "in cases where A is B," *as a condition*, the Consequent being evolved from it; it turns upon it only *as a limitation*, showing in how many cases the reasoning is applicable. The reasoning does rest exclusively upon the Major Premise, where the corresponding phrase, " in cases where M is N," *is* a true *condition*, the Consequent being evolved from it, and the whole argumentation being governed by the Axiom of Reason and Consequent.

This error has led Dr. Thomson into a more serious one. Not perceiving that Hypothetical Reasoning is distinct in kind from Categorical, being governed by a different Axiom of Thought, he has overlooked the principle that, *from affirming the Consequent of a Reason, no Conclusion can be drawn*, and has presented the following as a valid Syllogism : —

In cases where C is D, M is N;
In cases where A is B, M is N;
∴ In cases where A is B, C is D.

But here the Minor Premise only affirms that " M is N," which is the Consequent of the hypothesis in the Major Premise; and therefore the Conclusion is illogical; the Middle Term is not distributed. This can be easily seen from the following example, the Conclusion of which is evidently a *non sequitur*.

If you whip him, the boy cries;
If you take away his toys, the boy cries;
∴ If you take away his toys, you whip him.

Then, in a Conditional Syllogism, it is *only* the Major Premise which is a Conditional Judgment; for the reasoning turns upon the relation of Reason and Consequent, and this relation, being once affirmed in the Major Premise, affords all the material requisite for the Inference. Both the Minor Premise and the Conclusion must be Categorical; the Major contains all the Terms which appear in either of them; whereas, the Minor Premise of a Categorical Syllogism contains a new Term, which did not appear in the Major. If, then, both Premises, or one Premise and Conclusion, are Conditional Judgments, the reasoning is, in fact, Categorical, and depends upon the Axioms of Identity and Non-Contradiction. This is easily seen in the case of a Disjunctive Syllogism, whose form is determined by the Axiom of Excluded Middle.

    Every A is either X or Y;
    But B is A;
    Then B is either X or Y.

Here the reasoning is evidently Categorical; the Minor Premise introduces a new Term, B, not contained in the Major Premise, and therefore the Conclusion is also Disjunctive.

Endeavoring to prove that, in a Disjunctive Syllogism, not only the Major, but the Minor Premise or the Conclusion, may be a Disjunctive Judgment, Dr. Thomson presents the following as a valid example: —

    C, D, and E are B;
    C, D, and E = A;
    ∴ A is B.

This is not a Disjunctive Syllogism at all, as neither of the three Judgments is Disjunctive; the three Concepts which constitute the Middle Term are not taken disjunctively, but collectively; that is, one of them does not exclude the others, but requires the presence of the others, in order to constitute the Predicate. They form one compound Term. Thus, let $C, D,$ and $E = M$, and make the substitution. Then the Syllogism assumes this form, and is evidently Categorical.

    M is B;
    M = A;
    ∴ A is B.

The Axiom of Reason and Consequent is explicated, as we have seen, into these two principles; — *to affirm the Reason or the Condition is also to affirm the Consequent or the Conditioned;* and *to deny the Consequent is also to deny the Reason.* The application of these principles gives us, from the same Major Premise, two, and only two, valid Moods of the Hypothetical Syllogism, — namely, the *Modus Ponens* and the *Modus Tollens.* Thus: —

If A is B, C is D.

MODUS PONENS.	MODUS TOLLENS.
A is B ;	C is not D ;
Then C is D.	Then A is not B.

The following are examples of these formulas: —

MODUS PONENS.

If matter is essentially inert, every change in it must be produced by mind ;
But matter is essentially inert ;
Then all changes in it are produced by mind.

MODUS TOLLENS.

If the moon shines by its own light, it must always be full ;
But it is not always full ;
Then it does not shine by its own light.

We have said that there are only two valid Moods, because, from denying the Reason, or from affirming the Consequent, nothing follows. The Consequent may follow from some other Reason than the particular one assigned in the Major Premise ; and the original Axiom only affirms the necessity of some Reason or other, not of any particular one. It is true, that the Minor Premise may be quantified with the predesignations *all*, *some*, or *this*, and corresponding Conclusions will follow. The different forms which thus result may, if we please, be called *Moods* also.

The Major Premise, or Sumption, in either of the preceding examples, may be converted by Contraposition ; and the result will be, that what was the *Modus Tollens* becomes the *Modus Ponens*, and *vice versa*. These two Moods are thus shown to be really one ; and this is precisely what we should expect, for the two principles by which they are governed are only two explications of one Axiom of Thought. Thus, the last preceding example, which is now the *Modus Tollens*, becomes the following, if we contrapone the Sumption: —

If the moon is not always full, it does not shine by its own light;
But it is not always full;
Then it does not shine by its own light.

Here the Subsumption posits what is now the Reason, (though both are negative in form,) and therefore the Conclusion posits the Consequent. Hence the reasoning has now become the *Modus Ponens*.

Summing up what has been said, it appears that the Hypothetical Syllogism is subject to these three Special Rules: —

1. It consists of three Judgments, and only three; but in these Judgments there may be more than three Terms.

2. In respect to Quantity and Quality, the Sumption must always be Affirmative and Universal, while the Subsumption may vary in either of these relations.

3. The Conclusion is regulated, both in Quantity and Quality, by that member of the Sumption which is not subsumed, agreeing with it in both these respects in the *Modus Ponens*, and differing from it in both in the *Modus Tollens*.

The Sumption in the last example (after Contraposition) may seem not to conform to the second of these Rules; for it appears to be Negative in Quality. But if closely examined, the negative particle *not* will be found to belong to each of the two parts (Reason and Consequent) taken separately; while the Sumption, as a whole, *affirms* the connection of these two negative parts with each other.

Agreeably to what has been said, a *Disjunctive Syllogism is one of which the Major Premise is a Disjunctive Judg-*

ment, while the Minor Premise and the Conclusion are Categorical Judgments. The Axiom of Excluded Middle, by which this sort of Syllogism is governed, affirms that, of *two Contradictories*, one must be true and the other must be false. Accordingly, if the Major Premise presents *three* or more Disjunct Members, the Axiom will not be immediately applicable; these three or more Members are only *Contraries* with respect to each other, and they must be reduced to *two Contradictories*, before we can obtain a ground of inference, from positing or sublating one of them, to sublating or positing the other. The number of such Members can always be thus reduced by considering, for the moment, two or more of them as one. After this reduction is accomplished, the Minor Premise and Conclusion appear in their true character, not as Disjunctive, but as Categorical Judgments. For example:—

Complete Formula.	*Reduced Formula.*
A is either B, C, or D;	*Let B or C* = *X.*
But A is neither B nor C;	A is either X or D;
Then A is D.*	But A is not X;
	Then A is D.

This formula, as reduced, presents the universal type of Disjunctive reasoning. As its two Disjunct Members are Contradictories of each other, the Axiom of Excluded Middle authorizes us, from positing either one of them, to sublate the other. This is called the *Modus ponendo tollens*, and it has two forms, according as we posit one or the other of the two Disjunct Members. The same Axiom

---

* A story is told to illustrate the sagacity of a dog. Following his master by the scent, the animal came to a place where three roads met, and having ascertained by his nose, at two of them, that the object of his search had not taken either of the two, he immediately darted off by the third, without pausing to try whether this path also was scentless. The story is unquestionably a fiction; but, if true, the dog must have reasoned by this form of the Disjunctive Syllogism, in the *modus tollendo ponens*.

permits us, from sublating either of the two, to posit the other. This is called the *Modus tollendo ponens*, and has two forms like the other. Hence, every Disjunctive Syllogism affords, from the same Major Premise, two valid Moods, each containing two forms. It is obvious, that the remaining Term, A, of the Major Premise, may be quantified as *all* or *this*, and the Conclusion will appear accordingly as Universal or Singular. The two Moods and four forms of a Disjunctive Syllogism are exhibited in the following example: —

Major Premise. Every Judgment is either Affirmative or Negative.

MODUS PONENDO TOLLENS.

First form. This Judgment is Affirmative;
Then it is not Negative.

Second form. This Judgment is Negative;
Then it is not Affirmative.

MODUS TOLLENDO PONENS.

First form. This Judgment is not Affirmative;
Then it is Negative.

Second form. This Judgment is not Negative;
Then it is Affirmative.

For those who are fond of mnemonic hexameters, Hamilton has presented all four forms in the following verses: —

Ponendo tollens. Falleris aut fallor; fallor; non falleris ergo.
Falleris aut fallor; tu falleris; ergo ego nedum.
Tollendo ponens. Falleris aut fallor; non fallor; falleris ergo.
Falleris aut fallor; non falleris; ergo ego fallor.

Three Special Rules have been framed for Disjunctive Syllogism, though they are so obvious that their formal enouncement is hardly necessary.

1. A regular Disjunctive Syllogism must consist of three Judgments only, in which, if the Major Premise be reduced to its proper logical form, there can be

only three Terms, all of which must appear in the Major Premise.

2. The Major Premise must be Universal and Affirmative; the Minor Premise may be of either Quality and of either Quantity.

3. The Conclusion must be of the same Quantity, but of opposite Quality, with the Minor Premise.

Agreeably to what was said in treating of Disjunctive Judgments, each Mood of a Disjunctive Syllogism may be resolved into a Hypothetical Syllogism, and then its two forms appear as the two Moods of the Hypothetical reasoning. For instance, the example last cited may be thus transformed: —

If any Judgment is not Affirmative, it is Negative.

Modus Ponens.	*Modus Tollens.*
This Judgment is not Affirmative;	This Judgment is not Negative;
Then it is Negative.	Then it is Affirmative.

As a Dilemmatic Syllogism consists of a Hypothetical and a Disjunctive combined, and as these two may be combined in several different ways, the resulting forms are numerous and complex. Most of them are really compound, and a full analysis would need to resolve them into several simple and subordinate Syllogisms. It would be tedious to analyze them all, and this is not necessary, as the principles already established for the Hypothetical and the Disjunctive Syllogisms taken separately, still govern them when taken in connection; and the learner in each case may make the analysis and apply the principles for himself. What follows is to be regarded only as illustrating the method to be pursued.

What has already been presented as a type of the Dilemmatic Syllogism is, in fact, only a Hypothetical disguised, as the Disjunction is not resolved, and therefore its

Disjunct Members, whether two or more, may be regarded as a single Term.

If A is B, C is either D or E.

Modus Ponens.	Modus Tollens.
But A is B ;	C is neither D nor E ;
∴ C is either D or E.	∴ A is not B.

In practice, however, the Disjunction is usually resolved, in the *Modus tollens*, by two subordinate (abridged) Syllogisms, by which it is first separately proved that *C is not D*, and that *C is not E;* and then the Conclusion of the compound *Modus tollens* follows, that *A is not B*. Thus:—

If man cannot be virtuous, either he must be unable to know what is right, or unable to will what is right.
But he is not unable to know what is right, *for he is intelligent;* and he is not unable to will what is right, *for he is free.*
Therefore, he can be virtuous.

Hence, the Dilemma was called by the old logicians the *Cornutus* or *horned syllogism*, because, in the Sumption, the Disjunct Members are opposed like horns to the assertion of the adversary; with these, we throw it from one side to the other in the Subsumption, in order to toss it altogether away in the Conclusion.

Krug remarks: "The *Cornutus* and *Crocodilinus* of the ancients must not be confounded with the Dilemma which we are here speaking of. The former were *sophismata heterozeteseos*, *sophisms of counter-questioning;* the latter is a legitimate mode of reasoning." But it may be shown that the old *Cornutus* is a legitimate Dilemma in Form, and is of the type which we are now considering, the fallacy being in the Matter. The *Litigiosus*, for instance, which is one illustration of this old fallacy, may be thus resolved.

Protagoras agreed for a large sum to educate Euathlus as a lawyer, one half of the price to be paid down, and the other half on the day when the pupil should plead and gain his first cause. Some time elapsed, and Protagoras, thinking that his disciple intentionally delayed the completion of his contract, sued him in court for the remainder of the fee, and propounded this Dilemma.

If Euathlus is to be released from the payment of this sum, it must be either because the judgment of this court will be in his favor, or against him.

But if the judgment is in his favor, then he has pleaded and gained his first cause, and the money is due me under the contract.

If the judgment is against him, the money is due me under the decision of the court.

Thus, both the Disjunct Members of the Consequent being disproved by subordinate Syllogisms, the Conclusion of the compound *Modus tollens* follows, that Euathlus is not to be released from the payment.

The Dilemma is here correct in Form, but there is a Material Fallacy in the Major Premise, since the Disjunction is not complete. There is a third horn to it, as Protagoras had no right, under the contract, to invoke the judgment of the court at all, so that the judges ought to have dismissed the case without a hearing. *Before a judgment was rendered*, Protagoras had no ground of action.

Euathlus is said to have retorted upon his antagonist, by propounding a Dilemma in the same Form in which it had just been urged against him. "If the decision be favorable to me, I shall pay nothing under the sentence of the court; if adverse, I pay nothing in virtue of the compact, because I shall not have gained my first cause."

"In sifting a proposed Dilemma," says Krug, "we are to look closely to the three following particulars: —
1. Whether, in the Sumption, the Consequent is a legiti-

mate inference from the Antecedent; 2. Whether the Disjunction in the Consequent is complete; 3. Whether, in the Subsumption, the Disjunct Members are properly sublated. The following Dilemma is faulty in each of these respects.

"If Philosophy be of any value, it must procure for us power, riches, or honor.

"But it procures neither of them. Therefore, &c.

"Here, 1. the inference is wrong, as Philosophy may be worth something, though it does not secure any of these external advantages; 2. the Disjunction is incomplete, as there are other goods, besides the three here enumerated; 3. the Subsumption is false, as Philosophy has often been the means of procuring these very advantages."

In another form of the Dilemma, the Sumption is a Hypothetical Judgment with more than one Antecedent, and the Subsumption is a Disjunctive of which these several Antecedents are the Disjunct Members.

If A is B, C is D; and if E is F, C is D;
But either A is B or E is F;
∴ C is D.

Here, the several Antecedents have *the same* Consequent, and therefore the Conclusion is Categorical. If they had *different* Consequents, the Conclusion would be Disjunctive. Thus: —

If A is B, C is D; and if E is F, G is H;
But either A is B or E is F;
∴ Either C is D, or G is H.

In this case, the *Modus tollens* is also valid; if we disjunctively deny the Consequents, we may, in the Conclusion, disjunctively deny the Antecedents.

Either C is not D, or G is not H.
∴ Either A is not B, or E is not F.

In the preceding case, where the Antecedents had *the*

same Consequent, if we deny this one Consequent, we must deny the Antecedents taken collectively, and not disjunctively; then the Syllogism will be exclusively Hypothetical, as neither Judgment will be disjunctive. Thus: —

If A is B, C is D; and if E is F, C is D;
But C is not D;
∴ Then A is not B, *and* E is not F.

The nature of a Disjunction is, that any one of the Disjunct Members exists, or is posited, only by the non-existence, or sublation, of all the others. Hence, the particles, *either — or*, have a Disjunctive force; but the corresponding negative particles, *neither — nor*, have a Conjunctive force, as they denote the exclusion of *both* or *all*, and not merely the exclusion of *one* on condition of the inclusion of all the others. *A is either B or C*, means that *A is B* only on condition that *A is not C*. But *A is neither B nor C*, means that *A is not B and is not C*.

It has been remarked, that the *Modus tollens* of the Dilemma, in the form in which it was here first proposed, is nothing but a Negative induction.

If A is B, C is either D, E, or F;
But C is neither D; E, nor F;
Then A is not B.

This can be resolved into a Categorical Syllogism of Induction. Thus: —

C is not D, is not E, and is not F;
But these are all the possible cases of A being B;
Then A is not B.

3. Defective and Complex Syllogisms.

It has already been mentioned, that men do not usually speak or write complete Syllogisms; nay, it is almost only in treatises on Logic that we find Syllogisms completely enounced, or with all their parts expressed. The abridged form is preferred on all ordinary occasions, because at least one of the three Judgments is so obvious, both to the speaker and the hearer, that it would be a waste of time and words — a sin against brevity, and even against perspicuity — to propound it openly; for unnecessary words do not elucidate, but obscure, the Thought. We usually express a single process of reasoning by *two* Judgments, connected by an illative particle, *because*, *then*, *therefore*, &c. ; sometimes only by a conjunctive particle, *and*. The following are instances of reasoning thus enounced.

Aldebaran is a star; therefore, it shines by its own light.
No avaricious person can be happy; because he who is never free from fear cannot be happy.
A liar ought not to be believed; and this witness has been proved to be a liar.

Such sentences as these are called Enthymemes, because they are abridged statements of a process of reasoning, one of the three Judgments necessary to constitute the Syllogism being ἐν θυμῷ, *in the mind*, but not expressed. In the first case, the suppressed Judgment is the Major Premise, — *all stars shine by their own light;* in the second, it is the Minor Premise, — *an avaricious person is never free from fear,* the Conclusion also, as is frequently the case in Enthymemes, being placed first, instead of last; in the third case, the suppressed Judgment is the Conclusion, — *this witness ought not to be believed.*

An Enthymeme, then, is not a peculiar kind of Syllogism, but only an abridged expression of a Syllogism. Of course, the doctrine of Enthymemes properly belongs, not to Logic, but to Rhetoric, for it concerns expression, not thought; and it would never have been obtruded into the former science but for the authority of Aristotle, who employed the name, indeed, in a different and now disused meaning, signifying by it "a reasoning from signs and likelihoods."

Hitherto, we have treated only of the so-called *Monosyllogism*, — that is, of a Syllogism considered as one independent whole, without reference to the continuous *chain of reasoning*, of which, in an abridged form of expression, it usually constitutes a single link. Many truths — most of the theorems in Geometry, for instance — can be proved only by a Chain of Reasoning; — that is, by a connected series of Syllogisms, the several portions of which are dependent upon each other. A Conclusion of one may become a Premise of the next succeeding Syllogism, and is then called, in reference to its successor, a Prosyllogism; while the latter, in reference to the one which preceded it, is called an Episyllogism. A Prosyllogism, then, is *a Syllogism whose Conclusion is a Premise of that which follows;* and an Episyllogism is *one whose Premise is a Conclusion of that which precedes*. As, in a hierarchy of Concepts, the same class-notion is at once a Genus to the class below and a Species to the class above; so, in a Chain of Reasoning, the same Syllogism is at once a Prosyllogism and an Episyllogism in its opposite relations. Only that which contains the primary or highest reason can be exclusively called a Prosyllogism; only that which enounces the last or lowest consequent is exclusively an Episyllogism.

The Syllogism constituting a Chain may be either partly complete and partly abbreviated, or all equally abbreviated. In the former case, the complex Syllogism which results is called an Epicheirema; in the latter, it is called a Sorites.

A Syllogism is called an Epicheirema, when, to either or both of its two Premises, there is attached a reason for its support. The Premise with such a rider annexed is, in fact, a Prosyllogism abbreviated, — that is, an Enthymeme used to prove one of the branches of the main Syllogism. Thus: —

M is P; The flesh of ruminants is good for food;
S is M, because it is N; These animals are ruminants, because they have cloven hoofs;
∴ S is P. ∴ These animals are good for food.

Here, the Enthymeme, which is a rider of the Minor Premise, may be thus explicated into a complete Prosyllogism.

All animals which have cloven hoofs are ruminant;
These animals have cloven hoofs;
∴ These animals are ruminants.

It has already been said, that every Syllogism may be regarded as an application of the general and self-evident principle, that *a part of a part is a part of the whole*. If, in the application of this principle, we do not stop at the first or proximate whole, but, before drawing any expressed Conclusion, proceed step by step to remoter parts and more comprehensive wholes, and, in the Conclusion, finally place the smallest part under the largest whole, the complex abbreviated reasoning thus formed is called a Chain-Syllogism, or *Sorites*. It may be aptly symbolized by a series of concentric circles.

1. A is B;
2. B is C;
3. C is D;
4. D is E;
Therefore, A is E.

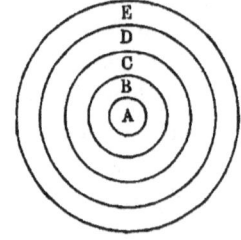

A Sorites of this sort may be described as *a series of Enthymemes with suppressed Conclusions, in which the Predicate of each is the Subject of the next, and the Conclusion of the whole is formed from the first Subject and last Predicate of the Premises*. The Conclusion being thus formed,

DEFECTIVE AND COMPLEX SYLLOGISMS. 223

it is evident that there must be as many Middle Terms
(i. e. Terms intervening between the first Subject and last
Predicate, that is, again, between the smallest part and the
greatest whole which the reasoning connects) as there are
Premises minus one; consequently, *every Sorites may be
explicated into as many distinct Syllogisms as there are
Premises minus one.* The first Judgment in the Sorites is
the only Minor Premise that is expressed; each of the
other Minor Premises is the Conclusion of the separate
Syllogism next preceding. Hence, each of the Judgments
in the Sorites except the first is the Major Premise of a
distinct Syllogism. The preceding Sorites, for instance,
may be thus explicated into three Syllogisms, the correctness of the explication being made very evident by a reference to the diagram.

I.	II.	III.
2. B is C,	3. C is D,	4. D is E,
1. A is B;	*A is C;*	*A is D;*
∴ *A is C.*	∴ *A is D.*	∴ *A is E.*

An invalid Mood occurring anywhere in the series
before the last Syllogism would not only be wrong itself,
but, as furnishing a Premise to its successors, would vitiate
all that follow. Hence, in a Sorites, out of all the Premises, only the one *first* expressed may be *Particular;* because, in the First Figure, to which all the separate Syllogisms belong, the Minor Premise may be Particular, but
not the Major; and all the Judgments in the Sorites,
except the first and the Conclusion, are Major Premises.
In the Sorites, also, only the *last* Judgment may be *Negative;* for if any other of its Judgments were Negative, the
Syllogism formed from the next following Judgment would
have a Negative Minor Premise, which the First Figure
does not admit. A Sorites in the *Modus tollens,* then, can
be stated only in one form; — from denying the last Con-

sequent of the last Antecedent, we go back to denying this same Consequent of the first Antecedent. Thus, if we say that *D is not E*, we must conclude that *A is not E*.

The three distinct Syllogisms already given are not all that may be formed from the given Sorites. Instead of beginning with the *first* Judgment, and thereby finally concluding that *A is E*, we may begin with the *second* Judgment, first concluding that *B is D*, and then that *B is E;* and again, beginning with the *third*, we may conclude that *C is E*. Hence, from a Sorites with four Premises, we may form in all six distinct Syllogisms. If there were five Premises, there would be ten resultant Syllogisms. "The formula," says Dr. Thomson, "for ascertaining the number of Conclusions is this: — Let the number of Premises $= n$; the number of terms $= n + 1$; then the number of Conclusions $= \dfrac{n(n-1)}{1.2}$."

Goclenius invented another form of the Sorites, to which his name has been attached; it is the same as the common form, except that the Premises are reversed. Referring to the diagram again, it is evident that, instead of beginning with the Terms of least Extension, represented by the innermost circles, we may begin with the more Extended Terms in the outer circles. Then the Subject of each Judgment becomes the Predicate of the next; while, in the common form, it is the Predicate of the former which becomes the Subject of the latter. The Goclenian Sorites is thus stated: —

D is E,
C is D,
B is C,
A is B ;
∴ A is E.

Here, Extension is more prominent, as we start with the wider Terms; hence, this form is better suited for deduction. In the common form, Intension predominates, as the narrower Terms come first; Induction naturally assumes this Form.

"A 'pretty quarrel' long existed amongst logicians," says Dr. Thomson, "which of the two was to be called *progressive* and which *regressive*. It was a mere strife about words. If we are discovering truth by the inductive method, the Aristotelian form is progressive; if we are teaching truth, or trying our laws upon new facts, we use deduction, and the Goclenian form is progressive. In an apt but familiar figure, — if I am on the ground floor, and wish to fetch something that is above, my going up stairs is my progress towards my object, and my coming down is a regression; if the positions of myself and the thing are reversed, going down would be progress, and returning up, regress. The inductive truth-seeker is on the ground-floor of facts, and goes up to seek a law; the deductive teacher is on a higher story, and carries his law down with him to the facts.

"This will be clearer from a pair of examples.

Goclenian or descending Sorites.
Sentient beings seek happiness;
All finite beings are sentient;
All men are finite beings;
Caius is a man;

Therefore Caius seeks happiness.

Aristotelian or ascending Sorites.
Caius is a man;
All men are finite beings;
All finite beings are sentient;
All sentient beings seek happiness;

Therefore Caius seeks happiness."

By way of recapitulation, the chief principles and rules of the Aristotelic doctrine of Syllogism are brought together in the following Conspectus.

CONSPECTUS OF THE ARISTOTELIC

MEDIATE INFERENCE OR SYLLOGISM	SYLLOGISMS
is that act of Thought whereby the relation of the two Terms of a possible Judgment to each other is ascertained by comparing each of them separately with a Third Term.	CATEGORICAL, in which each of the three Judgments can be expressed under one or the other of these two Formulas:— *A* is *B* ; *A* is not *B*.

GENERAL CANON	This Canon is explicated
of Categorical Syllogisms. In so far as two Notions, (Concepts or Individuals,) either both agree, or, one agreeing, the other does not agree, with a common Third Notion, in so far these Notions do, or do not, agree with each other.	I. A Syllogism must contain three Terms, and no more. II. A Syllogism must contain three Judgments, and no more.

THE FIGURE	Let S = Subject of the
of a Syllogism is determined by the relative position of the Middle Term in the two Premises.	Figure I. M P ; S M ; ∴ S P.

THE MOOD	VALID
of a Syllogism is the value of its three Judgments in respect to their Quantity and Quality, as indicated in each case by the four Judgments, A, E, I, and O.	Fig. I. A A A ; *Barbara.* E A E ; *Celarent.* A I I ; *Darii.* E I O ; *Ferio.*

REDUCTION	
of the valid Moods of the three lower Figures to those of the First Figure may be accomplished by performing the processes indicated by the following letters in the names of those Moods.	B = Reduce the Mood to *Barbara.* C = " " *Celarent.* D = " " *Darii.* F = " " *Ferio.*

GENERAL CANON	This Canon produces, from
of Hypothetical Syllogisms. To affirm the Reason or the Condition is to affirm the Consequent; and to deny the Consequent is also to deny the Reason.	*Major Premise,* *Modus Ponens.* A is B ; ∴ C is D.

GENERAL CANON	This Canon produces, from
of Disjunctive Syllogisms. Of two Contradictories, one must be true and the other must be false.	*Major Premise,* *Modus ponendo tollens.* 1. A is B; ∴ A is not C. 2. A is C ; ∴ A is not B.

DOCTRINE OF SYLLOGISM. 227

ARE EITHER

OR CONDITIONAL,

in which the Major Premise, and only the Major Premise, is a Conditional Judgment; and these are subdivided into

Hypothetical;	Disjunctive;	Dilemmatic or Hypothetical Disjunctive.
Major Premise,	Major Premise,	Major Premise,
If A is B, C is D.	A is either B or C.	If A is B, C is either D or E.

into these six General Rules.

III.	IV.	V.	VI.
The Middle Term must be distributed in at least one of the Premises.	One Premise at least must be Affirmative.	If either Premise is Negative, the Conclusion must be Negative.	Neither Term must be distributed in the Conclusion, if it was not distributed in the Premise.

Conclusion; P = Predicate of the Conclusion; M = Middle Term. Then,

Figure II. P M;	Figure III. M P;	Figure IV. P M;
S M;	M S;	M S;
∴ S P.	∴ S P.	∴ S P.

MOODS.

Fig. II.	Fig. III.	Fig. IV.
E A E; *Cesare.*	A A I; *Darapti.*	A A I; *Bramantip.*
A E E; *Camestres.*	I A I; *Disamis.*	A E E; *Camenes.*
E I O; *Festino.*	A I I; *Datisi.*	I A I; *Dimaris.*
A O O; *Baroko (Fakoro).*	E A O; *Felapton.*	E A O; *Fesapo.*
All Negative Conclusions.	O A O; *Bokardo (Dokamok).*	E I O; *Fresison.*
	E I O. *Ferison.*	
	All Particular Conclusions.	

m = Transpose the Premises.
s = Convert simply.
p = Convert *per accidens.*
k = Reduce *per impossibile* for Baroko & Bokardo;
Convert by Contraposition for Fakoro & Dokamok.

Barbara, Celarent, Darii, Ferioque, prioris;
Cesare, Camestres, Festino, Baroko, secundæ;
Tertia Darapti, Disamis, Datisi, Felapton,
Bokardo, Ferison habet; Quarta insuper addit
Bramantip, Camenes, Dimaris, Fesapo, Fresison.

the same Premise, two valid Moods.

If A is B, C is D.
Modus Tollens.
C is not D;
∴ A is not B.

the same Premise, two valid Moods, each having two forms.

A is either B or C.
Modus tollendo ponens.
 1. A is not B;
 ∴ A is C.
 2. A is not C;
 ∴ A is B.

CHAPTER VIII.

THE HAMILTONIAN DOCTRINE OF SYLLOGISMS.

SIR William Hamilton's innovations in the doctrine of Syllogisms, which had been generally received up to this time, are not limited to such as are the direct consequences of his theory of the thorough-going quantification of the Predicate. On several minor points, also, he has considerably modified the Aristotelic doctrine. These changes, it is true, were probably suggested by his system of quantifying the Predicate; but they are not so closely connected with it as to prevent them from being received, even by those logicians who, wholly or in part, reject that system. All of them deserve consideration, as they involve a discussion of some incidental questions of much interest, affecting the whole theory of Logic.

As to the order of enouncement, the old doctrine was, that the Premises, as their name imports, should precede the Conclusion. Hamilton observes that the reverse order is more natural, that it more faithfully represents the progress of the mind in the investigation or discovery of truth, and that it effectually relieves the Syllogism from the imputation, which has been thrown upon it for more than three centuries, of being founded upon a mere *petitio principii*, or a begging of the question. "Mentally one," he says, "the Categorical Syllogism, according to its order of enouncement, is either *Analytic*, if what is inappropriately styled the 'Conclusion' be expressed first, and what are inappropriately styled the 'Premises' be then stated as its *reasons;* or *Synthetic,* if the Premises precede and, as it were, effectuate the Conclusion." In the Analytic order, the "Conclusion" would be more properly called the *Quæsitum,* and the "Premises" should be denominated the *Proofs.*

Now, the Analytic order, it is argued, is the more natural, because the Problem or Question, which it is the purpose of the Syllogism to solve or answer, and which is therefore the leading thought in the mind, is propounded first. When we are in doubt whether A is, or is not, B, it is surely more natural to argue, A *is* B, because A *is* C, and *all* C *is* B, than to reason in the old order, placing the solution of the Problem *last.* "In point of fact, the Analytic Syllogism is not only the more natural, it is even *presupposed* by the Synthetic." As already stated, the Syllogistic process in the mind is really one and undivided, consisting only in the *inference* of the Conclusion from the Premises. But in order to state this single process in words, we must analyze it, and therefore the Conclusion, which is the compound result, ought to be stated first, so as to admit of analysis. It may be stated generally, that a process of investigation or research, looking towards truth not yet discovered, is always Analytic. The most that can be said for the Synthetic method is, that it may be successfully used for teaching, or proving the truth that is already known. To adopt an old illustration, in order to find out for ourselves how a clock is made and how it does its work, we must take it to pieces; having done this, the best way to teach another person how to make a clock is to take those pieces and put them together again.

The common objection to the validity of the Syllogistic process is, that the Conclusion is virtually contained in the Premises, so that we have to assume it to be true in the very propositions by which we attempt to prove it. This objection is thus forcibly stated by Mr. Mill. "When we say, —

All men are mortal;
Socrates is a man;
Therefore, Socrates is mortal;
it is unanswerably urged by the adversaries of the Syllogistic theory, that the proposition, 'Socrates is mortal,' is presupposed in the more general assumption, 'All men are mortal'; that we cannot be assured of the mortality of all men, unless we were previously certain of the mortality of every individual man; that if it be still doubtful whether Socrates, or any other individual you choose to name, be mortal or not, the same degree of uncertainty must hang over the assertion, 'All men are mortal'; that the general principle, instead of being given as evidence of the particular case, cannot itself be taken for true without exception, until every shadow of doubt which could affect any case comprised with it is dispelled by evidence *aliunde;* and then, what remains for the Syllogism to prove? that, in short, no reasoning from generals to particulars can, as such, prove anything: since, from a general principle, you cannot infer any particulars but those which the principle itself assumes as foreknown."

But if the Syllogism be stated in the Analytic form, it is obvious that this objection is inapplicable. When we argue, —
Socrates is mortal,
Because Socrates is a man,
And all men are mortal, —
we do not assume the point which ought to be proved, but we prove that it is right to predicate *mortality* of Socrates, by showing that Socrates belongs to the class *man*, all the members of which are universally admitted to be *mortal*. We appeal to the admitted Universal truth only *after* we have established, what is here the main point of the argument, the applicability of the truth to this case, — the fact that Socrates *is a man*. Mr. Mill mistakes the compara-

tive importance of the two Premises; in Analytic reasoning, — in drawing an inference for the purpose of investigation or discovery, — the proof turns chiefly upon the Subsumption; and Aristotle therefore correctly places this Premise first. Thus, if I am in doubt with respect to a new substance which I have found, whether it be fusible or not, the doubt may be resolved by ascertaining that *this substance is a metal.* Only after this fact is ascertained, and then only in order to complete the thought, or to silence cavil, I refer to the admitted truth that *all metals are fusible.* Men usually reason in this manner, as is shown by the frequent recurrence of such Enthymemes as these: *This iron is not malleable, for it is cast-iron; The man is dishonest, for he has taken what is not his own; this line is equal to that, for they are both radii of the same circle,* &c. There is certainly a mental reference in such cases to a Major Premise, — to the well-known truths, that *No cast-iron is malleable, All radii of the same circle are equal,* &c. But precisely because such Premises are well known and obvious, though thought, they are not usually expressed.

The bald truisms which are usually taken as examples of the Syllogistic process are unfortunately chosen, as they render more plausible the imputation that this process itself is futile and needless. Any kind of reasoning appears puerile, when it is applied only to establish a puerile Conclusion. Nobody wishes any proof of the fact that Socrates was mortal. Adopt any supposition which will make it appear that there was a real doubt in the case, and that the point to be determined was one of some importance, and the Syllogism employed loses its frivolous aspect, and seems grave and pertinent. Suppose that the impulsive Athenians of his day had made the same mistake in relation to Socrates, that those of a later time committed in regard to Paul and Barnabas, and had begun to offer sacrifices to him as an immortal being; it would have been dignified and conclusive on his part to argue with them, as the Apostle did, by saying, "*We are men* of like passions with you," and worship is due only unto God. The first question for the inquirer or disputant is, not whether this case has already been decided, and therefore included under this General Rule, which is supposed to be already found; but under what Class-notion can this case be put, which shall afford a General Rule that will be applicable for the solution of the doubt. The difficulty is, how to find the right Rule, and not, as Mr. Mill supposes, how to interpret it when found. The astronomer proceeds in this manner, when he seeks to know whether a comet, which has just appeared in the heavens, will return at a future period, or disappear forever. By determining three or more points in its path, he ascertains either that its orbit is an ellipse or an hyperbola; this is the Subsumption, and when found, the question is really answered, for the application of the Sumption — that the ellipse is a curve which returns into itself, while the hyperbola does not — is so obvious, that it is unnecessary, except for a child, to be reminded of it. But though not expressed, the thought without it is certainly incomplete, and the main question is not answered.

Mr. Mill's doctrine is, that "we much oftener conclude from particulars to particulars directly, than through the intermediate agency of any general proposition." For example, "it is not only the village matron, who, when called to a consultation upon the case of a neighbor's child, pronounces on the evil and its remedy simply on the recollection and authority of what she accounts the similar case of her Lucy."

We have already observed (page 9) that a Concept may be derived from *one* object, as well as from many similar ones; that is, it may not represent an actual, but only a possible, class or plurality of things. The hasty and sweeping inductions of the vulgar are of this character; they are often generalizations from a single instance. The medicine which they have once successfully tried is believed by them to be a panacea. The unhesitating confidence with which the village matron pronounces, not merely on *one* case of measles or whooping-cough in her neighbor's family, but on every one that occurs in the village, proves that she has generalized her Lucy's case.

All general truths are not learned by induction from particulars. They are sometimes first obtained by Intuition, as in the case of axioms and other necessary truths, or by reasoning from the causes or conditions on which they depend; and then, individual truths are proved by deduction from these generals. Most of the truths of pure mathematics are thus acquired. To borrow an example from Hobbes, — because we know how a circle is generated, namely, by the circumduction of a body one end of which is fixed, we know that all radii of the same circle are equal. Most of the beautiful *applications* of algebraic theorems to the solution of arithmetical and geometrical problems were first ascertained to be possible long after the general theorems themselves were discovered. Such metaphysical principles as these, *Every event must have a cause, All attributes presuppose a substance, Space is infinite and indestructible*, were not first made known to us by induction, and cannot be proved by that method. Yet the objection to the Syllogistic process, that the Major Premise could not be posited if the truth of the Conclusion were not already known, has neither force nor relevancy, if it be not proved'that all general truths are obtained by induction, and that the induction was so perfect that it must have consciously included the very case which we are now seeking to deduce from the general rule.

Hamilton's next innovation in the theory of Logic — and it is one which was propounded by him at an earlier day than his doctrine of the quantification of the Predicate — was to draw attention to the fact, that reasoning does not proceed, as had formerly been taught, solely in the Quantity of Extension, but also in the Quantity of Intension, the relations of whole and part, on which he considers that the whole process depends, being reversed in these opposite Quantities. It has already been mentioned, that, in one sense, the Predicate of every Judgment includes the Subject, and therefore, as the greater or more Extensive Term, it was called the Major, and the Subject was designated as the Minor Term. As thus construed, the Judgment, *Man is an animal*, means that the class *Man* is included under, or forms a part of, the class *animal*. But in another sense, — that is, in the Quantity of Intension, — the Subject includes the Predicate, and the relations of whole and part are reversed. Interpreted Intensively, this Judgment signifies that all the attributes of *animal* are contained in or among — form a part of — the attributes of *man*. The Subject is now the Major Term, and the Predicate is the Minor; and the rule being still adhered to, that the Major Premise must be stated first, the order of the Premises is reversed.

Hamilton gives the following example of reasoning in Extension.

      All responsible agents are free agents;
      But man is a responsible agent;
      Therefore, man is a free agent.

The Premises are stated in this order on the supposition that "free agents," as the more Extensive class, is the whole or the Major Term, that "man," having the least Extension, is the smallest part or the Minor Term, and that the Middle Term, "responsible agent," as intermediate between the two, is made the Subject of the former, as contained under it, and the Predicate of the latter, which is only a part of it. In other words, *man* is a part of that

Term *responsible agent*, which is itself a part of the Term *free agent;* and therefore, as a part of a part is a part of the whole, *man is a free agent.*

Now reverse the Premises.

> Man is a responsible agent;
> But a responsible agent is a free agent;
> Therefore, man is a free agent.

Here, the notion *free agent*, which was the greatest whole, becomes the smallest part; and the notion *man*, which was the smallest part, becomes the greatest whole. " The notion *responsible agent* remains the Middle quantity or notion in both, but its relation to the two notions is reversed; what was formerly its part being now its whole, and what was formerly its whole being now its part."

Hence, in the First Figure (but not, as we shall see, in the two other Figures), the order in which the two Premises are placed always indicates the Quantity in which we are reasoning. If the Major Premise contains the Subject of the Conclusion, then this Subject is the Major Term, and the reasoning is in Intension. But if the Predicate of the Conclusion appears in the first Premise, then this Predicate is the Major quantity, and the reasoning is in Extension.

But as this indication is a faint one, and may mislead in the case of the Second or the Third Figure, it is easy to change the phraseology of the Judgments, so as to enounce explicitly whether the reasoning concerns the Intensive, metaphysical, whole (the whole of the Marks connoted), or the Extensive, logical, whole (the whole of the Individuals and Species denoted). Thus, for the latter, we may say, —

> All responsible agents are included in the class of free agents;
> But man is a responsible agent;
> Therefore, man is included in the class of free agents.

And the reasoning of Intension may be thus stated: —

The notion or Concept, man, includes the notion of responsibility;
But the notion of responsibility includes that of free agency;
Therefore, the notion, man, includes the notion of free-agency.

It is the more remarkable that nearly all the logicians since Aristotle should have contemplated exclusively reasoning in Extension, as Aristotle himself seems to have regarded reasoning in Intension as coextensive with the former, even if not paramount to it. Hamilton has only restored the doctrine of the great founder of Logic, which had been strangely overlooked by nearly the whole tribe of his commentators and followers. As already remarked, the *being in a Subject* and the *being predicated of a Subject* are used by Aristotle as synonymous phrases. " A is predicated of all B," means *All B is A;* "*A is in* (or *inheres in,* ὑπάρχειν) *all B*," also means *All B is A.* The meaning evidently is, that, in the Quantity of Intension, the Predicate is in the Subject because it constitutes a part, and only a part, of the Intension of the Subject. *Animal* is in *man,* because *man* has all the attributes or Marks of *animal,* and other attributes also.

But the relation of *whole* and *part* is not precisely the same thing in the one Quantity as in the other. In Extension, the *whole* is the Genus, and the *parts* are the subordinate Species; and the first Rule for the division is, that the parts, or the co-ordinate Species, must exclude each other. But in Intension, the *parts* are not Species, but attributes or Marks; and these do not exclude each other. Each part or attribute here interpenetrates, so to speak, and *informs*, the whole. *Black* is a part of *negro* in the sense of being only one of his attributes, since he has many others, such as being *long-heeled, prognathous,* &c.; but it is a part which colors the whole, for the negro is *black all over.* But if we consider the Extension, if the Genus *man* is subdivided into the co-ordinate Species *white man* and *black man*, these parts exclude each other; no one man can belong at the same time to both Species, — can be both white and black.

Hence the maxim, that *a part of a part is also a part of the whole,* is not a universal maxim of all reasoning; as it refers only to co-exclusive parts, it is applicable only to reasoning in Extension. The corresponding maxim for reasoning in Intension is, that *a Mark of a Mark is also a Mark of the thing itself,* — of the *whole* thing; *nota notæ est nota rei ipsius. Free agency,* which is a Mark of *responsibility,* is also a Mark of *man,* because *responsibility* is a Mark of the whole *man.* On the other hand, reasoning Extensively, we say, *men* are a part or class of *responsible agents,* and are, therefore, also a part of *free agents,* because *responsible agents* are a part of *free agents.*

By not attending to this distinction, Hamilton was betrayed on one occasion into propounding as a valid syllogism one, which, if the language be construed literally, is illogical; and into censuring as illogical another, which, as stated, is certainly irrecusable. It is true that the error consisted entirely in the use of language. As he understood them, his approbation of the one and his censure of the other are correct; but from his use of language, no other person would so understand them. In his Lectures on Logic, while illustrating the Special Rule of an Intensive Syllogism (page 223, Am. ed.), that the Sumption must be Affirmative, and the Subsumption Universal, he states the following as a valid Syllogism : —

" S comprehends M ;
  M does not comprehend P ;
  Therefore S does not comprehend P."

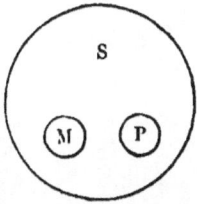

If the language be interpreted literally, the Conclusion here is illogical; for it is evident, from the diagram which we have annexed, that, though *S comprehends M*, and *M excludes P*, it may yet be true that *S comprehends P*.

On the same page, he censures the following as a *non sequitur*, though the diagram here annexed demonstrates it to be valid.

S does not comprehend M;
But M comprehends P;
Therefore S does not comprehend P.

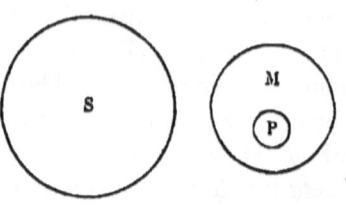

But instead of the proposition "S comprehends M," substitute the meaning which was intended, that *S has M for one of its Marks* or attributes, and make the corresponding change throughout, and Hamilton's verdict upon the two Syllogisms becomes correct. M, though only *one* of the attributes of S, affects or colors *the whole* of S; therefore, P, which is *not* an attribute of M, — does not affect any part of M, — is not an attribute of S; — S does not include P among its attributes. The Syllogism which is approved corresponds, in Form, to the following, which is evidently valid.

A negro has a black skin;
But a black skin is not an invariable sign of a brute intellect;
Therefore, a negro is not necessarily brutish in intellect.

And the Syllogism which is rejected is the following: —
    A negro is not white;
    But whites are civilized;
    Therefore, a negro is not civilized.

In fact, the mode of symbolizing Syllogisms by circles, as

well as the maxim, *a part of a part is also a part of the whole*, is inapplicable to the Intensive Syllogism; for here the "parts" are Marks or attributes; and these are not co-exclusive. They are not *partes extra partes*.

It is with some reason, then, that Mr. DeMorgan objects to considering the Intension of a Concept as a *quantity*. In the vague sense of being susceptible of *more* and *less*, it is a quantity; but so far as it is incapable of exact *measurement*, it is not a quantity. "As to extent," he says, "200 instances bear a definite ratio to 100, which we can use, because our instances are *homogeneous*. But different qualities or descriptions can never be numerically summed as attributes to any purpose arising out of their number. Does the idea of *rational animal*, two descriptive terms, suggest any useful idea of *duplication*, when compared with that of *animal* alone? When we say that a chair and a table are more furniture than a chair, which is true, we never can cumulate them to any purpose, except by extracting some homogeneous idea, as of bulk, price, weight, &c. To give equal quantitative weight to attributes, as attributes, seems to me absurd; to use them numerically otherwise, is at present impossible." Perhaps this is only saying that a logician's idea of *quantity* is not the same as a mathematician's; to the latter, it is always numerically definite, or may be made so; to the former, it is never so. Perhaps, if Mr. DeMorgan had kept this fact steadily in view, a good many of his attempted innovations in Logic might have appeared, even to him, irrelevant.

Hamilton has made no specific innovation in the doctrine of the Figures, but his speculations upon the subject have thrown a flood of light not only upon the essential nature of these varieties of the Syllogism, but upon the theories of former logicians in respect to them. To Aristotle, on account of his peculiar method of stating a Judgment, — with reference to the Intension instead of the Extension of its Terms, that is, placing the Predicate first and the Subject last, — the Middle Term was intermediate between the two others, not only in nature, but in position. Thus, the following are only two different expressions of the same Syllogism.

Aristotle's form.

P inheres in (is predicated of) all M ;
M inheres in all S ;
∴ P inheres in all S.

Later or common form.

All M are P ;
All S are M ;
∴ All S are P.

Here, in Aristotle's form, P, one of the Extremes, appears first, and S, the other Extreme, comes last; M, the Middle Term, in both of its expressions, being intermediate, or coming between them. In the later form, it is not so. As a consequence of this mode of statement, in his definition of the Second Figure, Aristotle says that the Middle Term is, by its position, the *first;* to us, on the contrary, it is the last. In fact, in his reduction of the Second and Third Figures to the First, Aristotle seems to have had in view, not only the establishment of the *dictum de omni et nullo* as the universal principle of all Syllogistic reasoning, but the restoration of the Middle Term to its proper intermediate position. He was evidently thinking most of reasoning in Intension, and his followers of what is more frequent in use, though not more natural, — reasoning in Extension. In the later form, if the Minor Premise is stated first, the Middle Term becomes intermediate in position, as in the Aristotelic formula.

In this exposition of Aristotle's mode of enouncement, as contrasted with that of the later logicians, Hamilton has merely followed Barthélemy St. Hilaire ; in what follows, he is more original.

" When logicians," he says, " came to enounce propositions and Syllogisms in common language, the Subject being usually first, they had one or other of two difficulties to encounter, and submit they must to either; for they must either displace the Middle Term from its intermediate position in the First Figure, to say nothing of reversing its order in the Second and Third; or, if they kept it in an intermediate position in the First Figure (in the Second and Third, the Aristotelic order could not be kept), it behooved them to enounce the Minor Premise first." Most of the older logicians adopted the latter alternative, stating the Minor Premise first in all the Figures; and this seems the more natural order, if the Syllogism is used for the purpose of investigation and discovery. At a later period, when instruction, disputation, and proof came to be the chief purposes for which Syllogisms were formally enounced, the former alternative was adopted, and the Middle Term lost its proper intermediate position, the Major Premise being placed first in all the Figures.

In the First Figure, according to any mode of enouncement, the Middle Term must be the Subject of one of the Extremes (the two Terms of the Conclusion), and the Predicate of the other. Hence, in this Figure, there is a determinate Major and Minor Premise for reasoning in either Quantity, and but one direct or proximate Conclusion. *If, in the Major Premise, the Middle Term is Predicate to the Subject of the Conclusion, then, in each of the three Judgments, the Subject includes the Predicate, and the reasoning is in the Quantity of Intension. If, on the contrary, in the Major Premise, the Middle Term is Subject to the Predicate of the Conclusion, then, in each of the three Judgments, the Predicate includes the Subject, and the reasoning is in the Quantity of Extension.* The relative position of the two Premises is really unimportant as respects the nature of the reasoning; this depends upon the nature of the Middle Term, as including, or included under, the Subject of the Conclusion. But following the established order of logical Quantity, that the greater should be placed first, the Middle Term as Subject, and the Predicate of the Conclusion as Predicate, should be the first or Major Premise for reasoning in Extension; and the Middle Term as Predicate, with the Subject of the Conclusion as Subject, should be the first or Major Premise in Intension. Thus: —

<table>
<tr><td>In Extension.</td><td>In Intension.</td></tr>
<tr><td>M is P;</td><td>S is M;</td></tr>
<tr><td>S is M;</td><td>M is P;</td></tr>
<tr><td>∴ S is [included under] P.</td><td>∴ S is [includes] P.</td></tr>
</table>

Here, the relation of the Terms to each other in the Premises determines their relation to each other in the Conclusion. If, in the Premises, M is included under P, and S included under M, then, in the Conclusion, S must be included under P. But if, in the Premises, S includes M, and M includes P, then, in the Conclusion, S must include P. Hence, in the First Figure, there can be but one direct Conclusion.

In the two other Figures, it is not so. The Middle Term is not Subject of one and Predicate of the other Extreme, but is either, as in the Second Figure, Predicate of both, or, as in the Third, Subject of both. Consequently, in each of these Figures, the Middle Term either includes both the Extremes, or is included under both. As there is nothing, then, to determine the relative Quantity of the two Extremes to each other, either may be considered as Major in the Conclusion; — we may conclude either that *S is P*, or that *P is S*.

Though the First Figure has but one direct or immediate Conclusion, we may, by the medium of Conversion, obtain from it another Conclusion, which is then properly called *indirect* or *mediate*. Thus, in the formulas just given, having concluded directly that *All S is P*, we may then conclude indirectly, or mediately, that *Some P is S*. But in the other Figures, there are two indifferent Conclusions, neither of which is more direct or immediate than the others. If *A is B* and *C is B*, we may conclude, with equal propriety and directness, either that *A is C*, or *C is A;* for there is nothing in the Premises to indicate whether A includes, or is included under, C. And in like manner in the Third Figure; if *B is A* and *B is C*, the two Conclusions, *A is C* and *C is A*, are equally competent and equally immediate. Of course, what has been called the *Fourth* Figure is merely the First, with its indirect Conclusion enounced as if it were direct or immediate; it is a hybrid reasoning, with its two Premises in one Quantity, and its Conclusion in the other. Hence the Fourth Figure is properly abolished.

In fact, all difference of Figure is unessential, — a mere accident of form. As it is demonstrated in the Hamiltonian analysis, that a Judgment is a mere equation of its two Terms, it makes no difference which is stated first, — which is Subject or which is Predicate; $A = B$ and $B = A$ are the same equation. Quantify the Predicate throughout, and this becomes evident. As all Conversion is then reduced to *Simple* Conversion, we have only to convert simply (retaining the subordination of the Terms) the Major Premise of the First Figure in Extension, in order to produce the Second Figure; convert its Minor Premise, and we have the Third. In Intension, this is merely reversed; convert the Minor for the Second, and the Major for the Third.

To make the Syllogistic process depend upon the mere *position*, either of the two Terms as Subject or Predicate, or of the two Premises as enounced first or second, or of the Conclusion as expressed first or last, is to reduce Reasoning to a mere accident of expression, and cause it to vary with the genius of different languages, or even with the mental peculiarities of individuals. Reasoning is a process of Thought, not of language. It depends solely upon the relations of inclusion and exclusion, of subordination and superordination, of Intension and Extension, existing between two Concepts and a Third; and it must be regulated by universal laws, irrespective of differences of language and peculiarities of mental habit. The order of enouncement is a convenient, though conventional, mode of indicating these relations to other persons, and even a safeguard against confusion and error in the successive elaboration of them in our own minds. But the actual inference, the mental process as such, is entirely independent of this order.

To show further the unessential character of variation by Figure, Hamilton pointed out the manner of abolishing the distinction of Subject and Predicate, and thereby reducing all Mediate Inference to what he calls the Unfigured Syllogism. Any Syllogisms whatever may find adequate, though awkward, expression under this form. The two following instances will suffice.

Fig. I. *Darii*, reduced to an *Unfigured Syllogism.*

All patriots are brave;

Some persecuted men *are patriots;*

∴ Some persecuted men are brave.

All patriots and some brave men are equal;

Some persecuted and *some patriots* are equal;

∴ Some persecuted and some brave men are equal.

Fig. II. *Camestres.*

All animals *are sentient;*

Nothing unorganized is *sentient;*

∴ Nothing unorganized is animal.

All animals and *some sentient things are equal;*

Any unorganized and *any sentient* are not equal;

∴ Any unorganized and any animal are not equal.

In this Unfigured Syllogism, as Hamilton remarks, "the

dependency of Extension and Intension does not subsist, and accordingly the order of the Premises is wholly arbitrary. This form has been overlooked by the logicians, though equally worthy of development as any other; in fact, it affords a key to the whole mystery of Syllogism. And what is curious, the Canon by which this Syllogism is regulated (what may be called that of logical Analogy or Proportion) has, for above five centuries, been commonly stated as the one principle of reasoning, whilst the form of reasoning itself, to which it properly applies, has never been generalized. This Canon, which has been often erroneously, and never adequately enounced, in rules four, three, two, or one, is as follows: — *In as far as two notions (notions proper or individuals) either both agree, or one agreeing the other does not, with a common third notion; in so far these notions do or do not agree with each other.* This Canon thus excludes, — 1. an undistributed Middle Term, as then no *common* notion; — 2. two negative Premises, as then no agreement of *either* of the other notions therewith."

A convenient, though somewhat mechanical, rule for drawing the correct Conclusion from any pair of Premises is the following, which was first stated by Ploucquet, and after him by Mr. De Morgan. *Erase the symbols of the Middle Term, the remaining symbols show the inference. Deleatur in præmissis medius; id quod restat indicat conclusionem.* Thus, in the two Syllogisms just given and reduced to the Unfigured form, strike out from the Premises, what I have italicized, all that relates to the Middle Term, and what remains of the Premises is the Conclusion. But it should be mentioned that this Rule, though valid for all the Aristotelic moods, does not hold good, as we shall see, for all the moods recognized under the Hamiltonian system.

Perhaps the most striking, and certainly the most convenient, improvement which Sir William Hamilton has made upon the labors of former logicians, is his system of notation, — a masterpiece of ingenuity in symbolization as respects perspicuity, completeness, and simplicity. It is valid for any system, and it manifests, at once, nearly all the alterations and improvements which he has made in the Aristotelic doctrine. It shows at a glance the equivalent Syllogisms in the different Figures, the convertible Syllogisms in the same Figure, and points out the two meanings which can be given to every Syllogism as interpreted according to its Extension or its Intension, in reference to the logical or the metaphysical whole. Even as a mnemonic contrivance, it is second in ingenuity and usefulness only to the famous quatrain of hexameters, which contains the whole doctrine of the Reduction of the Moods of the lower Figures to the first Figure.

The purpose of any system of notation is to manifest, by the differences and relations of geometrical quantities (lines or figures), the differences and relations of logical forms.

A Proposition or Judgment is here indicated by a straight horizontal line, its two Terms or Extremes being placed at the extremities of that line, and represented, as usual, by letters.

If, as in the Unfigured Syllogism, there is no distinction of Subject and Predicate, this line is made of equal thickness throughout. But if this distinction is introduced, then, as it is possible to read the Judgment in two ways, according to the Extension or the Intension of its Terms, (the Subject, in the latter case, including the Predicate, and in the former, being included under it,) the line is made wedge-shaped. Its broad end then represents the Subject of Extension or Breadth, and the thin end, that of Intension or Depth. A line gradually diminishing or increasing from end to end aptly indicates the relation between two Quantities which are always co-existent, and in inverse ratio to each other. As the employment of letters following upon each other in the same alphabet might suggest that one was invariably subordinated to the other, instead of being its subordinate in one Quantity and its superordinate in the other, Hamilton uses for the Extremes the Latin C and Greek Γ, each being the third letter in its own alphabet; as usual, M stands for the Middle Term. Thus: —

is read, C —— Γ
 C and Γ are equal.

C ▭— Γ

may be read in two ways; Extensively, *C is included under* Γ; Intensively, Γ *is included in C:* — or, in the usual manner, *C is* Γ, and Γ *is C*, merely remembering, without saying so, that Extension is signified in the former case, and Intension in the latter.

Negation is indicated by a perpendicular stroke drawn through the line, thus: ▬—|—. The line without this stroke may be regarded as the Affirmative Copula; with the stroke, as the Negative Copula. A colon (:) annexed to a Term shows that it is distributed, or taken universally; a comma (,) so annexed, that it is undistributed or Particular. When a Middle Term has a colon on the right, and a comma on the left, it is understood that it is distributed when coupled in a Judgment with the Term on the right, and undistributed when coupled with the other.

A line drawn beneath or above three Terms indicates the Conclusion (or the Copula of the Conclusion) deduced from the two Premises which those Terms constitute. In the Second and Third Figures, since there may be two equally direct or immediate Conclusions, they are represented by two such lines, the one above, and the other below the Premises. Thus: —

C, ▬—, M: ▬—, Γ This is a Syllogism in the Second Figure, which may be read in either of the following ways.

Extensively.	Intensively.
Some C is some M;	All M is some Γ;
Some Γ is all M;	Some M is some C;
∴ Some Γ is some C; *or*	∴ Some C is some Γ; *or*
∴ Some C is some Γ.	∴ Some Γ is some C.

C,———, M: —+— : Γ This is a Negative Syllogism in the First Figure, which may be read in either of the following ways; but in either way, it has only one *direct* or *immediate* Conclusion, though a Second Conclusion may be obtained from it *indirectly*, by converting simply the proper or direct Conclusion.

Extensively.	Intensively.
Some M is some C;	No M is any Γ;
No Γ is any M;	Some C is some M;
No Γ is some C; *or*,	Some C is not any Γ; *or*,
indirectly,	*indirectly*,
Some C is not any Γ.	Not any Γ is some C.

The following diagram presents the whole Hamiltonian doctrine of Figure, together with the distinction between the Analytic and the Synthetic order of enouncement. After the explanations which have been given, it will be easily understood.

As a Judgment has been designated by a line, a Syllogism, which is a union of three Judgments, is appropriately typified by a triangle, a union of three lines, of which the base represents the Conclusion, and the other two lines, the Premises. As the direction of the arrows indicates, we may proceed either in the usual or Synthetic order, from the Premises to the Conclusion, or in the reverse order, which is Analytic, from the Conclusion to the Premises. As there is no valid reason for always placing the Major Premise first in order, the diagram shows that either Premise may have precedence in this respect, so that what has been called the Fourth Figure is here identified with the Indirect Moods of the First.

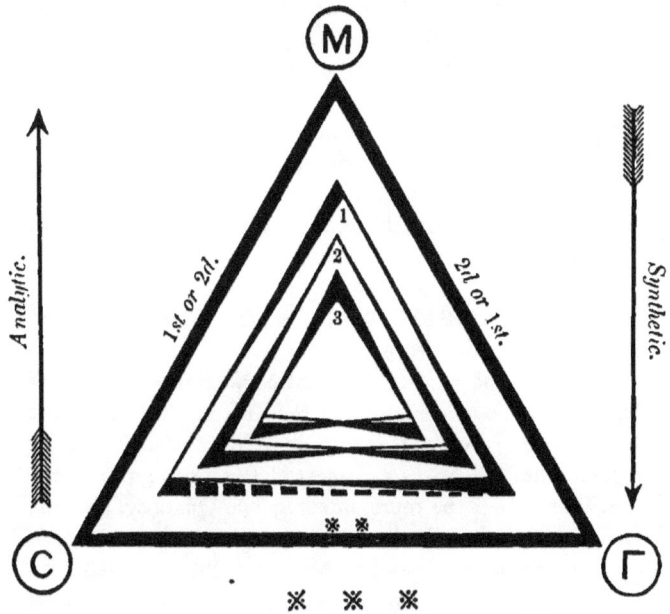

The Unfigured Syllogism is properly represented as including all the others, as any Syllogism of either Figure may be easily expressed in this form. In like manner, the triangle representing the First Figure is made to include the two typifying respectively the Second and Third, as either of the latter may be readily reduced to the former. And again, the essential unity of the Syllogistic process, and the unessential nature of variation by Figure, are appropriately signified by a single triangle comprehending all the varieties of form.

"The double Conclusions, both equally direct, in the Second and Third Figures, are shown in the crossing of two counter and corresponding lines. The Direct and Indirect Conclusions in the First Figure are distinctly typified by a common and by a broken line; the broken line is placed immediately under the other, and may thus indicate that it represents only a reflex of — a consequence through — the other (κατ' ἀνάκλασιν, *reflexim, per reflexionem*). The diagram therefore can show, that the Indirect Moods of the First Figure, as well as all the Moods of the Fourth, ought to be reduced to merely *mediate* inferences ; — that is, to Conclusions from Conclusions of the conjugations or Premises of the First Figure."

If we have the two Premises, *All C is some M*, and *All M is some Γ*, and consider that *some M* is a Mark of (or, is included in) *all C*, and *some Γ* a Mark of *all M*, then we are reasoning in the Quantity of Intension ; and, according to the Axiom that *a Mark of a Mark is also a Mark of the thing itself*, the proper and direct Conclusion is, *All C is some Γ*. But if we conclude that *Some Γ is all C*, according to the Fourth Figure or the Indirect Moods of the First, *Some Γ* does not appear as a Mark of *all C*, but as included under it, — as a Subject of Extension ; the Premises, then, would be represented in one Quantity, and the Conclusion in the other. " But though always coexistent, and consequently always, to some amount, potentially inferring each other, still we cannot, without the intervention of an actual inference, at once jump from the one Quantity to the other, — change, *per saltum*, Predicate into Subject and Subject into Predicate. We must proceed *gradatim*. We cannot arbitrarily commute the Quantities, in passing from the Quæsitum to the Premises, or in our transition from the Premises to the Conclusion. When this is apparently done, the procedure is not only unnatural, but virtually complex and mediate, *the mediacy being concealed by the concealment of the mental inference which really precedes* " ; — indicated by the broken line in the diagram.

One other species of Hamiltonian notation should be noticed, as it brings to light very clearly the virtual equivalence of those Moods in the several Figures which are indicated, in the old mnemonic hexameters, by names beginning with the same capital letter. Four straight lines are all that is needed for such a notation. Three of these are horizontal, to represent the Terms; and one perpendicular, or the want of it, at the beginning of the comparison, to express the Quality of Affirmation or Negation. "Quantity is marked by the relative length of a terminal line within, or its indefinite excursion before, the limit of comparison. This notation can represent equally *total* and *ultratotal* distribution, in simple Syllogism and in Sorites; and it shows at a glance the competence or incompetence of any Conclusion."

"Of these, the former, with its converse, includes Darii, Dabitis, Datisi, Disamis, Dimaris, &c.; whilst the latter, with its converse, includes Celarent, Cesare, Celanes, Camestres, Cameles, &c. But of these, those which are represented by the same diagram are, though in different Figures, formally the same Mood." "In all the other geometrical schemes hitherto proposed, whether by lines, angles, triangles, squares, or circles, the same complex diagram is necessarily employed to represent an indefinite plurality of Moods."

The application of Hamilton's doctrine of the thorough-going quantification of the Predicate to the explication of the Syllogistic theory produces, as might have been expected, a great enlargement of the number of Moods. If there are but *four* fundamental Judgments, the number of *conceivable* Moods that can be framed from them, by taking them three and three, is *sixty-four* *; excluding from these

---

* The computation is easily made. The four letters **A, E, I, O,** give us four different Major Premises; each of these may have four different Minor Premises;—hence there will be sixteen pairs of Premises. But each of these pairs may be conceived to have four different Conclusions: whence, 16 × 4 = 64 conceivable Moods.

the invalid Moods, as offending against one or more of
the general Rules of the Syllogistic process, there remain
only *fourteen* as valid in some one of the first three Figures; — *nineteen*, if we admit the Fourth Figure; — *twenty-
four*, if we include also the anonymous indirect Moods.
But under the Hamiltonian doctrine of *eight* fundamental
Judgments, we have *five hundred and twelve* * conceivable
Moods. Excluding from these all that offend against the
General Canon, (as by having an undistributed Middle,
two Negative Premises, or collecting more in the Conclusion than was distributed in the Premises,) there remain
thirty-six valid Moods, of which *twelve* are Affirmative and
twenty-four Negative. On this doctrine, each Affirmative
Mood yields two Negative ones, as each of its Premises
may be successively negatived. Figure now appears in its
true character, as an unessential variation; but as each of
these valid Moods can, if we please, be thrown into either
of the three Figures, there are $36 \times 3 = 108$ valid Moods,
reckoning as such all the modifications of statement of
which they are susceptible. But to show how trifling are
the changes thus effected by carrying what is really one
Mood through each of the three Figures, I borrow a concrete example from Mr. Baynes.

Fig. I.	Fig. II.
All man is some animal;	Some animal is all man;
Every Celt is some man;	Every Celt is some man;
∴ Every Celt is some animal.	∴ Every Celt is some animal.

Fig. III.
All man is some animal;
Some man is every Celt;
∴ Every Celt is some animal.

* Computing as before, from eight Judgments we have eight different
Major Premises, each of which may have eight different Minor Premises,
whence $8 \times 8 = 64$ pairs of Premises; and as each of these may have
eight different Conclusions, there are $64 \times 8 = 512$ triplets of Judgments,
or conceivable Syllogisms.

Hamilton's General Canon has already been enounced in the mode of statement in which it is directly applicable to the Unfigured Syllogism. As applied to the Figured Syllogism, wherein we have to consider the two counter Quantities of Extension and Intension, it should be thus expressed: — " What worse relation of Subject and Predicate subsists between either of two Terms and a common Third Term, with which one at least is positively [affirmatively] related, that relation subsists between the two Terms themselves." As already stated, this Canon is only a succinct statement of the six general Rules which have been laid down as fulfilled in every valid case of Mediate Inference; and it is, also, only a restatement of the two Primary Axioms of Pure Thought, the laws of Identity and Non-Contradiction, with the necessary conditions and limitations which determine their application. As these Rules and Axioms were found to hold good under the Aristotelic doctrine of four fundamental Judgments, they are also valid under the system which increases the number of these Judgments to eight. No Syllogism can be invalid which accords throughout with this Canon, and every illegitimate process, either directly or indirectly, openly or covertly, violates it.

But we must accurately determine which is the "*worse relation*" of Subject and Predicate that can subsist between either of two Terms and a common Third Term. When there are but four Judgments, the corresponding principle, that the Conclusion follows the " *weaker* part," admits of easy interpretation; Particular Quantity is weaker than Universal, Negative Quality is weaker than Affirmation. But with eight Judgments, the various degrees of better or worse, stronger or weaker, must be more precisely ascertained. Always considering Negation as weaker than Affirmation, we now say that the *best* (strongest) Quantity of Affirmation is the *worst* (weakest)

Quantity of Negation. In other words, we affirm *best* when we affirm *all*, and affirm *worst* when we affirm only *some*; on the contrary, we deny *best* when we deny only *some*, and deny *worst* when we deny *all*. On account of this inverse relation of the two Quantities, an Affirmative Mood with a *Particular* Conclusion may be changed, by merely negativing one of its Premises, into a Negative Mood with a *Universal* Conclusion. But though the Quantity is thus altered from Particular to Universal, this is not a change from worse to better, but from worst to worst; for though a Particular stands lowest in the scale of Affirmation, a Universal stands lowest in the scale of Negation. The seeming exception only confirms the rule, and proves that the Canon is universally applicable. Take the following instance : —

C : ———, M : ——— : Γ   Some M is all C ;
——————————,   All Γ is all M ;
                       ∴ Some Γ is all C.

    Some blacks are all slaves ;
    All of African descent are all blacks ;
    ∴ Some of African descent are all slaves.

Now, if we negative this Syllogism by negativing the Minor Premise, the Conclusion changes from Particular to Universal, thus : —

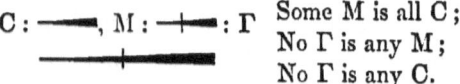

C : ———, M : —+— : Γ   Some M is all C ;
                             No Γ is any M ;
                             No Γ is any C.

    Some blacks are all slaves ;
    No Caucasian is any black ;
    ∴ No Caucasian is any slave.

This change, though from Particular to Universal, is really from the worst of Affirmation to the worst of Negation. But such changes are infrequent, as, in the intermediate relations, the commutation is only from equal to equal, and the predesignations of Quantity, in their inverse signification, remain externally the same. Out of the twenty-four valid Negative Moods, only four cases are found of a Particular quantification disappearing in the Negative Conclusion. Hamilton gives the following arrangement of the eight Judgments in the order proceeding from best to worst.

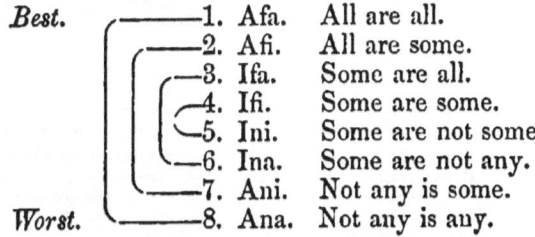

Best. 1. Afa. All are all.
2. Afi. All are some.
3. Ifa. Some are all.
4. Ifi. Some are some.
5. Ini. Some are not some.
6. Ina. Some are not any.
7. Ani. Not any is some.
Worst. 8. Ana. Not any is any.

With these explanations, the following list of the twelve valid Affirmative Moods in each of the three Figures, and the 24 valid Negative Moods in the First Figure, all expressed in the Hamiltonian notation, will be found intelligible.

In this Table, the Quantity of the Conclusion is marked only in the cases already considered, wherein the Terms obtain a different Quantity from that which they held in the Premises; accordingly, when not marked, the quantification of the Premises is held as repeated in the Conclusion. The symbol ⌢, placed beneath a Conclusion, indicates that, when the Premises are converted, the Syllogism remains in the same Mood; ✕ shows that the two Moods between which it stands are convertible into each other by converting their Premises. The Middle Term is said to be *balanced*, when it is Universal in both Premises. The Extremes, or Terms of the Conclusion, are *balanced*, when both alike are distributed; *unbalanced*, when one is, and the other is not, distributed. Accordingly, of the

256 MEDIATE INFERENCE OR SYLLOGISM.

SCHEME OF NOTATION—
TABLE OF SYLLO-

A. AFFIRMATIVE MOODS.

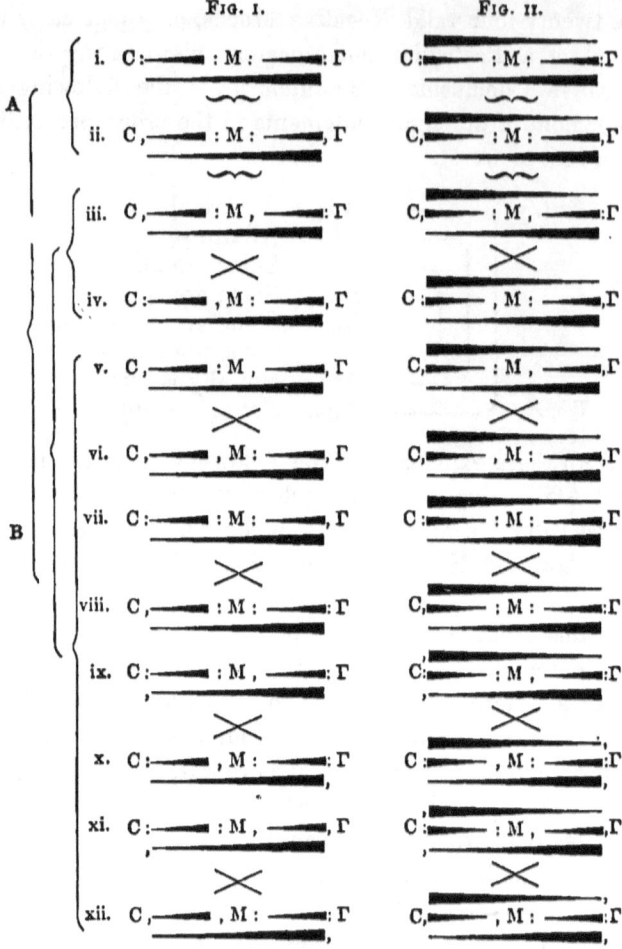

Note.—A. i. and ii. are *Balanced*. B. The other moods are *Unbalanced*. Of these,

THE HAMILTONIAN ANALYSIS. 257

FIGURED SYLLOGISM.
GISTIC MOODS.

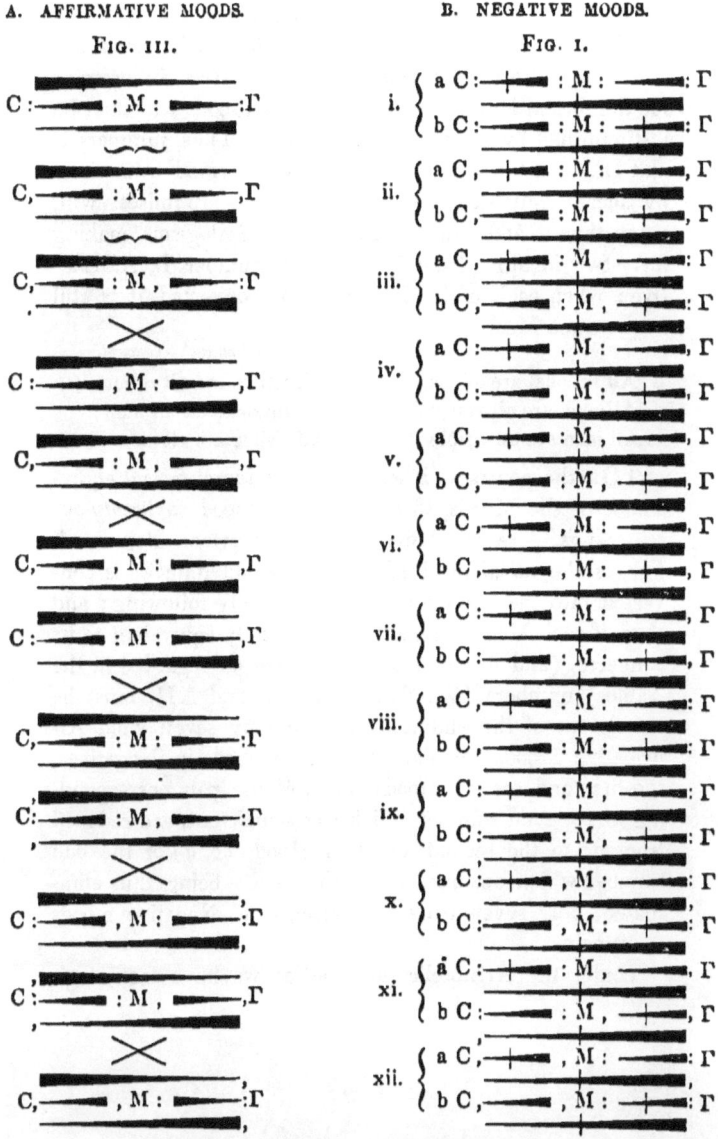

iii. and iv. are unbalanced in terms only, not in propositions; the rest in both.

Moods in the Table, numbers I. and II. are balanced as respects both Terms and Propositions; in III. and IV., only the Terms are unbalanced; in the remainder, both Terms and Propositions are unbalanced.

"If we apply the Moods to any *Matter*, however abstract, say letters, there will emerge *forty-two* Syllogisms; for the formal identity of the balanced Moods will then be distinguished by a *material* difference." Thus, numbers I. and II., with the four Negative Moods formed from them by successively negativing each of their Premises, will, when thus treated, yield six additional Syllogisms, making forty-two in all. Take for instance, number I., Affirmative; when each of its Judgments is converted, it is still in the same Mood.

Converting each Judgment.

I. All rational are all risible;   All risible are all rational;
   All men are all rational;   All rational are all men;
∴ All men are all risible.   ∴ All risible are all men.

"On the contrary, if we regard the mere *formal* equivalence of the Moods, these will be reduced to *twenty-one* reasonings, — seven Affirmative and fourteen Negative." For, of the unbalanced Moods, every odd number is converted into the even number immediately following; and thus, if each Mood is regarded as formally equivalent to its converse, (and numbers I. and II. are so regarded in the Table,) numbers IV., VI., VIII, X., and XII. must be struck out of the enumeration, and only seven valid Affirmative Moods remain. In like manner, in Negatives, the first and second Moods (*a*, *b*) of the pair corresponding to the even number which was struck out, are reduced from or to the second and first Moods (*b*, *a*) of the odd number which was retained. Five pairs being thus eliminated, only seven pairs — fourteen valid Negative moods — remain.

Under the Aristotelic doctrine, as we have seen, logi-

cians found that the six general Rules, which they had
enounced as governing all Mediate Inference, did not suffice to determine which of the Moods were valid, and
which invalid, in each of the four Figures. The variations
of Figure depend upon the relative position of the Middle
Term as Subject or Predicate to each of the two Terms
of the Conclusion; and *special* Rules were necessary to
prevent these variations from conflicting with the two
principles which, according to the Aristotelians, determine
the implicit quantification of the Predicate. These principles are, — 1. That in all Affirmative Judgments the
Predicate is Particular; and, 2. That in all Negative Judgments the Predicate is Universal. Now, in the Second
Figure, the Middle Term being Predicate in both Premises, the logicians were compelled, in order to prevent the
infringement of the General Rule, that *the Middle Term
must be distributed in at least one of the Premises*, to enact
the Special Rule, that, in this Figure, *one of the Premises,
and consequently the Conclusion also, must be Negative*.
But under the Hamiltonian system of the thorough-going
quantification of the Predicate, since the Middle Term can
be distributed when it is the Predicate of an Affirmative,
just as well as when it is the Predicate of a Negative
Judgment, this Special Rule is both useless and false.
And so with all the other Special Rules for each of the
Figures. They are needless, because they were formed
only on the supposition that the Predicate could be but
partially quantified; they are false, because the thorough-
going quantification of the Predicate brings to light many
valid forms of Syllogism which violate each of these rules.

The following demonstration of the falsity of these Special Rules is borrowed in part from Mr. Baynes's "New
Analytic of Logical Forms."

The Rules of the First Figure are, — 1. That the Sumption must be Universal; 2. That the Subsumption must

be Affirmative. Quantify the Predicate, and neither of these holds good.

First Rule falsified.

Some men are some fleet-footed ;
All rational is all man ;
∴ Some rational is some fleet-footed.

Second Rule falsified.

All idealists are some philosophers ;
No sensualist is any idealist ;
∴ No sensualist is some philosopher.

The Rules of the Second Figure are, — 1. That one of the Premises must be Negative ; 2. That the Sumption must be Universal. Both are abrogated by a quantified Predicate, thus: —

First Rule falsified.

All risible is all man ;
All philosophers are some men ;
∴ All philosophers are some risible.

Second Rule falsified.

Some mortal is all man ;
All rational is all man ;
∴ All rational is some mortal.

The Rules of the Third Figure are, — 1. That the Subsumption must be Affirmative ; 2. That the Conclusion must be Particular.

First Rule falsified.

All free agents are all responsible ;
No free agent is any brute ;
∴ No brute is any responsible.

Second Rule falsified.

All triangles are halves of parallelograms ;
All triangles are all trilaterals ;
∴ All trilaterals are halves of parallelograms.

All the Special Rules being thus abrogated, the unity

and simplicity of the Syllogistic process become manifest. Hamilton's Supreme Canon, which is a mere compend of the six General Rules, appears as the universal and all-sufficient law of Mediate Inference, and the science of Logic is freed from the encumbrance of a mass of needless distinctions and superfluous details. As Figure is demonstrated to be an unessential variation, all the Rules for Reduction are swept away. In fact, the process of Reduction is so far simplified by allowing all Judgments to be converted simply, that, if we still need to have recourse to it in order that the reasoning may appear in its most obvious and natural form, the requisite changes suggest themselves, and the work may be performed without the aid of rules.

Some observations are necessary, however, in respect to the applicability of the different Figures to those two directions of the reasoning process which are called Deductive and Inductive. This subject has been so well explained by Mr. Baynes, that I borrow his language. We have seen that the characteristic of reasoning in Intension — or *Comprehension*, as it is more frequently called — is, that the Predicate is contained in the Subject; of reasoning in Extension, that the Subject is contained under the Predicate. "This being remembered," says Mr. Baynes, "it will appear that in the Second Figure, where the Middle Term as Predicate contains both the Subjects *under it*, *Extension* will predominate. In the Third, where the Middle Term as Subject is contained under, and therefore *comprehends in* it both the Predicates, *Comprehension* will prevail. In the First Figure, again, where the Middle Term is both Subject and Predicate, Extension and Comprehension balance each other. The First Figure is indifferently competent to either.

"Reasoning, however, proceeds not only in different wholes, but in different *aspects* of the same whole. We may, it is evident, regard any whole, considered as the complement of its parts, in either of two ways; for we may, on the one hand, look from the whole to the parts, and reason accordingly downwards; or, on the other hand, look from the parts to the whole they constitute, and reason accordingly upwards. The former of these ·easonings is called *Deductive*, the latter *Inductive*. De-ᴊuctive reasoning is founded on the maxim, 'What belongs to the containing whole belongs also to the contained parts'; *Induction*, on the contrary maxim, 'What belongs to the constituent parts belongs also to the constituted whole.' Thus, in Deductive reasoning, the whole is stated first, and what is affirmed of it is affirmed of the parts it contains; in other words, a general law is laid down, and predicated of the particular instances to which it applies. In Inductive reasoning, the parts are first stated, and what is predicated of them is also predicated of the whole they constitute; in other words, the particular instances are first stated as facts, and then the law they constitute is evolved.

"This being the nature of these counter and correlative reasonings, it appears to us, that, though each kind is competent in either whole (Extension or Comprehension), yet the reasoning in the whole of Extension is more naturally allied to the *Deductive*, and that in Comprehension to the *Inductive*. For, in the whole of Extension, the reasoning proceeds from the general to the special, — from the abstract to the concrete, — from general laws to the particular instances which are contained under them; while in that of Comprehension, on the other hand, the reasoning proceeds from the special to the general, — from the concrete to the abstract, — from the particular instances to the general laws, whose operation they exemplify.

"Considering these kinds of reasoning in relation to the Figures, it will appear, then, that since Extension prevails in the Second, that will be so far more suitable for Deductive reasoning; and since Comprehension prevails in the Third, that Figure will so far be more adapted for Inductive reasoning; while, since Extension and Comprehension prevail equally in the First, that Figure will be equally fitted for either kind of reasoning.

"The relation of the Figures to these different kinds of reasoning will be best illustrated by an example. We will take first the Second Figure:—

FIG. II.
Deductive Reasoning: Quantity of Extension.

Endowed with reason is all man.
European, Asiatic, African, American, are all man.
European, Asiatic, African, American, are endowed with reason.

"Here the reasoning is *Deductive*, for the law is first enounced, the individual instances are next brought under it, and it is then affirmed of them; it is *Extensive*, for it proceeds from the wider notion through the narrower to the individual. Let us now take the same Terms and treat them Inductively, beginning with the individuals. The reasoning will then be in the whole of Comprehension, and will naturally appear in the form of the Third Figure:—

FIG. III.
Inductive Reasoning: Quantity of Comprehension.

European, Asiatic, African, American, are all man.
European, Asiatic, African, American, are endowed with reason.
Endowed with reason is all man.

"Here the reasoning is *Inductive*, for, beginning with the individuals in the Premises, we arrive at the law (with which we started in the previous Syllogism) in the Conclusion; it is *Comprehensive* or *Intensive*, for it proceeds from the concrete to the abstract, from a greater totality of attribute to a less. In other words, in either Quantity (Extensive or Intensive), we reason from the greatest whole; but in the Quantity of Extension, the greatest whole is the most abstract notion (i. e. the widest law), whereas in that of Comprehension, the greatest whole is the most concrete notion (i. e. the individual instance). But proceeding thus from the widest law, the reasoning is necessarily Deductive, while on the other hand, proceeding from the individual instance, it is as necessarily Inductive.

"We may give the same example in the First Figure, to illustrate (what will now be quite obvious) that it is indifferently competent to either reasoning: —

FIG. I.

Deductive Reasoning: Quantity of Extension.
All man is endowed with reason.
European, Asiatic, African, American, are all man.
European, Asiatic, African, American, are endowed with reason.

Inductive Reasoning: Quantity of Comprehension.
European, Asiatic, African, American, are all man.
All man is endowed with reason.
European, Asiatic, African, American, are endowed with reason.

"The Second and Third Figures are indeed naturally respectively connected with Deductive and Inductive reasoning; for in the Second, we judge the likeness or unlikeness of two parts, as they are contained or not contained by a common whole; while in the Third, we judge the likeness or unlikeness of two wholes, as they severally contain or do not contain common parts."

In respect to Hypothetical and Disjunctive reasoning, Hamilton has followed Kant in declaring that all Mediate Inference is one, — that which has been denominated Categorical; all the so-called Conditional Syllogisms are reducible to Immediate Inferences. Their characteristic feature is, that they have no Middle Term; the agreement or disagreement of the two Terms of the Conclusion with each other is ascertained, not by comparing each of them separately with a third Term, which is a mediate process, but directly, from a single Premise, here incorrectly styled a Major Premise. This Premise consists, not of two Terms merely, but of two Judgments, called respectively the Antecedent and the Consequent; a relation of mutual dependence is affirmed to exist between these, by virtue of which the Axiom of Reason and Consequent becomes applicable to the case. This Axiom, as has been shown (page 54), is directly explicated into the two Laws, — 1. That *to affirm the Reason or the Condition is also to affirm the Consequent;* and, 2. That *to deny the Consequent is also to deny the Reason.* *A ratione ad rationatum, a negatione rationati ad negationem rationis, valet consequentia.* The single Premise affirming that this relation of Reason and Consequent exists between the Judgments which are its two parts, this Axiom compels us to infer *immediately*, or without the aid of a third Term, both that the Consequent follows when the Antecedent is posited, and that the Antecedent is denied when the Consequent is sublated.

The reduction of a Hypothetical Judgment to a Categorical shows very clearly the Immediacy of the reasoning in what is called a Hypothetical Syllogism. Thus, *If A is B, C is D*, is equivalent to

All cases of A is B are cases of C is D.
∴ { Some cases of A is B are cases of } C is D.
{ This case of A is B is a case of }

In such reasoning, as Kant remarks, the Premise does not afford a *proof* of the Conclusion, but a *ground or manner of proving it;* it is then only an explication of the meaning of the Premise, when we say that the Consequent holds good when the ground or Reason exists, and that the Reason does not exist if the Consequent does not hold good. Hence, this kind of reasoning may properly be referred to the doctrine of Exponibles. All the Matter which we are reasoning about is embraced in the one complex proposition that is here called the Premise; and all that the reasoner has to do is to explicate or interpret this proposition. Considered as an Exponible, the Conditional Judgment, *If A is B, C is D*, may be interpreted in two ways, — 1. as a Restrictive; 2. as an Exclusive. The first of these interpretations yields, by the Immediate Inference of Subalternation, what is called the *Modus ponens* of Conditional Reasoning; the second yields, also Immediately, the *Modus tollens*.

1. Thus, Restrictively, in affirming that, if *A is B, C is D*, we do not say, C is *always* D, but only, "All C, *when A is B*, is D," the italicized clause being the Restriction, and answering to a limiting adjective, — say, *yellow* : *All yellow C is D*. Then, by Subalternation,

Some yellow C } is D.
This yellow C }

Again, the same Judgment, *If A is B, C is D*, yields, by the Immediate Inference of Contraposition, *If C is not D, A is not B*. This is an Exclusive; it affirms that

A is B *only when* C is D; then, Immediately,
A is not B *when C is not D*.

In fact, all reasoning is hypothetical; the Syllogism, *as such*, does not affirm its Conclusion absolutely, but only its dependence on the Premises. *If* the Premises are true, the Conclusion follows. Any Immediate Inference, also, may be stated hypothetically. Take that by Subalternation, for instance : —

All A is B;
∴ Some A is B.

Stated hypothetically thus : —

If all A is B, some A is B;
∴ Some A, or this A, is B.

It is unnecessary to consider separately the case of Disjunctive reasoning; for it has already been proved (page 131) that Disjunctives are only complex Hypotheticals.

CHAPTER IX.

OF FALLACIES.

A FALLACY is any instance of unsound or invalid reasoning which has a deceptive appearance of correctness and truth. If it be such that the writer or speaker is himself deceived by it, it is called a Paralogism; if framed by him for the purpose of deceiving others, while he is himself aware of its unsoundness, it is a Sophism. Those of the former class are what we have most to dread; for on account of the necessary dependence of Thought on Language, we often commit them in our silent meditations, while we are attempting to discover the truth or to disintricate it from error. The danger is greatly enhanced by the symbolic or algebraic use of Language, whereby we employ words for the moment as mere signs, without spreading out their signification before the mind, and thus are often deceived by their ambiguity and vagueness. Sophisms are comparatively of rare occurrence, as one who wishes to deceive can do so more easily and effectually by false statements than by false reasonings. It is more difficult to weave invalid but specious arguments, knowing their incorrectness, than to reason correctly from wrong premises. Formerly it was otherwise; the great use of disputation by the ancient sophists and the Schoolmen, as a logical exercise and a means of education, tended to create a special art of sophistry, and has left on record a multitude of logical puzzles for the amusement of later times. Dexterity in framing and solving these sophisms was reckoned a scholarly accomplishment, and one of the special fruits of a university education. Nowadays this species of mental gymnastics has fallen into entire disrepute, as men prefer to sharpen their wits on graver matters and subjects of more immediate interest.

The purpose of the doctrine of Fallacies, as it is now taught, is to familiarize the mind with those instances of erroneous reasoning which are most likely to lead our own thoughts astray in the search after truth and the elimination of error. For this end, a classification of Fallacies is desirable. The earliest attempt, of which we have any distinct knowledge, thus to reduce them to system, was that of Aristotle; and the chief endeavor of later logicians has been to ascertain, develop, and illustrate his meaning. Even the phraseology which he employed became consecrated, as it were, by long use in the Schools; and the chief dispute among modern writers has been, whether a particular Fallacy is rightly designated by this or that technical name. A more unprofitable logomachy can hardly be imagined. Our business is to teach Logic, and not to write a commentary upon Aristotle. The classification framed by him, though a marvellous work for the time, evincing the prodigious acuteness and comprehensiveness of view for which his intellect was so remarkable, must still, if viewed under the lights of modern science, be regarded as crude and imperfect. A better arrangement can be effected, not by laying aside his phraseology altogether, but by employing his technical terms, when they are convenient, under the conventional meaning which has long been assigned to them, and by striking out many of his distinctions, and introducing others in their place which have been suggested by later experience. The use of classification, it must be remembered, is merely subsidiary; the main purpose is to become familiar with the characteristics of those forms of erroneous reasoning which most frequently occur in practice; and this can be best accomplished by dividing them into species, and discriminating these species from each other.

It should be observed that, strictly speaking, the consideration of Fallacies is extralogical. We have already laid down the Rules of correct or valid Inference; any argumentation which violates one or more of these Rules is invalid. But an open violation of one of them, as, from its very obviousness, it is not likely to deceive anybody, is not usually called a Fallacy. A classification of what are properly denominated Fallacies would depend on an enumeration of those circumstances which are most likely to deceive us — to cover up the violation of a Rule — in the formation of our Judgments and Inferences; and a disquisition on these circumstances would form a valuable chapter of Psychology, or in a Treatise on the practical Conduct of the Understanding. The chief source of these errors is the ambiguity of language, both as respects the meaning of single words (*æquivocatio*) and the construction of sentences (*amphibolia*). Then the ultimate remedy for them is to be found in the study of language; it would be a part of the doctrine of Hermeneutics, or the science of Interpretation. But as certain prominent classes of them frequently perplex and vitiate our reasonings, a description of such is not entirely out of place as an appendage to the science of Logic.

We observe in the first place, then, that Aristotle was wrong, and his authority has misled most of the later logicians, in forming a distinct class of the Fallacies of language. His first distinction is between those *in dictione*, which arise merely from the improper use of words as arbitrary signs of thought, and which, therefore, generally disappear when the proposition is translated into another language, and those *extra dictionem*, which are in the Thought itself, whether in its Matter or its Form, and therefore adhere to the Thought, however it may be expressed. He enumerates six classes or subdivisions of the former; but the division is a faulty one, as the six can be reduced to two, namely, the ambiguity of single words, or the ambiguous construction of sentences. But we object generally, that the erroneous use of language is of no logical import whatever, if it be not employed to hide some defect in the reasoning. The ambiguity of words may cloak, but does not constitute, the sophism. If the suspected Syllogism does not contain an undistributed Middle, or four Terms instead of three, or an Illicit Process, or some other violation of logical Rule, it is a sound Inference, however faulty may be the language in which it is expressed. Accordingly, it will be found, that all the instances given in the books to illustrate the six classes of what may be briefly termed Verbal Fallacies, resolve themselves, when the ambiguity is detected, into logical *quadrupeds*, as Syllogisms with *four* Terms have been derisively called, or some other form of violating one or more of the Canons of Pure Logic. Take the following illustration, from Mr. De Morgan, of the Fallacy of ambiguous words, Aristotle's first subdivision.

All *criminal actions* ought to be punished by law;
Prosecutions for theft are *criminal actions;*
Therefore, prosecutions for theft ought to be punished by law.

Here the Middle Term, *criminal actions*, is ambiguous; in the Sumption, it means *immoral deeds;* in the Subsumption, it is a technical phrase for *a particular class of legal proceedings*. Substitute these definitions for the phrase defined, and it is apparent that the pretended Syllogism is a quadruped.

Take the following as an instance of Aristotle's second subdivision, — ambiguous construction.

All that glitters is not gold;
Tinsel glitters;
Then, tinsel is not gold.

Here, in the Sumption, the Middle Term is apparently distributed by the predesignation *all;* but it is not so in reality, as the negative particle ought to be construed as qualifying *all*, and *not all* means *some are not*. But if we read, *Some things that glitter are not gold*, the Middle is not distributed in either Premise.

The class of Verbal Fallacies, then, should be abolished, as all instances of invalid or erroneous reasoning, being either an open or a concealed violation of the Laws of Thought, are necessarily *extra dictionem*, or independent of language. Then the most general division of them will be into Formal and Material Fallacies, "according as the source of deception lies in the act of Thought itself, or in the object upon which, or the circumstances under which, it is exercised." This distinction may be well expressed by saying that, in every Fallacy, the Conclusion either *does, or does not, follow from the Premises*. If it *does not* so follow, it is clear that the fault is in the *reasoning*, and in that alone; the error concerns only the *Form* of Thought, so that these alone are Logical Fallacies strictly so called. If the Conclusion *does* follow from the Premises, we must search for the deception in the *Matter* of the Thought; that is, we must consider what we are reasoning about, and what is the Conclusion which we wish to establish. Such consideration is properly extralogical; but as the purpose of examining both classes of these Fallacies is the same, namely, to guard the mind against error in its own processes, and as the consideration of only one class of Fallacies would very imperfectly answer this end, we subordinate strict method to convenience, and take into view all cases of defective and sophistical argumentation. While considering both of these classes of Fallacies, the ambiguities of language which hide them, and which originally led the reasoner astray, will incidentally come into notice, and the exposure of them thus effected will be, in a practical point of view, the most valuable result of the discussion.

The subdivision of Fallacies in the Form of Thought, the Conclusion being illogically drawn, is easily effected, as it must have reference to the six General Rules, which are all embodied in Hamilton's one Supreme Canon of Mediate Inference. But the classification thus made is not easily adhered to, as it will often be found that the same Fallacy involves a violation of two or more of these General Rules. The subject being once properly distributed into parts, however, the question is of little moment whether a particular case is rightly assigned to this or that class, if it may fairly be placed under either. The Rules most frequently violated are those which require, — 1. That a Syllogism should consist of only three Terms; 2. That the Middle Term should be distributed in at least one of the Premises; 3. That neither Term can be distributed in the Conclusion, if it was not taken universally in the Premises; 4. That the Conclusion must be Negative, if either Premise is Negative; 5. That at least one Premise must be Affirmative. Besides the five kinds of Fallacies arising from violations of these Rules, two others should be mentioned, being the two invalid Moods of Hypothetical Inference: — 6. From denying the Antecedent, or, 7. From affirming the Consequent, no Conclusion can be drawn. A number of other classes might be framed, arising from violation of the various Rules of Immediate Inference, — the Laws of Conversion, Opposition, Infinitation, for instance. But as such errors are neither frequent nor insidious, they need not be considered here.

1. To the class of Syllogisms which are invalid because they consist of more than three Terms may be referred all the cases which are usually placed under the head of *ambiguous Middle*. If an ambiguous word or phrase is employed as the Middle Term in the Major Premise in one of its

significations, and in the Minor Premise in a different signification, it is evident that it does not afford us any means of ascertaining the relation of the Extremes to each other. Having only compared A with M, and B with N, we cannot tell whether A is, or is not, B. Cases of this Fallacy are more numerous, and more apt to deceive, than those of any other class. They are the more insidious, because terms in frequent use, and which are constantly employed by the vulgar in ordinary conversation, are precisely those which are most apt to become ambiguous; but on account of their familiarity, we fancy that we are perfectly acquainted with them, and therefore never suspect that they are leading us astray.

Most political Fallacies are of this order. That very common phrase, *the government*, means both "the system of laws under which we live and the machinery by which these are administered," and "the members of the administration for the time being, whose duty it is to carry out this system and to work this machinery"; or it may mean certain measures, or a favorite policy, of these administrators. Hence what Jeremy Bentham calls "the official malefactor's screen";—"Attack us, you attack the government." It may well happen that we best manifest our attachment to *the government* in the former sense, by a vehement opposition to it in the second meaning; or, if the administrators are really able and well disposed, but are pursuing a mistaken policy in one respect, that we best show our regard for them personally, by laboring to convince them of their error.

Still more ambiguous is that which is so much talked and written about,—*the Church*. How many controversies might have been spared, and how many volumes remained unwritten, had it been remembered that, at least in all countries where a religious establishment exists supported by law, "the Church" may have these six different meanings : — 1. a place of meeting for worship ; 2. all the people engaged as worshippers ; 3. only the faithful who, in in every age, since the advent of the Redeemer, have constituted the mystical Body of Christ ; 4. the inferior clergy by whom the ceremonies of worship are conducted ; 5. the superior clergy, who may be regarded as the heads of the Church ; 6. rules and customs respecting the modes of worship. As Bentham remarks, *church* is often made to mean *churchmen*, and *law* to signify *lawyers*, by the easy device of "substituting for men's proper official denomination the name of some fictitious entity, to whom, by customary language, and hence opinion, the attribute of excellence has been attached."

If it were allowable to make a new use of one of Bacon's technical appellations, another large class of these sophisms might be called Fallacies of the Forum. These relate chiefly to *money*, *currency*, *prices*, *interest*, *profits*, and other terms of frequent use in commercial and financial transactions. *Money* may mean either *specie*, or *bank-notes*, or *currency* consisting of a mixture of these two, or *credit*, or *capital*, or *that portion of capital which is offered for loan*. An individual merchant is said to be in want of *money* wherewith to pay his debts, when his only real lack is of credit, capital, or merchandise, *money* serving no other purpose in the affair than that of the *carts* by which the merchandise is transported. Again, *interest* is usually spoken of as if it were the interest *of money;* whereas a little reflection will satisfy any one, that money (if the name be applied, as it usually is, to specie, to bank-notes, or to a combination of the two) yields neither profit nor interest ; whether it is in the hands of an individual or a corporation, whether in the pocket or in a safe, it is a part of the owner's *dead capital*, and therefore he usually aims to get along with the use of as little of it as possible. Again, money is usually considered as the measure of wealth; and then, by a very common metonomy, *the measure* is confounded with *the thing measured*. Hence the following sophism, which may be said to have directed the commercial legislation of all civilized countries, down, at least, to the time of Adam Smith.

Any increase of the money in a country is an equivalent enlargement of its wealth.
Laws to protect native manufactures against foreign competition tend to increase the money in the country.
Therefore, such laws tend to increase the nation's wealth.

But Adam Smith demonstrated that laws directed solely to keeping specie at home, only tend to make the country poorer; and his arguments being at last generally admitted to be conclusive, there arose the opposite Fallacy of universal Free Trade, which now controls the legislation of England, and is gaining ground in many other quarters.

Laws which do not increase the quantity of money in the country are at best useless.
A Protective System does not increase this quantity.
Therefore, a Protective System is useless.

Of course, the answer to this argument is, that measures which do not prevent specie from going abroad may yet make the people more wealthy and prosperous, by enabling them, in their foreign trade, to exchange manufactures for raw material, — that is, the products of skilled labor for those of rude labor, — that is, again, the fruits of the industry of one man for those of the industry of three or four men. And it is precisely this system, — fostering the growth of native manufactures and allowing the production of raw material to take care of itself, — and not the prevalence of the doctrine of Free Trade, which has been the great source of England's prosperity.

Another frequent source of this Fallacy — the introduction, through the ambiguity of language, of four Terms into a Syllogism — is the doctrine that the primary or etymological meaning of a word is its only proper signification, or that it is the standard to which modern usage ought to conform. This sophism is the more frequent, as it affords an opportunity for a little display of erudition; numerous instances of it can be found in what is otherwise an ingenious and excellent work, Tooke's "Diversions of Purley." Thus, *right* comes from *rectus*, and that from *rego*, — to rule or govern; hence an alleged confirmation of the doctrine of Hobbes, that *right* is only a creature of positive law, another unfounded assumption being then allowed to slip in, that the only kind of law is human, not divine. Again, most of the words which are now significant of the operations of Mind were originally applied to some of the forms or changes of Matter; and this fact has been held to countenance the doctrine of materialism. But that *spirit* once signified *breath*, and *animus*, ἄνεμος, *air*, does not afford even a presumption that such is their present meaning. The secondary or usual sense of a word has often travelled so far away from its primitive application as to have lost sight of it altogether, though we may be able to point out the stopping-places in its long journey.

I cannot help thinking that Sir William Hamilton has unconsciously glided into a Fallacy of this sort in his criticism of Dr. Reid's definition of memory. Reid says, "Memory is an *immediate* knowledge of things past"; meaning thereby, as it seems to me, a *present* knowledge of the past. This, at any rate, is a very common use of the word; an action is said to be *immediate* which takes place now, at once, or without delay. But *immediate* is also the opposite of *mediate* or *vicarious;* we are said to have an immediate knowledge of a thing when we know it *directly* or *in itself*, in contradistinction from knowing it vicariously, or through the medium of an image or representation of itself. In this sense, Hamilton argues very properly that an *immediate* knowledge of the *past* is impossible; and Reid, I think, would have agreed with him; while Hamilton would not have denied that memory is *present* knowledge, or *knowledge* which exists at the present time.

Another source of ambiguity, which is well exposed by Whately, is the supposition that *paronymous* or *conjugate* words — as the substantive, verb, adjective, and adverb formed from the same root — necessarily agree in meaning; whereas, they often depart widely from each other in signification. Thus, what is *imaginary* is *unreal;* but an *image*, as formed from wood or stone, is a reality. *To apprehend* is *to lay hold of*, or *to come to a knowledge of;* while *apprehension* often signifies *fear*, dread.

What Aristotle calls the Fallacy of Accent (he should have explained it as an ambiguity which may be resolved by accent) may be illustrated by the difference between *gal'lant* and *gallant*´; the former means *brave, high-spirited;* the latter, *courteous* or *devoted to women*. It is more difficult to resolve by accent the curious ambiguity of the phrase, *not the least*, where the two meanings are opposites of each other. Thus, "not the least difference" may mean either "no difference at all," or, "a very considerable, perhaps the greatest, difference." In the former case, the phrase is elliptical, standing for "not any, not even the least, difference." *The least* is excluded or negatived, as in the phrase "*not* the least," both by *nothing* and by *the greatest*.

As De Morgan remarks, "a statement of what was said, with the suppression of such tone as was meant to accompany it, is the *fallacia accentus*. Gesture and manner often make the difference between irony or sarcasm and ordinary assertion. A person who quotes another, omitting anything which serves to show the *animus* of the meaning; or one who without notice puts any word of the author he cites in Italics, so as to alter its emphasis; or one who attempts to heighten his own assertions, so as to make them imply more than he would openly say, by Italics, or notes of exclamation, or otherwise, is guilty of the *fallacia accentus.*"

2. The Fallacy of Undistributed Middle does not occur so frequently, and is not so insidious, as that of Ambiguous Middle. We may fall into it unawares by overlooking the difference between the Collective meaning of the word *all* = " all taken together," and its Distributive meaning, in which *all* signifies " each and every." Thus, *all* the Senators (taken collectively) try impeachments; *all* the Senators (i. e. each and every Senator) are chosen by the State legislatures.

> All these exercises will fatigue me;
> This performance is one of them;
> Therefore, this performance will fatigue me.

Another ambiguity, which may serve to cloak this logical fault, is passing from the Composite to the Divisive, or from the Divisive to the Composite, meaning of a proposition. If we take together those members of the sentence which ought to have been taken separately, it is called the sophism of Composition; if we take separately what is true of all only when they are united, it is the sophism of Division. A ludicrous instance of the latter is found in most of the old text-books on Logic.

> Two and three (taken compositely) are five;
> Two and three (taken divisively) are odd and even;
> Therefore, five is odd and even.

An instance of the former is what may be called the Spendthrift's Fallacy.

> All of these contemplated expenditures (taken separately) are of trifling amount;
> Therefore all of them may be incurred (together) without ruining me.

The lazy person reasons in the same manner, in respect to the waste of an hour or two of time, or to missing this or that favorable opportunity. It behooves such persons to remember, that the predesignation *any one* is not the equivalent of *all* taken collectively.

This is the nature of the famous old Fallacy called σωρός, *a heap*, whence the name *Sorites* applied to a different and legitimate argument. Does one grain of corn make a heap? No. Do two grains make a heap? No. Do three grains? No. And in like manner, we may ask a series of questions, successively adding unity to the number, till the respondent is at last obliged to contradict himself, and confess what he has just denied, that a single grain of corn makes the only difference between what is not, and what is, a heap. The same sophism was denominated by the old logicians the *Calvus*, because illustrated by a series of questions beginning with the inquiry, whether pulling *one* hair out of a man's head made him bald. Horace used it to ridicule the fashion of valuing ancient authors simply on account of the antiquity of their productions.

> "Iste quidem veteres inter ponetur honeste,
> Qui vel mente brevi vel toto est junior anno,
> Utor permisso, caudæque pilos ut equinæ
> Paulatim vello, et demo unum, demo etiam unum,
> Dum cadat elusus ratione ruentis acervi,
> Qui redit ad fastos, et virtutem æstimat annis,
> Miraturque nihil nisi quod Libitina sacravit."

But while laughing at an old sophism, we may be found ridiculing a modern paralogism. I have recently heard this very argument gravely reproduced in a learned Academy, during a debate on an important question of science. The answer to it is obvious; — not *one alone*, but *one added to the previous* 999, constitutes a heap.

The Fallacy of the Composite and Divisive sense is apt to be repeated by the incautious in estimating the probability of two events happening conjointly. Though each of them, taken separately, is more likely than not to happen, the probability of their occurrence together is of a very inferior character. Thus, the probability of the first being represented by $\frac{2}{3}$, and that of the second by $\frac{5}{9}$, that of their joint occurrence is the *product* of these two fractions, or $\frac{10}{27}$, or much less than $\frac{1}{2}$, which represents an even chance. So we are often misled by the use of the word *tendency*. We rightly say that a given result *tends* to happen only when there is more than an even chance of its occurrence; if there is less than an even chance, it *tends not* to happen. This is the form of a common blunder in the doctrine of *means* or *averages*. Thus, *all* persons who have attained the age of twenty-four survive *on an average* till they are sixty-two years old. But *no one person*, now aged twenty-four, has a right to expect that this average will be exemplified in his particular case. On the contrary, his chance of attaining the precise age of sixty-two, no more and no less, is very much less than his chance of dying at some other age. *All* (collectively) *tend* to the average; but *no one* tends to the average. This is no paradox; for the average is only a compensation of errors, and therefore remains the same whether the errors are great or small, provided only that they are equally distributed on all sides of the average; and such equality of distribution is the direct consequence of the fact, that *no one* error has any tendency to be on one side of the average rather than on any other side. No one tends to the average, but tends equally, or indifferently, to depart from it.

Mr. Darwin, in his theory of "the Origin of Species by Natural Selection," is guilty of both of these forms of the Fallacy. He first argues, that the specific Marks of Species, both in the animal and vegetable kingdoms, *tend* to vary, because, perhaps in one case out of ten thousand, a child is born with six fingers on one hand, or a cat with blue eyes, or a flower grows out of the middle of another flower. Collecting many instances of such sports of nature or monstrosities, he bases his whole theory upon them, forgetting that the vastly larger number of normal growths and developments proves that the *tendency* is to *non-variation*. Then, secondly, because perhaps one out of a hundred of these abnormal Marks is transmitted by inheritance, he assumes that these freaks of nature *tend* to perpetuate themselves in a distinct race, and thus to become permanent Marks of distinct species. Thirdly, as either of the two preceding points, taken singly, affords no basis whatever for his doctrine, he assumes that their *joint* occurrence is probable, because he has made out what is, in truth, a very faint probability that each may *separately* happen. But if the chance of a variation in the first instance is only one out of a thousand, and that of the anomaly being handed down by descent is one out of a hundred, the probability of a variation established by inheritance is but one out of a hundred thousand. As the theory further requires the *cumulation* of an indefinite number of such variations one upon another, the formation of a new species by the Darwinian process may be safely pronounced to be incredible.

3. The third class of Fallacies, those which arise from a violation of the Rule that neither Term must be distributed in the Conclusion if it was not distributed in the Premise, are frequent enough, but will deceive no one if they are not ambiguously expressed. If it is the Predicate of the Conclusion which is illogically distributed, the error is called an Illicit Process of the Major Term; if the Subject, an Illicit Process of the Minor Term. Of these, the former is more common and insidious; for as the Quantity of the Predicate is not expressed in the ordinary use of language, we are apt to forget that, in a Negative proposition, it is always presumed to be Universal, and in an

Affirmative, if nothing be said to the contrary, it is *usually* Particular. In what the Aristotelians call *Indefinite* propositions, the Quantity of neither Term is expressed; but if Affirmative, both Terms are commonly understood to be distributed; for most propositions of this sort are either Definitions, or statements of a general law; and in both of these cases, the Universal quantification of each Term is easily supplied in thought. Thus, *Falsehood is wilful deception*, is easily and properly construed to mean, *All falsehoods are all wilful deceptions;* and *Matter gravitates*, to mean, *All matter is all that gravitates.* But statements of a general law must be carefully distinguished from statements of the application of such a law to a particular class of cases; thus, *Stones gravitate*, means only, "*All* stones are *some* gravitating substances."

All birds are winged;
The bat is not a bird;
Then the bat is not winged.

Here, the Conclusion is logically false, for it contains an Illicit Process of the Major Term. The Sumption is understood to mean only that "All birds are *some* winged things"; the bat, therefore, though not a bird, may be (as here it happens actually to be) one of the *other some* winged things, while the illogical Conclusion declares it to be *not (any) winged thing.*

No slave has his rights;
All slaves are persons of African descent;
Therefore no person of African descent has his rights.

The Illicit Process is here of the Minor Term; for the Conclusion denies of *any*, what the Premises authorize us to deny only of *some* Africans.

In both these cases, the Fallacy is so obvious that it cannot deceive any one who thinks clearly. But the ambiguities of language may so cloak the deception as to render its exposure difficult. Most insidious in this respect is the ambiguity between what is *true absolutely*, and what is *true* only in some respect, τὸ ἁπλῶς ἢ μὴ ἁπλῶς. From this confusion of language two modes of false reasoning result, the first of which is denominated by the Aristotelians the *fallacia a dicto secundum quid ad dictum simpliciter*. It consists in inferring something as true of the subject simply, or without limitation, which is true of it only in some respect. Thus, *Man is immortal* (in respect to his soul); *therefore, man is immortal* (absolutely, both as to soul and body). The second has been called the *fallacia accidentis*, because it confounds an *accidental* attribute with what is *essential* or principally intended. But as it is the exact converse of the former, it should rather be called the *fallacia a dicto simpliciter ad dictum secundum quid*. Thus, to take the converse of the former instance, *Man is mortal* (*man* being here understood, as usual, to be a living organism); *therefore, man is mortal* (as respects his soul). Aristotle gives the following illustration, which is puerile, though it might well puzzle a beginner: —

Socrates is not Coriscus (in any sense);
But Coriscus is a man (this being one of his characteristics);
Therefore, Socrates is not a man.

The most difficult cases to be resolved are those in which giving the name of the genus, to which the subject belongs, is confounded with giving the name of its species. Thus,

He who calls you a man speaks truly;
He who calls you a knave calls you a man;
Then he who calls you a knave speaks truly.

A ludicrous instance of the former mode of the Fallacy is found in most of the text-books: —

What you bought yesterday you eat to-day;
But you bought raw meat yesterday;
Then you eat raw meat to-day.

Perhaps both forms of this Fallacy are best resolved by

considering that the ambiguity resides in the Copula.
When one thing is predicated of another, it is seldom understood that the Predicate is thereby entirely identified with the Subject, as the proposition would then be merely tautologous, *A is A*. But unless it is so identified, we cannot affirm of the Predicate *all* that might be affirmed of the Subject. The logical rule as usually enounced, that no Term must be *distributed* in the Conclusion if it was not distributed in the Premises, is defective; for it only insures that the *Quantity* shall be the same. The *sense* ought also to be the same throughout, whether absolute or relative, whether in one respect or in many, whether essentially or accidentally. An adequate enouncement of the rule would be, that *no more and no less, in any respect*, must be collected in the Conclusion than was given out in the Premises. In order to know how much was so given out, we must consider the meaning of the Copula, *is*, in each separate case. Mr. De Morgan says: " The most common uses of the verb are, — 1. absolute identity, as in 'the thing he sold you *is* the one I sold him,'— this is the *dictum simpliciter;* 2. agreement in a certain particular or particulars understood," *dictum secundum quid*, "as in 'he is a negro,' said of a European in reference to his color; 3. possession of a quality, as in 'the rose is red'; 4. reference of a species to its genus, as in 'man is an animal.' All these uses are independent of the use of the verb alone, denoting existence, as in 'man is [i. e. exists].'" In most cases, these meanings are not interchangeable; and whenever they are not, a Fallacy may be founded upon the difference between any two of them.

But the enumeration is imperfect; several additions may be made to it, by observing, what has been already remarked in treating of Contradiction, "that two Judgments properly contradict each other only when that which is affirmed by the one is denied by the other, — 1. in the same respect; 2. in the same manner; 3. in the same degree; 4. at the same time." Thus, Mr. De Morgan's instance of absolute identity is unhappily chosen; for if the limitation of *time* is taken into account, " the horse which he sold you," being ten years old, is not absolutely *the same* horse which I sold him, as that was only six years old. All Fallacies of this class may be easily resolved by merely completing in expression what was previously only implied in thought. We thereby prevent any more or less stress being laid upon an accident, or upon any view of the subject, in the Conclusion, than was done in the Premises.

The use of wine is destructive to the health;
Therefore its use ought to be forbidden.

As stated, this Enthymeme may seem indisputable; but there can be no practical application of it, unless it is understood to mean that *any* use of wine is pernicious, and hence that it ought *always* to be forbidden. This is the fallacy of arguing against the *use* of a thing merely from its liability to *abuse*. The proper caution is, that no change whatever in the Terms employed must take place during the process of inference.

In ordinary language, few terms are so loosely used, or so often improperly applied, as *the same*, *all*, *always*, &c. Hence the logicians were obliged to form a separate class of Fallacies, which they called those *fictæ universalitatis*. People say *the same*, when they mean *similar;* *all*, when they mean only *most;* and *always* signifies to them the same as *frequently*. They do not even mention the excuse which the Psalmist alleges when conscious of his exaggeration, — " I said *in my haste*, All men are liars." It was once considered a difficult question, whether a stocking, which had been so much darned that not a thread of the original fabric remained, was, or was not, the same stocking. But it can present no difficulty to one who considers that *sameness* or *identity* is an absolute term, which can neither be affirmed nor denied except in an unqualified sense; and that all which can be truly predicated of what comes short of sameness is *similarity*.

"We might suppose that most persons have no idea of a universal proposition; but use the language, never intending *all* to mean more than *most*. And in the same manner, principles are stated broadly and generally, which the assertor is afterwards at liberty to deny, under the phrase that he does not *carry them so far* as the instance named. It would not do to avow that the principle is not always true; so it is stated to be *always true*, but not capable of being *carried* more than *a certain length*. Are not many persons under some confusion about the meaning of the word *general?* In science, it always has the meaning of *universal;* and the same in old English. Thus the Catechism of the Church of England asserts that there are two sacraments which are *generally* [universally] necessary to salvation,—meaning, necessary for *all of the genus* in question, be it man, Christian, member of the Church, or any other. But in modern and vernacular English, *general* means only *usual*, and *generally* means *usually*." *

An opposite error, but one proceeding from the same source, viz. from confounding the Universal with the Particular, is committed by many Americans and some Englishmen in respect to the word *quite*. Its proper meaning is *completely*, *entirely*, as "quite contrary principles"; but it is often used in the sense of *very*, as "quite warm," "quite cold," "quite recent."

The word *same*, in ordinary parlance, is applied to all objects for which a single description will serve, or which are included under *one* Concept. Thus we say, "This writing is on the *same* paper with that," meaning the *same kind* of paper; "This erroneous reasoning is the *same* Fallacy with the other," meaning the *same kind* of Fallacy.

* De Morgan's *Formal Logic*, p. 272.

A description or Concept, as we have seen, is an *imperfect* enumeration of the qualities of a whole class of objects; and it is only because the enumeration is imperfect that *many* can be ranked under *one* class. A perfect enumeration, if such were possible, — a list of *all* the qualities, — would cause each Individual (if this were not a contradiction in terms) to constitute a class by itself.

" Nothing, perhaps," says Dr. Whately, "has contributed more to the error of Realism, than inattention to this ambiguity. When several persons are said to have *one and the same* opinion, thought, or idea, many men, overlooking the true, simple statement of the case, which is, that they are all *thinking alike* [or *similarly*], look for something more abstruse and mystical, and imagine there must be some *one thing*, in the primary sense, though not an Individual, which is present at once in the mind of each of these persons; and thence readily sprung Plato's theory of Ideas, each of which was, according to him, one real, eternal object, existing entire and complete in each of the Individual objects that are known by one name.* Hence, first in poetical mythology, and ultimately, perhaps, in popular belief, Fortune, Liberty, Prudence (Minerva), a Boundary (Terminus), and even the Mildew of Corn (Rubigo), became personified, deified, and represented by statues; somewhat according to the process which is described by Swift, in his humorous manner, in speaking of Zeal, in the ' Tale of a Tub,' ' how from a notion it became a word, and thence, in a hot summer, ripened into a tangible substance.' "

But Dr. Whately seems to depart from his own prin-

* " When abstract truth is contemplated," asks Dr. Price, " is not the very object itself present to the mind ? When millions of intellects contemplate the equality of every angle in a semicircle to a right angle, have they not all *the same* object in view ? Is this object nothing ? Or is it only an image or kind of shadow ? These inquiries carry our thoughts high."

ciples, when he proceeds to remark, that " *Sameness*, in
the primary sense, does not even necessarily imply *Similarity;* for if we say of any man that he is greatly altered
since such a time, we understand, and indeed imply by
the very expression, that he is *one person*, though different
in several qualities; else it would not be *he*." Surely,
what we mean by Personal Identity is sameness of *substance* under great differences of *phenomenal manifestation*.
Sameness here does not imply Similarity, merely because
it implies a great deal more; — namely, absolute *oneness*
of substance, under the greatest diversity of outward appearance. The Person is not different at different times,
but his attributes and actions are. But perhaps this is
what Dr. Whately really means, though it is not the obvious construction of his language. He seems to consider
the Person, and his outward character or manifestation, as
one.

The Fallacy of over-hasty generalization is very frequent,
as Bentham remarks, in political reasoning. It consists in
attributing to an individual person or thing certain attributes which appear in many or most others which have
been loosely ranked in the same class with the object in
question, and thereby designated by the same name. Thus,
a pamphlet entitled " The Crimes of Kings" was published
in Paris in 1792, in order to prove that Louis XVI. ought
to be put to death. In like manner, " The Cruelties of
Catholics " was the title of a book published in England as
an argument against Catholic Emancipation. Most political harangues abound in arguments of the like character;
but they are evidently addressed to the passions rather
than the intellect, as they cannot deceive any one who is
cool enough to be able to think.

To the ambiguity between what is true absolutely, and
what is true only in some respect, may be referred the
famous sophism of Eubulides, called $\Psi\epsilon\nu\delta\acute{o}\mu\epsilon\nu\sigma$, the Liar.

According to Diogenes Laertius, Chrysippus the Stoic wrote six different treatises upon this logical puzzle, and Philetas of Cos studied himself to death in the vain attempt to solve it. "If you say that you lie, and say so truly, then you do lie; but if you say so falsely, then you speak the truth. In either case, therefore, the same assertion is both true and false." But if any one says, "I lie," his assertion is not a *dictum simpliciter;* for a lie is only possible *secundum quid.* He who lies must lie about something, in some particular affirmation or denial; otherwise, his assertion is as meaningless as the remark that "something is very like." Like what?* If he means only, "I have lied in some former assertion," there is no contradiction; if he means, "I lie now, in saying that 'I lie,'" he really makes two affirmations, of which the one, the *oratio obliqua,* is vague and meaningless, and the other, the *oratio directa,* improperly characterizes this one as a falsehood, — improperly, for that which has no significance cannot be either true or false.

This sophism has been stated in a different and inferior form, as follows: —

"All the Cretans are liars."
But Epimenides, who says this, is himself a Cretan.
Therefore, as he is a liar, this saying is not true.
But if the saying is not true, Epimenides may have spoken the truth.
Then the saying is true; — and so on, as before.

But here the Major Premise does not support the Conclusion, unless it is construed to mean that the Cretans are *always* liars, — that they *cannot* speak the truth. And even if this were true, one who is himself a Cretan could not say so, for then he would speak truly, and so contradict himself. Of a similar nature is the following puzzle.

* Mansel's *Notes to Aldrich,* p. 145.

"No rule holds true without some exceptions."
But this very remark is a rule.
Then it has exceptions.
Then there are rules without exceptions.

Here the reasoning, as such, is correct, and the absurdity to which it leads demonstrates what has been properly called the Fallacy of *universal scepticism*. As Sir James Mackintosh remarks, "universal scepticism involves a contradiction in terms; it is a belief that there can be no belief." He who denies *every* assertion thereby denies his own denial, and so contradicts himself. The Major Premise in this very puzzle is such a self-contradictory assertion; I cannot make a *true* general remark, that *all* general remarks are *false;* or, what is the same thing, that they "have exceptions."

4 & 5. Little need be said to illustrate the remaining classes of Fallacies, as they are of infrequent occurrence, and are easy to be detected unless cloaked by some of the ambiguities of language which have already been exposed. Those which respect the Quality of the reasoning may well be considered together. The two Rules are, that at least one of the Premises must be Affirmative, and that the Conclusion must be Negative if either Premise is Negative. These Rules may be violated in appearance, when they are not so in reality. For instance: —

No one is rich who has not enough;
No miser has enough;
Therefore no miser is rich.

Here, both Premises are seemingly negative; but they are not really so, for the negation of having enough is a part of the Predicate, and therefore does not affect the Quality of the Judgment, which depends on the Copula. Instead of *not having enough*, substitute the equivalent phrase, *wanting more*, and the seeming incorrectness is removed.

OF FALLACIES. 291

> No one who wants more is rich;
> Every miser wants more;
> Therefore no miser is rich.

As has been shown in treating of Exponibles, the Exclusive proposition, "None but Whites are civilized," is really complex; it contains one direct assertion, respecting *all non-Whites*, that they are *not* civilized, and one implied assertion, that *some* Whites are civilized. Then the following syllogism is valid, though each of its three Judgments appears to be negative.

None but Whites are civilized; = No non-White is civilized;
The Hindoos are not Whites; = The Hindoos are non-Whites;
The Hindoos are not civilized.

Two ludicrous instances, which have often been repeated in the books, are enough to illustrate the Fallacy which arises from a violation of the fifth Rule, though both of them can be referred also to one of the other classes which have been already considered.

> Nothing is heavier than platinum;
> Feathers are heavier than nothing;
> Therefore, feathers are heavier than platinum.

This sophism cannot puzzle even a beginner, and is of the same character in the following.

> No cat has two tails;
> Every cat has one tail more than no cat;
> Therefore, every cat has three tails.

The Fallacy *plurium interrogationum*, as it was called, may be brought under this head by being referred to the *ambiguous construction* of sentences. It is a mere trick, which consists in asking *two* or more questions as if they were *one;* then the respondent is entrapped whether he answers in the Affirmative or the Negative, as either will be inappropriate to one or the other of the two interrogatories. Of course, the Fallacy is solved by dividing the questions and answering them separately. The standard illustration is asking a man " whether he has *ceased* beating his father." Lawyers are often guilty of this sophism while examining a witness in court, by insisting that he shall give what they call " a *categorical* answer"; — that is, that he shall say either Yes or No. But to the question as they propound it, either Yes or No will be a false answer. A question often involves a real duplicity under a seeming unity, as the uncertainty may regard, not the *meaning*, but the *extension*, of the Terms employed; and the same ambiguity may lurk in a categorical proposition, or in the answer to an interrogatory. The distinction between Contraries and Contradictories, and the relation between Sub-Contraries, must be kept in view. He who denies that *all* are lost, does not thereby deny that *some*, perhaps *many*, even *all but one*, have perished. *Some are not* may mean *perhaps all are not*, or *some certainly are*. To assert or deny a particular *motive* for an action, is still to leave the question undecided as to the concurrence of many motives, and to say nothing about their comparative strength. Most of our actions proceed from a mixture of motives, and the agent himself may not be able to say which was the principal. Men easily deceive themselves in this respect, as their memory, their vanity, or even their remorse, may mislead them; and the mistake is especially frequent when conscientious or religious motives are in question.

Those who made it their business to invent logical puzzles, and to entrap an opponent in disputation, often secured their Premises beforehand, by requiring their interlocutor to answer a series of questions. Socrates was a great master of this eristic art; but though it may fairly and profitably be employed in the communications of a teacher with his pupils, a free use of it may reduce an opponent to silence without convincing him. In Plato's Dialogues, Socrates often appears in no better light than a satirical disputant quibbling about the meaning of words. The following instance of the Fallacy *plurium interrogationum*, which I borrow from Fries, would not puzzle any one if it were not stated in the form of questions and answers.

Is it not true that you must have lost that which you once had, but which you have no longer? Yes.

Did you not have ten counters when you commenced the game? Yes.

Have you ten counters now? No.

Then you have lost ten counters.

But he still had eight, having lost only two; to deny possession of the whole is not necessarily to deny that you have a part. But if obliged to answer simply Yes or No, the respondent could not avail himself of this distinction.

6 & 7. From Dr. Whately's convenient collection of "examples for the exercise of learners," to which I have been indebted for several of the preceding illustrations, I borrow the following instances of violation of the Canons of hypothetical reasoning.

If penal laws against Papists were enforced, they would be aggrieved;

But they are not enforced;

Therefore, the Papists are not aggrieved.

Though this argument was often gravely repeated in Parliament, and elsewhere, during the debates on Catholic Emancipation, it is, of course, entirely invalid by the rules of Logic; for from denying the Antecedent in a Hypothetical Judgment, no Conclusion follows, since the Consequent may still be true from some other reason than the one here specified. In this case, though the penal laws were not enforced, the Catholics had a right to feel aggrieved that these laws should be permitted to remain in the statute-book, as this was an insult to them personally, and to their faith.

We ought to give one day in seven to religious duties, if the Fourth Commandment is obligatory on us;
But we are bound to set apart one day in seven for religion;
Therefore, the Fourth Commandment is obligatory on us.

The Canon here violated is, that from affirming the Consequent no Conclusion can be drawn, since the Consequent may have resulted from some other reason than that specified in the Antecedent. A little attempt is here made to cloak the Fallacy, by inverting the natural position of the Antecedent and the Consequent in the Major Premise.

We pass now to a consideration of those fallacious reasonings which are correct in Form, since the Conclusion is logically drawn, but are faulty in Matter, either from some error or undue assumption in the Premises, or some mistake as to the point to which the argumentation ought to be directed. An exhaustive classification of Material Fallacies is not to be expected, as they are numerous and varied in form, and derive their characteristics chiefly from the particular Matter of the special sciences which first suggested them. The only proper classes of them which have been separately considered by logicians are those which, ever since Aristotle's time, have been technically designated as the *petitio principii*, the *ignoratio elenchi*, and the *non-causa pro causa;* to which may be added several miscellaneous sophisms of so puzzling a character that the old logicians called them the Inexplicables.

1. The vulgar equivalent for *petitio principii* is *begging the question;* and the common explanation of it is, that it consists in assuming, in the course of the argument, the very point which ought to be proved. Its most deceptive application is what is called *reasoning in a circle*, in which Premises are first assumed, and subsequently proved by means of the very Conclusions which they had been used to establish. This error is more difficult of detection in proportion as the circle is more extended, or as more Syl-

logisms are employed before the reasoner comes round to the very point that he started from. As Krug remarks, "to the Circle there are properly required two probations, which are so reciprocally related that the Antecedent in the one is proved by its own Consequent in the other. The proposition A is true because the proposition B is true; and the proposition B is true because the proposition A is true. A Circle so palpable as this would, indeed, be committed by no one. The vice is usually concealed by the interpolation of intermediate propositions, or by a change in the expression." "Thus," says Hamilton, "Plato, in his *Phædo*, demonstrates the immortality of the soul from its simplicity; and, in the *Republic*, he demonstrates its simplicity from its immortality." Theologians, also, sometimes fall into this error, by first proving the authority of the Church from the testimony of the Scriptures, and then seeking to establish the authenticity of the Scriptures by the testimony of the Church; and the Fallacy escapes notice, because one branch of it is found, perhaps, in a polemic tract on Church government, and the other half in a treatise on the Evidences.

Strictly speaking, all valid reasoning proceeds *ex concessis*. Two Premises must be *assumed*, or taken for granted; and these two, taken in conjunction, necessarily involve the Conclusion. Thus much must be conceded to those who claim that every Syllogism presupposes the truth of what it is brought forward to establish. But then it is presumed that there is no undue assumption;—that the two Premises, which we now posit, either have been already proved, or that they are universally admitted truths, or that they have just been conceded, *pro hac vice*, by the opponent. As Mr. Mansel remarks, "the *petitio principii* is a *material*, not a *formal* Fallacy, and consists in assuming, in demonstration, a non-axiomatic principle as axiomatic, or in dialectic disputation, a non-probable principle as probable." It consists not in mere assumption, then, for that is necessary, but in *undue* assumption. That branch of it which is called *reasoning in a circle* is, from the nature of the case, not a vice which can be committed in a single Syllogism, but only in a series of Syllogisms constituting a chain of proof. That which vitiates a single Syllogism is reasoning from Premises, one, if not both, of which either is in more need of proof than the very proposition which we seek to prove by it, or it is that proposition itself only veiled in other words, or it assumes two Terms to be mere equivalents of each other, when they really have not the same meaning. We must not reason like the physician in Molière, who accounts for opium producing sleep by saying that it has a soporific virtue. The argument that *locomotion is not an attribute of all animals, since sponges cannot change their place*, contains the undue assumption that *sponges are animals*. Indeed, the Fallacy in this case becomes obvious when the argument is explicated into a regular Syllogism. And this is usually so in what is popularly called *begging the question;* the argument is stated as an Enthymeme, and the suppressed Premise is that which contains the undue assumption.

A *petitio principii* is involved in every case of reasoning which depends upon an Imperfect Disjunction, though such cases might also be properly referred to other kinds of Fallacy. A Disjunction must be assumed to be perfect, or the Dilemma which is founded upon it is obviously invalid. Of this character is the famous sophism of Diodorus Cronus, which professes to demonstrate the impossibility of motion, and which has probably occasioned more discussion than any other logical puzzle on record. It occupies a high place among those which were formerly called the Inexplicables. Dr. Whately seems tacitly to admit that it is insoluble; for, though he justly criticises an attempted explanation of it by Aldrich, he proposes nothing to take its place. The sophism may be thus stated.

If motion is possible, a body must move either in the place where it is, or in a place where it is not.
But a body cannot move in the place where it is; and of course, it cannot move where it is not.
Therefore, motion is impossible.

It is hazardous to differ from Mr. Mansel upon any logical question; but the solution of this sophism which he has adopted and improved seems to me unsatisfactory. He says, "The true solution is, that the disjunctive premise is false. 'The place where a body is,' is contradictory of 'the place where a body is not'; as 'Englishmen' is contradictory of 'not-Englishmen'; but 'moving in the place where it is,' is no more contradictory of 'moving in the place where it is not,' than 'an army composed of Englishmen' is contradictory of 'an army composed of not-Englishmen.' As it would be false to say, 'Every army must be composed of Englishmen or not-Englishmen,' to the exclusion of the third possibility of a mixed force, so it is false to say, 'Every body must move in the place where it is, or in the place where it is not,' to the exclusion of the third possibility of *moving partly in the one and partly in the other*. This solution is substantially given by Hobbes." *

Hobbes even gives a diagram to prove that a body — *quantulumcunque sit*, however small it may be — "cannot, all at once, so leave the whole of its former place that *a part of it shall not be in* that portion which is common to *the two places*, namely, the one which is left and the other which is reached." But the difficulty cannot be thus evaded. *A part* of a body cannot be in two places at once, any more than *the whole*. For suppose that which moves to be a mathematical point, as in the geometer's conception of the generation of a line. Such a point, of course, being indivisible, cannot be "partly in the one and partly in the

---
* Mansel's *Notes to Aldrich*, p. 144.

other" place. A whole cannot move unless every point in it moves also. Every individual must be, as Mr. Mansel acknowledges, either an Englishman or a not-Englishman. Reduce the army to a single soldier, and the difficulty of moving him, according to this sophism, is still insuperable.

The following solution, I believe, has not before appeared in print. The Major Premise of the sophism is not true except with a proviso or limitation, which is improperly suppressed; so that the Fallacy may properly be referred to the class *a dicto secundum quid ad dictum simpliciter*. "A moving body, *at any one indivisible moment*, must be either where it is, or where it is not." When the proviso here italicized is expressed, the proposition is true, the reasoning is sound, and the conclusion is correct. *In any one indivisible moment, motion is impossible;* for motion requires time as well as space. The Axiom of Excluded Middle, that a thing must be, or not be, in a certain place, does apply to *a body;* but it does not apply to *a moving body*, and this is what covers up the Fallacy. For in order to be *moving*, it must, at the second indivisible instant, be where it was not at the first instant. Hence, we do not violate the Axiom when we deny the Major Premise as originally stated; for "a moving body" *is* that which *has been* where it *now is not*. The difference of tense (time) makes it possible for the same thing *to be* and *not to be*. The law of Excluded Middle itself, as we have seen, is true only when the qualification *at the same time* is understood.

A solution which is substantially similar to the one here given is proposed by Mr. De Morgan. Movement is *change*, and so requires *two* places; a body is not moved *in* a place, but *from* one place *to* another.

2. *Ignoratio elenchi* is what we should now call *answering to the wrong point*. It is proving something which does not really controvert your antagonist's position, though it is assumed to do so. An *Elenchus* is a Syllogism which

will confute the argument of your opponent; and *ignoratio elenchi* is ignorance of what will so confute him, — ignorance of the fact that your Conclusion, even if it were established, would not contradict his Conclusion. This error in reasoning is so common, that special precautions have, in some cases, been adopted in order to obviate it. Thus, in Law, the only object of what is called *special pleading* is, to ascertain the precise point at issue, or to prevent irrelevancy of evidence and argument by binding both parties in the suit to address themselves to what is really the sole point in controversy. A *Demurrer* has been happily explained to be equivalent to the remark, "Well, what of that?" Even granting the facts stated in the declaration to be true, it may be insisted that these facts give the plaintiff no ground of action; and hence, that it was an *ignoratio elenchi* to state them at all.

As the Port Royal logicians remark, the passions of men afford the reason why this sophism is so common in controversy. "We dispute with warmth, and often without understanding one another. Passion or bad faith leads us to attribute to our adversary that which is very far from his meaning, in order to carry on the contest with greater advantage; or to impute to him consequences which we imagine may be derived from his doctrine, although he disavows and denies them. All this may be reduced to this kind of sophism, which an honest and good man ought to avoid above all things."

Logicians have distinguished and described certain kinds of argument which are valid, and may fairly enough be used, provided that it is clearly seen and admitted that they have no bearing upon the main question. The Fallacy consists in referring such arguments to a wrong Conclusion, in urging them as if they established the real point of controversy, whereas they actually tend only to direct censure or laughter against those who hold the opposite opinion, or to some other equally irrelevant object. Let the reasoning which tends directly to prove the main point at issue be called the *argumentum ad rem*. Then the *argumentum ad hominem* is that which convicts your opponent of inconsistency, ignorance, bad faith, or illogical reasoning. Any or all these charges may be well founded, but they are aside from the purpose; for the doctrine which is in dispute may be well founded, though its supporter is deficient in all the qualities of a good reasoner. The *argumentum ad verecundiam* appeals to our reverence for some high authority, or some venerable institution, as a means of silencing an opponent, but not of convincing him that he is mistaken in opinion. The *argumentum ad populum* is a similar appeal to the passions or prejudices of common people; it is a fair inference that proper arguments are wanting, when such appeals are permitted.

To these must be added the *argumentum ad ignorantiam*, which is asserting that your own position is correct, unless your opponent can show some valid reason to the contrary. This mistake is often committed with reference to alleged occurrences which appear to us strange and improbable, or which we may even believe to be impossible. The Fallacy consists in denying that the thing is so, merely because we do not know *how* it is so. But if this reasoning were correct, we ought to deny that the human will has any control over a single movement of our animal organism, or even that the grass grows; for, certainly, no one can tell *how* a mere volition moves the arm, or *how* the green herb in the spring-time absorbs inorganic matter and assimilates it to itself. But our ignorance of one thing, the *modus operandi*, is no disproof of a very different thing, the *opus operatum*. The king of Siam was illogical in denying that water could become ice, merely because, within his experience, a liquid had never become solid. The inconceivable is no sure indication of the impossible. Sir Wil-

liam Hamilton even undertakes to show, that all which *is*
conceivable in thought lies between two extremes, both of
which are inconceivable, but of which, as they are contradictories of each other, one must be true.

But lest this exposition should seem to favor credulity
and superstition, it should be observed, that the paralogism
here exposed is usually met by a counter argument just as
untenable as the one which it is brought forward to confute. Because neither I nor you know *how* a certain
phenomenon is produced, I am not justified in arbitrarily
assigning it to a certain cause, whether natural or supernatural, and then calling upon you to accept this explanation for want of a better. This also would be an appeal
to ignorance, — an attempt to found knowledge upon ignorance. To take an instance from the reputed wonders
of animal magnetism ; — perhaps I do not know *how* the
table tips; but you are not *therefore* to assume that spirits
from the other world are tipping it. It is an *ignoratio
elenchi* to argue, that your hypothesis must be well founded
because I am not able to invent a better. Your business
is to support your own Conclusion by valid reasoning, not
to rest it merely on my inability to prove the opposite.

This Fallacy pervades all the speculations of those whom
Dr. Whewell calls the uniformitarian school of geologists.
They argue that the geological phenomena now visible,
many of which are of stupendous magnitude, *can be* accounted for by the ordinary working of physical causes
now in operation, if we only assign a sufficient lapse of time
for the cumulation of their results. It is unnecessary, they
say, to suppose that there was any cataclasm, any violent
disruption of what is the usual course of nature in our own
days, in order to account for the elevation of vast mountain
chains, the sinking of continents, or the dislocation of strata
many miles in thickness; the same causes, which are now
altering the level of a continent at the rate of an inch in a

century, can have piled up the Andes or the Himalayas, if you give them time enough. Perhaps so; and yet it may be questioned which is the more violent supposition, the sudden and irresistible outbreak of a power whose operations, at least on so grand a scale, have never since been witnessed, or the undisturbed lapse of those countless millions of ages on which the imaginations of geologists love to dwell. But this is not the real question. Their *ignoratio elenchi* consists in multiplying proofs that slow-working causes *might have* effected all these stupendous results, and then jumping at the Conclusion that these causes *did* so produce them. They propound this Dilemma:— Accept this solution of the problem, or propose a better one. We may logically decline to do either. An ingenious mechanic, witnessing for the first time the uniform motion of the hands over the dial-plate of a clock, if challenged to explain, without inspecting the works, *how* this equable and long-continued motion could be produced, might easily invent a combination of springs, wheels, and pinions, which would be adequate for the purpose; but it would be extravagant for him to assume that the machinery thus invented by himself was an exact copy of the works which he had not been allowed to examine. He could only say, the results in question *might be* brought about by my apparatus; but I cannot tell how they are actually produced. Science does not rest on hypothesis, and is not content with *possible* explanations of phenomena.

The well-known rule in controversy, that the burden of proof rests on him who maintains the affirmative, because it is difficult, or impossible, to prove a negative, rests on the considerations here alleged. In order to prove a negative, it must be demonstrated that not one out of many different contingencies admits the positive. Thus a survey of the whole field is necessary, and the exclusion of the opposite hypothesis from every point in it must be made certain. On the other hand, the proof of the positive is established at a single point; no wide range of search is requisite. To borrow an illustration, it is easy to demonstrate that the book *is* in the room; we have only to produce it. But to prove that it *is not* there, "it must be made certain, first, that every book in the room has been found and examined, secondly, that it has been correctly examined. No one, in fact, can prove more than that he cannot find the book; whether the book be there or not, is another question, to be settled by our opinion of the vigilance and competency of the searcher." The geologists say their opponents *cannot find* any proof that the ordinary working of Nature's laws *could not*, in an indefinite lapse of years, produce the effects in question. What is that to the purpose? Our *inability to find* a needle in a hay-mow is no proof that the needle is not there.

Indirectly, indeed, many negatives are established by a single positive; it is thus that an accused person in court makes a triumphant defence by proving what the lawyers call an *alibi;* direct testimony that *he was* in Manchester, on the night in question, is an indirect demonstration that *he was not* in any part of Birmingham, where the crime must have been committed. Here, the testimony required is positive in character, though it tends indirectly to a negative result; hence, it is easily obtained. Sometimes, indeed, when there are but few possible cases, so that the field for search is very limited, we may be required to prove a negative directly. This is the nature of the geometer's demonstration *per impossibile*, as it is called. Failing to obtain direct proof that the angle A is equal to the angle B, we remember that only three suppositions are possible; and then, by demonstrating that it cannot be either greater or less, we indirectly prove that it must be equal. In like manner, after it has been proved that the accused person committed a homicide, it is a *presumption* in law that the act was done "with malice prepense"; in other words, the law puts upon the accused the burden of proof that he did *not* do it maliciously. But this seemingly harsh presumption of law rests, as Mr. De Morgan remarks, upon the fact, that there are so few alternatives to the supposition of wilful murder; in order to disprove malice, the accused is only required to make out either mishap, insanity, or heat of blood. He is not put to hunting for a needle in a hay-mow, under penalty of being hanged if he fails; but, out of four possible cases, he is obliged to disprove the single fatal supposition by direct evidence that his case is some one of the three others.

Most rhetorical artifices may be referred to the class of the *ignoratio elenchi*. Thus, says Dr. Whately, "when the occasion or object in question is not such as calls for, or as is likely to excite in those particular readers or hearers, the emotions required, it is a common rhetorical artifice to turn their attention to some object which *will* call forth these feelings; and when they are too much excited to be capable of judging calmly, it will not be difficult to turn their passions, once roused, in the direction required, and to make them view the case before them in a very different light. When the metal is heated, it may easily be moulded into the desired form. Thus, vehement indignation against some *crime* may be directed against a *person* who has not been proved guilty of it; and vague declamations against corruption, oppression, &c., or against the mischiefs of anarchy, with high-flown panegyrics on liberty, rights of man, &c., or on social order, justice, the constitution, law, religion, &c., will gradually lead the hearers to take for granted, without proof, that the measure proposed will lead to these evils, or to these advantages; and it will in consequence become the object of groundless abhorrence or admiration."

Under this class of Fallacies also may be ranked the

error of adopting an argument which proves either *too little*
or *too much*. In one of these cases, however, the error is
by no means so serious as in the other. The reasoning
which proves too little may be good as far as it goes; it
conduces to the end in view, and, taken in conjunction
with another argument also partial in its effect, it may
establish the whole doctrine in question. But the argument which proves too much is invalid throughout; *Falsus
in uno, falsus in omnibus*, is a sound logical maxim. If
any portion of the Conclusion is evidently false, the reasoning which led to it, considered in itself alone, must
be essentially and altogether vicious; since from correct
premises, and by valid inference, no error whatever can
possibly be deduced.

When the main purpose is to disprove a particular doctrine, it is not enough to refute one or more arguments
that have been alleged in its support; this is merely con-
futing your opponent, and not the proposition which he
maintains, and which may be supported by better reasons
than he has been able to adduce. In like manner, to state
objections, though they may be perfectly valid ones, to a
specific plan of action, is insufficient to prove that this plan
ought to be rejected; for it may well be that some action
is unavoidable, and yet that strong objections may be urged
against every mode of action that can be devised. When
the Necessitarian says that the doctrine of the freedom of
the human will is inconceivable, Sir William Hamilton
justly replies, that the argument proves too little; for it is
at least equally inconceivable that the will should *not* be
free. Unbelievers, says Dr. Whately, "may find numerous objections against various parts of Scripture, to some
of which no satisfactory answer can be given; and the
incautious hearer is apt, while his attention is fixed on
these, to forget that there are infinitely more and stronger
objections against the supposition that the Christian religion

T

is of *human* origin; and that, where we cannot answer all objections, we are bound in reason and in candor to adopt the hypothesis which labors under the least."

3. A full illustration of the Fallacy, *non causa pro causa*, would carry us too far into the domain of the physical sciences, and therefore would be more in place as a chapter of Applied Logic. Only the more frequent and obvious errors of this class can be noticed here. Prominent among these are the common blunders of reasoning *post hoc, ergo propter hoc;* of mistaking physical laws for efficient causes; and of applying the doctrine of the Necessitarian or Fatalist as a motive of action, or rather of inaction, in our ordinary concerns.

An invariable antecedent is a *sign*, but often it is indisputably not a *cause*, of the phenomenon which it precedes. As that which *leads the mind to expect* a certain event, it may be regarded as a *causa cognoscendi;* but this is very different from the *causa essendi*, which is the ordinary signification of the word *cause*. Cicero states this distinction very clearly: — *Causa autem ea est quæ id efficit cujus est causa. Non sic causa intelligi debet, ut, quod cuique antecedat, id ei causa sit, sed quod cuique efficienter antecedat.* In this sense, deliberation is certainly not the cause of the action which follows it, nor is one beat of the pulse the cause of the subsequent beats. In fact, two successive states of the same substance are seldom regarded even by the vulgar as cause and effect. But since we necessarily think a cause as immediately preceding its effect, or as simultaneous with it, the mind is prone, especially in the case of obscure and anomalous phenomena, of which the true cause cannot easily be discovered, to consider any antecedent event as such a cause. This is the origin of the belief in omens, and many other superstitions of the vulgar. An accidental conjunction in time between some private or public calamity, and the appearance of a meteor or a comet, or the occurrence of an earthquake, is regarded as indicating a causal union of the two events. The science of medicine, at least in that branch of it which is called therapeutics, is little else than an application of the maxim, *Post hoc, ergo propter hoc.* The wisest physician cannot tell, in any one case, whether the recovery of the patient took place because he swallowed the drugs, or in spite of them, or whether they were powerless in respect either to good or evil. A harsh application of this fallacious rule consists in judging the wisdom of a man's conduct by its consequences, or the uprightness of his intentions by the immediate results of his action upon the happiness or misery of those around him. A brave and able commander is not always successful in battle, and a conscientious and kind-hearted man may be compelled by a sense of duty to inflict suffering and death. *Practical* men, as they are called, who profess to be guided only by experience, and to rely upon facts instead of theories, are especially liable to this class of errors. In their eyes, the disorders and other evils which follow some long-delayed reform are attributable to the reform itself, and not to its undue postponement.

Forming an induction from too small a class of cases, and disregarding negative instances, are the frequent source of this confusion between an antecedent phenomenon and an efficient cause. The most common of all the superstitions of the vulgar, the belief that Friday is an unlucky day for beginning any new enterprise, may be traced to this origin. And it should not be forgotten, that the prognostications of evil thus formed very often bring about their own fulfilment; fearful and dispirited men can make little effectual effort to avert danger. The belief in the hereditary transmission of diseases of mind and body, at least in the unreasonable extent to which it now prevails, is formed in this manner, and tends in this way to verify itself. Gout and insanity run in families where a perpetual apprehension of them exists, and where, perchance, habits of life are actually transmitted from father to son which are likely to induce and foster such diseases. But even in these cases, a careful enumeration might satisfy one that, of all who are within the unlucky circle, at least as many escape the dreaded calamity as those who suffer from it. Were it otherwise, indeed, the circle would continue to enlarge itself in successive generations, till few could hope to escape the hereditary taint. As Dr. Johnson remarks, the one prophetic dream which comes to pass is remembered and spoken of, while the ninety and nine which fail of accomplishment are forgotten.

"In minds not habituated to accurate thinking," says Mr. Mill, "there is often a confused notion that the general *laws* are the *causes* of the partial ones; that the law of general gravitation, for example, *causes* the phenomenon of the fall of bodies to the earth. But to assert this would be a misuse of the word *cause;* terrestrial gravity is not an *effect* of general gravitation, but a *case* of it; that is, one kind of the particular instances in which that general law obtains." A Law of Nature is only a general fact, or, rather, a general statement comprehending under it many similar individual facts. Hence, such a Law *does not account for*, or *explain*, the phenomena of Nature; it only *describes* them. Thus, it is not a Law of Hydrostatics which causes water to remain at the same level in the two arms of a bent tube; but the fact that water stands at this level is ranked among many other facts, which are comprehended under the general statement *called a Law* of Hydrostatics.

The process of Thought by which we pass from a Physical Law to an individual case happening under it is one of Deduction, and is therefore governed by the *dictum de omni.* Because *all bodies* tend to fall towards the common centre of gravity, therefore *this body* thus tends to fall. Hence, the statement of the Law is that which *makes us believe* that the individual event will happen; and this, by a very natural confusion of Thought, is mistaken for the *cause* which *makes the event happen.* But the relation in the former case is that between Premises and Conclusion; in the latter, between Cause and Effect; the former is a law of Thought, the latter is a law of things; the one is the *causa cognoscendi,* the other, the *causa essendi.*

The Fallacy here exposed is one of much interest, as it is that which lies at the bottom of every scheme of Materialism, — every attempt to account for the origin of species, and the general phenomena of the universe, without bringing in any other agency than that of mere Physical Laws, or what it was once the fashion to call "Second Causes." Such a theory is not only insufficient, or unsupported by the requisite evidence; it is founded upon a mere confusion of Thought, and is illogical and absurd. There is no such thing as the *agency* or *action* of a Law; except as a figure of speech, we might as well predicate *locomotion* of an *idea,* or speak of *bilateral triangles.* "Second Causes" are no causes at all; they are mere fictions of the intellect, and exist only in Thought. A *cause* in the proper sense of the word, that is, an *efficient* cause, as original and direct in its action, must be a *First* cause; that through which its action is transmitted is not a cause, but a portion of the *effect,* — as it does not act, but is acted upon.

The *Ignava Ratio,* or do-nothing argument, is a fallacious application of the Necessitarian theory. According to this theory, all occurrences whatever have their environment of circumstances, with which they stand in necessary and fixed relations by an absolute law; and the state of the universe at any one moment, in all its parts, from the creation of a world to the stirring of an aspen-leaf, could not possibly have been different from what is. Every occurrence has its cause, of which it is the necessary result, and to which it is necessarily proportioned, even in the minutest respects. Every event, of course, is surrounded by other events, and must be considered as being at the same time both antecedent and consequent, — as necessarily resulting from those which preceded it, and necessarily followed by those which come after it, — and thus as forming one link in an adamantine chain which extends from eternity to eternity. As Mr. Mill himself, an enlightened and consistent advocate of this theory, remarks, "there is no Thing produced, no event happening, in the known universe, which is not connected by a uniformity, or invariable sequence, with some one or more of the phenomena which preceded it; insomuch that it will happen again as often as these phenomena occur again, and as no other phenomenon having the character of a counteracting cause shall coexist. These antecedent phenomena, again, were connected in a similar manner with some that preceded them; and so on, until we reach, as the ultimate step attainable by us, either the properties of some one primeval cause, or the conjunction of several. The state of the whole universe at any instant we believe to be the consequent of its state at the previous instant; insomuch that one who knew all the agents which exist at the present moment, their collocation in space, and their properties, — in other words, the laws of their agency, — could predict the whole subsequent history of the universe, at least unless some new volition of a power capable of controlling the universe should supervene." *

The confutation of this astounding theory is the business of the metaphysician or the theologian; we have no concern with it here, except to point out the Fallacy of regarding it as justifying inaction, or as demonstrating the

* Mill's *Logic*, 3d ed., Vol. I. p. 358.

hopelessness of any endeavor on our part to control the course of natural events. The *Ignava Ratio* is thus stated by Cicero, in the form of an argument against taking any measures for the restoration of one's health.

If it is fated that you shall recover from the present disease, then you will recover whether you call in a physician or not. If it is fated that you shall not recover, then, with or without a physician, you will not recover.
But either the one or the other of these two contradictories is fated.
Therefore, it will be of no use to call in a doctor.

As Cicero remarks, if this reasoning were correct, our whole life would be reduced to a state of hopeless inactivity; as it would prove the inutility of any endeavor to bring about a desirable result, or to avert a threatened calamity. The Turks, who are fatalists, so understand it, and reduce it to practice by refusing to take any precautions against a pestilence, or to remove a lighted match from its dangerous proximity to a powder-magazine. But they only show thereby that they are incapable of following out correctly the logical consequences of their own doctrine. Calling in medical aid furnishes a new antecedent, and thus presents a new case for the determination of Fate. It may also be fated that I should send for a physician, and, with his aid, that I should recover; or it may be fated that he should not be called in, and, *as a consequence of this neglect*, and not as a necessary result of the disease alone, that I should die. Fate is only a concurrence of causes and an assemblage of conditions; supply a new cause, take away one of the necessary conditions, and the result will be different, though it will still be a fated or necessary result. Zeno aptly confuted this Fallacy, when he was whipping a slave, who called out, in excuse for his fault, that it was fated for him to steal; " And so it is for me to whip you," was the reply.

Most of the sophisms once called Inexplicable have been already resolved in treating of the different classes of Fallacies to which they were respectively referred. It is only necessary to consider here the famous argument, called the Achilles, proposed by Zeno the Eleatic, as Mr. Mansel says, " to support the leading tenet of Parmenides, of the unity of all things, by showing that the identity of rest and motion is a necessary result from the contrary opinion." It might more aptly be adduced to prove that extension is not infinitely divisible, for if it were so, according to this argument, motion would be impossible. The sophism is thus stated.

The swiftest runner can never overtake the slowest, if the latter has ever so little the start. Suppose, for instance, that Achilles runs ten times as fast as a tortoise, and that the tortoise is one mile in advance at the outset. While Achilles is traversing this mile, the tortoise has advanced $\frac{1}{10}$th of a mile farther; before his pursuer has passed over this $\frac{1}{10}$th, the tortoise has advanced $\frac{1}{100}$th, and then, again, $\frac{1}{1000}$th, and so on forever, always being some fraction, however small, of a mile in advance.

Dr. Whately seems to have been entirely puzzled by this sophism, as he does not attempt a solution of it, but merely remarks that it "furnishes a confirmation of the utility of an acquaintance with the Syllogistic form, in which form the pretended demonstration cannot possibly be expressed." But this confession, as Mr. Mansel observes, " is in fact a surrender of the Syllogistic criterion, as a means of discriminating between sound and unsound reasoning. On the contrary, nothing is easier than to exhibit the reasoning in a Syllogism, and to show thereby that the fallacy does not lie in the Form, but the Matter. Thus, representing the whole space to be traversed by a,

'Any space equal to $\frac{a}{10} + \frac{a}{100} + \frac{a}{1000}$, &c. is infinite (being the sum of an infinite series).

'The space to be passed before Achilles overtakes the tortoise is equal to this sum.
'Therefore, it is infinite.'

" The whole logical mystery of this famous Fallacy lies in this, that *the major premise is false*. The sum of an infinite series may be, and in this case is, finite. This premise is equally false, whether space is, or is not, divisible *ad infinitum*." *

Fries remarks that the sophistry is here covered up by the mode of stating the problem. The question really asked is, when will Achilles have passed over the particular extent of ground which the tortoise, at any one moment, *has already left behind him;* and this question, on account of the infinite divisibility of space and time, may be repeated *ad infinitum*. The true question, at what point will Achilles *overtake* the tortoise, is not allowed to come into view. The space between the two parties, however small, is, *in thought, though not in reality*, infinitely divisible; and the series of constantly diminishing terms into which it is mentally broken up, though infinite in number, is finite in amount, the sum of the series being equal, of course, only to the small space originally divided. Any finite quantity may be broken up into an infinite number of terms, if these terms become infinitely small. The confusion of thought consists in mistaking the sum of the terms of such a descending series, composed of infinitesimals, for the sum of an infinite series the terms of which are not infinitely small. It is only this latter sum which is necessarily an infinite quantity.

* Mansel's *Notes to Aldrich*, pp. 141, 142.

CHAPTER X.

APPLIED LOGIC.

APPLIED Logic, as it will be here understood, includes both what has usually been called the Doctrine of Method, and what Sir William Hamilton terms Modified Logic. Its object is the proper regulation of the Thinking Faculty, not only in forming individual cognitions, but in the more complex processes required for the construction and advancement of Science. Pure Logic, as we have seen, is concerned only with the Forms of Thought; it considers these as given, or already formed, and regards only the necessary and fundamental laws, emanating from the mind itself, which have concurred in their formation and which regulate their use. Applied Logic has regard also to the Matter of Thought, — to the infinitely numerous and diversified objects of cognition which Nature furnishes us, — and considers by what general processes these are brought within the grasp of mind, or are made intelligible, or, what is the same thing, are put under the Forms of Thought. The laws which govern these processes are not universal and necessary, as in the former case, but are contingent and varied, depending, in part, on the diverse and multiform characteristics of the objects of cognition, and, in part, on the powers and limitations of the human mind itself. To avoid the vagueness and perplexity which result from attempting to grasp too much, Applied Logic treats directly only of the latter, — that is, of the formation of Science so far as this depends on the nature of the human intellect, leaving to the special sciences the duty of adapting their own procedures to the nature of the peculiar objects of study with which they are immediately concerned.

This division, however, like many others in Science, cannot be always accurately preserved. The processes through which the mind acts can be exemplified only in their application to various classes of objects, and as varying somewhat with the nature of those objects. The practical distinction will be, that Applied Logic regards the peculiarities of what we are thinking about only so far as these illustrate, and in some measure direct, the processes of thinking. It considers primarily how the mind acts, and only secondarily what it is acting upon.

Science is a body of truths relating to any well-defined object or class of objects, so arranged as to be easily comprehended and retained, and conveniently used. The merits at which it aims are Completeness, Thoroughness, and Method. Its objects are the numberless things which Nature furnishes us for study.

What we call *Nature* is an assemblage of objects and a succession of events. The mind, on account of the limitation of its faculties, and the endless number and variety of these objects and events, cannot grasp and consider them all at once. Neither can it undertake to study successively each individual thing by itself; for a lifetime might be so spent, before we could obtain even a small fraction of the knowledge which is requisite for the proper guidance of life. The first necessity, then, which is imposed upon us by the constitution of the mind itself, is to break up the infinite wealth of Nature into groups and classes of things, with reference to their resemblances and affinities, and thus to enlarge the grasp of our mental faculties, even at the expense of sacrificing the minuteness of information which can be acquired only by studying objects in detail. The first efforts in the pursuit of knowledge, then, must be directed to the business of Classification. Perhaps it will be found in the sequel, that Classification is not only the beginning, but the culmination and the end, of human knowledge.

We will first consider the mental processes through which we gain a knowledge of real Objects, — that is, of Objects which coexist in space, leaving for subsequent inquiry the question, how far these processes must be modified in constructing a science of Events which succeed each other in time.

It has already been remarked, that the beginning of all knowledge is in single acts of the Perceptive or Acquisitive Faculty, which operates either through the external senses, thus constituting External Perception, or through that notice which the mind takes of what is passing within itself, this being denominated Consciousness, or Internal Perception. In either case, one indivisible act of the Perceptive Faculty gives us to know only one phenomenon. A succession of such acts relating to one Object furnishes a number of cognitions of the qualities or attributes of that Object; and these qualities we unite together, and bind up into one whole, through the conception, which the mind furnishes, of *Substance*, or *that in which the qualities inhere.* Thus, suppose the Object presented is an apple; the eye tells me that it is red; the touch, that it is spherical and moderately hard; the muscular sense, that it has weight; the taste, that it is subacid, &c.; and these qualities I unite into one whole by the conception of *one substance* in which they all inhere, and call the aggregate thus formed *apple.* The reason why just these qualities, and no others, are united into the whole is, that they all are, or may be, received at one time, under the same circumstances, and appear to proceed from one Object, as they are referred by me to one definite locality in space.

Take another instance from Internal Perception. I am conscious, either at once or in succession, of joy or pain, of a thought, reminiscence, or volition, of a sensation of hunger, coldness, &c.; and these separate Intuitions I put together into one whole through the Intuition, which enters into each of them, that they are *mine*, or that they all belong to the one person which I call *myself*. Here, the Intuition of *Self* is the unifying principle, or that through which the aggregation of many into one is accomplished, just as, in the former case, it was the conception of *Substance*.

Manifestly, then, the first step towards the formation of science is a Synthesis, a putting together of the Matter of several Intuitions into that one whole which we call an Individual Object. This Object itself, though called an Individual, as if it were one thing, has in truth only a virtual unity; it is really complex, consisting of many parts and many qualities, which were at first separately perceived; but having often been perceived together, or in combination, they become so firmly united that the perception of a few, perhaps of only one, of its parts or qualities immediately calls up the imagination of all the others, that is, of the whole. Thus, I am said to perceive the apple, when, in fact, I perceive only its shape and color; but this shape and color immediately suggest all its other qualities, and the complex Intuition thus formed, partly perceived and partly imagined, is what is called, though improperly, a single perception of one thing. The wholes thus formed are of all degrees of complexity, either having as many parts, qualities, and uses as a house or an intricate machine, or as few as a spot of purple cloud in the sky. They may be either real or factitious, the conception and belief of *actual existence* being one of the parts or elements of the former, but not of the latter. Each of these wholes is, or might be, designated by a Proper Name, belonging to this one thing and to nothing else.

But as the number of such Objects and Names would be endless, we seek, as has been said, to bring them within the grasp of the mind by throwing them into groups and classes. The first step of the process directed to this end is the reverse of the former one; we must now begin by Analysis. The many complex wholes, called Individual Objects, which we have previously formed by a procedure so easy and so frequently repeated that we are almost unconscious of it, must now be resolved into their constituent parts and properties, in order that, by an abstraction of their dissimilar elements and restricting the attention to those which are similar, classes may be formed, all the members of which have some like or equivalent attributes. The process of Classification, then, is an Analysis immediately followed by a Synthesis into groups, this Synthesis being directed by the Comparative or Elaborative Faculty of the mind, the chief function of which is the perception of relations, and especially the relations of likeness and unlikeness. Having formed one set of classes, called the Infimæ Species, because they are composed of Individuals only, we then proceed, in an exactly similar way, to group these groups into Genera; and so on, erecting a hierarchy of Concepts, until we at least approximate a Summum Genus, or that thought which embraces all conceivable things. The highest generalization usually attempted is that which arranges all existence, whether actual or potential, under the three heads, Man, the Universe, and God who is Absolute Being and Absolute Cause.

Evidently, then, the universal procedure of Science is an Analysis followed by a Synthesis, the result of the whole being a more or less complete Classification. All the problems which Science has to solve may be reduced to these two questions: What Classes ought to be formed? and, Does this or that Object possess the special attribute or attributes which entitle it to be ranked under a certain

Class? Isolated cognitions — the knowledge, for instance, that this particular attribute does, or does not, belong to this particular thing — are not entitled to be called Science, until they are arranged in some Class, or subsumed under some comprehensive Law.

There is a confusion in the application of the terms Analysis and Synthesis, which may be best resolved by borrowing a passage from Sir William Hamilton. " It is manifest, in general, from the meaning of the words, that the term Analysis can only be applied to the separation of a whole into its parts; and that the term Synthesis can only be applied to the collection of parts into a whole. So far, no ambiguity is possible, — no room is left for abuse. But there are different kinds of *whole* and *parts;* some of the wholes, like the whole of Comprehension (called also the *Metaphysical*), and the whole of Extension (called also the *Logical*), are in the inverse ratio of each other; so that what in the one is a *part,* is necessarily in the other a *whole.* It is evident, then, that the counter processes of Analysis and Synthesis, as applied to these counter wholes and parts, should fall into one, or correspond; inasmuch as each in the one quantity should be diametrically opposite to itself in the other. Thus, Analysis, as applied to Comprehension, is the reverse process of Analysis as applied to Extension, but a corresponding process with Synthesis; and *vice versa.* Now, should it happen that the existence and opposition of the two quantities are not considered, — that men, viewing the whole of Extension or the whole of Comprehension, each to the exclusion of the other, must define Analysis and Synthesis with reference to that single quantity which they exclusively take into account; — on this supposition, I say, it is manifest that, if different philosophers regard different wholes or quantities, we may have the terms Analysis and Synthesis absolutely used by different philosophers in a contrary or reverse sense. And this has actually happened. The ancients, in general, looking only to the whole of Extension, use the terms Analysis and Synthesis simply to denote a division of the Genus into Species, — of the Species into Individuals; the moderns, on the other hand, in general, looking only at the whole of Comprehension, employ these terms to express a resolution of the Individual into its various attributes."

The words *analytic* and *synthetic*, Hamilton further observes, "are, like most of our logical terms, taken from Geometry"; and the applications of them in this science are thus admirably illustrated by Dr. Whewell. In *discursive* processes of reasoning, he remarks, "we obtain our conclusions, not by looking at our conceptions steadily in one view, which is *intuition*, but by passing from one view to another, like those who run from place to place (*discursus*). Thus, a straight line may be, at the same time, a side of a triangle and a radius of a circle; and in the first proposition of Euclid, a line is considered first in one of these relations, and then in the other, and thus the sides of a certain triangle are proved to be equal. And by this 'discourse of reason,' as by our older writers it was termed, we set forth from those axioms which we perceive by intuition, travel securely over a vast and varied region, and become possessed of a copious store of mathematical truths." In such geometrical reasoning, he continues, "we introduce at every step some new consideration; and it is by combining all these considerations that we arrive at the conclusion, that is, the demonstration of the proposition. Each step tends to the final result, by exhibiting some part of the figure under a new relation. To what we have already proved, is added something more; and hence this process is called *Synthesis*, or *putting together*. The proof flows on, receiving at every turn new contributions from different quarters; like a river fed and augmented by many tributary streams. And each of these tributaries flows from some definition or axiom as its fountain, or is itself formed by the union of smaller rivulets which have sources of this kind. In descending along its course, the synthetical proof gathers all these accessions into one common trunk, the proposition finally proved.

"But we may proceed in a different manner. We may begin from the formed river, and ascend to its sources. We may take the proposition of which we require a proof, and may examine what the supposition of its truth implies. If this be true, then something else may be seen to be true; and from this, something else, and so on. We may often, in this way, discover of what simpler propositions our theorem or solution is compounded, and may resolve these in succession, till we come to some proposition which is obvious. This is geometrical *Analysis*. Having succeeded in this analytical process, we may invert it; and may descend again, from the simple and known propositions, to the proof of a theorem, or the solution of a problem, which was our starting-place."*

We have said that an Individual Object, as thought, is a Synthesis of parts and attributes. But it is not an arbitrary Synthesis, — not a putting together of any elements whatever, such as mere caprice may have induced us to select. Imaginary Objects, it is true, may be thus built up at pleasure; mere fancy may construct a centaur, a griffin, or any other imaginative creation, recognizing it at the moment to be unreal. But if *actual existence* is one of the elements of the combination, that is, if the Object thus thought is understood to be a *real* Object, our conception of it must be a Synthesis of such parts and properties only as we know it actually possesses. *Truth* may be defined to be the conformity of our mental representations to the things which they are intended to represent; and in Applied Logic, where we are concerned not only with the

* *Philosophy of the Inductive Sciences*, Vol. I. p. 144.

Form, but with the Matter, of Thought, *truth* is the chief object in view, — the first requisite of Science. The Synthesis in thought is true only when it corresponds to the combination which exists in nature.

In like manner, the Classification which is to serve the purposes of Science cannot be arbitrary. In the construction of Science, the first, and perhaps the most difficult, question which we have to answer is, What classes ought to be formed. " The power of framing classes," says Mr. Mill, " is unlimited, as long as there is any (even the smallest) difference to found a distinction upon. Take any attribute whatever, and if some things have it and others have it not, we may ground upon this attribute a division of all things into two classes; and we actually do so, the moment we create a name which connotes the attribute "; — as the class of *white* things, and that of things *not-white*. " The number of possible classes, therefore, is boundless; and there are as many actual classes (either of real or imaginary things) as there are general names, positive and negative together."

The relations and connections of the various attributes with each other must guide us in selecting those upon which the Classification is to be founded. The purpose of the arrangement is, that all the individual objects included in any one class shall have as many common or similar elements as possible ; — that they shall resemble each other in numerous and important respects. Now it is found that certain attributes always carry along with them, or are constantly found in company with, many other attributes ; — not merely those which are necessarily thus connected as derivative from them by necessary inference, but many others, of which we can only say that nature always puts them together. On the other hand, certain attributes have no such regular companionship, but are found indifferently in connection with entirely different sets of elements. Among inorganic bodies, for example, the metallic property is an instance of the former class; among animals, the possession of a vertebrated column or backbone. There is good reason, then, for forming a class of Metals, and a class of Vertebrates, because we are sure that each of these classes will have many common properties, besides the single one from which their name is derived. On the contrary, the same color or the same magnitude is not found in constant companionship with many other qualities, so that it would be comparatively useless to form a class of white objects, or a class of animals three feet high. Such classes would be found to include the most dissimilar and heterogeneous members.

It is evident even from these few examples, that the quality selected as a principle of Classification is not usually an obvious or conspicuous trait. The casual observer would generally think that it was small and insignificant. Thus, the Botanist, disregarding the size, shape, and color of trunk, branches, and leaves, founds an important classification of plants upon the minute and rudimentary cotyledons, or seed-coverings. All the Monocotyledons are Endogens, and therefore have in common all the numerous traits of that great tribe or family; while the Dicotyledons are all Exogens. On the other hand, the number and relative position of the stamens and pistils, on which Linnæus founded his artificial system, are not found to be invariably joined with any important features in the organization of the vegetable kingdom. It should be observed, however, that classifications are framed for different uses; and the peculiar nature of the purpose in view may justify an arrangement that would be otherwise indefensible. Thus, the alphabetical order is the only convenient one for a dictionary; but only such classifications of words are properly scientific as are found in Logic and Grammar.

In order to carry on the Classification, and erect a hierarchy of Concepts of many ascending steps, it is absolutely essential that the Infima Species, or class first formed, should embrace only those individuals which have, at least, several common attributes. There must be, at least, as many of these attributes as will furnish a Specific Difference for each step in the ascending scale.

Passing now from the science of coexistent objects to that of events which succeed one another in time, we come upon a totally different principle of connection. In the former case, it was the Concept of *substance;* in the present one, it is that of *causation.* It belongs to Metaphysics rather than to Logic to explain the peculiar nature of the relation of Cause and Effect. Here it is enough to say, that the connection between them is conceived to be absolute or necessary; where the Cause exists, the Effect *must* follow, and the presence of the Effect is inconceivable unless the Cause immediately precedes it. But *causation,* as well as *substance,* is incognizable through the perceptions of sense. In the outward world, at least, we never can perceive the *nexus,* the bond of union which *compels* the Effect to follow. We believe that it exists, and that the connection is a necessary one; but we are compelled to infer its existence from the invariableness of the sequence in time between the two events. If heat is applied to wax, the wax always melts; if poison in sufficient quantity is taken into the stomach, the man invariably dies. Hence we are led to believe that the heat *causes* the melting, and the poison *causes* the death; or, in other words, that the subsequent event is the *necessary* result of some *power* or *force* in the antecedent, which, though it cannot be perceived by us, inevitably produces this phenomenon. If heat be a true Cause, the melting of the wax *must* follow; but as far as our experience, and, if human testimony may be believed, as far as all human experience has gone, the melting always *does* follow; therefore, the heat is the Cause. On such reasoning as this, all our evidence of *physical causation* — i. e. of Causation in the material universe — depends. But it is obvious that the reasoning is illogical and the evidence is insufficient. Human experience is limited; it extends only to a certain number of cases, — no matter to how many, as the number is certainly finite. Any number of instances of actual measurement would never satisfy the geometer that the three angles of a triangle *must* equal two right angles. It is conceivable — nay, the case has actually happened — that, after one hundred millions of favorable instances occurring in uninterrupted succession, the hundred-million-and-first instance should be an exception, or one of an opposite character. Mr. Babbage tells us that his Calculating Machine may be so adjusted that, when put in regular motion by the descent of a weight, it will present to the eye successively the series of natural numbers, 1, 2, 3, 4, 5, &c.; that, if we should have patience and time to watch it long enough, we should find that it would present this series in one unbroken chain from 1 up to 100,000,000, each term exceeding its antecedent by unity. Now an induction extending successively to 100,000,000 terms, without a single inconformable instance being discovered, would be regarded by most persons as equivalent to a demonstration that the law of the series was universal or absolute. But in fact, the next number presented, after 100,000,001, instead of being 100,000,002 would be 100,010,002, and the next term would be 100,030,003. Human experience, then, as it is limited to a finite number of cases, can never establish an absolute law, or prove that a certain result is *necessary*. As the very idea of Efficient Causation involves that of the *necessary* consequence of the Effect, it follows that the range of human experience in the material universe does not extend to the discovery of Causes properly so called.

In all the Physical Sciences, then, *causation* should be

understood to mean only *constant conjunction in time*. We cannot even declare that this conjunction is absolutely *invariable;* all that can be said is, that it *has been* invariable so far as human observation has extended, and we may firmly believe that no instance will ever be found to the contrary. But this is not a *necessary* belief; its contradictory neither violates any Law of Thought, nor any of the primitive and ineradicable laws of human belief. The assumed invariability of what are called "the laws of nature" rests upon no foundation whatever but uniform experience, and is absolutely certain, therefore, only to the extent of that experience. That a Law of Nature may hereafter be violated, or be altogether changed, is not merely *conceivable;* we say as much as that of any Judgment which does not contradict one of the Axioms of Pure Thought. Such a violation or change must be pronounced to be *possible*, though not probable. Our only reason, for instance, for believing that sugar always will be soluble in water, and that powdered chalk, under the same circumstances, will always be insoluble, is, that, though a vast number of experiments have been tried, we have not, *as yet*, known or heard of one instance to the contrary.

But in the strict meaning of the word *cause*, — that is, *efficient cause*, — what is called the Law of Causation is absolute; it is, in the strictest meaning of the term, *impossible* that any event should take place without a true Cause. I do not say that the contradictory of this Law would violate any Axiom of Pure Thought; for as we are now concerned, not with the Form, but with the Matter, of Thought, these Axioms are inapplicable. But it may be said that the Law of Causation is held to be inviolable by what I have here called "the primitive and ineradicable laws of human belief." It is, for instance, just as impossible for us to believe that an event should take place without a Cause, as it is to believe that any particular space should be annihilated, or that what I am now conscious of does not really exist as a mental phenomenon. He who can believe that space has limits or boundaries beyond which there is no space, or that he himself does not exist as a thinking being, may also believe that a physical event can take place without a Cause; no sane person is capable of crediting either of these propositions.

The distinction here established would seem to authorize some change of the phraseology usually employed in Physical Science. What has hitherto been denominated, not only by physicists, but by people generally, a *cause*, might more properly be called a constant *condition*, of the phenomenon. What the physical inquirer is really in search of, when he is inquiring after what he calls the *cause* of any event, is a constant *antecedent* of it, which, being discovered, will ever afterwards enable him, should not the sequence of antecedent and consequent be altered, (and of this he justly entertains no fears whatever,) to predict the recurrence of the phenomenon. To him, the Law of Causation, to adopt Mr. J. S. Mill's language, means only this: " For every event, there exists some combination of events, some given concurrence of circumstances, positive and negative, the occurrence of which will always be followed by that phenomenon." Under this view, the so-called Laws of Nature might more properly be denominated General Facts, as the word " law " generally implies what is absolute or necessary. But as any sweeping change of scientific phraseology is hardly to be expected, the language heretofore in use must continue to be employed, though under protest from those who understand the impropriety of its application. There may be Laws of Nature which are absolutely invariable; but it is certain that none such have been, or ever can be, discovered. Human science is merely able to establish certain General Facts, which are indisputably true only to the extent of our experience.

We shall hereafter examine some of the reasons which have caused a higher degree of certainty and generality to be attributed to these Facts than they actually deserve.

It is manifest from what has been said, that Science is made up of two sorts of cognitions, — those in which the objects are given as contingent phenomena, and those in which the objects are given as necessary facts or laws. The former are called *empirical*, as they are derived from experience, and are true only to the extent of that experience. Their origin is also said to be *a posteriori*, because they are *subsequent* to experience. The latter are said to be *a priori* in origin, for although first manifested on occasion of experience, they are truly prior to it; for if they had not previously existed, as native to the mind and inwrought into its very constitution, experience itself would not have been possible. We have already had examples of such, in our notions of *substance, cause, space, time,* &c. These may be expressed, as here, each by a single term which is significant of one act of the mind, — an indivisible Intuition or Thought; or they may be resolved into one or more Judgments, as statements of *necessary laws*. Thus, the cognition of *substance* may be resolved into this Law, that *every real attribute or quality presupposes some substance in which it inheres*. *Cause,* as already mentioned, furnishes the universal and absolute Law of Causation, that *every physical event or change must have a cause.* The Intuition of *space* yields many necessary Judgments, thus: *Every physical object must exist in space; Space is indestructible, even in Thought, as a whole, or in any of its parts; Space is boundless;* &c. The notion of *Time* also is resolved into several necessary laws, thus: *Every event must take place at some determinate point in time; Time necessarily flows on in one continuous lapse; Time is boundless both before and after,* or, as the Schoolmen say, both *a parte ante* and *a parte post;* &c.

These necessary Laws must be regarded as mere explications of their respective *a priori* cognitions; they are not inferences from such cognitions, but are involved in them, so that it is impossible to have a full and adequate conception of the one — that is, to fully understand the meaning of the term — without the other. In neither form, as one conception nor as a judgment, can they be derived from experience; for experience can only tell me of what is true in certain cases, — namely, those cases which I or other persons have actually witnessed; while these Laws are known to be absolutely true for *all* cases past, present, and future. All the maxims of experience are reversible in thought; that is, I can conceive that their opposites or contraries should be true; — I can conceive, for instance, that fire should not burn, that water should not drown, that stones should fall upwards instead of downwards, that "when the brains were out, the man should *not* die." But these necessary cognitions *a priori* are not reversible in thought; I cannot conceive that an attribute should exist without a substance, or that space should be annihilated, or have limits affixed to it, or that a physical event should take place without a Cause. Moreover, as has been said, these cognitions are prerequisites of experience, without which experience itself would not be possible. As no body can exist without space, no quality without a substance, I could not have my *first* experience of either, — that is, I could not know body to be body, or quality to be quality, — unless these cognitions were already present to the mind, although then first drawn out and made distinct to consciousness. As the capacity of being exploded must be conceived to exist in the gunpowder *before* the actual explosion can take place, although this capacity was latent up to that moment, so the cognition of *space* must have been in the mind before we could have a conception of *body*, and the cognition of *time*, before we could have that of an *event*, since every event must be in time.

And yet these cognitions are not, like the Axioms which we formerly considered, mere Laws of *thought;* for they are necessarily apprehended as actual and immutable Laws of real *things.* It is true, that the attribution of these Laws to actual phenomena is an act of thought; so is all cognition, whether of external events and things, or of abstract universal principles. Berkeley and other Idealists, then, who hold that what we call external realities exist only in the mind, may consistently maintain that these *a priori* cognitions are merely necessities of thinking thus and so. But the Realist, who believes in the objective validity of our external perceptions, who holds that things are what they seem to be, cannot consistently deny the objective reality of those Forms and Laws without which any external existence would be impossible, — which are, in fact, necessary conditions of the reality of such existence. Hence I cannot but regard Kant's elaborate attempt to reduce these cognitions to mere Laws of Thought as inconsistent with his own doctrine. He affirms that we have no knowledge of external realities, and are, therefore, incompetent to pronounce whether they do, or do not, possess certain attributes; and yet he declares that "things in themselves" have a real existence apart from our thoughts. He admits the distinction between *noumena* and *phenomena,* between things as they are and things as they appear, and asserts the reality of the former, though they are wholly incognizable to our minds. But if they are absolutely incognizable, how does he know that they do not exist under the Laws of space, time, and Cause; and if they are real, how can they exist except under those Laws which are the conditions of all reality? To deny the objective validity of these Laws is to contradict the primitive testimony of consciousness, and to cut away the foundations of all philosophy, whether dogmatic, critical, or sceptical, by impeaching the correctness of those principles and arguments by which the sceptic himself attempts to show the reasonableness of his doubts. I have no better and no other reason for affirming that two straight lines cannot enclose a space, than for pronouncing that space itself exists in some other manner than as a mere law of the perceptive faculty. The doctrine of the Idealists is at least intelligible; for I can imagine the annihilation or non-existence of objects in space; but the non-existence of space itself is literally unthinkable. It is a mere paradox to assert the reality of the objects, whose existence is contingent, and deny that of space, which exists by necessity. And the argument is worse than the doctrine which it is offered to support; since the only reason alleged for believing space and time to be unreal, is the impossibility of thinking that they are unreal.

In conformity with what has been said, it might seem that the doctrine of the formation of Science would properly fall into two great divisions; the one relating to the acquisition of contingent knowledge by means of experience, and the other to the attainment of necessary knowledge by the development and application of those primitive truths which are revealed to us in the very constitution of our minds. And, in a certain sense, this division exists. Geometry and Arithmetic, as the sciences of continuous and discrete quantity, are applied most directly, and in their purest form, to the conceptions of space and time, in which these two modes of quantity are most clearly manifested, not being modified or confused by the presence of other attributes. The lapse of time cannot be conceived or expressed except by the idea of *number*, or discrete quantity; and the extent of space, in like manner, is necessarily conceived as continuous quantity. And in both cases, our conception of pure quantity is most distinct, because there are so few other attributes of space and time with which it might become confused. But these two sciences are not restricted to the consideration of pure space and time, and do not exhaust our conceptions of them. They relate to space and time only so far as these are *magnitudes*, or things to be measured; and they relate to everything else, *so far forth* as any other thing is susceptible of measurement. Mathematics itself is the science of relative magnitude. Thus, Algebra, which is the highest form of mathematical generalization, is the science of *pure* magnitude, or quantity in the abstract, and thus includes both Geometry and Arithmetic, since its principles and formulas are alike and indiscriminately applicable both to space and time. Thus the expression for the square of the sum of two quantities, $(a+b)^2 = a^2 + 2ab + b^2$, holds true alike for continuous and discrete quantity, for space and time; since it is equally an expression of the truth, that the square erected upon the sum of two lines may always be resolved into two smaller squares and two rectangles, corresponding to the formula; and also of that which is only another aspect of the same truth, viz. that the arithmetical expression for the square of the sum of two numbers may be resolved in precisely the same manner.

It does not appear, then, that what are called the demonstrative sciences owe their attribute of logical certainty to the peculiar nature of the subjects about which they are conversant. It is not because space and time are at once necessary conceptions of the intellect and immutable laws of real things, that the mathematician is able to build up his vast fabric of pure truths, which are absolutely certain and are independent of any verification by experience. The science of pure quantity, which seems to me the only proper definition of mathematics, is also the science of real things, but so far only as these are affected by quantity and thus subject to measurement, and so far only as this measurement is executed with that ideal precision and accuracy which are presupposed in every mathematical investigation. The necessary and *a priori* cognitions of the human mind do not constitute a department of science by themselves, but are interwoven with the empirical elements of our knowledge. Their office is not constitutive, but regulative. They determine the limits of the understanding, prescribe its functions, and regulate its belief. Whatever is apprehended under the relations of Quantity, is subject to the immutable laws of Quantity. Whatever is known as an event or change, is governed by the necessary laws of Causality and Time. Attributes or qualities are apprehended under the law of Substance, which determines the mode of their existence. It is only by abstraction, or disjoining in thought what cannot be separated in reality, that a separate science can be created of necessary cognitions *a priori*, as in that branch of Metaphysics which is called Ontology.

Going back to the physicist's conception of Cause, that is, Invariable Antecedence, we observe that the method of distinguishing invariable sequences from accidental ones is by analysis. Every event has many antecedents and a crowd of concomitant circumstances. We seek to ascertain which of these are necessary conditions of the phenomenon by analyzing them; that is, by trying the experiment over again, leaving out each time one or more of the attendant circumstances; if the same result still follows, the circumstances thus left out are not the causes which we are in search of, but were only accidental concomitants, that did not at all affect the issue. Proceeding in this manner, step by step, we come at last to some of the original antecedents, which being omitted, the event no longer takes place. Then, in common parlance, we are said to have discovered the *cause* of the phenomenon; strictly speaking, it is only, so far as we know, its invariable antecedent, or a condition of its existence, — perhaps only a condition of our knowing that it exists. The whole method is tentative, and is evidently exposed to error, as it is only an application of that fallacious mode of reasoning which has been exposed as the sophism *post hoc, ergo propter hoc.* Hence, the conclusion is not held to be established for the purposes of science, until the experiment has been tried, or the observation repeated, under every possible variety of circumstances. But a large experience, especially if confirmed by some analogy between this phenomenon and others that are known to follow similar antecedents, may establish the conclusion beyond all reasonable doubt.

As our knowledge of the phenomena of succession increases, the Concepts which we form of individual objects and classes of objects become larger and more complex. Our conception of any corporeal thing must include not only those obvious qualities, such as shape, color, specific gravity, texture, &c., which it manifests on nearly all occasions, but the changes to which these are subject when it is brought in contact with other substances under different circumstances, and also those changes in other bodies of which its presence may be a constant antecedent. "The ideas," says John Locke, "that make up our complex notions of corporeal substances are of these three sorts. First, the ideas of the *primary qualities* of things, which are discovered by our senses, and are in them even when we perceive them not; such are the bulk, figure, number, situation, and motions of the parts of bodies, which are really in them, whether we take notice of them or no. Secondly, the sensible *secondary qualities,* which, depending on these, are nothing but the powers those substances have to produce several ideas in us by our senses ; which ideas are not in the things themselves, otherwise than as anything is in its Cause. Thirdly, the aptness we consider in any substance to give or receive such alterations of primary qualities as that the substance so altered should produce in us different ideas from what it did before ; these are called *active and passive powers;* all which powers, so far as we have any notice or notion of them, terminate only in sensible simple ideas. For whatever alteration a loadstone has the power to make in the minute particles of iron, we should have no notion of any power it had at all to operate on iron, did not its sensible motion discover it; and I doubt not but there are a thousand changes, that bodies we daily handle have a power to cause in one another, which we never suspect, because they never appear in sensible effects."

"Powers therefore justly make a great part of our complex ideas of substances. He that will examine his complex idea of *gold*, will find several of its ideas that make it up to be only powers; as the power of being melted, but of not spending itself in the fire, of being dissolved in *aqua regia*, are ideas as necessary to make up our complex idea of *gold*, as its color and weight; which, if duly considered, are also nothing but different powers. For to speak truly, yellowness is not actually in gold, but is a power in gold to produce that idea in us by our eyes, when placed in a due light; and the heat which we cannot leave out of our idea of the sun is no more really in the sun, than the white color it introduces into wax. These are both equally powers in the sun, operating, by the motion and figure of its sensible parts, so on a man, as to make him have the idea of *heat*, and so on wax, as to make it capable to produce in a man the idea of white." *

A fourth class of the elements that form our Concepts of individual objects consists of the *Relations* in which these objects stand to other things. These, of course, are numberless, and therefore are a great source of the indistinctness and imperfection of this sort of knowledge. Every object may be compared with every other object in nature, and with every Concept which the mind has previously formed;

* *Essay on Human Understanding*, Book II. Chap. 23, §§ 9 and 10.

and of the countless Relations thus brought to our notice, many are essential to an adequate knowledge of the related object. Most of Aristotle's Categories are an imperfect attempt to classify these Relations, and place them under their *summa genera*. Some of them, such as those of Quantity, Place, and Time, are definite and admit of accurate determination; as such, they are the objects of the Exact Sciences. Others, like those of Quality, Posture, and Modes of Being, Doing, and Suffering, are wholly indeterminate, at least in this respect, that their various sorts and degrees are shaded into each other imperceptibly, or without any natural lines of demarcation. These, of course, can be grouped into classes only in some rough and arbitrary way, the divisions not being marked out by nature. As our knowledge of them is thus vague and incomplete, our conclusions or inferences concerning them must be uncertain, and the Sciences under which they fall may be said to be occupied with Contingent Matter.

In Applied Logic, the test of the adequacy of a Concept is its more or less complete enumeration of the essential qualities of the real thing, or class of things, which it denotes. Any attempt to ascertain and enumerate all of these empirically, or by successive observations and experiments, is hopeless; a lifetime would not suffice to accumulate more than a small fraction of such knowledge of a single object. Thus, its active and passive powers, as they are termed, or, more properly, the fixed Relations of antecedence and consequence which subsist between the changes affecting it and those affecting all other substances, could be ascertained only by placing it in juxtaposition with every other thing singly, and with every conceivable combination of other things. Apply heat or water to some one substance taken separately, and only two or three series of changes would be observed, such as its greater or less fusibility, solubility, absorption of heat or fluid, capability of being oxidized, &c. But apply the same agents to it in combination with one or more other substances, and series of very different phenomena may be manifested. By reason of the endless number and variety of such possible observations and experiments, the results of them in a vast majority of cases being individual truths of no special interest or importance, no one can think of engaging in them by detail, or with a view of exhausting the round of possible inquiry and trial; and hence our knowledge must always fall infinitely short of the truth of things. The most important single facts of this character now known to man were accidentally discovered; they are the fruits, not of study and research, but of mere chance. Hence we seldom know the history of such discoveries, or the person who made them. Centuries after the attractive power of magnetic iron had been known, some one, we know not who, happened to observe its polarity, or quality of pointing constantly to the north; and the result was the invention of the mariner's compass. The ancients were familiar with the obvious qualities of nitre, sulphur, and charcoal; but some obscure alchemist, some time in the fourteenth century, happened to mix them together in the right proportions, and the explosion which ensued taught the world the secret of gunpowder. The art of printing was hit upon by a similar lucky chance. Yet "these three things," says Lord Bacon, " to wit, Printing, Gunpowder, and the Mariner's Compass, have changed the whole face and state of things throughout the world; the first in literature, the second in warfare, the third in navigation; whence have followed innumerable changes; insomuch that no empire, no sect, no star, seems to have exerted greater power and influence in human affairs than these mechanical discoveries."

But as much the greater number of casual observations of individual things reveal only unimportant relations and qualities, there is no encouragement to pursue and record them methodically, in the hope of hitting at last upon some one of interest and value. Yet Lord Bacon, misled by a few brilliant examples, such as those just cited, seems to have required, as the first step towards carrying out his new system of inductive research, a "Natural and Experimental History, sufficient and good, as the foundation of all." This "History" was to be a complete record of individual observations and experiments, omitting nothing on account of its seeming triviality and obviousness, to be subsequently digested into "Tables and Arrangements of Instances, in such method and order that the understanding may be able to deal with them."* Upon this vast store of crude material, towards furnishing which he himself made a respectable beginning in his *Historia Naturalis et Experimentalis ad condendam Philosophiam*, and his *Sylva Sylvarum, or a Natural History*, all the subsequent processes of his Inductive Method were to be expended. "Since there is so great a number and army of particulars," he observes, "and that army so scattered and dispersed as to distract and confound the understanding, little is to be hoped for from the skirmishings and slight attacks and desultory movements of the intellect, unless *all* the particulars which pertain to the subject of inquiry shall, by means of Tables of Discovery, apt, well arranged, and as it were animate, be drawn up and marshalled; and the mind be set to work upon the helps duly prepared and digested which these Tables supply." †

Bacon failed to observe that the minds of all men naturally and inevitably proceed in great part by this method, as is evinced by the construction of language. As we have seen, all *words* properly so called are only the General Names of the groups and classes into which we marshal and digest our individual observations; — yet with this

* *Novum Organon*, Book II. Aph. x. † Id. Book I. Aph. cii.

improvement upon the system that Bacon recommends, that the Concepts thus framed include only the original and essential attributes, the others being left out as of no account, and needlessly burdening the memory by their vast number. If experiment or casual observation should hereafter determine that one of these omitted elements is really of interest and importance, it will then henceforward constitute an integral part of the Concept. Every one's notion of the *magnet* now includes its attribute of *polarity*.

Derivative attributes, it has been mentioned, are not expressly included in the Intension of a Concept, because they are implied and virtually contained in their primaries. Thus, the numberless properties of every geometric figure are reduced, in the Concept which bears the Name of that figure, to the two or three qualities, constituting its Definition, from which they may all be derived by necessary inference *a priori*, or without the aid of actual observation and experiment. Down to the time of the Baconian reform in the processes of physical science, it seems to have been imagined that individual substances or bodies, like geometric figures, had each its one or two *essential* properties, which being known, all the others could be immediately deduced from them by a purely logical process, without any aid from experience. This, in fact, was the meaning of the word *essence*, that internal constitution of a body which makes it what it is, or from which all its attributes necessarily flow. Change the *essence* of the body, then, and you thereby change all its properties. To the eye of Omniscience, doubtless, there is such an essence; but it must ever remain unknown to man's finite capacities, on account of the endless number of unknown attributes with which it is intermingled. Those qualities alone appear to us essential which are known to be constantly associated with a few others, either because these others can be deduced from them by necessary inference, or because they have always been found together in a large experience. In the latter case, of course, the conclusion is contingent or uncertain, being necessarily true only to the extent of our previous observation. In the former case, the conclusion is absolute, if, by the hypothesis, all other qualities are excluded from the Concept except those which are certainly known. In geometry, for instance, the Concept or definition of any solid body includes only its shape and magnitude, and supposes that these are accurately determined; abstraction is made of all its other qualities, because these are not susceptible of perfect determination, and we know only from experience how far they associated with each other.

If the Matter of Thought, then, includes real existences, or such objects and events as are actually presented to us in nature, our conclusions respecting them, being derived only from experience, must always be subject to doubt. As we know them only imperfectly, our inferences respecting them can never be logically certain. But if the Concepts are limited to imaginary objects, consisting only of a few perfectly determinate qualities, our conclusions respecting them will be absolute, though they will be applicable only in the realm of pure abstractions. Bacon was right, then, in maintaining that the Physical Sciences, so far as they extend to the knowledge of real objects, are dependent solely upon observation and experiment. "Man, being the servant and interpreter of Nature, can do and understand so much only as he has observed, either in fact or in thought, of the course of Nature; beyond this, he cannot understand or do anything."

We can now see what are the preliminary classifications upon the formation of which all Science depends, and can point out the principles which regulate this formation.

1. We form classes of *real things* or Natural Objects, arranging them according to the similarity of their attri-

butes, and selecting by preference, as the basis of the classification, those qualities which are invariably found conjoined with the greatest number of other uniform qualities; as the presence of one of these constant elements enables us to infer, in anticipation of experience, that it will be found in conjunction with those others. The science of Natural History, in its various departments, consists exclusively of such classifications, together with such descriptions and definitions as are subsidiary to them.

2. We classify the *qualities* themselves, according to their similarities, irrespective of the real objects in which they inhere. Thus, we form classes of colors, sounds, shape, and dimension, degrees of consistency, specific gravity, &c. Sometimes a single set of these arrangements is found important enough to be made the basis of a distinct science, as in the case of Acoustics and Optics; more frequently, several sets of them are grouped together for scientific consideration, as is the case with the chemical qualities of substances.

3. We classify *events* according to the uniformity of their succession in time. These, if regarded as mere sequences of phenomena, may be referred to the subsequent head of Relations; if regarded as the active or passive powers of bodies, they may be placed under the preceding head of Qualities. A constant order of succession is often erroneously supposed to be a necessary sequence, because the mind superadds in such cases its pure conception of the necessary relations of Cause and Effect; and hence sciences based upon such classifications are improperly termed sciences of causation. Several departments of Physics, such as the sciences of Mechanics and Hydrostatics, and some divisions of the moral sciences, such as Politics and Civil History, are made up chiefly of classifications of this sort.

4. We classify the *relations* of things, irrespective of the

other Qualities and differences of the things related. Thus, Geography is, in the main, a classification of the Relations of the different portions of the earth's surface to each other; Astronomy takes a similar view of the Relations between the different members of the solar and stellar systems. A large portion of the sciences of Law and Politics has regard to the different Relations which subsist between human beings, such as those of husband and wife, parent and child, rulers and subjects, countrymen and aliens, &c. The mind takes special cognizance only of a very few of the countless Relations which comparison and reflection bring to light. We select those only which happen to be of special interest to us, through the guidance which they afford for our future conduct, the wonder and curiosity which they excite, or the bearing which they may have in any way upon our welfare.

It is not meant that each one of the Classes and Sciences which we form consists exclusively of one or the other of the four species here enumerated. Indeed, the division itself is a very imperfect one, for the Dividing Members, as we have intimated, do not exclude each other; a Concept of Real Things includes a view of their Qualities, their active and passive Powers, and their Relations; and the two latter may be comprised under the name of Qualities. But these four, sometimes separately and sometimes in combination, are the elements which we group together into classes, out of which those higher classes, or hierarchies of Concepts, which we call Sciences, are subsequently erected. In every case, the classifying principle is similarity, or uniformity of succession, those Objects and Qualities being united which resemble each other in certain respects, and those events being reduced to the same head which uniformly follow one another under similar circumstances. The education of every human being consists in the gradual acquisition of a large stock of these elementary

Concepts, which are taught to him in learning the use of his mother-tongue, while exercising at the same time his powers of observation and reflection.

The advancement of Science depends on the success of the attempts which man is constantly making to enlarge and improve the classifications which are the bases of these Concepts. By detecting hitherto unobserved similarities and conjunctions in time, we extend the generalizations and reduce the number of classes, thereby bringing the infinitude of objects and events which nature offers us more nearly within the grasp of the human intellect. Sometimes the principle itself, or the Ground of Division, which determines the classification of a whole set of phenomena, is altered; as we find a greater number of the attributes of these phenomena to be in constant companionship with some one or more traits hitherto disregarded as of little account, a differently constituted hierarchy of Concepts, founded upon these traits, is adopted. This may be called an improvement in the Method, rather than an actual enlargement of the domain, of Science. Thus the Natural System was substituted for the Linnæan classification of plants, and an improvement almost equally extensive was made by Cuvier in the arrangement of the animal kingdom. But most of the questions and problems which Science encounters in its progress relate to successive improvements and extensions of the classification which, in all its main features, was long since formed, and not to the substitution of an entirely different one in its place. The fixedness of language, which stereotypes, as it were, the names and phraseology appropriated to the old division, is a great obstacle to the introduction of a new one, which would require a new set of words. The principal object of the researches of Science is to determine whether this or that object, or class of objects, has the special characteristics which entitle it to be placed in a certain class, and therefore to be called by the name of that class. For instance: — Is the lightning to be placed in the class of electrical phenomena? Can the revolution of the planets be reduced to the phenomena of falling bodies? Is light the undulatory movement of an ether? Are the processes of digestion and assimilation reducible to the ordinary action of chemical affinities? Ought the relation of a motive to a volition to be classed with the relations of cause and effect, or with those of mere antecedence and consequence?

Such questions relate, for the most part, not to some one object or event, but to whole classes of phenomena, and therefore presuppose a classification already formed. Sometimes, indeed, one particular phenomenon of an anomalous character may now be observed for the first time; and then the purpose of the inquiry is, to refer it to its proper class, and call it by its right name. But such inquiries belong usually to the education of a child, who has not yet acquired the amount of knowledge long since possessed by his elders, and embodied by them in language through the appropriation of names to the different Concepts. But Science advances almost exclusively by the resolution of problems which concern whole classes of objects, and a single phenomenon is observed and experimented upon only as a typical specimen of its class, and therefore, as leading to conclusions which affect all that are called by the same name. Thus, Franklin experimented with his kite upon a particular thunder-cloud, but only because this one represented to his mind the whole class of meteorological phenomena whose characteristics he was investigating. This, indeed, is the difference between the intellect of a common man and that of a philosopher. The latter flies at once to generalities; the former wonders at the individual case, and seldom goes beyond it.

"From the moment an isolated fact is discovered," says

Hamilton, " we endeavor to refer it to other facts which it resembles. Until this be accomplished, we do not view it as understood. This is the case, for example, with sulphur, which, in a certain degree of temperature, melts like other bodies; but at a higher degree of heat, instead of evaporating, again consolidates." Another example may be taken from the General Fact, which some will call a Law of Nature, that all bodies give out heat on passing from a gaseous to a liquid, or from a liquid to a solid, state; in other words, that contraction of bulk is attended or occasioned by loss of heat, and expansion of bulk by addition or absorption of heat. Yet clay is known to contract from the application of heat; and though water contracts in bulk when it is cooling down to as low a temperature as $40°$, yet as it falls below that point it expands again, and in the act of congelation there is a sudden and considerable increase of bulk. Our natural love of unity, or disposition to reduce corresponding phenomena to one class or Law, does not allow us to rest in the consideration that such cases are anomalous, or isolated exceptions. We seek either for a new expression of the Law, which shall cover also these apparent exceptions, or for the discovery of some attribute of these now isolated cases which shall harmonize them with the Law as already expressed. When the facts are thus generalized, or brought together under one Concept and name, " our discontent is quieted," Hamilton continues, " and we consider the generality itself as tantamount to an explanation. Why does this apple fall to the ground? Because all bodies gravitate towards each other. Arrived at this General Fact, we inquire no more, although ignorant now, as previously, of the *cause* of gravitation; for gravitation is nothing more than a *name* for a General Fact, the *why* of which we know not. A mystery, if recognized as universal, would no longer appear mysterious."

We now see how it is that the successive discoveries, and consequent enlarged and improved generalizations, of Science are embodied, as fast as they are made, in language, so that we learn them through the simple mode of gradually acquiring the use of our mother tongue. This is done to some extent by the actual introduction of new words and names, these being necessary to designate the new groups and Concepts which the improved classification requires. But it is effected still more largely by modifying and enlarging the connotation of words already in use. For a time, these new elements of phraseology are in current use only among a small circle of scientific inquirers, whose labors have made them necessary. But gradually they creep out into the ordinary dialect of the market, the parlor, and the newspaper, and are naturalized there, and taught to children as fast as children learn to speak. How much more knowledge is now necessarily acquired in learning the use of the English language, than was gained from such learning only one or two centuries ago!

The same considerations of interest and convenience, of immediate relation to the curiosity or the physical wants of men, which determine us to classify and name some of our individual observations and experiences, to the exclusion of many others, also guide us in the selection of those groups of Concepts which we enlarge, develop, and methodize into distinct Sciences. As many objects and events do not need to be classified because they are not worth remembrance, so the classification of many others needs not to be extended beyond the first and most elementary stage, because a Science elaborated out of them would neither interest us nor minister to our necessities. We do not chronicle petty occurrences, we do not study out and subsequently generalize the insignificant relations of unimportant objects to each other. But as circumstances change and knowledge is enlarged, what formerly seemed trivial often assumes a new dignity and interest, or is unexpectedly found to be subservient to some great purpose. A new Science, or department of Science, is thus formed, perhaps to be carried up by subsequent discoveries and generalizations higher than any of those formerly cultivated. How many new departments of study and research have thus been opened within the last few generations! The Sciences of Geology, Ethnology, Comparative Philology, and Political Economy are hardly more than a century old. The moderns know more than the ancients, not so much because they know the same things more perfectly, as because their investigations are extended over a larger range of objects.

Hence it is easy to see why the numerous attempts that have been made to classify the Sciences, and thereby to reduce them into one complete and orderly system of human knowledge, have not been more successful. The Sciences have not been formed on any predetermined and systematic plan, with a view of covering the whole ground of inquiry; but they have grown by a natural and irregular development, corresponding both to the ever increasing wants and stimulated curiosity of those who prosecute them, to the different aptitudes of the various classes of objects to be digested into system and divided by obvious lines of demarcation, and especially to the facility with which our conclusions respecting these objects may be drawn without the aid of observation and experience. Such a survey of all that is possible to be known, compared with all that is actually known, as Bacon attempted to make in his treatise on the "Advancement of the Sciences," must always disclose, as it did to him, many *lacunæ*, or gaps which it is necessary to fill, before man can be said even to have entered upon all the avenues which lead to truth. Divisions of the Sciences, like those which have been devised by Bacon, Locke, Ampère, Comte, Wilson, and others, must always be imperfect, or, if they approximate completeness, must always indicate at least as many blanks as there are departments already occupied. Whether we try to distribute the various branches of knowledge, as Bacon did, according to the different faculties of the mind which they respectively call into play; or, with Locke, according to the several ends in view; or, with Descartes, as followed by Comte, according to the order of their development, as determined by their degrees of simplicity; — some Sciences will appear redundant, others as defective, and many as having an equally good title to be ranked under two or three different heads.

As one of the best specimens of these attempts at classification, we may take Dr. Thomson's account of the arrangement proposed by Comte, on the basis of Descartes's aphorism, that knowledge should advance from the simpler to the more complex phenomena.

"Mathematics, or the science of quantities, is at once the most simple in its elements and the most general in its application, entering, more or less, into all the sciences of Nature, and constituting almost the whole of that which comes next it in the order of dependence. Astronomy, or the science of the heavenly bodies, is the application of mathematical truths to the laws of matter and motion; matter and the motions of material bodies being the new conceptions which belong to this science. Physics, being the science, or rather group of sciences, which is conversant with the general laws of the world, so far as they relate to beings without life or organization, would come next; and it imports, in addition to the conceptions of Astronomy, those of light, of heat, of sound, of electricity, of magnetism, and many others. Chemistry would rank next, which is the science of the decomposition and combinations of the various substances that compose and surround the earth. Next in order of complexity would rank Physiology, founded on the additional conception of vegetable and animal life. To this would succeed Anthropology, or the science of man's nature; and to this, Social Science, which ascertains the laws that govern men when combined in cities and nations. Each of these departments may be divided into many branches; as Physics into Acoustics, Optics, Electricity, and the like; or Social Science into Morals, Politics, Political Economy, Law, and the like.

"On comparing scientific works, differences in the mode of teaching the same subject become apparent. In one, the pure theory of Astronomy is presented; in another, the striking features of its historical progress as a science, with speculations on the historical sequence of the phenomena themselves; in a third, the practical applications of which the Science admits in respect to the comfort and progress of mankind. This threefold mode of treatment runs through all the Sciences, and in a table of them might well be expressed. The classification would thus embody all that is valuable of another system of classes, that according to the purpose towards which the Science was directed.

"A classification which advances on Descartes's principle, from the more simple to the more complex subjects, which commences from the notions of extension and quantity, and proceeds through material things up to living, intelligent, and moral agents, ought to coincide with the order in which the sciences themselves have reached maturity. And this it certainly does. Mathematics had made good its ground when Astronomy was yet in its infancy; Physics began to obtain a sure footing later than either; whilst the Sciences which relate to Life are still very immature; and some of the main problems of Social Science are yet matter of controversy even in our own days."

It is an obvious imperfection of this scheme, that it takes no notice of the numerous branches of that Science, Natural History, which, as it depends solely upon observation, and thus gives us our first knowledge of all the objects of study, would seem to constitute the basis of all the other Sciences. In explanation of this defect, Comte remarks, "we must distinguish between the two classes of Natural Science; — the abstract or general, which have for their object the discovery of the Laws which regulate phenomena in all conceivable cases; and the concrete, particular, or descriptive, which are sometimes called Natural Sciences in a restricted sense, whose function it is to apply these Laws to the actual history of existing beings. The first are fundamental; and our business is with them alone, as the second are derived, and, however important, not rising into the rank of our subjects of contemplation. We shall treat of Physiology, but not of Botany and Zoölogy, which are derived from it. We shall treat of Chemistry, but not of Mineralogy, which is secondary to it." But this remark is inconsistent with the previous assertion, that this order of classification "coincides with the order in which the Sciences themselves have reached maturity." In the order of time, certainly, Zoölogy and Botany had been cultivated to a considerable extent before men had obtained more than the crudest notions of the physiological processes of animal and vegetable life; just as Civil History, the basis of another department, had been very fully treated before it first suggested the idea of Social Science. In what may be called the logical order, or the order of ideas, however, it is true that the Sciences which embody principles and general results take precedence of those which afford only the material of knowledge.

CHAPTER XI.

DEMONSTRATIVE REASONING AND DEDUCTIVE EVIDENCE.

WE have already said, that the principal object of the researches of Science is, to determine whether this or that object, or class of objects, has the special characteristics which entitle it to be placed in a certain class, and called by a certain name.

Most of such questions, if they relate only to one thing, or to a very few things, are answered directly, and without difficulty, by observation or intuition. We answer one of them, in fact, whenever we perceive any object and call it by its appropriate Common Name. For instance; — this thing which I now hold in my hand I call a *pen*, a *rose*, or an *apple*, because I perceive that it has the attributes which are the Marks connoted by that name. In like manner, I pronounce the animals now before me to be *dogs*, *horses*, or *cows*, according as I recognize their distinctive qualities.

Writers like Dr. Brown, Mr. J. S. Mill, and Mr. Bailey, who have laboriously attempted to restrict the range and depreciate the utility of the Syllogistic process, have seemingly failed to notice the fact, that we must reason syllogistically whenever we use language with any perception of its meaning, — that is, when we call anything by its appropriate name. If I had not already spread out before my mind the Marks which constitute the Intension of the Concept *apple*, or *rose*, I could not designate the object now presented to me by that appellation. This process of reasoning, which we are performing almost every moment of our lives, and therefore so quickly and easily that its several steps are taken almost unconsciously, is thus spread out into the formal process.

The Concept or Class-notion *apple* has, as Marks, a nearly spherical shape, a red color, a moderate hardness, and a certain smell;

This object has all these Marks;

Therefore, this object is an apple.

This is what Hamilton calls Reasoning in Intension, for, in each of the Premises, the Predicate is contained in the Subject. Moreover, the Reasoning is not only logical, — *i. e.* valid in Form, but it is also Demonstrative, — *i. e.* absolutely certain in respect to its Matter. It is Demonstrative, because the Major Term, which is here the Subject of the Major Premise, is a Concept or Class-notion, which, being a mere creation of the mind, cannot have any other Marks or qualities than those which we voluntarily attribute to it. As we know by Intuition, that the object has *all* the Marks which we included in the Concept, it is certain that it should be designated by the name of that Concept, — that is, that it should be included under its Extension.

On the other hand, if the Reasoning is made to concern, not a mere Concept in the mind, but a class of *real things*, which, as we have seen, always have an unknown and unknowable number of qualities and relations, then I cannot be sure that the object in question possesses *all* these qualities, but can only doubtfully infer that it has *all*, because I know that it possesses *some*, of the more important of them. An element of uncertainty is introduced; the Reasoning ceases to be Demonstrative, and becomes merely Probable or contingent. For instance; — if, in the Major Premise of the preceding Syllogism, we say, not "the Concept or Class-notion *apple*," but "*All apples*" — *i. e.* All the actual objects which we have been accustomed to call *apples* — "have a nearly spherical shape, a red color, a moderate hardness, and a certain smell"; then, though "this object has all these Marks," I cannot be sure that "it is an apple." It may be only a wax counterfeit, and the deception would instantly be detected by *the taste*, which quality was not included in the enumeration. The Reasoning is still valid in Form, but the Major Premise is false; it covers up the Fallacy *fictæ universalitatis*. In order to be sure that an object is properly ranked under a given class, we must be certain that it contains *all the original and essential qualities* of the objects denoted by the class-name; and this certainty, in the case of *real things*, is unattainable. In our conception, we may arbitrarily restrict the meaning of the word *apple*, so as to exclude the quality of *taste;* and in this sense, the wax counterfeit is properly called an apple. But in speaking to others, the word would be understood to signify all the qualities possessed by the real things, viz. this sort of fruit; and in this meaning, the wax substitute is not an apple.

We can now see why the Reasonings of the mathematician are Demonstrative, while those of the zoölogist, the botanist, and other naturalists who deal only with real things, are merely Probable or contingent. The Form is always the same; Reasoning, as such, must always be Syllogistic; and when the rules of Pure Logic are duly observed, the Consequence, or the mere deduction of the Conclusion from the Premises, must be absolutely certain. The difference, then, concerns the Premises only, the truth of which, as we have seen, is not guaranteed by the principles of Logic. The universal rule, that the Middle Term must always be distributed, requires that the predesignation *all*, or *none*, should appear in at least one of the Premises. Now, our knowledge of real things is derived solely from experience; and experience, as has been mentioned, must be restricted, from its very nature, to a limited number of examples. In respect to real objects and events, it can never extend either to the inclusion or the exclusion of *all;* it can never pronounce with certainty either upon *all*, or *none*. Only with reference to a certain class arbitrarily formed by the Understanding, — to the very things which I am now thinking of, or which I have actually observed, and to none others, — to the things which are included under this Definition, and to these only, — can the finite understanding of man, so far as it is enlightened only by experience, safely pronounce upon *all* or *none*. Without such limitations, naturalists, and all others who seek to educe Science from mere experience, can never speak of *all* or *none*, without falling into the Fallacy *fictæ universalitatis*.

The mathematician deals only with certain Concepts of Quantity, whether continuous or discrete, which are precisely limited and determined by the Definitions that he employs. The propositions which he establishes do not concern circular objects and triangular objects, which are real things, but circles and triangles, which are imaginary things as conceived by the Understanding, and which are restricted by their Definitions to the possession of those qualities only which Thought voluntarily attributes to them. Hence, the conclusions which the mathematician forms respecting them are not liable to be vitiated by the intrusion of any unexpected and counteracting elements. Any theorem, therefore, which is proved of *one*, must hold good of *all;* any property which cannot belong to *one*, can be possessed by *none*, of the class thus defined. The same measure of certainty which the student of nature obtains by Intuition respecting a single real object, the mathematician acquires respecting a whole class of imaginary objects, because the latter has the assurance, which the former can never attain, that the single object, which he is contemplating in Thought, is *a perfect representative* of its whole class; he has this assurance, *because the whole class exists only in Thought*, and are therefore all actually before him, or present to consciousness. For example; this bit of iron, I find by direct observation, melts at a certain temperature; but it may well happen that another piece of iron, quite similar to it in external appearance, may be fusible only at a much higher temperature, owing to the unsuspected presence with it of a little more, or a little less, carbon in composition. But if the angles at the basis of this triangle are equal to each other, I know that a corresponding equality must exist in the case of every other figure which conforms to the Definition of an isosceles triangle; for that Definition excludes every disturbing element. The conclusion in this latter case, then, is Universal, while in the former, it can be only Singular or Particular.

Conclusions which are demonstratively certain and absolutely universal can be obtained only when we are reasoning about abstract conceptions. In the case of natural objects and events, which can be *known* only through experience, we approximate universality and certainty in reasoning only by the aid of Induction and Analogy. The lack of certainty is a consequence of the lack of universality. No doubt affects the few instances which I am now actually observing, or which are present to sense or consciousness. Of these, I am as certain as of any conclusions in arithmetic or geometry. The doubt comes in only when I attempt to extend the conclusion from *some*, which I have examined, to *all* others, of which I know nothing, except from testimony, Induction, or Analogy. And this doubt is inevitable; no matter how many cases have been examined, experience can never extend to *all*. The fact that all matter gravitates, or has weight, is a truth which rests upon as large a testimony from experience as has ever been collected. Yet the chemist will readily admit that it is not only conceivable, but we may almost say *probable*, that some of the imponderable agents, as they are called, — heat, light, electricity, &c., — may at last be found to be material; and the astronomer has not yet proved entirely to his satisfaction, that the law of gravitation is universal throughout the stellar system. From the nature of the case, he would say, the fact does not admit of absolute proof.

It appears, then, that the range of Deductive reasoning and Demonstrative proof is not confined to pure Mathematics. Whenever the objects about which we reason are pure Concepts, or mere creations of the intellect, strictly limited by Definition, and thus guarded against reference to things actually existent in Nature, our conclusions respecting them, if obtained in strict uniformity with logical rules, are as absolute as the truths of the multiplication-table. But Mathematics, it must be admitted, afford vastly the larger number of conclusions of this class; in no other science is Demonstrative reasoning either carried so far, or so fruitful in results. This peculiarity seems to be due to the nature of those Concepts, *quantity*, *space*, and *number*, with which the mathematician deals. Two of these, *quantity* and *number*, are universal attributes, as they belong to all things, both to objects of sense and consciousness; and the third, *space* or extension, is an attribute of all external things. They are suggested to us on a greater variety of occasions than any other qualities, and thus are more frequent objects of contemplation, and more fully determined. "Propositions concerning numbers," as Mr. Mill observes, "have this remarkable peculiarity, that they are propositions concerning all things whatever, — all objects, all existences of every kind, known to our experience. All things possess quantity; consist of parts which can be numbered; and, in that character, possess all the properties which are called properties of numbers."

Again, the various modes, properties, and relations of *quantity*, *space*, and *number* admit of being more accurately

defined and clearly determined than those of any other
class of ideas; they are separable from each other by lines
of demarcation that cannot be overlooked or mistaken.
Differences of *degree*, with which we are chiefly concerned
in the case of all other qualities, are not by any means so
definite, as they are shaded into each other by imperceptible gradations; their minute differences are inappreciable
either by the senses or by the understanding. But the
difference between two *quantities*, whether of number or
extension, may be reduced as low as we please, and still
remain as distinct to our apprehension as if it were world-
wide.

But the chief peculiarity of these three Concepts, which
causes them to afford so broad and fruitful a field for Demonstrative reasoning, is the measureless variety of accurately determinable relations in which all their modes stand
to each other. Any one quantity stands in a perfectly conceivable ratio — whether it can be exactly expressed in
numbers or not — to every other quantity, and also has a
countless number of peculiar relations in which it stands to
many at once. Attempt to enumerate, for instance, the
properties of the number 9; — that it is the square of 3,
the square-root of 81, the double of $4\frac{1}{2}$, the half of 18,
&c., — and we soon abandon the undertaking in despair.
And when we come to think of the relations of these relations, as in the doctrine of proportions, it becomes evident
that the properties of quantity are too great to be numbered. The field of investigation is infinite.

These innumerable and perfectly definite relations, which
subsist between distinct quantities, furnish an inexhaustible
number of Middle Terms, through which we obtain, by
Mediate Inference, such Conclusions as are not apparent at
a glance, or by direct Intuition. When the geometer, for
instance, cannot determine directly the distance from one
point to another, he constructs a triangle, the base of which,

with its adjacent angles, as accessible, can be easily measured; and he can then deduce the required distance, or the height of the triangle, from the known relations which exist between it and the quantities which he has thus directly determined. In like manner, the value of one or more unknown quantities, symbolically represented in an algebraic equation, is deduced from some of the given relations which subsist between them and the known quantities, with which they are taken in connection. Indeed, the peculiar function of algebraic science is to determine *general* relations between different groups and classes of magnitudes, these general ratios, proportions, and analyses being subsequently applied by the geometer and the arithmetician to the solution of *particular* problems. The mere construction of a geometrical diagram enables us to see the use which is made of one or two *known* relations between several quantities, as means of determining indirectly *other* relations between them which cannot be directly measured. The diagram is only a means of making clear to our apprehension the fact, that the same straight line, or length already determined, is at once the base of a triangle, the radius of a circle, the side of a square, &c.; then this line may be used as a Middle Term, or means of proving syllogistically what the other properties and dimensions, hitherto unascertained, of this triangle, circle, and square must be. Thus to ascertain a new property of a former object of Thought is to advance a step in the classifications which the mind is continually forming, enabling us to refer this object, perhaps hitherto anomalous, to its proper class. The diagram, indeed, is a Singular instance; but what it enables us to discover is a General Truth; for, as already remarked, we know that this one instance is a perfect representative of its whole class, since that class exists only in our Thought, and is therefore perfectly known. The little triangle which I am contemplating as drawn on paper corresponds perfectly, *in all particulars that can be essential for the Reasoning,* to the magnificent one, having as its base line the diameter of the earth's orbit, which the astronomer, when he would determine the distance of a fixed star, imagines to be erected in the heavens.

These considerations appear to me to evince very clearly, that the peculiar cogency and fruitfulness of mathematical reasoning do not arise, as Kant maintains, from the fact that it concerns nothing but Space and Time, and that Space and Time exist only in our minds. The sole object of this sort of reasoning seems to be *quantity* in its various forms; and reasoning would be equally Demonstrative, if it related to any other single attribute of things considered abstractly, or as we conceive it apart from all other properties with which it is united in the actual constitution of things. The fact that Quantity is a universal attribute, belonging to all objects of Thought whatever, explains the broad scope and general applicability of mathematical reasoning; while its peculiar fruitfulness, or the vast number of truths which it brings to light, appears to proceed from the countless number and definite character of the relations which subsist between different quantities. No other attribute presents itself so universally, or in modes at once so numerous and so distinct, capable alike of indefinite augmentation and diminution. The field is boundless, and we advance over any portion of it with the precision and certainty in every movement which admit neither error nor doubt.

The views which have now been presented enable us to refute the doctrine, originally proposed, as Mr. Stewart thinks, by Leibnitz, that the certainty of mathematical reasoning depends upon the fact, that all the evidence on which it is supported may be resolved, in the last analysis, into the perception of *identity;* — "the innumerable variety of propositions which have been discovered, or which *remain* to be discovered in the science, being only diversified expressions of the simple formula, $a = a$." It is true that this theory correctly presents the *form*, not only of mathematical reasoning, but of all reasoning whatever; for we have shown that every Affirmative Judgment, in a certain sense, or with reference to the *denotation* of the Concepts which it concerns, is an equation of its two Terms. The formula, *A is B*, to which all conceivable Affirmative Judgments may be reduced, is resolvable, *in this sense*, as *B* equals *A*, into $A = A$. But the peculiar cogency of mathematical evidence cannot be explained by the possession of an attribute which does not distinguish it from Moral Reasoning. In reference to the *connotation* of its Terms, a Judgment does not express an equation, but the inclusion of an object in a class, and the consequent possession by that object of the peculiar attributes of that class. In this sense, the signification is, not that the Subject *equals* the Predicate, but that it *possesses* one or more of the attributes of the Predicate, or *possesses* the Predicate itself as one of its own attributes. The doctrine which we are considering owes its plausibility to a confusion of the significance of these two very different words, *identity* and *equivalence*. When the geometer proves the area of a circle to be equal to that of a triangle having the circumference for its base and the radius for its altitude, he certainly does not mean that it is *identical* with such a triangle, but only that it is *equivalent* to it in a single respect, — viz. *in magnitude;* they are not identical, for, *in shape*, they are wholly unlike. Take even a simpler case, which seems more nearly resolvable into an expression of identity: $4 = 2 + 2$. Even here, the meaning is not that the two members of the equation are identical, but only that the Concept or group *four* is equivalent *in one respect* — viz. the possession of an equal number of units — to the two groups *two* and *two*. It is plain that *one* group cannot be *identical* with *two* groups, or that *two* distinct acts of the mind, each conceiving or grasping together *two* units, cannot be literally the same thing as *one* mental act conceiving *four*.

The essential distinction between Pure and Applied Mathematics consists in this, that, in the former, our thoughts never go beyond the conception of pure *quantity*, or magnitude in the abstract, considered in either of its two modes, *space* or *number;* while in the latter, the additional qualities of *weight, attraction, impenetrability, elasticity, density,* and many others, are brought in, not merely as they are conceived in the mind, but as they actually exist, or are manifested, in *real things*. These qualities also, so far as they are viewed in the former light, that is, abstractly, as mere Concepts strictly limited by Definition, may be reasoned about demonstratively; though it is only in respect to their *quantity* that the reasoning will have any wide range, or be fruitful in conclusions, since they have not the numerous and distinctly conceived relations which subsist between the innumerable degrees of Quantity. But if viewed as actual qualities of real things, our knowledge of them is derived merely from experience, and must therefore be subject to all the limitations and imperfections of knowledge so derived. No Judgments concerning them can be absolute or universal; they are objects only of Probable Reasoning. Previous to experience, we could not attribute *weight* to any material substance, much less to all such substances; that every particle of matter should attract, would seem no more probable than that it should repel, every other particle. This is the source of Dr. Whewell's error; because *weight, attraction, impenetrability,* &c. can be conceived abstractly, and therefore be strictly limited by Definitions, and so reasoned about demonstratively, he maintains that the Physical Laws of Motion are *necessary* truths, and "capable of demonstration, like the truths of Geometry." So they are, if viewed as mere Concepts, not necessarily having anything corresponding to them in the outward universe. But if regarded as *Physical* Laws, expressing the actual phenomena of real things, they are mere educts from experience, can be reasoned about only Inductively, and rest solely upon Probable evidence.

Deduction is not a happily chosen word to indicate the characteristic feature of reasoning from Universals to Particulars, as contradistinguished from *Induction*, whereby we reason from Particulars to Generals. In the Syllogism which expresses the Form of the latter process, the Conclusion is as much a *deduction* from the Premises, as in the former case. We may speak of a Law, or general rule, as deduced from several individual facts, with just as much propriety as of facts as deduced from the Law. In either case, the Conclusion may be said to depend upon the Premises in this sense, that the latter authorize us to proceed to the former. But it is a mere figure of speech, and not a very happy one, to speak of the Conclusion as so involved in the Premises, that the one can be *drawn out of*, or *deduced*, from the other. The process is rather an *explication* of what was previously in the mind, whereby two acts of Thought are brought into harmony with each other. The Subsumption either includes one or more individuals in a class, or excludes them from it; and the Conclusion then states explicitly what is virtually or implicitly thought in that act of inclusion or exclusion. The process of reasoning is not so much a mode of evolving a new truth, as it is of establishing or proving an old one, by showing how much was admitted in the concession of the two Premises taken together, or what follows from the act of bringing them into harmony. The Conclusion is not authorized by either of them taken singly.

Hence it is a still graver mistake, and one which has

given rise to much misunderstanding, to speak of the Conclusion as *deduced* from *one* of its antecedents, from the Major Premise only. A Sumption or General Rule is a necessary part of every Syllogism; but it does not by any means follow, that this Rule alone implicitly contains all the particular Conclusions which are ordinarily said to be drawn out of it. The Conclusion is drawn *in accordance with* the Rule, and the latter may, in one sense, be said to afford a *proof* of the former, inasmuch as it evinces that the Conclusion, *if the truth of the Minor Premise or Subsumption is granted*, cannot be denied without overthrowing a general principle the truth of which is presupposed, as resting upon the evidence either of Intuition, or of a Primary Law of Thought, or of previous Demonstration. In one sort of Immediate Inference, that of Subalternation, the Premise may be rightly viewed as containing the Conclusion, as a whole contains one of its parts, and the latter may therefore be held to be *deduced* from the former. But the relation between the Subalterns and the Subalternate is very different from that which subsists between the Sumption and the Conclusion in a case of Mediate Inference. In the latter case, the gist of the reasoning does not depend upon any Maxim or First Principle, but upon the discovery of a Middle Term, with which both Terms of the Conclusion are separately compared. This Middle Term is the name of a Class, and the new truth which is developed by the reasoning consists in the Subsumption of the Subject of the Conclusion into that Class, and the consequent discovery that it possesses all the attributes or properties which are connoted by its Name. For example: — the geometer, wishing to ascertain the size of a certain angle, finds that it is one of the angles of an equilateral triangle; this is the Subsumption, and when it is accomplished, the discovery is really made and the problem solved, for the Conclusion that the angle measures 60° immediately follows, *in accordance with* the General Truths already demonstrated, that the three angles of an equilateral triangle are equal to each other, and that their sum is 180°. But no manipulation, no analysis, of these Truths previously demonstrated would enable him to evolve from them, without the aid of the classification given in the Minor Premise, the measure of this particular angle. When the Sumption, instead of being, as in this case, a General Theorem previously demonstrated, happens to be one of those Maxims which are called Axioms in Geometry, it is still more evident that it is a meagre and barren Rule, from which no fruitful and significant Conclusion can properly be *deduced.*

I accept, then, to its full extent, the doctrine originally propounded by John Locke, and adopted and defended in our own day by Dugald Stewart, that the Axioms of Geometry, and the other very general maxims which are usually considered as First Principles in our researches, "are not the foundations on which any of the Sciences are built, nor at all useful in helping men forward to the discovery of unknown truths." If Reasoning were an organon of *discovery*, a means for the advancement of truth, its characteristic feature would appear in the Subsumption, which places the Subject of inquiry, hitherto anomalous, or of uncertain classification, under a Concept, or, what is the same thing, in a class, the attributes of which are known; and the *proof* that it possesses one or more of the attributes of that class then appears by citing the General Rule, which is the Major Premise. In other words, each of the two Premises in a Syllogism has its own appropriate function; the Minor announces a discovery, a new truth, which is always a truth of classification, and the Major cites an Axiom, or some other general rule, previously well known, which *proves* some consequence of this new truth, or enables us to acquiesce, with more or less confidence, in the announcement of this consequence. If the Major is an Axiom properly so called, or a truth previously demonstrated, — in either case, having absolute universality and certainty, — then the Conclusion, if the Subsumption is correct, is demonstrated ; but if it is merely a general rule obtained by Induction or Analogy, the Conclusion is merely probable.

The correctness of this analysis will appear, I think, from an examination of either of the following Syllogisms.

1. All electricity may be silently drawn off from any charged body, by bringing near to it a sharp-pointed rod.
Lightning is electricity.
∴ Lightning may be so discharged.
2. The nervous fluid will not travel along a tied nerve.
Electricity will travel along a tied nerve.
∴ Electricity is not the nervous fluid.
3. All alternate angles made by one straight line cutting two parallel lines are equal.
A B C and B C E are alternate angles.
∴ A B C and B C E are equal.
4. Things which are equal to the same thing are equal to each other.
A B and B C are each equal to C D.
∴ A B and B C are equal.
5. Happiness is desirable.
Virtue is happiness.
∴ Virtue is desirable.

It is evident that no one of the General Rules which form the Major Premises of these Syllogisms can be "at all useful in helping men forward to the discovery of unknown truths." The real discovery is announced in the Minor Premise, and the connection of the two Premises in one act of reasoning is the means of *proving* the Conclusion, and of assuming it into its proper place under the General Rule. It does not appear, then, that Reasoning as such, or as an act of Pure Thought, is a means for the advancement of knowledge. This doctrine, indeed, follows immediately from the principles that have been already laid down. Reasoning as such is one of the processes of pure Thought which determine the *Form*, but not the *Matter*, of our knowledge. The Matter of Thought is obtained by Intuition,— by observation through the senses or through consciousness. The fact or truth thus discovered is *announced* in the Subsumption, not as first made known by it, or as deduced from what was previously known, but in order to be *proved* through the Reasoning process; that is, *to be brought into harmony with our previous knowledge as stated in the Major Premise, and that the same consequences may be attributed to it which are already known to follow from all the cases included under that general statement.*

Accordingly, what Hamilton remarks of the whole doctrine of Logic may be applied to the theory of Reasoning, which is but one of the departments of this science. We cite again, in reference to one of the parts, what has been already quoted in reference to the whole. "An extension of any science through [pure Reasoning] is absolutely impossible ; for, by conforming to the logical canons, we acquire no knowledge, — receive nothing new, but are only enabled to render what is already obtained more intelligible by analysis and arrangement. [Reasoning] is only the negative condition of truth. To attempt by mere [Reasoning] to amplify a science, is an absurdity as great as if we should attempt, by a knowledge of the grammatical laws of a language, to discover what is written in this language, without a perusal of the several writings themselves. But though [Reasoning] cannot extend, cannot amplify, a science by the discovery of new facts, it is not to be supposed that it does not contribute to the progress of science. The progress of the sciences consists not merely in the accumulation of new matter, but likewise in the detection of the relations subsisting among the materials accumulated; and the reflective abstraction by which this is effected" must follow the laws of Reasoning.

We are now prepared to understand and appreciate Locke's doctrine, which has been accepted and ably supported by Mr. Bailey and Mr. J. S. Mill, that "the immediate object of all our reasoning and knowledge is nothing but particulars." Locke argues that "the perception of the agreement or disagreement of our particular ideas is the whole and utmost of all our knowledge. Universality is but accidental to it, and consists only in this, that the particular ideas about which it is are such as more than one particular thing can correspond with and be represented by. But the perception of the agreement or disagreement of any two ideas is equally clear and certain, whether either, or both, or neither, of those ideas be capable of representing more real beings than one, or no."*
Mr. Mill says: "We much oftener conclude from particulars to particulars directly, than through the intermediate agency of any general proposition. We are constantly reasoning from ourselves to other people, or from one person to another, without giving ourselves the trouble to erect our observations into general maxims of human or external nature." †

The only question here concerns the proper use of words. The process of comparing one individual object or event with another, and thereby ascertaining some relation between them, is unquestionably the first step to knowledge, and the only means of enlarging our stock of knowledge. But the particular fact thus learned is a fact of *observation*, not of *reasoning*. Certainly I do not need to reason, nor, in the strict and technical sense, to *think*, in order to per-

---
* *Essay on Human Understanding*, Book IV. Chap. 17, § 8.
† *System of Logic*, Book II. Chap. 3, § 3.

ceive that John is taller than William. A brute perceives this fact as well as I do, and acts upon it, as in distinguishing his master. Even if we carry the process one step further, and form a *Judgment*, by subsuming the individual object of intuition under a class, through perceiving that it affects our senses just as some other objects ranked under that class have done, still we are engaged only in enlarging and generalizing our knowledge, and not in *reasoning* properly so called. But when we take one step more, and proceed to attribute certain qualities to that individual thing, which are not now directly perceived in it, but are supposed to exist in it, because we have noticed them in other objects of the same class, we are properly said to reason; the act is one of Mediate Inference. But this act does not properly *enlarge* our knowledge, but only explicates it, by bringing out explicitly into Thought what was already virtually contained in it. By putting an object into a class, we have *already* virtually attributed to it all the qualities which belong to that class.

This doctrine is not inconsistent with what has already been maintained, that an act of Reasoning is necessary to enable us to call anything by its appropriate Common Name. Mere observation cannot teach us what is the proper appellation of any object which is now for the first time perceived; its name is not stamped upon it, — is not one of its qualities directly perceptible either by sense or consciousness. But by the joint action of our faculties of perception and comparison, we are made aware that the new object resembles a certain class of previously known objects in all the particulars which are connoted by the name of that class, and *therefore*, that the object may be properly subsumed into that class, and called by its name.

The doctrine of Locke and Mill, then, appears true to this extent; — that we certainly *compare* one individual thing with another, and only by such comparison can discoveries be made and knowledge advanced. But that simple comparison, and the consequent perception of a relation of likeness or unlikeness, is not an act of *reasoning*. We do not, in the technical sense of the term, "*conclude* from particulars to particulars." Before this particular discovery can be made available for the purposes of Science,— before it can be brought into union and harmony with our previous stock of knowledge, an act of Pure Thought — of Mediate Inference, or Reasoning properly so called — is necessary. We must become aware that at least one of the two Individuals which were compared together is a typical specimen or representative of a whole Class, and the corresponding Conclusion must be reached, that the other Individual possesses some one or more of the essential attributes of that Class. To advance to this Conclusion is, in one sense, an unimportant step; for it contains nothing new, — it does not increase our knowledge. Having learned the individual fact, that "A and B are both equal to C," we do not really make any progress, except in the way of systematizing our knowledge, when we add the very obvious corollary, that "they are equal to each other," since this is but one instance under the General Rule, that "all which are equal to the same thing are equal to each other." But in another respect, this step is far from being unimportant. Though we have already *virtually* attributed all the qualities of the class to the individual when we have included that individual in the class, so that the technical Conclusion only draws out explicitly what was already implicitly thought, a new act of classification is thus completed, and the memory is disburdened of particulars by an act of arranging and harmonizing our knowledge. First to bring out into distinct consciousness the truths which are already, so to speak, within our reach, but in a confused and undeveloped state, and then to place them under their appropriate heads or classes in a methodized system of knowledge, is the peculiar office of Reasoning. The Conclusion, when once drawn, is obvious enough; otherwise it could not be said to be demonstratively proved. But far the greater part of our knowledge exists in this half latent semi-developed state; only by an act of Reasoning can it be drawn forth, proved, and made available for use in further inquiry. In respect to utility, it matters little whether our stores are positively enlarged, or our previous acquisitions are developed, systematized, and rendered more efficient. I believe that no new truth was ever discovered by a direct process of pure Reasoning; and, on the other hand, that, without the aids and appliances furnished by such Reasoning, no progress beyond the most elementary steps of Science would have been practicable. Good observers discover new facts, but good reasoners do most to educate and instruct mankind.

Of course, the fact of observation on which the Reasoning is based, and which it is the office of the Reasoning to develop, is not necessarily one perceptible by sense. The mere thinker, who, by some lucky chance or by dint of patient reflection, hits upon some relation, hitherto unobserved, between two abstract ideas, is just as much a discoverer, as the chemist who first finds that a metal is the basis of an alkali; otherwise, no progress could be made in pure mathematics or any other abstract science. The naked fact, that the square upon the hypothenuse of a right-angled triangle is equal to the sum of the squares on the two other sides, was observed and known long before Pythagoras first succeeded in proving it, by showing, through a series of Middle Terms, that it is really involved in and harmonizes with some elementary principles, the whole compass and meaning of which had not before been duly developed. The fact was first made known by reflective observation, — perhaps by sensible experiment; but it did not become a step in the progress of Science till it had been proved, or subsumed under some broader principles, and thus assigned its due place in a system of knowledge, by an act of pure Reasoning.

To those who have fully considered the doctrine which was laid down at the commencement, that Logic is not an organon for the discovery of truth, and that it is exclusively concerned with the Form, and not the Matter, of Thought, this discussion may seem to have been needlessly prolonged. But it has so long been supposed that the admission of the inapplicability of the Syllogistic process to the discovery of truth was tantamount to a confession of the entire inutility of the science, that it seemed worth while, even at the expense of some repetition, to prove that this supposition was wholly groundless, and to show precisely what is the utility of the ends to which mere Reasoning is subservient. When Mr. Locke says, " I am apt to think that he who should employ all the force of his reason only in brandishing of Syllogisms will discover *very little* of that mass of knowledge which lies concealed in the secret recesses of nature," we have a right to answer, in the words of an acute logician, Mr. J. Walker, of Dublin, that " he expresses himself with needless caution. Such a man will certainly not discover *any* of it. And if any imagined that the mere brandishing of Syllogisms could increase their knowledge, as some of the Schoolmen seemed to think, they were indeed very absurd." But to those who consider how limited the range of human knowledge would be, if it were confined to isolated facts of observation resulting from the comparison of one individual thing with another, having no connection with each other, often seemingly at variance, not systematized, not summed up into general truths, and hence incapable of communication by language, it will be evident that, without the capacity and the constant exercise of Reasoning, mankind would have advanced but little beyond the condition of the brutes.

It may be useful to enumerate the different classes of General Rules which are the Major Premises of all Syllogisms, and, as such, are not so much the First Principles whence all our Conclusions are derived, as they are the Ultimate Truths in which all Reasoning terminates.

1. The first of these classes consists of the Primary Laws of Pure Thought, and those secondary or derivative maxims into which, in different sciences and for different purposes, these Primary Laws are explicated. In Logic, as we have seen, both the supreme Canons of Mediate Inference, such as the *Dictum de omni et nullo*, and the special Rules of various sorts of Syllogisms, are all resolvable, in the last analysis, into these Laws of Thought. In like manner, the Axioms properly so called of Geometry, that "if equals are added to equals, the wholes are equal," "if equals are subtracted from equals, the remainders are equal," &c., are only varied expressions, explications, or immediate consequences, of the Laws of Identity and Non-contradiction.

2. The foregoing maxims are merely analytic or explicative. The next class consists of synthetic or ampliative Judgments. These are necessary intuitions of pure reason, or universal truths known *a priori*, as resulting from the constitution of the mind itself. Such are the Judgments, that every event must have a cause, that space is infinite, that substance underlies all material attributes, &c. With these I am inclined to rank what have been called Axioms — more properly, Assumptions — of geometrical science, as they are propositions which the geometer must assume to be true, though they cannot be demonstrated; for example, — two straight lines cannot enclose a space; a straight line is the shortest distance between two points; two straight lines cut by a third line at equal angles, if produced, will never meet.

3. We also reason demonstratively from Definitions, that

is, from explications of the Intension of any Concepts which we see fit to frame. Of course, such Judgments are purely analytic, and if they contain no unfounded assumption, that the signification thus assigned to the Names of the Concepts is that which is usually affixed to them in the common use of language, or that the Marks enumerated are *all* the original and essential qualities of the real things which these Names denote, the Conclusions at which we arrive must be demonstratively certain.

4. The laws, or positive precepts, which emanate from any sufficient authority, whether human or divine. These are not Judgments, but commands, and, as they are to be obeyed at all hazards, and on all occasions, the only question which can arise respecting them concerns their interpretation. Of this nature are the injunctions of conscience, the laws of the land, and the commands of God, as made known in his revealed word. Apart from any doubt which may arise concerning the signification of the terms in which they are expressed, any Conclusion legitimately deduced from such commands must be absolutely valid, since universality is of the very nature of law.

5. Universal propositions previously demonstrated.

6. Truths of generalization, based upon observation and Induction or Analogy. These are true only to the extent of our experience, which, as we have seen, never extends to *all* or *none*. Consequently, these propositions rest only upon probable evidence; and though such evidence be sufficient for moral certainty, they are not available for Demonstration strictly so called. We may *assume* them to be universally true, and upon such assumptions may rest perfectly valid syllogisms; but the Conclusion in such cases will have no other or higher certainty than belongs to the Major Premise.

It should be observed, however, that, when we thus speak of merely *probable* evidence, the epithet is used only in its technical sense, and it is not meant that we have necessarily less confidence in it than in mathematical Demonstration. " The word *probable*, when thus used," says Dugald Stewart, "does not imply any *deficiency* in the proof, but only marks the peculiar nature of that proof as contradistinguished from another species of evidence. It is opposed, not to what is *certain*, but to what admits of being demonstrated after the manner of mathematicians. This differs widely from the meaning annexed to the same word in popular discourse; according to which, whatever event is said to be *probable* is understood to be expected with some degree of doubt." Perhaps the clearest distinction between Demonstrative and Probable evidence consists in the fact, that the former does not admit of degrees, as a proposition is either demonstrated absolutely, or not at all; while the latter may exist in any degree, from the faintest shade of probability up to moral certainty.

This seems the proper place for the explanation of the technical terms, or Second Intentions of Judgments, that are used in the construction of Science. Most of these, however, are of infrequent occurrence, except in the mathematical sciences. All propositions are either *Theoretical* or *Practical;* — the former are purely speculative, the truths which they enounce being merely objects of contemplation by the mind, as having no reference to action or conduct; the latter have regard to something which is to be done or omitted, to some performance or mode of procedure. Propositions are also said to be *demonstrable*, if they require or admit of proof; they are *indemonstrable*, if they are self-evident, or intuitively known.

An indemonstrable judgment, if theoretical, is called an *Axiom;* if practical, it is styled a *Postulate*. A demonstrable judgment, or one which is announced as needing proof, if theoretical, is called a *Theorem;* if practical, it is a *Problem*. A *Thesis* coincides very nearly with a Theorem; it is a judgment proposed for discussion and proof. A *Corollary* is a truth announced as an immediate consequence or collateral result of another judgment that has just been proved, and therefore as not needing any separate proof for itself. A Judgment which does not properly belong to the science in which it appears, but is borrowed from some other, is called a *Lemma;* one which merely illustrates the science, but is not an integral part of it, is a *Scholion.* An *Hypothesis* is a judgment not known to be true, but accepted for the time as a provisional explanation of some phenomena, and as liable to be modified or rejected altogether on the production of further evidence. A *Theory*, sometimes incorrectly used as a synonyme for *Hypothesis*, is a comprehensive and methodical arrangement of some large group of phenomena under their supposed Causes and Laws, offered as at least a provisional account of them and mode of reducing them to system. " *Theoriarum vires,*" says Bacon, " *arctâ et quasi se mutuo sustinente partium adaptatione, quâ quasi in orbem cohærent, firmantur.*"

CHAPTER XII.

INDUCTION AND ANALOGY.

ANY act of Reasoning strictly so called presupposes the universality of its Sumption or Major Premise. If I am not absolutely certain that *all* A are B, then, though the Subsumption that C is A be undoubtedly true, I cannot be sure that C is B.

Now it has been repeatedly proved, that universal Judgments cannot be derived from mere experience, which is competent to pronounce upon *some*, or *many*, but never upon *all*, or *none*. But as we cannot have any knowledge of *real things*, or actual existences, except by means of experience, it follows that such things are not objects of Reasoning in the proper sense of the term, — that is, of Demonstrative Reasoning, in which the Conclusion is accepted with absolute certainty. From the enumeration which has just been made, it appears that, with the unimportant exceptions of legal precepts and a few truths known *a priori*, all Major Premises must be either mere analytic judgments obtained by explicating our own abstract conceptions, or general rules that are true only to the extent of our experience. We may *assume* such rules to be universally true, and the Reasoning will then become perfect or Demonstrative *in Form;* but as the Conclusion can never be purged from the shade of uncertainty thrown upon it by the imperfect evidence of the universality of its Major Premise, such Reasoning is rightly considered as merely *probable* or *contingent*. We may *suppose*, also, that the real existences perfectly correspond to the abstract conceptions that we have formed of them, and, in this way, may seem to obtain absolute Conclusions about matters of fact. This is commonly said to be reasoning from hypotheses; but just so far as such reasoning is Demonstrative, it concerns only the Concept, which cannot be more than an imperfect representation of the reality.

For illustration, I borrow from Mr. Bailey's "Theory of Reasoning," page 2, the following examples of Probable or contingent Reasoning.

1. "I am walking, I will suppose, on the sea-shore, and, perceiving a quantity of sea-weed lying on the beach, while the water is at the moment a quarter of a mile from it, I conclude that the tide has ebbed, and left the weed where I perceive it lying."
2. "I notice the print of a small foot on the sand, and I feel pretty sure that it was made by a child."

Each of these instances may be resolved into *the Form* of perfect or Demonstrative Reasoning, and it will then be seen that the uncertainty which attaches to the Conclusion arises solely from the doubt, which experience, however often repeated, is incompetent to remove, as to the absolute universality of the Major Premise.

1. All sea-weed found within the space usually covered by the sea at high water must have been left there by the ebbing of the tide;
This bunch of sea-weed was so found; therefore, &c.
2. No small foot-shaped imprint on the sand can have been left by anything else than the foot of a child;
This is a small foot-shaped imprint on the sand; therefore, &c.

"In these several cases," says Mr. Bailey, "my mind is determined by the sight of present phenomena, conjoined with knowledge previously acquired, to believe something which I do not actually perceive through the organs of sense;—something past, something future, or something distant; or, in other words, to believe that some event has happened, will happen, or is happening, although beyond the sphere of my observation." In short, it is an attempt to make the Thinking faculty do the work of the Perceptive faculty; to gain a knowledge of an external fact by a mere process of Thought, instead of acquiring it by observation through the senses. Such an attempt can have but imperfect success; its result is not properly denominated *knowledge*, but *belief*, or *opinion*. The inference is rightly said to rest upon *moral*, or *probable*, evidence.

It is contended by some, that the mind actually rests such inferences upon the amount of evidence which has really been collected, though conscious that it is incomplete, and does not go through the Form of *assuming* a Major Premise which is absolutely universal, and which, if we were only sure that it was well founded, would render the Conclusion certain. Thus, to recur to one of the instances just cited, Mr. Bailey argues that the Premise from which the mind actually draws the inference is what he terms the *Collective Fact*, viz. that, *in all the cases which I have ever observed or heard of*, all sea-weed so found has been left by the tide,—and not the *General Law*, announced without this limitation, which affirms as much absolutely of *all* sea-weed so found. He maintains that the General Law itself, just as much as the particular case in question, is an inference from the Collective Fact. To rest the inference respecting the individual case upon the General Law, does not make the Conclusion a whit more probable, than to rest it upon the Collective Fact on which this General Law itself is founded.

Perhaps the question is one which does not merit much discussion. Obviously it matters not whether the mind, in seeking for competent proof of this particular inference, proceeds by throwing what evidence it possesses into *the*

Form of perfect or Demonstrative reasoning, through the assumption of a Major Premise which is not free from doubt; or whether it forbears any undue assumption in the Premises, and adopts a process of inference which is confessedly imperfect even in Form. Taking a doubtful assertion for a Premise, it thus preserves the Form of valid reasoning.

> All men are fallible;
> The author of this book is a man;
> Therefore the author of this book is fallible.

Restrict the statement in the Major Premise, so that it shall express no more than what is known to be true, and the Reasoning thus becomes invalid through an undistributed Middle.

> All men, *so far as observation has extended,* have been fallible;
> Therefore this author is fallible.

As a fact, however, I believe the first of these forms is much more frequently in use. For proof in any particular case, we usually refer to a Law of Nature, the universality of which is expressed with as little hesitation as if it were a Law of Thought. The usual form of Enthymeme employed is the following: — This bit of iron will melt, because *all* iron is fusible; This water will boil at 212°, because water *always* boils at that temperature; These men must die, for *all* human beings are mortal. In truth, with the exception of those who have made a special study of the theory of Reasoning, nobody thinks of restricting the universality of such statements by the qualifying clause, "so far as has been observed," or "according to all known experience." And it is not mere carelessness in the use of language, or the proneness to exaggeration which has already been pointed out for censure, that causes such statements to be made without their proper limitations. Very few are conscious, even after reflection, that there is any exaggeration in the case; and there is none, except what is implied by adopting the Form, without the substance, of Demonstrative Reasoning.

Induction and Analogy are the two processes of thought by which we endeavor to make our Judgments about whole classes of real objects, or actual existences, approximate the absolute certainty and universality of our Judgments about abstract conceptions. Hence they are, what Pure Reasoning is not, *organa* for the discovery of truth and the actual advancement of knowledge. But just so far as they are means to these ends, they lose the character of Pure or Demonstrative Reasoning; the Syllogisms to which they are reducible are faulty either in Matter, as having a Major Premise the universality of which is merely *probable*, or in Form, as containing an undistributed Middle. The question whether they are entitled to be called *Reasoning* is hardly worth discussing here, as it concerns only the use of words. Logical or Demonstrative Reasoning they are not; but they may be denominated Probable Reasoning, or Philosophical Presumptions.

It should be mentioned, however, that what may be termed Logical Induction, the *plena enumeratio* of the logicians, which deduces a General Rule from what is known to be true of *every* individual in the class, belongs to Pure Reasoning strictly so called. Conclusions drawn from such Premises as the following, are Demonstrative or absolutely certain; but these only generalize our knowledge, or alter its expression; they do not enlarge it.

Mercury, Venus, the Earth, &c. are all the Planets.

Peter, James, John, Matthew, &c. are all the Apostles.

This mode of Reasoning has already been analyzed; but it is not what is understood by Induction in the processes of Science. Logical Induction concludes from *each one* to *all;* Induction properly so called concerns the Matter of Thought, and concludes from *some* to *all.*

The difference between Induction and Analogy has been clearly stated and illustrated by Kant. In order to enlarge our knowledge beyond the bounds of experience, we must either conclude from *many* things to *all* others of the same Species, which is Induction; or we must conclude from the known agreement of two things in *several* qualities, that they agree also in *some other* quality which is not directly known. In our progress from the Particular to the General, Induction proceeds upon the principle, that *what certainly belongs to many Individuals of the same kind, also probably belongs to all the other Individuals of that kind;* the principle of Analogy is, that, *if two things agree in many respects, they probably agree also in some other respect.* Because *some one* quality *exists in many* things, therefore *it exists in all* of the same kind; this is Induction. Because *many* qualities in this are the same as in that, therefore *one* other quality in this resembles that; this is Analogy. In other words, Induction concludes from *one in many* to *the others*, by way of Extension; Analogy, from *many in one* to *the others*, by way of Intension.

The following are instances of Induction : —

1. In many cases in which water has been analyzed, it has been found to consist solely of oxygen and hydrogen; therefore, all water is made up from these two elements.

2. Very many animals have been examined, and these, without a single exception, have been found to possess a nervous system; therefore, all animals have a nervous system.

3. Most bodies expand in bulk, if heated; therefore, heat always produces expansion, if it be not counteracted by some other cause.

The following are instances of Analogy : —

1. The planets Venus and Mars resemble the earth in many respects, as in size, density, time of rotation on the axis, distance from the sun, receiving light and heat from

it, &c.; therefore, they probably resemble it in one other respect, in being inhabited by living beings.

2. Fossil skeletons that are found in the rocks bear a close resemblance in very many respects to the skeletons which, as we know, once belonged to recently living animals; therefore, they resemble them in one other respect, in that these fossils are the remains of animals which were formerly living upon the earth.

3. In many respects, as in complexity of parts, nice adjustment and mutual dependence of these parts one upon another, delicacy of finish, symmetry, and adaptation to many useful ends, the human hand resembles some ingenious machines, which we know to have been contrived and fashioned by the exercise of mind; therefore the hand was so contrived and fashioned.

4. The argument of Origen and Bishop Butler is, that if the Scriptures and the constitution of Nature are alike in this respect, that they proceeded from the same Author, we may well expect to find the same difficulties in the former as are found in the latter.

It is plain that what is here called Analogy is the same mental process which is described and analyzed by Aristotle as " reasoning from Example." He gives the following as an instance of this sort of argument. If we would prove that it is not expedient for the Athenians to make war upon the Thebans, who are their neighbors, we may reason from the analogous case, that the war against the Phoceans, who were their neighbors, was fatal to the Thebans. He says that Example is not founded, like Syllogism, upon the relation of the whole to its parts, nor, like Induction, upon the relation of the parts to the whole, but upon the relation of one part to another, because the one is more perfectly known than that other. The Aristotelic Induction proceeds from *all* the individual cases, while Example is founded only upon *some* of them, perhaps, as above, upon a single instance.

Comparatively little need be said of Analogy, as the Conclusions to which it leads are evidently not Demonstrative, but merely Probable. Strictly speaking, there is no *proof* whatever, because two things resemble each other, however nearly, or in however many respects, that the resemblance extends to a single point other than what has been actually observed. The existence of one quality, it is true, may be necessarily implied in that of another, either by the Laws of Thought, or by the *a priori* laws of the human mind; as one geometrical property of a body may be deduced from another, or as its divisibility may be inferred from its extension. This is Demonstrative Reasoning, but it is merely explicating our knowledge, and not directly adding to it; and certainly it is not reasoning from Analogy, which proceeds from similarity in *some* respects to similarity in *one* other, or in *many* others. Analogical conclusions may have any degree of probability, varying from a merely permissible hypothesis up to what may fairly be called moral certainty. Because this kind of inference is often greatly abused, for some degree of resemblance may often be detected between two things apparently most dissimilar,— skill in such detection, when the inference is ludicrously improbable, constituting *wit*,— I am inclined to think that the force of which it is susceptible is generally underrated. Slight Analogies are worth nothing, except to show that the coexistence of two or more qualities is barely *possible*, no belief whatever being justly created that it is *probable*. On the other hand, the Analogy may be so perfect that the Conclusion founded upon it may be accepted with as full faith as if it rested upon an extensive and cautious Induction, with which, indeed, it is frequently confounded.

To recur to the instances just cited. . The supposition that the other planets are inhabited rests upon an Analogy which is so faint and imperfect, that it does not afford sufficient ground for making up any opinion on the subject, either for or against the hypothesis. The resemblance is but slight, even in the few particulars that are cited; and we have no evidence that there is any similarity whatever in a vast number of other respects, many of which are essential to the existence of life under any of the forms with which we are acquainted. On the other hand, the Analogy between the skeletons that exist only in a fossil state, and those of animals now living, is so broad and perfect, that a man's sanity or sincerity would be questioned who should affect to doubt that the former also once walked the earth or swam in the seas. These fossils do not differ more from the extant types than many of the latter do from each other, while in the numberless points of Analogy the resemblance is perfect. And the conclusion in the third case, founded upon the Analogy between the human hand and a contrivance of man's device, is still more indisputable. If, without the aid of mind, without foresight or design, the mere fortuitous concourse of atoms, in the lapse of a past eternity, could have formed a *living* tree, fish, or elephant, then, we say, that same rudderless and purposeless crowd of primeval atoms, in the lapse of a past eternity, could have formed, *what is much easier*, a *fossil* tree, fish, or elephant. We are here pointing out the analogous character of two arguments, each founded upon Analogy, but pointing to different Conclusions; and we find the resemblance between them so perfect, that it is impossible to maintain the validity of the Conclusion in the former case, and deny it in the latter.

The definition which is ordinarily given of Analogy, that it means proportion, or a similarity of relations, does not differ from the one here propounded. Thus, it is said, when we affirm the relation of the fins of a fish to the water to be the same [similar] to that of the wings of a bird to the air, that we are judging from Analogy. So we are; we are pointing out what is perhaps an unexpected resemblance amid apparent diversity. However unlike fins are to wings, we still pronounce that they agree in this, the adaptation of the former to the animal's motion through the water being very similar to the fitness of the latter to effect motion through the air. From this equality of fitness for corresponding purposes, we reason analogically that, if one was contrived by intelligence, the other was also.

Induction, says Mr. Mill, "may be summarily defined as Generalization from Experience. It consists in inferring from *some* individual instances in which a phenomenon is observed to occur, that it occurs in *all* instances of a certain class; namely, in all which resemble the former in what are regarded as the material circumstances." This last qualification is an important one, and has not received sufficient notice from those who have speculated upon the theory of Induction. The process would be invalid and nugatory, *if we did not presuppose the correctness of the preceding Classifications that have been formed of the objects of Science*. A conclusion from *some* to *all* would not hold, would not have even the slightest shade of probability, if it were applied to a Class formed of the objects now contained in this room, or of those embraced within my present field of vision, or of things having no common attribute except that they are of the same color, or the same size. But such a conclusion becomes extremely probable, even morally certain, when applied to a Class, like that of *metals* or *stars*, having many common characteristics which are definite and peculiar. Thus, having ascertained of only two metals, iron and copper, that they are conductors of electricity, it would be a tolerably safe Induction, that *all* metals are such conductors. Having found that one thunder-cloud was electrical, Franklin at once safely leaped to the conclusion, that all such clouds had that property. We have already seen that the Classifications formed of the innumerable objects of thought cannot be arbitrary, but must be framed to embrace as many common or similar elements as possible. The numberless properties of a geometric figure can be deduced by necessary inference from the one or two leading properties of it which are selected to form its Definition. And the hope always is, in forming a Classification of real objects or events in Nature, to hit upon some attribute as the basis of the arrangement with which all the other qualities of it are connected by some necessary, though to us invisible, tie.

This appears to afford the solution of a problem which has puzzled many inquirers; — how it is, that we often safely frame an Induction from a single instance, while, in other cases, the conclusion is precarious, though supported by a multitude of affirmative examples. Thus, the chemist, having discovered a new metal, ascertains by a single experiment its specific gravity, degree of hardness, toughness, &c., and then safely concludes that every other specimen of the metal, which may afterwards be obtained, will be found to possess these qualities in the same degree. On the other hand, a multitude of instances of recovery from a specific disease after the administration of a particular drug are insufficient to establish the universal efficacy of the medicine in what appear to be similar cases. In Meteorology, also, and in the several branches of Natural History, though the Induction may be very extensive, and conducted with all possible caution, the general conclusions have only that low degree of probability which is indicated by calling them *empirical laws*. The reason of this difference evidently is, that the Classifications in the science of Chemistry approach very nearly to perfection, the qualities determinable by chemical analysis being definite, strongly marked, and constant in their forms of combination with each other; while Medicine, Meteorology, and Natural History are, and probably must ever remain, sciences very imperfect in

Classification, as the objects with which they are concerned have an indefinite multitude of ill-determined attributes, shaded into each other by imperceptible degrees, and combined in the most irregular manner. The lines, and even the principles, of division of the objects of these sciences are merely provisional, and are frequently changed, so as to adapt them to the progress of observation, or in the hope of hitting upon some qualities which may be found in more constant relations with the other leading properties than those which have hitherto formed the basis of the Classification. Of course, the Induction becomes extremely precarious, when we are not sure that the instances over which it extends agree with each other in all material circumstances.

It is evident, moreover, that the smaller the Class is, or the nearer that it comes to an Infima Species, the stronger is our assurance that, in reference to this Class, the conclusion from *some* to *all* will hold good. The Induction is safer, for instance, from some to all lumps of iron, than from some to all metals; and it is still more certain in reference to all specimens of one kind of iron, wrought or malleable, than with respect to all sorts of that metal. As the Extension and Intension of the Class-name are in inverse ratio to each other, that is, as the number of attributes connoted is greater in proportion as the number of objects denoted is less, the similarity of the members of the Class to each other is increased as the number of those members is diminished; and the greater the similarity, the safer the Induction, because it is then more probable that the resemblance extends to the material or essential circumstances. As the Intension is greater, the Induction is founded upon a larger number of qualities, that is, upon a more perfect resemblance; and as the Extension is less, the Induction extends to fewer objects, and is therefore more likely to be well founded. The gap between *some* and *all* is not so great, when even *all* denotes only *a few*. We cannot safely reason, from the process of treatment which has been effectual in one case of fever, to the efficiency of the same treatment in any other instance, merely because the symptoms of no one fever-stricken patient have anything more than a general resemblance to those of another; and the internal peculiarities of the malady, of which the outward symptoms are only the faint and easily mistakable indications, are still more unlike.

Thus much, however, is certain, that if the Classification is correct, if the cases brought together are really parallel in all the essential circumstances, — and we must presuppose as much as this before we can reason from Induction at all, — then we firmly believe, and assume it even as an axiomatic truth, that "the course of nature is uniform," that "natural events are governed by constant general laws," that "what has been will be," and that "what has been even in one instance has been in all other instances." These are only different modes of expressing one and the same Universal Truth, — one invincible conviction of the human mind. This Truth is the ultimate Major Premise, upon which all reasoning from Induction depends, or which is taken for granted in all such reasoning. The simplest and most indisputable case of such reasoning depends upon this Maxim, just as much as the latest and broadest general conclusion that has been propounded in physical science, though this conclusion may be so questionable that it is propounded only as an hypothesis. I could not be sure, for instance, that the identical piece of coin now in my hand still possesses the same weight, malleability, hardness, purity, &c., which I ascertained from actual observation that it had only five minutes ago, if it were not for this irresistible belief in the uniformity of nature's laws. Whatever doubts may perplex or weaken the inference from some to all, these doubts do not concern the Primary Truth upon which all such inferences are based, but relate solely to the correctness of the Classification over which the inference extends. Is it certain that we have classified rightly? that the cases brought together are really parallel in all essential respects? If so, one instance is just as good to base an Induction upon as ten thousand; for we have an irresistible conviction that, as the law thus operates in one case, it *must* so operate in all. What is the ground of our assumption of this General Truth? How came we to be convinced thus absolutely that nature's course is uniform? He who can answer this question has solved the great problem in the philosophy of Induction.

Dr. Reid, Mr. Stewart, and most of the other Scotch philosophers, attempt to resolve our assumption of this Maxim into an ultimate fact, into an original and instinctive law of the human mind. Experience is constantly tending to confirm it, but they hold that we believe in it previously to all experience. They do not identify it with the principle of Causation, — with the law that every event must have a Cause, — but maintain that it is a distinct and independent Axiom. Dr. Brown even goes so far as to attempt to resolve the law of Causality itself into this Axiom. He asserts that we are obliged to refer every event, every beginning to be, to some Cause, *because* we have an instinctive anticipation of the uniformity of nature's laws. My own opinion, as will be seen hereafter, is exactly the reverse of Brown's theory. It seems to me that our irresistible conviction of the truth of this Maxim, that nature's course is uniform, is resolvable into our necessary belief of the law of Causality; that the latter is the primitive judgment *a priori*, and the former is secondary and derivative; that a process of Thought, an act of Reasoning, if not an appeal to experience, always precedes, and is used to confirm or prove, our assertion that nature's course is uniform, while we affirm at once, antecedently to all experience, and without any attempt at proof, that every event must have a Cause.

But however this may be, the doctrine in which Brown agrees with Reid and Stewart, that we have an instinctive and *a priori* conviction that nature's laws are unchangeable, appears plainly indefensible. *Entia non sunt multiplicanda præter necessitatem;* it is a cardinal maxim in philosophy, that no principle can be admitted as an ultimate fact until it is clearly shown that it cannot be explained as derivative. Indirectly, therefore, this doctrine is refuted by the proof, which will subsequently be attempted, that this principle is resolvable into the law of Causality. But still further: — any conviction, which is *a priori* in its origin and character, must be universal, necessary, and immediate. Now without going so far as Comte and Mill, who maintain, with respect to this principle, that "far from being the first Induction we make, it is one of the last," that "it was only acquired gradually, and extended itself, as observation advanced, from one order of phenomena to another," and that "there are cases, in which we reckon with the most unfailing confidence upon uniformity, and other cases in which we do not count upon it at all"; — without adopting these assertions, I say, it may safely be pronounced, that we do not accept this principle at first, or in all cases, unless it is justified by some reflection or experience; that is, until we have satisfied ourselves that it is a necessary consequence of some intuitive and imperative belief, or have verified it by subsequent observations. Through the law of the Association of Ideas, it is true, the recurrence of any phenomenon *suggests* all the circumstances by which it was originally accompanied; it may even *incline us to believe* that these circumstances, also, will recur in the same order as before. Even the dog cowers at the sight of the whip which has once or twice been used to punish him. But this is very far from an immediate and necessary conviction that any of these former concomitants *must* so recur. We stop to analyze the case and make distinctions; we separate the conjunctions that are believed to be invariable from those that are merely casual, and accept the former only because we recognize one of the events either as a Cause, or what is believed to be the regular concomitant of a Cause, of the other.

"Every person's consciousness," says Mr. Mill, "assures him that he does not always expect uniformity in the course of events; he does not always believe that the unknown will be similar to the known, that the future will resemble the past. Nobody believes that the succession of rain and fine weather will be the same in every future year as in the present. Nobody expects to have the same dreams repeated every night. On the contrary, everybody mentions it as something extraordinary, if the course of nature is constant, and resembles itself, in these particulars. To look for constancy where constancy is not to be expected, as, for instance, that a day which has once brought good fortune will always be a fortunate day, is justly accounted superstition. The course of nature, in truth, is not only uniform, it is also infinitely capricious. Some phenomena are always seen to recur in the very same combinations in which we met with them at first; others seem altogether capricious."

On the other hand, the doctrine of Comte and Mill, that our conviction of the uniformity of nature's laws, which is the ground or principle upon which all Induction rests, is itself obtained by Induction, appears to be an evident begging of the question. How can any mental operation be used as a means of discovering and verifying a principle which must be taken for granted before that operation itself can be performed? To obtain a number of Conclusions by adopting a certain Maxim as a Major Premise, and then to use those very Conclusions as a means of proving that Maxim, is evidently reasoning in a circle. Mr. Mill is perfectly aware of this objection to his doctrine, and frankly states it in the strongest terms. " Can we prove a proposition," he asks, "by an argument which takes it for granted? And if not so proved, on what evidence does it rest?"

But though aware of the objection, it does not appear that Mr. Mill has been successful in his endeavors to obviate it. He rather augments the difficulty, by admitting that the Maxim " was not, of course, derived from *rigid* Induction, but from the *loose and uncertain* mode of Induction *per enumerationem simplicem*." Then the Premise rests upon *less* satisfactory evidence than the Conclusion, and yet the latter is based exclusively upon the former. Is not this a contradiction? How can the superstructure be more stable than the very foundation on which it rests?

Induction by simple enumeration "consists in ascribing the character of general truths to all propositions which are true in every instance that we happen to know of." Thus, we say that "*All* ruminating animals divide the hoof," merely because no instance to the contrary has, *as yet*, been discovered. But "to Europeans, not many years ago, the proposition, 'All swans are white,' appeared an equally unequivocal instance of uniformity in the course of nature. Further experience has proved that they were mistaken." Then the presumption in favor of what is still the accepted rule, in the present state of our knowledge, that all ruminating animals divide the hoof, would not be held to outweigh the testimony of one unimpeachable witness, who should declare that, in some hitherto imperfectly explored region, he had discovered a solid-hoofed ruminating animal. How can the evidence of these merely provisional truths, which are liable to be overturned at any moment, be the same with that which supports the validity of the Maxim upon which the most rigorous Inductions depend?

Mr. Mill answers, that even this precarious Induction, that something is universally true because we have never known any instance to the contrary, may become a valid ground of belief when it is preceded by the assurance, that, "if there were in nature any instances to the contrary, we should have known of them." An empirical law, he argues, "of which the truth is exemplified at every moment of time, and in every variety of place or circumstance, has an evidence which surpasses that of the most rigid Induction, even if the foundation of scientific Induction were not itself laid, as we have seen that it is, in a generalization of this very description." As to the admissions made in the passage which has just been quoted from Mr. Mill, that we do "not always expect uniformity in the course of events," and that "the course of nature, in truth, is not only uniform, it is also infinitely capricious," it is claimed that the progress of Inductive Science has already explained away these apparent exceptions. This progress has been so great, it is argued, that we now know directly that the Maxim holds good of far the greater number of phenomena, "the utmost that can be said being that of some we cannot positively, from direct evidence, affirm its truth; while phenomenon after phenomenon, as they become better known to us, is constantly passing from the latter class into the former; and in all cases in which that transition has not yet taken place, the absence of direct proof is accounted for by the rarity or the obscurity of the phenomena, or our deficient means of observing them, or the logical difficulties arising from the complication of the circumstances in which they occur."

But even when the doctrine is thus limited and explained, it does not appear to be relieved from the two fundamental objections which have been urged against it, first, that it founds the principle of Induction upon Induction itself, which is reasoning in a circle, and secondly, that it bases a stronger conviction upon a weaker one, a higher probability upon a lower one. Granted, if you will, that Induction itself, a rude Induction, gradually *leads us to believe* in rigorous scientific Induction; this may explain the genesis of the phenomenon, or how it was that we were first led to employ this organon of discovery. But before we can accept the fruit of the Induction with the strong and unhesitating conviction which we now accord to any well-established Law of Nature, we must not only know how we were first induced to believe that such a Law exists, but we must find some valid principle which may fairly be accounted a *proof* of its existence. Certainly such proof cannot be obtained by reasoning in a circle. Mill and Comte would have us believe, that our invincible conviction of the universality of the Law of Gravitation rests upon no firmer basis than the opinion, which, indeed, is daily gaining ground, and which the progress of mere Physical Science evidently tends to confirm, that everything in nature is subject to law, so that it takes place by a physical necessity, and might be predicted with unerring confidence, if we had a perfect knowledge of its antecedents. "Every event has some invariable and unconditional antecedent"; — if we hesitate to admit this proposition in all its generality, Mr. Mill thinks we cannot consistently believe that all matter gravitates, that oxygen is necessary for the support of animal life, or even that fire will burn and water drown. We maintain that the latter propositions are incontestable, while the former, the principle of the universality of law, is merely a hypothetical conclusion, though an extremely probable one. Accordingly, to base the latter upon the former is to make the superstructure stronger than its own foundation. Mr. Mill himself is compelled to admit, with respect to one very large class of phenomena, those of the human will, that at least one half of the speculative world, even in our own day, do not believe in the universality of law, or that every event is necessarily determined by its antecedents. And with regard even to physical events, a large and increasing number of philosophers, among whom are ranked Bishop Berkeley, Dr. Samuel Clarke, and Dugald Stewart, hold that none of them are subject to law, in the sense of being absolutely determined by their physical antecedents, but are the results of volition, which is free to modify them at any moment. But without adopting this theory, he is a bold advocate of the perfectibility of Physical Science who will maintain that the probability of ultimately discovering that phenomena still so apparently irregular and inconstant as those of the weather, of health and disease, the countless peculiarities of individual plants and animals, and the equally numerous idiosyncrasies of human intellect and character, are subject to fixed and definite laws, is so great, that we may safely rest upon it all our confidence in the physical laws that have already been established; — that this probability is the measure and the test of all the certainty that has hitherto been obtained in Physical Science.

Let us examine, then, the only remaining theory, which is, that the ultimate Ground of Induction is the Law of Causality, or the judgment that every event must have a Cause, — not merely a constant physical antecedent, but an *efficient* Cause. It is only necessary to show, that the Law of Causality is readily and naturally explicated into the Maxim that nature's course is uniform, so that the absolute and imperative conviction, which belongs to the former as an *a priori* cognition of the human mind, is transferred, by an easy association of ideas, to the latter, though not logically belonging to it.

Take the simplest case of Induction, by which we are led to expect that any physical object will always continue to manifest the same qualities that have hitherto been observed in it, unless it is exposed to some new influences, or a new antecedent is brought in. Here the assumption evidently is, that the qualities of the same thing are permanent, unless some Cause intervenes to change them; and this assumption is logically certain, for it is an Immediate Inference from the Law of Causality, that no change whatever can take place in anything without a Cause. The coin *must* retain the same attributes which it was recently observed to possess, *if there has not been some Cause of alteration.* This proviso is the source of doubt which must always arise when an unquestionable abstract truth is applied to real objects or actual events. We never can be sure that such a Cause of change has not intervened; but we are morally certain that it has not, if there has been no apparent alteration of the circumstances of the case, no seeming exposure to new influences. To this extent, then, we can safely reason from the past to the future, or from *some* to *all*, when satisfied that the Classification is correct, — that is, that no new occurrence or Efficient Cause has destroyed the resemblance of the observed instances to the expected ones, or of *some* to the *others*.

The next sort of Induction, though a little more complicated, is easily resolved into the same Law of Causality. It has already been shown that among the other properties of any particular substance must be ranked its active and passive powers, that is, the changes in other bodies of which its proximity has been a constant antecedent, or the changes to which it is itself subject when brought into relation with other substances under different circumstances. These active and passive powers, regarded as mere sequences of phenomena, may properly be reduced to the preceding head of *qualities;* they form, as we have seen, one class of the attributes of every substance, and, as such, enter into the Intension of the Concept which denotes that substance. In truth, what are called *secondary qualities* are only the powers which bodies possess to excite certain sensations in us, when brought into relation with our organs of sense. And in like manner, the capacity of gold to be melted on the application of a sufficient degree of heat is an integral part of our complex notion of this substance. *Powers* being nothing but *qualities*, then, the Law of Causality is applicable just as in the former case; these powers *must* be fixed or constant in their operation, if a new Cause has not supervened to alter them. The general maxim is one of absolute certainty, but in its application to a given case we never can be sure that the proviso in it has been rigidly fulfilled. This doubt must always remain, and is usually more serious, and less capable of being reduced by further observation and experiment, as regards the powers, than with respect to the other qualities, of bodies. The circumstances to be observed in order to prevent the intrusion of a new antecedent are more numerous and complex; we cannot so easily be assured that the cases are strictly parallel. The unexpected presence of a little more or less carbon may have diminished the fusibility of the metal; if a large mass of iron be near, the action of the magnetic needle is disturbed.

Still further;—it is now known that the merely physical antecedents and other circumstances are not the Efficient Cause of the phenomenon, but are believed to be its regular concomitants only because their presence, thus far, has been invariably followed by the effect. Accordingly, whatever assurance we may possess that the outward circumstances are unchanged, it is still possible that the real Cause may be so far modified that the expected result will no longer be produced. The doubt which thus rests upon the case cannot be dispelled by any precautions whatsoever. The cases may be strictly parallel in every visible respect, as tested by the nicest observations; but if the physical antecedent was only the occasion, and not the Cause, the phenomenon may not be repeated, as it is always possible that the true Cause may now for the first time exist under different combinations. To recur to the illustration taken from Mr. Babbage's machine;—though, in countless instances, each number presented has been greater than its immediate predecessor by unity, yet as this constant precursor was not the true Cause which determined the number that was to come after it, it is always conceivable that the next presentation should be of an entirely novel character.

We can now see why it is that the Maxim which is the Ground of Induction, and on the assumption of which the validity of all our reasoning about real objects and actual events depends, appears so unquestionably true that we regard it as an Axiom. To say that nature's course is uniform, and that all events are subject to law, is only to assert our intuitive conviction, that every phenomenon must have an Efficient Cause, that, while the Cause remains the same, the effect *must be* constant and proportional to it, and hence, that, whenever the true Cause is discovered, we are enabled to predict unerringly the recurrence of the effect. The relation between a true Cause — that is, an *efficient* Cause — and its effect, is radically unlike that between a physical antecedent and its physical consequent. No absolute conviction, no law of the human mind, manifesting itself anterior to all experience, and thereby first rendering experience possible, asserts any connection between antecedent and consequent like that which exists between Cause and effect. The relation between the two former, that of mere succession in time, is contingent, resting solely upon experience, and liable to be overturned at any moment by subsequent experience; between the two latter, it is a Causal relation, and, as such, is absolute and unchangeable, for it is irreversible even in thought. What do we mean when, as a ground of reasoning from *some* to *all*, we assert that nature acts uniformly, or that all physical events are subject to law? Not, surely, that a given antecedent must always be followed by that particular phenomenon which, according to all experience *thus far*, has been its invariable consequent. This is the only conclusion which mere Induction aims to establish; but it is not competent to serve as the Ground of Induction itself, or as that Premise which must be taken for granted before reasoning by Induction is possible. But we mean only that the sequence in question is necessary, if the antecedent is the Efficient Cause (or the invariable concomitant, sign, or precursor of such Cause) of the consequent. We mean only to assert the existence of an irreversible law, and not necessarily that such law has already been discovered. Comte and all his followers will tell us that no event, however extraordinary and unexpected, is to be deemed a *miracle*, — that is, a violation of law, — because the presumption is, that further research will either reveal a new law, or an improved expression of an old one, under which the occurrence, however strange and marvellous, may naturally be subsumed. He will say, — to adopt a well-worn illustration, — that the conversion of water into a solid was a miracle to the King of Siam; but with our larger experience, it is no miracle to us, for we have even discovered the law, — that is, the constant antecedent, — under which the formation of ice takes place. What is this but to assert that our conviction of the universality and permanence of law, so far from being derived from experience, so far from resting on that very process of Induction of which it is the sole support, is strong enough to contradict all experience, and to maintain its place as an Axiom, though contradicted by the largest and most cautious Induction which human science has ever framed? Not even the resurrection of a dead man, says the Positivist, would be a violation of law; — then his conviction of the permanence of nature's laws overrides all the evidence of experience, and contradicts the whole tenor of modern Inductive science.

What is called *physical necessity* is nothing but a conviction that the relation of an Efficient Cause to its effect is unalterable, coupled with the assumption, which is a natural one, but still illogical, either that the particular antecedent or concomitant phenomenon is itself the Cause, or is so closely connected with it that its presence must always be followed by the recurrence of the effect. The only ground of this assumption is the invariability of the succession in time, or the fact that, so far as our experience, or as all human experience, has extended, the one phenomenon has always been the immediate consequent of the other. That this ground is insufficient to justify us in calling the succession a necessary one has already been abundantly proved. The Positivists, in their desire to eliminate the notion of *cause* altogether, although they are compelled to retain the word and all the associations connected with it, refuse to attribute the phenomenon to any single antecedent. The invariable sequence, they say, exists between a consequent and the sum of its several antecedents, all of which must concur before we can be sure of the presence of the effect. In other words, what they call a *cause* is only an assemblage of the *conditions*, all of which must be fulfilled before the phenomenon can be reproduced. "The real Cause," says Mr. Mill, "is the whole of these antecedents; and we have, philosophically speaking, no right to give the name of *cause* to one of them, exclusively of the others." And again, "the Cause is the sum total of the Conditions, positive and negative, taken together; the whole of the contingencies of every description, which, being realized, the consequent invariably follows." Among these "negative" conditions, or rather, as the sum of them, he ranks "the absence of preventing or counteracting Causes." In conformity with this view, the distinction between *agent* and *patient*, between something which acts and some other thing which is acted upon, is formally abolished, as it is denied that there is any *action* in the case. An inevitable corollary of this doctrine is, that there is no *power* or *efficiency* in any one of the antecedents the exertion of which necessarily creates the effect. Yet the denial of any such causal agency entirely refutes the hypothesis that there is any necessary connection between the two events, and leaves their union merely a contingent one, liable to be dissolved or contradicted by subsequent experience. By rejecting the doctrine of Efficient Causation, the Positivist theory throws away all evidence of the permanence and universality of nature's laws.

This conclusion will appear still more obvious when it is demonstrated, as can very easily be done, that every process of Inductive Reasoning, however rigidly conducted, and however verified by subsequent observations, is still resolvable, in the last analysis, into the despised "Induction by simple enumeration," which Lord Bacon calls *mera palpatio*, or groping in the dark. The best evidence which physical science has been able to collect in support of the most generally recognized Laws of Nature amounts only to this, that they are found to be true in every instance that we happen to know of. Mr. Mill admits that Induction necessarily commences with this very imperfect evidence; and he should have added, that it also proceeds and ends with it, finding no other or stronger basis on which to rest its conclusions.

Nearly all the additional evidence which the advancement of science procures for those conclusions which were at first avowedly accepted as inferences from Induction by simple enumeration, (perhaps from an enumeration only of a few instances, or even from a single case,) arises either from extended observation and experiment, from an improved classification of the objects about which we reason, or from what Dr. Whewell calls, by a happily invented phrase, the *consilience* of several Inductions. The process of Induction, when considered as an operation of mind, or as a sort of inference, is essentially one and the same, and perfectly determinate in character. There are not several *kinds* of it, though there are various *degrees* of caution, precision, and thoroughness with which it is carried out. It is always employed with reference to a *class* of objects, qualities, or events, whether that class be well or ill formed, that is, whether the members of it do, or do not, agree with each other in all material respects; and it always proceeds from *some* to *all* of that class, whether the conclusion thus formed does, or does not, coincide or harmonize with other conclusions obtained by a perfectly similar process, though from other data, and with a different purpose in view. The village matron, undertaking to prescribe for the illness of her neighbor's child from what she judges to be the similar cases that have happened in her own family, and Sir Humphry Davy, anticipating that his mode of analyzing potash into the oxide of a new metal would not only hold good of all other lumps of potash besides the very one he was experimenting upon, but would be found practicable, and would lead to similar results, in the case of other alkalis and earths, are both alike reasoning from Induction by simple enumeration. The only difference is, that the diseases which affect the human frame are very numerous, and, as they have but few recognizable symptoms, can be but imperfectly classified at best, and a village matron would probably classify them very ill, so that her inference from *some* to *all* would be wrong; while the alkalis are few in number, and have determinable and strongly marked common qualities, so that the corresponding inference in their case was entirely safe.

Attempts have been made at various times to frame what

may be called a "Logic of Induction," or a full analysis
and description of the operations by which we proceed to
the discovery of physical laws. Lord Bacon, who made
the earliest and most remarkable endeavor of this sort,
hoped to furnish a method of scientific investigation which
should be so complete and accurate as to constitute an organon of discovery, and reduce all intellects to a level,
making success in the search after truth a matter merely
of time and labor. Taught by experience that discoveries
cannot be thus made by rule, but are generally the results
of a tentative process many times repeated, and a happy
combination of circumstances, the later followers of Lord
Bacon have attempted merely to analyze and describe the
process by which discoveries have been made, without hop-
ing to indicate any sure method of adding to their number.
But even this endeavor, though aided by all the lights of
modern physical science, and prosecuted by such eminent
thinkers as Sir John Herschel, Dr. Whewell, and Mr. J.
S. Mill, has had but very limited success. The results do
not agree; though the same compound phenomena are presented for examination, they are analyzed by these three inquirers into very different elements and processes of thought.
These theorists do not even hold the same opinion as to
the nature of the process which they have to separate into
its elements, or, in other words, as to what constitutes Induction. Dr. Whewell, fearful of resting the whole certainty of physical science upon so narrow and unstable a
basis as reasoning in respect merely to all the cases that we
happen to know of, boldly restricts the name of Induction
to what seems to be a mere generalization of the facts
already observed, but as now seen under a new light because succinctly comprehended in one general formula;
and appears to lose sight altogether of the necessity, if
science is to fulfil its office of anticipation and prediction,
of extending the generalization to *all* the objects and events

of a given class, whether they have yet been observed or not. Mr. J. S. Mill, who has more confidence in the precautions and the means of verification by which men of science test and confirm the rude Inductions of the vulgar, justly asserts that Dr. Whewell's mere "Colligation of Facts," far from being the type of Induction generally, "is not Induction at all," but only a new description of the phenomena. He undertakes to analyze and reduce to system these precautions and means of subsequent verification, and to show that, when they are duly observed and practised, scientific Induction differs in kind, and not merely in degree, from Induction by simple enumeration, and, though based merely on experience, establishes its conclusions with the highest certainty of which the human mind is capable. But experience, from its very nature, cannot extend beyond a limited number of cases; and as even the most cautious and rigorous Induction avowedly has no other foundation than experience, either the absolute universality of the Laws of Nature is not scientifically established, or it must be deduced from *a priori* considerations respecting the relation of an Efficient Cause to its effects. The consilience of several Inductions merely extends the enumeration to a larger number of cases; but any such extension, of course, cannot include *future* instances, nor in any way enlarge the domain of possible experience. In fact, most of the scientific processes, which are ably analyzed by Mr. Mill, have reference to the use of Induction as an organon of discovery, and not as a medium of proof; they point out the inferences which we ought to make, but they do not render any more stable the foundation by which all such inferences are supported. And any improvements in the modes of observation, or in the classification of the things observed, are merely preparatory to the process of Induction, and do not in any way affect the essential nature of that process.

Putting aside the terminology invented by Dr. Whewell, and also that recommended by Mr. Mill, as not even their authority has sufficed to bring either into common use, it may be said that there are but three phrases generally employed to designate those results of Induction which constitute the highest generalizations of science. These are a *General Fact*, a *Law of Nature*, and a *Cause*, this last being now usually understood to mean nothing more than an *Invariable Antecedent*. Unfortunately, even these three phrases are so wavering and uncertain in their signification, that they are often employed as synonymes, while hardly any scientific person is consistent in the use which he makes of them, and no two writers upon the philosophy of the physical sciences agree with each other in the attempt to limit and define their meaning.

The first of the number, a General Fact, though employed with somewhat more precision and consistency than the other two, is yet of narrow and indeterminate range, and is grudgingly used, because it is modest in pretension, and does not feed the pride of science, or gratify the vanity of the inquirer into the secrets of nature. It coincides with what Mr. Mill calls an Empirical Law, or the result of an Induction by simple enumeration. Thus, it is properly a General Fact that all horned animals are ruminant, that all quadrupeds are viviparous, that every living thing is produced from an egg, that opium and alcohol intoxicate, &c. But the phrase is sparingly used, because we are not content simply to point out a new characteristic of a whole class of objects, or to form a new class of facts by tracing their hitherto unsuspected agreement with each other, so far as our observation has extended, in some latent attribute. We aspire to the much higher praise of determining a new "Law of Nature," which *must* hold true on *all* occasions, whether observed or not, and the discovery of which is therefore equivalent to a revelation of another of the immutable purposes of the Almighty. The General Fact is admitted to be true only so far as our observation has extended, or at any rate to afford comparatively but a slight presumption that it will be found to hold good in cases as yet unobserved. But as already remarked, the narrower and the more definite the class, the stronger is this presumption. Thus, that every antelope is ruminant, is a far more probable conclusion than that all horned animals are ruminant; we admit very readily that all the mammalia are produced from eggs, but not so readily that the whole animal kingdom are thus produced.

A Law of Nature, in its more definite signification, is employed to designate a group or series of General Facts, relating to the same subject or class of subjects, and differing from each other by some mode of proportional variation, so that the place of every member of the series may be easily deduced from one numerical formula. Such are Kepler's laws of the planetary motions, the law of definite, reciprocal, and multiple proportions in Chemistry, and of phyllotaxis in Botany. The General Facts may be known, long before their relation to each other, or their *law* of proportional variation, is discovered. Thus, the General Fact that the leaves of the apple-tree are disposed in cycles of fives, and so that the spiral line connecting their points of insertion passes twice round the stem for each cycle, their arrangement being thus conveniently denoted by the fraction $\frac{2}{5}$, was ascertained, and a corresponding General Fact for many other species of plants was equally well known, before the "Law" was discovered, that the resulting fractions fall into a series, any one of which has for its numerator the sum of the two preceding numerators, and for its denominator the sum of the two preceding denominators. So, also, the General Facts in Optics, that the angle of refraction, measured from the perpendicular to the surface of any medium heavier than air, is always less than the angle of incidence, and is not proportional to it, were commonly known, and even Tables had been laboriously formed, giving experimental measures of refraction for the various angles of incidence, and for different media, many centuries before Snell, in 1621, superseded the use of many of these Tables by discovering the simple Law of Nature, that the ratio of the sines of the angles of incidence and those of refraction is constant for the same medium. Every measurement of refraction as formerly given in those Tables was a General Fact, including every case of a ray of light falling upon the given medium at the given angle; and this Fact was obtained, of course, by reasoning Inductively, that as the refraction for this angle of incidence and this medium had been actually observed to be of this magnitude in *some* cases, (namely, in all that had been observed,) it would be found of the same magnitude in *all* such cases. Snell's discovery of the "Law" took the place of an immense number of such Facts, by summing them all up in one general proposition or formula, thereby rendering any detailed mention of them unnecessary.

Such a discovery as this by Snell is what Dr. Whewell, by a happily selected phrase, calls a "Colligation of Facts"; and the process by which it is arrived at — the *method*, if there be one, of making such a discovery — is what he denominates Induction. Mr. Mill very properly objects, that it is not Induction at all. It is an act of generalization, founded on direct intuition of the relations which the cases actually before us bear to each other, and not professing to extend beyond these cases. Consequently, it does not *enlarge* our knowledge, as Induction always does, but only grasps up together into one Concept the knowledge which we already possessed; and it accomplishes this through perceiving that this group of General Facts, instead of being entirely heterogeneous, as they at first appeared, are really linked together by some common relation, the expression of which reduces them to unity in the Understanding, and so renders them more easy to be remembered and more convenient to be used.

It is true, as Mr. Mill remarks, that a real act of Induction usually goes along with the Colligation, as subsidiary to it. In this case, Snell not only took for granted the previous Inductions, which, as we have seen, are expressed in the separate General Facts that he grouped together in his formula, but also, having ascertained by actual observation that this formula held true for refraction in *some* media, he reasoned Inductively that it would hold true for *all* media, or, in other words, that it was the *universal* Law of refraction.

It ought also to be remarked, that the discovery of the Law which colligates the General Facts does not change the nature of the evidence on which those Facts depends, or raise them out of the rank of Probable, into that of Demonstrative, judgments. These Facts are still nothing but truths of Induction, just as much after the discovery of the Law as they were before it. The discovery, it is true, makes the previous Inductions somewhat more probable than they were before; but it does not by any means demonstrate them. The degree of probability is increased through the discovered *consilience* of the Inductions, as this consilience amounts to increasing the basis of enumeration on which each of them rests. A number of conclusions affecting a group of kindred subjects are mutually strengthened, when it is found that the separate Induction leading to each one of them harmonizes in one respect, or in several respects, with the Inductions leading to all the others; for such harmony is precisely what we expect, in view of the Maxim on which all Inductive reasoning depends, that nature's course is uniform. Each Induction stands more firmly, when it not only rests on its own foundation, but is indirectly supported by the foundations of its neighbors.

According to the view here given, a Law of Nature is a generalization of the second order; in some respects, it bears the same relation to General Facts, that a General Fact bears to Individual Facts. I say "in some respects"; for this statement does not convey the whole truth. A Law of Nature is not a mere truth of classification; it is not merely a Genus of which the several General Facts are the Species. If it were, then the tabulated measures of refraction, or any other mere collection of General Facts relating to the same class of subjects, might be called a Law. But it is not so; a Law may be contained in such a Table, but it is concealed there, and when discovered, the Table itself becomes useless. The discovery, as I have said, consists in a perception of the truth, that the group of General Facts falls naturally into a series, in which the place or power of any term is easily deduced from a single brief formula. The effort of mind by which such a discovery is made is rather an Intuition, or a happy conjecture, than an Induction. The kind of conviction which attends the discovery, when made, is not mere probability, but certainty. With reference to the General Facts actually before us, we *know* that the Law is there, for we see it just as soon as we have learned where to look for it. But the *universality* of the Law, the extension of it to *all* other General Facts, not now observed, of the same class, is the result of an Induction; and the establishment of the Law also takes for granted the validity of the preceding Inductions on which each separate General Fact depends. Here, as elsewhere, whenever we attempt to extend our knowledge beyond what is actually observed, our only guide is Induction by simple enumeration.

The process of hunting for a Law of Nature amid a group of General Facts is essentially tentative, resembling an attempt to find the meaning of a riddle; we try one guess after another, and at last stumble upon the right one when we least expected it. Success is usually obtained, not by trying to extend the survey, or to contemplate the largest possible number of cases, but by restricting the field of search to a few well-chosen instances, and attempting to find a pattern or construction which these few will precisely fit. To take an example from a quarter where we should least expect to find one, — from pure mathematics; Newton discovered the Binomial Theorem, which is a true Law of Nature according to our definition, probably by simple inspection of a few of the lower powers of binomials, the law of the exponents being obvious enough, and that of the coefficients offering but little difficulty to his marvellous insight. He certainly discovered and used the Theorem long before he endeavored to demonstrate it, or to trace it to its true mathematical principles. There is reason to believe that not a few of the general theorems of the higher mathematics have been discovered in a precisely similar manner.

Why the Law should be suddenly revealed to a single happy glance, when it had previously escaped the most laborious research, is a curious problem, which perhaps admits of no complete solution, though the process may be elucidated in a few particulars. The essential characteristic of such a Law is a series proceeding by some uniform gradation, the relation between two or more consecutive terms in any part of it being the same as that existing between the corresponding terms in any other part. This relation may be simple or complex, recondite or obvious. Each term may be an increment of its predecessor by the addition of a constant quantity, or may be a simple multiple of it, or may be related to it through some of the periodic magnitudes connected with a varying angle, such as the sine, tangent, secant, &c.; or the law of progression may be covered up, as it were, by a constant quantity added to each of the terms; or the numbers, as we have them, may be the complex results of two or more independent series multiplied into each other, in which case there are two or more independent Laws to be discovered. Two difficulties, then, are to be overcome, either one of which would seem to be insuperable if the other had not been previously mastered; we must properly arrange the terms of the series before the Law of it can be discovered, but a knowledge of the Law is indispensable before we can with certainty make such an arrangement. In a contest with so many and so serious difficulties, it is not surprising that success at last should often seem attributable quite as much to accident, as to sagacity and dogged perseverance.

Kepler has furnished an instructive narrative of his successive attempts to reduce to Law the astronomical observations of Tycho, constructing many formulæ by hypothesis, finding that one after another would not fit, and, after each disappointment, trying again with unwearied patience. At last, his perseverance was rewarded with the discovery of the great Laws which deservedly bear his name, as they are the foundations of the whole modern science of astronomy, for they sum up in three sentences all recorded astronomical observations. He also attempted, in a similar way, to detect the Law concealed in the measured angles of refraction, by comparing them with the angles of incidence through a variety of constructions by triangles, conic sections, &c.; but all without success. Where he failed, Snell succeeded, twenty years later, merely by turning his attention from the direct measures of the angles to the ratio of their sines. The law was then manifest at a glance. Such instances are needed to remind us, that the well-known fable of Columbus and the egg is not a caricature, but a faithful representation, of many of the greatest discoveries in science. What Dr. Whewell happily calls "the *ex-post-facto* obviousness of discoveries, is a delusion to which we are liable with regard to many of the most important discoveries."

The validity of a Law of Nature thus discovered, as it were, by a happy casualty, is regarded as sufficiently established by comparison with but very few of the observed data from which it was educed. Thus, Dalton's magnificent generalization, coextensive with all matter, and now verified by almost countless analyses, that chemical elements combine only in definite, reciprocal, and multiple proportions, was first suggested to him during his examination of only two compounds; "and was asserted generally," says Dr. Whewell, "on the strength of a few facts, being, as it were, irresistibly recommended by the clearness and simplicity which the notion possessed." What is the ground of this bold anticipation of the universality of a Law as yet verified only by a very few examples, when, in the case of a General Fact, as already shown, a very extensive Induction may still leave us in doubt whether the supposed truth may not be contradicted by the next instance that arises? In general terms, the answer is obvious. Simple uniformities, such as are comprehended in a General Fact, may be merely accidental; to recur to an instance already cited, all ruminating animals now known divide the hoof; but as the number of such animals is not very great, this simple coincidence of two properties may be as casual as the experience of an individual observer who has never happened to see a squint-eyed person that had not also brown hair. But complex uniformities, such as are marshalled into the symmetrical series called Laws of Nature, and thus expressed in one formula, cannot be regarded as accidental. As the number of individual facts comprehended in one of these series is very great, it is incredible that mere chance should throw even a portion of them into symmetrical groups, bearing a constant ratio to each other. Hence, if we can detect but a portion, even a fragment, of such a series, we feel assured that it will prove to be continuous, that the Law will not change, that the uniformity will be carried out to the end. Only the action of a permanent and unvarying Cause, it is assumed, could so harmonize results. Nay, so strong is our assurance of the universality of the principle thus discovered, though it seems as yet very imperfectly verified, that, when an anomalous or inconformable instance actually arises, we seek at once for the means of eliminating it, or explaining it away, instead of allowing it to wrest the inchoate discovery out of our grasp and send us to the work of research again. We class the exception immediately among those apparent exceptions which really confirm the rule;—just as we now see that the rising of a balloon in the atmosphere does not contradict, but actually verifies, the Law of gravitation.

We come, then, to the conception of a physical Cause, as indicating the third or highest stage in the generalizations of science, and therefore as bearing the same relation to a Law of Nature, that such a Law bears to a General Fact. As thus understood, a Cause is simply a higher Law, under which several inferior Laws are subsumed; it appears as the original principle, of which these lower Laws are the derivatives by immediate and necessary consequence. Thus, the theory of gravitation, or the doctrine that every body attracts every other body with a force which is directly as its mass and inversely as the square of its distance, is the statement of a universal principle, under which not only Kepler's Laws of the planetary motions, but the Laws of falling bodies, of the equilibrium of fluids, &c., are subsumed in this sense;—that if we take for granted the existence of the force or physical Cause, termed *Gravity*, which this theory assumes, then these inferior Laws may all be deduced from it by Demonstrative Reasoning. That such Deduction is possible, is the only proof we have that such a force or Cause exists. The hypothetical force, for it is nothing more, represents the inferior Laws that are subsumed under it, merely because it is an expression of them in a single formula. It may well happen that two or more such formulas may be devised, differing essentially from each other, yet answering equally well all the conditions of the case, as the given Laws may logically be deduced from either of them. For instance: — all, or the greater part, of the Laws of vision and light may be explained with equal precision and accuracy either on the doctrine of emission, or on the undulatory theory. Two such hypotheses correspond to two very dissimilar engines, which different mechanics might invent, in order to cause the hands of a clock to make the required movements over the dial-plate, or the little balls in an orrery to counterfeit the motions of the solar system. It is no more necessary to suppose that such an attractive force as Gravity, or such a luminiferous ether as the undulatory theory treats of, actually exists, than it is to believe that a set of wheels and pinions, like that which moves an orrery, really produces the motion of the planets. All that the theory does for us is to *represent* the phenomena correctly; no one who understands the subject supposes that the hypothetical force or Cause, which is merely a convenient supposition for the theorist, actually *produces* those phenomena.

It is evident that such *Causes* as we are now speaking of are merely the highest generalizations of Physical Science, and that the invention of them — for they are rather *invented* than *discovered* — affords not the slightest additional evidence of the universality of those Laws of Nature which they represent, or which are subsumed under them. The proof, indeed, proceeds in the opposite direction; the only evidence we have that the right Cause has been assigned is, that it correctly represents the Laws which are placed under it. When it is demonstrated that the Law may be deduced from such a Cause, the real course of the argument is, from the admitted validity of the Conclusion to infer the soundness of the Premise. Gravity does not cause heavy bodies to fall to the ground, nor does it bind the planets to their orbits; but Gravity is rightly considered as a "physical Cause," in the technical sense of that phrase, because its hypothetical existence enables us correctly to represent in a single formula the phenomena of falling bodies and of the planetary motions.

The higher generalizations, then, depend exclusively, for proof of their correctness, on the validity of those which are next below them. When the proper Law of Nature is provisionally assumed, certain consequences can be demonstrated to follow which agree with the General Facts that were previously established on Inductive evidence; when the proper physical Cause is assumed, we can logically make certain Deductions from it which harmonize with the Laws of Nature which this Cause was invented to express. Neither the Law nor the Cause brings any additional evidence of its own, but both alike depend for proof, in the last analysis, on the validity of the Induction by simple enumeration by which we first collected their common basis, the General Facts. The process of verifying both consists in enlarging the Induction, but not in altering its character; both the Law and the Cause being *assumed* to be *universally* true, we make further Deductions from them, and still find these to coincide with the observed Facts. In other words, we first reason Inductively from *some* to *all*, and then, assuming provisionally that the principle holds true of *all*, we reason from it Deductively to *other some*, and find that these also are confirmed by observation, so that they reflect evidence upon the Law or the Cause of which they are the logical consequences. Turn the matter as we may, Induction by simple enumeration is still the basis of the whole procedure, and the discovery or invention of Laws of Nature, or physical Causes, only supplies names and formulas of expression for the successive steps of generalization, as we form one after another the proper hierarchy of Concepts.

We can now see more plainly than before the correctness of the doctrine already advanced, that the strong and unhesitating belief which we accord to any well-established Law of Nature, and which we indicate by saying that an event happening under it takes place by *a physical necessity*, is not due to the strength of the Induction through which the Law was discovered, but to our absolute *a priori* conviction of the fixedness of the relation which connects every effect with its *efficient* Cause. The Law is *discovered* by Induction; but it is *proved* by a different process, — by bringing it under a necessary *a priori* conception of the human mind, that of Efficient Cause, and thereby subjecting it to the principle of Causality, that every event *must* have a Cause, and must be proportional to that Cause.

In speaking of the use which is sometimes made of Inductive reasoning in pure mathematics, as in the case of Newton's discovery of the Binomial Theorem, Mr. Mill maintains that the process of thought in such cases is not an Induction properly so called, but is governed by certain "*a priori* considerations (which might be exhibited in the form of demonstration), that the mode of formation of the subsequent terms, each from that which preceded it, *must be* similar to the formation of the terms which have been already calculated." But it was certainly Inductive in this respect, that the observed regular formation of the first few terms of the series originally led Newton to anticipate that all the other terms must be formed in the same manner, and to act upon this anticipation, — that is, confidently to use the Theorem for a long time, — without giving himself the trouble to work out a demonstration of it. Undoubtedly he had a strong belief that such a demonstration was practicable; and this belief prompted him to acquiesce with greater confidence in the result of the Induction. For this very reason, this instance appears to be a typical and instructive case of Inductive reasoning. Pure Induction is exclusively an *organon* of discovery, a clew for anticipating facts not yet observed and truths not yet proved. The Ground of the Induction, that is, the proof, if it may be called such, or the source of the confidence with which we accept its conclusions, is an indistinct assurance, derived from *a priori* considerations, that the results might be demonstrated, if we were acquainted with all the circumstances of the case. Newton's assurance was founded on his indistinct anticipation of the truth, that the formation of the coefficients of the series must depend in some manner on the laws of the permutation and combination of numbers,— an anticipation which he did not stop to work out and verify. The physicist's assurance is based primarily, as we have seen, on his necessary conviction that every event or change must have an efficient Cause, a truth which is readily explicated into the maxim that Nature's course is uniform; and secondarily, upon his belief that the proportional variation of the successive terms in such a series as is called a Law of Nature is another consequence of the axiomatic principle of Causality, that effects must be proportional to their Causes. The physicist's anticipation cannot be verified, because, in the physical universe, Efficient Causes lie beyond the reach of human insight. We can discover nothing but Invariable Antecedents. But so strong is the bias which leads us to identify an Invariable Antecedent with an Efficient Cause, that the phraseology of Causation is still employed throughout our investigations, though it has been demonstrated over and over again, that constancy of sequence is no certain indication of causal efficiency. We still speak of physical *Causes*, of *agents* and their *action*, of *forces* and *powers*, although it is now admitted on all hands that we mean nothing by such language, when employed with reference to the material universe, except "constant relations of succession or of similarity." The very persistency of this inappropriate phraseology indicates quite clearly the source of our conviction that Nature's course is uniform, and her Laws unchangeable, except by Him whose infinite wisdom first established them, and whose unvarying purposes and modes of action they express.

CHAPTER XIII.

THE SOURCES OF EVIDENCE AND THE CAUSES OF ERROR.

INTUITION is not only the source in which all our knowledge originates, but it is the universal basis of certainty, or the sole ground of the confidence with which we accept any facts or truths as known. What we directly or immediately perceive, whether by the external senses or by consciousness, that we *know*. What is not thus directly perceived is entitled to be called *knowledge* only in a secondary or derivative sense; properly speaking, it is only an *inference* from our knowledge, and however legitimate this Inference may be, it is worth nothing if the truth of one or more Intuitions, on which it depends, be not previously taken for granted. Take even Demonstrative Reasoning, for instance, in which it is rightly said that the Conclusion is a necessary inference from the Premises. Still, before we can accept this Conclusion as certain, we must assume that both the Premises are true. Now, whatever be the nature of the Major Premise, the Subsumption must express, either directly or indirectly, a truth of Intuition. We can knowingly assert that a given object possesses a certain attribute, or bears a certain relation of likeness or unlikeness to some other object, only through our direct perception of this fact either by sense or consciousness; and such an assertion must enter into every act of Reasoning, as one of the grounds on which the Conclusion rests. Any Reasoning, then, by which we might attempt to doubt or deny the validity of our Intuitions, would be self-destructive; for in such Reasoning, the truthfulness of our Intuitive faculties must be presupposed, or taken for granted. We should, by such scepticism, deny the legitimacy of our own denial.

Intuition, therefore, is the highest source of evidence, and the ultimate foundation of all certainty. If we cannot accept, as absolutely true, what we immediately perceive, or are conscious of, then we can know nothing; we cannot even *know* that we do *not* know. But before we place this absolute reliance upon Intuition or Perception, we must carefully distinguish what it is that we really perceive, or, in other words, what that is of which we have an Intuition. In ordinary mental action, Inferences are so quickly and habitually drawn from Intuitions, and thereby so closely blended with them, acts of comparison and generalization also entering into the compound result, that it becomes extremely difficult to separate the pure Matter of Intuition, of which we are absolutely certain, from the heterogeneous ingredients which are thus united with it, and of which we are not by any means equally sure. Hence it is often said that our senses deceive us, when the truth is, that we are mistaken only in the Inferences which we have incorrectly drawn from the data actually furnished by the senses. Thus we are often deceived into accepting a counterfeit as a good coin; but the mental act which thus leads us into a mistaken belief is really compound, embracing an act of memory, one of generalization, and one of Reasoning. The little object placed in our hands for examination is perceived to have a certain color, weight, shape, stamp, &c.; and it is impossible that these qualities should be, *to us,* in any respect different from what they are perceived to be. But when we proceed to *compare* these qualities with others which we *remember* to have perceived at some other time in good coins, and to *infer* from their similarity that this supposed coin is not a counterfeit, it is evident that we are exposed to many sources of error. Even if we go so far only as to designate one of these qualities by its Common Name, — to say, for instance, that this coin is *yellow*, — we go beyond the Intuition, and, so far, become liable to mistake; it may well be that we have but an imperfect recollection and imagination of the color which is usually so called, and therefore may be mistaken in supposing that this color is so similar to it as to merit the same name. In like manner, any other comparison, as of the weight, shape, or stamp, as it requires either memory, if both objects be not actually before us, or a decision as to the degree of similarity, if they are both present to sense, must involve an element of uncertainty.

The question has been raised, whether external objects are directly perceived by us *as external*, or whether their externality is an Inference subsequently drawn from this perception as combined with others, and as governed by the necessary and *a priori* convictions of the mind. In other words, is the externality of the object, or the fact that it is something different from myself, that it is *not-me*, a constituent part of the Intuition, or only an Inference from it? If the former supposition be true, then I *know* that the external world exists, and any Reasoning upon the case, either for or against this knowledge, is superfluous, and even illogical; for as Reasoning must involve and depend upon Intuition, it cannot contradict Intuition. But if the latter supposition be correct, then the reality of the outward universe is not, strictly speaking, *known*, but only *inferred* through an act of the understanding, which, as it purports to relate to real objects, and not to a mere conception of the mind, certainly may be a mistaken one.

The question is an important one, but the full discussion of it belongs to Metaphysics, and not to Logic. We can only consider here the nature and the relevancy of the evidence adduced, regarded as illustrating the general laws of evidence. Thus much, I think, must be admitted, that the mind, in its adult state, is immediately conscious of the affections of its own bodily organism *as such*, — that is, as affections of the body, which is foreign to itself, or a part of the *not-me;* for we localize these affections, or refer them instantly, and without an act of reasoning, to the affected parts. Thus, I am immediately conscious of a pain, not merely as a pain, but as a pain in the foot, in the hand, or in the head, the Intuition extending to the locality, just as much as to the severity, of the affection. But it is said that the pain, being a sensation, can exist only in the sentient mind, and not in the unsentient matter of the body. Very true; but the question then arises, *Where is the mind?* You have no right to confine it to a certain part of the body, — to the brain, for instance. I say, that the mind *is* wherever it *feels;* for its feeling — its state of consciousness — is the only evidence that we have of its existence. It is present, at least, to the whole nervous organism. As we certainly feel at the tips of our fingers, it is little more than tautology to assert, that that which feels is existent at the tips of the fingers. It is admitted that this doctrine of the ubiquity of the mind to the body is incomprehensible; we cannot see *how* it is that the thinking being should be "all in every part" of its extended nervous organism. In like manner, many physical facts, especially those of electricity and magnetism, and whatever involves the action of what are called Polar Forces, are inconceivable; but this is no reason for doubting their reality, when they are evidenced by Intuition. But if the mind immediately localizes its sensations, if it perceives that the pain is *here*, and not *there*, then it is immediately conscious of its own body as extended, and therefore of space and externality.

This is a mere outline of Sir William Hamilton's doctrine of our immediate perception, or consciousness, of the external world. It appears to disprove very satisfactorily Kant's counter assertion, that space is wholly subjective, — a mere law of our perceptive faculty, which imposes the modes of its own being upon the constitution of the objects which it perceives. But while the Hamiltonian doctrine seems to hold good of the adult mind, it is not so clear that it would apply to the perceptions of an infant. It may be questioned whether, at the dawn of our existence, our sensations are distinctly referred to outward things, or that the perceptions by which they are accompanied appear to be anything else than states of our own consciousness. An infant's world, it may be suspected, lies entirely within himself; and if so, the subsequent reference of these perceptions to external realities must be produced, or aided, by experience and an act of Reasoning, and the knowledge or belief thus gained is no longer exclusively Intuitive.

Passing over this metaphysical question, however, it is to be observed that Memory, as a source of evidence, stands next in extent and importance to Intuition. In many cases, the two are so closely interwoven with each other, as we have just seen, that facts are often loosely said to be Intuitively known, when we have no better evidence of their existence than is afforded by Memory. Intuition, as such, is always *present*, relating only to what exists *now* and *here;* past Intuitions can be now known to us only by an act of remembrance ; and as the strength of a chain is the strength of its weakest link, that which we did know Intuitively, can be now accepted only on the strength of our belief that we remember rightly. In like manner, when we are judging of Individual Objects by comparison, or are ascertaining their relations to each other, or to a class of cognate Objects, the results of the observation will not be Intuitively certain, unless all the related objects are present, at one and the same moment, either to sense or consciousness; if *all* are not thus present, then, to the extent of this deficiency, objects actually observed must be compared with those which are merely remembered. Moreover, as Locke and Dugald Stewart have remarked, even in mathematical demonstration, we have not, at every step, the immediate evidence of Intuition, but only that of Memory. The whole science of geometry hangs together by a continued chain of Intuitive judgments; but in the case of any advanced theorem, it is not to be supposed that we can carry in mind, as simultaneously present to consciousness, all the truths, previously established, which must concur in order to support this particular demonstration. In by far the greater number of instances, we trust entirely to judgments resting on the evidence of Memory. At the close, before we can accept the Conclusion as demonstrated, we must remember the whole chain so perfectly as to be sure that nothing has been left out; we must recollect not only that we have proved, but how we proved, each point. Practically, then, the truths of geometry, and all other Conclusions dependent on a chain of Demonstrative Reasoning consisting of more than two or three links, must be accepted on the evidence of Memory quite as much as on that of Intuition. Of course, the Inductive Sciences, including, as they do, a vast collection of facts, are dependent, to a still greater extent, upon this source of evidence.

But the edifice of Science, when it is thus shown to be largely dependent upon individual recollections, would seem to rest on a very insecure basis. The defects of Memory, as every one is aware, are both numerous and grave. It is capricious, it often fails us when we most need its aid, and it exists in very different degrees in different persons. We might be tempted, at the first glance, to pronounce it one of the most untrustworthy of all our faculties. But on closer observation, it will appear that the faults with which it is chargeable are not so serious as we might at first sup-

AND THE CAUSES OF ERROR. 425

pose, and, especially, that they do not much diminish its usefulness, or the confidence which we place in it, as an indispensable means for the progress of Science. In the first place, its faults are rather negative than positive in character; we often forget, but we are very seldom mistaken in what we think that we distinctly remember. In truth, a remembrance, seemingly clear and distinct, of what we have but recently observed, especially if the phenomenon be of a simple and definite character, must be placed next to Intuition as a ground of certainty. The distinction between a pure Intuition now present to the mind, and a distinct recollection of a very recent one, experienced perhaps within the last hour, is theoretical rather than practical. In the ordinary conduct of life, no one would think of maintaining that the former was more trustworthy than the latter. Our judicial tribunals, in grave matters involving property and life, will not allow the clear and distinct recollections of a witness, though extending over a much longer period, to be even called in question. Still, the theoretical distinction exists; Intuition, as the basis of Demonstration, has absolute or logical certainty, and does not admit of degrees; while Memory is confessedly subject to error, and therefore is a source only of *probable* evidence, though, in its highest degree, it amounts to what is called *moral* certainty.

And here another distinction must be drawn. We must distinguish, as Hamilton has done, between the simple fact that we do remember, or think that we remember, a certain phenomenon, and the truthfulness of this act of remembrance, or our belief in the former actual existence of that phenomenon. The former is matter of direct Intuition, and therefore does not admit of doubt; the latter rests merely upon probable evidence, and may be a mistaken belief. Memory may be compared to a witness giving testimony in a court of justice; the judge and jury cannot doubt that he *does* testify to this or that occurrence, for they have sensible — that is, Intuitive — evidence of the fact; but they may well doubt whether he testifies *truly*, — whether the occurence in question ever took place. It is only in this last respect, the correctness of the representation of what we remember, that the faculty of Memory is said to be a source of merely probable evidence.

It is to be observed that the art of writing is a most valuable auxiliary to the faculty of Memory, inasmuch as a proper use of it may obviate, in great part, the uncertainty that would otherwise attach to this source of evidence. Remembrance is more perfect, that is, more clear and distinct, and thus more trustworthy, according as the Intuitions which it preserves and stores up are more recent. But a written record of the observations, taken at the time when they were made, or as soon afterwards as might be, keeps the evidence as perfect as it would be if Memory were not liable to be impaired by 'the lapse of time. The possession of such a record may enable even future generations to accept the evidence of the occurrence with as full confidence as if it had been observed by their contemporaries only a few days, or a few hours, before. Of course, the age and genuineness of the document must first be proved, just as we must first establish, on satisfactory grounds, the veracity and competency of the witnesses who testify to contemporary events which we have not ourselves observed. But this being done, and it is generally about as easy to do in the one case as in the other, the evidence remains as perfect after the lapse of centuries as it was at the time when the record was made. Time is thus deprived of its power to wipe out by degrees the recollection of events. Many facts in history, though of very old date, must be admitted to be now as firmly established as if they had taken place within the lifetime of the present generation. Thus, the fact that a deed of privileges, called the

Great Charter, was granted by King John to the English people, June 5, 1215, is even now as firmly established as that of the passage of the Reform Bill in 1832; and the precise nature and extent of the franchises granted are as fully known in the former case as in the latter, for in both cases the original parchment rolls, on which these title-deeds of freedom were first engrossed, and attested by the seals and signatures of those who were parties to them, are yet extant.

We dwell upon this point as one of some importance, because it has been wrongly maintained, in reference to what may be called the historical part of Christianity, that as the mere lapse of time slowly, but surely, wears away all historical evidence, the great *facts* on which our religious faith depends must become subject in future centuries to so much uncertainty as to be wholly unworthy of credit. The proper answer to this assertion is, that nothing less than a general conflagration, which should burn up all the written and printed records now in existence, could make these facts, to any appreciable extent, less certain thousands of years hence, than they are at the present day. Miracles were needed for the first establishment of Christianity; but only the ordinary course of God's providence is necessary to preserve its blessings to any number of future generations.

The two faculties of Intuition and Memory are the sources only of our individual experience. But the experience of an individual — what I have myself observed and remembered, or reduced to writing — is extremely limited, when compared with the vast fund of information that is opened to us by accepting the experience of our fellow-men, and combining it with our own. Not merely in our labors for the advancement of Science, but in the ordinary management of our every-day concerns, we are obliged to depend upon the Testimony and the Authority of others. Science grows by a combination of the labors of many minds and a long succession of generations. The lifetime of an individual might be spent in a vain endeavor to review, and verify by personal observation, all the data which support the conclusions in but one of its departments. Many of them, from the nature of the case, cannot be so verified; the occurrences of former times, and even those in our own day that took place under a peculiar combination of circumstances, such as may never be repeated, must be received on the Testimony of others, or be left entirely out of account, together with all the conclusions that are founded upon them. We must continually accept on trust what others have observed, and even the Inferences that they have drawn, without pretending to verify them for ourselves, or we must sit down in ignorance. And this remark is applicable not merely to the Inductive, but also to the Exact Sciences. In astronomical calculations, for example, very few of the data rest upon the evidence of our own senses, and we compute by the aid of a book of logarithms, the accuracy of which, at the present day, no one thinks of verifying by independent calculation.

Testimony and Authority ought to be sharply distinguished from each other, though they are often loosely used as synonymous. Properly speaking, we *accept* Testimony as to matters of fact, and *yield to* Authority in matters of opinion. Our confidence in the former depends mainly on our opinion of the veracity of our informant; in the latter case, we rely chiefly on the soundness of his judgment, the accuracy of his habits of reasoning, and the largeness of his information. We disbelieve Testimony, we reject Authority. The reason why these two sources of belief are so frequently confounded is, that the provinces of observation and of reasoning are not kept sufficiently distinct; the certainty of the Intuition is improperly extended to the

Inference which is drawn from it, and drawn so quickly and easily that it is mistaken for a part of the observation itself. When Dr. Cullen remarked, with as much truth as point, that "there are more false facts than there are false theories in the world," he did not mean to impugn the general disposition of men to tell the truth. He alluded to what are generally supposed to be *facts*, and which go by that name, but are really nothing but loose compounds of matters of opinion with those of observation. Probably what he had in mind was the insufficiency of the evidence on which the members of his own profession, that of Medicine, are often obliged to act. Thus, it is said that a patient is in a Consumption; this, *if true*, would be a fact; but the only known fact is, that certain symptoms were manifested from which it was *inferred*, perhaps wrongly, that the case was one of Consumption. Again, it is announced as a fact, that the use of a certain medicine cured the disease; when the truth is, that the dose was administered, and the man got well, perhaps in spite of the medicine. Men are so prone to confound their own crude conjectures with what they have actually seen or heard, that very few, except those who have been carefully trained to scientific habits of mind, can be trusted to report their own observations, until they have undergone a severe cross-examination. They do not intend to deceive others, but they have effectually deceived themselves. The reputed sciences of Phrenology and Animal Magnetism rested exclusively, in the opinion of their admirers, on a basis of observed facts, and hence were to be maintained, in spite of the arguments with which they were assailed, because facts are admitted to be a better test of truth than reasoning. But it became evident on severe scrutiny, that this basis was made up, for the most part, out of what Dr. Cullen calls " false facts."

On account of this frequent confusion of two very dissimilar things, it is commonly said, and with good reason, that before accepting Testimony, we ought to have satisfactory proof both of the *veracity* and the *competency* of the witness. But if people generally could be trusted to separate their Inferences from their observations, and to report the latter unmixed, it would evidently be enough to have assurance only upon the former point. In respect only to their quality or certainty, though not with regard to their extent or comprehensiveness, one man's Intuitions are as good as another's. The one, indeed, may see *more* than the other, because he knows where to look and what to observe. He will therefore have more to report, or, at any rate, more that is pertinent and useful. But the Testimony of the other, as far as it goes, will be equally valid and trustworthy, for it is equally a report of what has actually been observed, and the Intuitive faculty cannot deceive. The only doubt, then, which can properly affect the reception of Testimony, or the admission of other people's experience as at least of equal value with our own, is that which regards the disposition of the witness to tell the truth. Doubts respecting his competency as an observer can be settled by sifting the report itself, better than by inquiring into the abilities of him who made it.

The proper distinction to be made is, that the claims of Testimony to be accepted depend upon the evidence which is offered as to the Veracity of the witness, while those of Authority rest upon the proofs which we possess of the Competency of the person whose opinions we are invited to follow. The rules for forming an estimate either of the Veracity of an observer or the Competency of a judge are too obvious to need mention here, except in very general terms. "In regard to the honesty of a witness," says Esser, as translated by Hamilton, "this, though often admitting of the highest probability, never admits of absolute certainty; for though, in many cases, we may know enough of the general character of the witness to rely with perfect confidence on his Veracity, in no case can we look into the heart, and observe the influence which motives have actually had upon his volitions. We are, however, compelled, in many of the most important concerns of our existence, to depend on the Testimony, and consequently to confide in the sincerity, of others. But, from the moral constitution of human nature, we are warranted in presuming on the honesty of a witness; and this presumption is enhanced in proportion as the following circumstances concur in its confirmation. In the first place, a witness is presumed to be veracious in this case, in proportion as his love of truth is already established from others. In the second place, a witness is to be presumed veracious, in proportion as he has fewer and weaker motives to falsify his Testimony. In the third place, a witness is to be presumed veracious, in proportion to the likelihood of contradiction which his Testimony would encounter, if he deviated from the truth."

In respect to the Competency of the person to whose Authority we are requested to defer, the only important principle which needs to be here laid down is contained in the old adage, *Cuique credendum est in suâ arte*, — Trust each person in his own specialty. Eminence in one department of science, far from being an indication of superior power of judgment and reasoning in other departments, is often a disqualification for forming a correct opinion in them. The mind is prone to carry over the special forms and processes which are appropriate to one science into others, where they are out of place, and lead only to error. To adopt Bacon's expressive metaphor, it imports into a new sphere of research the rust and tarnish contracted in the workshop wherein it has chiefly labored. A distinguished mathematician, other things being equal, is not so competent to form an opinion upon some disputed point in the moral sciences, as one who is conversant with questions of this sort, though he has never gained distinction in them, and may be ignorant of the first principles of Algebra and the Calculus. "The merit of a mathematical invention," as Hamilton justly remarks, "consists in the amount of thought which it supersedes"; and hence it is matter of common remark, that those who are most capable of making such inventions, and profiting by them, are least fitted for reasoning by Induction and Analogy. Consequently, "Mathematics afford us no assistance either in conquering the difficulties, or in avoiding the dangers, which we encounter in the great field of *probabilities* wherein we live and move."

Hume's celebrated argument against the credibility of miracles is a fallacy which results from losing sight of the distinction between Testimony and Authority, between Veracity and Competency. He argues, that it is contrary to all experience that a Law of Nature should be broken, but it is not contrary to experience that human testimony should be false; and therefore we ought to believe that any amount of Testimony is false, in preference to admitting the occurrence of a miracle, as this would be a violation of Law. We answer, that the miraculous character of an event is not a matter of Intuition, but of Inference; hence, it is not to be decided by Testimony, but by Reasoning from the probabilities of the case, the only question being whether, in view of all the circumstances, the Conclusion is *competent* that the occurrence was supernatural. The Testimony relates only to the happening of the event considered merely as an external phenomenon; the question respecting the nature of this event, whether it is, or is not, a violation of Physical Law, whether it is an effect of this or that Efficient Cause, cannot be determined by Intuition and Testimony, but is a matter for Judgment founded on Reasoning, in view of all the circumstances of the case. If doubtful of our own Competency to form a correct opinion on this point, we may defer to the Authority of another, who is familiar with the kind of Reasoning by which such questions are settled. Now we have abundant evidence from experience, that no event whatever, regarded simply as an external phenomenon, can be so strange and marvellous that sufficient Testimony will not convince us of the reality of its occurrence. To the contemporaries of our Saviour, not even bringing a dead man to life would have appeared so incredible as the transmission of a written message five thousand miles, without error, within a minute of time. Yet this feat has been accomplished by the Magnetic Telegraph. Why do we decide, then, that the raising of Lazarus was, and the transmission of intelligence by telegraph is not, a miracle? Evidently not by Intuition, but by reasoning from the very different circumstances of the two cases. The *fact*, that the eyes of the blind were opened, or a storm was reduced to a calm, or the dead were raised, is established by Intuition and Testimony, which have established many other facts quite as wonderful; the *character* of this fact, whether miraculous or not, is to be settled in a very different manner. We say, then, that Hume's argument, which is based exclusively upon an appeal to experience and Testimony, is totally inapplicable to the question respecting the credibility of a miracle. Testimony has nothing to do with the correct inference of a Conclusion from its Premises.

We can touch only very briefly on the Criticism of recorded Testimony, and of writings in general. As we must avail ourselves, in the construction of Science, of the experience of former generations, in respect to which the Testimony of eye- and ear-witnesses is no longer directly accessible, we are obliged to consider the credibility of this Testimony as affected by the channels of transmission through which it has been passed. There are but two such channels, Tradition and Ancient Writings. The former of these may be left out of account; for if the lapse of time has been considerable, the probability that the Testimony, if transmitted merely by word of mouth, has been materially altered or falsified, is so great, that the report can be received only with extreme caution. But it has already been mentioned, that the invention of the art of writing has rendered it *possible* for the experience of a former generation to be handed down, through an indefinite lapse of centuries, in as perfect a state as that in which it was first communicated to those who were the contemporaries of the events narrated. This is possible, we say; the question whether it has been actually so transmitted is what we have to consider in the Criticism of Ancient Writings.

When a document purporting to be the recorded Testimony of certain individuals of a former generation is presented to us, we have first to inquire whether it is actually the handwriting, or the composition as taken down by dictation, or a faithful report, made at the time, of the substance of the evidence of the individuals whose names it bears, or to whom it is attributed. The establishment of either of these three points is the proof of what is called the *Genuineness* of the writing. It is comparatively unimportant which of the three is proved, as either of them gives us assurance that the document is a faithful record of the Testimony of the persons whose evidence is to be weighed. Thus, even if we were sure that the Testimony of the Evangelists was originally written out by their own hands, we certainly do not possess their autograph copies; still, the Gospels are Genuine, if we have sufficient evidence that they are faithful records, made at the time, (or correct transcripts of such records,) of what the Evangelists said.

But a second question must be answered before we can

accept the evidence furnished by the document. We must be satisfied, not only that the Testimony is Genuine,—that it was actually given by those from whom it purports to come, but that it is Authentic, — that this Testimony is a true and faithful narrative of what actually happened. Proofs of the Genuineness of the writing amount, at the utmost, only to bringing the witnesses into court and establishing their identity; proofs of the Authenticity must be found by sifting their evidence, and applying to it all the tests and means of verification which we possess, in order to ascertain whether they are telling the truth. If not Genuine, the document is said to be Spurious; if not Authentic, it is false.

As most of the tests and proofs of the Genuineness and Authenticity of a writing are such as readily suggest themselves to the inquirer, it is unnecessary to consider them here at any length. Generally, they may be divided into two classes, called respectively the External and the Internal Evidences of the point to be proved. The External Evidences of Genuineness are to be found either in other and admitted writings of the supposed author, or in the works of writers who were either his contemporaries, or nearly of the same antiquity; and the evidence is either direct, if the disputed writing is therein explicitly attributed to him, or indirect, if these works quote as his production passages which are found in the document. This indirect testimony has the greater force, for on account of its casual or incidental character there is less reason to suspect that it has been forged. The External Evidences of the Authenticity of the writing, considered as a narrative of facts, are too numerous to mention. They are found in allusions to the same facts, or to incidents obviously connected with them, by contemporary authors; in customs, traditions, and institutions, which have come down to later times, and the origin of which cannot be accounted for, except on the supposition that the reported events actually took place; in coins, medals, and inscriptions, belonging to the same age, or one immediately subsequent, and connected by equally close relations with the alleged facts; in the notoriety which such incidents must have obtained, the interest which must have been felt in them, and the consequent probability that falsifications and forgeries respecting them would never have been attempted, or would have been detected and disproved at the time.

Of the Internal Evidence, it has been justly remarked, that it is weak to establish either Genuineness or Authenticity, but powerful to disprove both. As Hamilton remarks, "We can easily conceive that an able and learned forger may accommodate his fabrications both to all the general circumstances of time, place, people, and language under which it is supposed to have been written, and even to all the particular circumstances of the style, habit of thought, personal relations, &c. of the supposed author." On the other hand, a single anachronism, well made out, in respect either to events, institutions, customs, or even the use of language, is as fatal to the document's claim to antiquity, as a well-established *alibi* is to the success of a criminal prosecution. Bentley's Dissertation upon the Epistles of Phalaris might have been limited to pointing out two or three of the numerous anachronisms which he detected in them, if his only object in writing it had been to prove that these alleged Epistles were an impudent forgery. In respect to the Authenticity of a narrative, it is to be observed, that the credibility of certain facts is one thing, and the proof of their actual occurrence is another. For establishing the former, Internal Evidence is sufficient; for the latter, it is powerless, being entirely inapplicable. By saying that a narrative of certain events bears with it Internal Evidence of its truth, we mean only that the events are possible, — that they are consistent with each other, — that they harmonize with what we know from other sources concerning the men of that country and that age, — that they are conformable to the ordinary course of things. All this may be true of an avowed fiction. Some of Shakespeare's plays, most of Scott's novels, have as much Internal Evidence of truth as any testimony given in a court of justice. They may have even more; for it is a common proverb that truth is often stranger than fiction. If we disregard all extraneous circumstances, and look only at the face of the narrative, Robinson Crusoe appears as true a story as Cook's Voyages, and Richardson the novelist is as faithful an historian as Hume.

As the evidence from the several sources that have now been mentioned may be of various degrees of strength, and as opinion is often drawn in opposite directions by conflicting testimony, we are naturally led to inquire whether there is any *measure of probability*, or any means of accurately estimating the *amount of belief* which ought to be accorded under different circumstances. This brings us at once to the Theory of Probabilities, or, as the mathematicians sometimes call it, the Doctrine of Chances. Only the outlines, or first principles, of the subject can be considered here, as the details are exclusively mathematical, and so do not come within our province.

It is first to be observed, that, in the calculation of Chances, as in every other department of pure mathematics, since the reasoning employed is Demonstrative in character, the correctness of the results obtained depends upon the truth of certain assumptions made in the outset; and the applicability of one of these results to any given case, or actual instance, turns upon the answer to the question whether this instance is exactly comprehended within the Definition of the Concept upon which the whole calculation is based. Thus, in calculating the probability of any one out of a given number of events, it is assumed that all the events considered are equally possible, — that no one has any advantage which would render it more likely to happen than the others. Practically, this supposition is never fulfilled. In illustrating their conclusions, the mathematicians have shown much ingenuity in selecting cases where the chances would seem to be equally balanced; but it is easy to show that they have never entirely succeeded. Their favorite case is that of putting a number of balls, equal in size, but different in color, into an urn, and then considering the probability of a blindfolded person drawing one of a certain color after a given number of trials. But suppose the number of balls is considerable, that all the white ones are first thrown in together, and then all the black ones; in such case, the chance of drawing a black ball at the first trial is obviously much greater than that of a white one. A dozen other suppositions might be made, depending on the size and shape of the urn, and the manner of throwing in the balls, any one of which would be fatal to a precise agreement of the actual with the calculated result. Another favorite case is that of throwing up a half-penny, to determine whether it will give head or tail; but here it is assumed that the two sides of the coin just balance each other, which, on account of the different imprints that they bear, is never the case. Even in the better chosen illustrations, then, the calculated result will be only an approximation to the truth. In ordinary cases in which the Doctrine of Chances is applied, as in gambling, it will be but a rude approximation; most of what are called games of chance are, at least in some faint degree, games of skill; and in the long run, though not necessarily in a few trials, skill will tell.

In most cases of the practical application of the Doctrine of Chances, the existence of numerous causes of error is admitted; but as we know nothing of the character of these causes, and do not see any reason why more of them should operate on one side than on the other, it is assumed that, in the long run, they will compensate each other, so that the result will agree with the calculation. But this is only the argument *ad ignorantiam*, the fallacy of which has already been noticed; because *we do not know any reason* why there should not be as many and as heavy errors on one side as on the other, it does not follow that there is no such reason. It was for a long time supposed, that the arithmetical mean of several distinct observations of the same astronomical phenomenon would afford the nearest approximation to a correct result, as there was no known reason why different observers should not err as much on one side as on the other. But it is now known that each observer has a constant tendency, distinctly appreciable in amount, to err in one direction; and if allowance is not made for this "personal equation," as it is called, the arithmetical mean is not the nearest attainable approximation to the truth.

What is called "the Method of Least Squares" has been adopted as a mode of finding the most probable result in those cases in which the arithmetical mean is not an applicable expedient for determining this probability. This Method proceeds upon the assumption that all errors are *not* equally probable, but that small errors are more probable than large ones. An easy corollary from this assumption is, that the most probable conclusion can be obtained by making, not the errors themselves, but the sum of the squares of these errors, of the smallest possible amount. To borrow an instance from Dr. Whewell: — Let the observed numbers be 4, 12, 14; and suppose it known that these numbers must be erroneous, as they ought to form an arithmetical progression. The question is, what arithmetical progression do they *most probably* represent. The following table shows that there are three such progressions which approximate the observed series, and also indicates which one of them, according to the Method of Least Squares, is the most probable.

		Errors.	Sums of errors.	Sums of squares of errors.
Observed Series	4, 12, 14			
1st Progression	4, 9, 14	0, 3, 0	3	9
2d "	6, 10, 14	2, 2, 0	4	8
3d "	5, 10, 15	1, 2, 1	4	6

We here see, although the first progression gives the least sum of errors, the third shows the least sum of the squares of the errors; and therefore, according to this Method, the third is the most probable of the three.

These remarks were necessary in order to obviate the inference which too many are inclined to draw, that, because the calculations in the Doctrine of Chances are made on strict mathematical principles, the calculated probability of an event, in any actual application of this Doctrine, must therefore be mathematically exact and absolutely certain. On the contrary, in any such application of the principles, the result is only a rough approximation to the truth.

It is also important to remember, that the application of the Theory of Probabilities only shows us what we ought to expect, or what, as rational beings, we are bound to believe, and does not reveal any Cause or Law that actually determines the occurrence. To speak technically, the calculated probability is subjective, and not objective; it reveals what may be called a law of thought, but not a law of things. "The subject-matter of calculations in the Theory of Probabilities," says Professor Donkin, "is *quantity of belief*. In every problem, a certain number of hypotheses are presented to the mind, along with a certain quantity of information relating to them; the question is,— In what way ought belief to be distributed among them?" The calculation of the chances does not assume to increase this "quantity of information," or to reveal any new data on which our judgment ought to be based; but only how we ought to judge and to act on the data that we already possess. The doctrine does not even assure us that the calculated result will be verified at the first trial, or at any subsequent trial; but it only shows us how we ought to expect the actual results to be distributed in the course of an infinite number of trials. The calculation does not relate merely to future events, the occurrence of which is still contingent; it may be applied also to the past, to determine the probability that the event did, or did not, take place. In cases of the latter sort, it is sufficiently obvious that the application of the Theory of Probabilities does not in any wise affect the event itself, which is already irrevocably determined either one way or the other; but only assumes, in our ignorance of what the actual result has been, to determine what we ought to believe respecting it.

Keeping this distinction in mind, we can explain the seeming paradox, that an event should be *sure* to happen at the first trial, though the chances were indefinitely great against its occurrence. Put into an urn any number of balls numbered consecutively from one upwards, — say 1,000. Of course, there are 999 chances to 1 against a blindfolded person drawing, at the first trial, the particular ball marked with any one of these numbers; and yet some one ball so marked *must* be drawn. But this is no violation of the law regulating what we ought to expect; for we ought not to expect any *particular* number to come at the first trial, though we are certain that *some* — we know not what — number must so come.

It is assumed in the Doctrine of Chances, that the various degrees of belief may be represented by numbers. An impossible event, as it has no probability whatever in its favor, is appropriately represented by zero. An event which is sure to happen, as the expectation of its occurrence is not broken or divided by any chance of failure, might be represented by any integral number; its most convenient, because the simplest, symbol is unity. Then all the degrees of probability between impossibility and certainty will be denoted by the fractions that may be interpolated between 0 and 1.

The first principle of the Doctrine of Chances is, that *the probability of an uncertain event is represented by the number of chances favorable to its occurrence, divided by the total number of chances whether favorable or unfavorable.* Thus, as a pack contains 52 cards, divided into four equal suits, into 12 pictured and 40 plain cards, and into 26 red and 26 black cards, the chance of drawing a heart at the first trial is $\frac{13}{52}$ or $\frac{1}{4}$; of a pictured card, $\frac{12}{52}$ or $\frac{3}{13}$; of a red card, $\frac{26}{52}$ or $\frac{1}{2}$. This last case represents an event which is entirely uncertain, the chances being equal for and against its occurrence. We may get rid of the fractional form by expressing the probability of an event in that mode which is called "the odds"; that is, we may take the numerator to express the chances for, and the difference between the numerator and the denominator to signify the chances against, the occurrence. This rule is an immediate corollary from the first principle as just stated, since the numerator gives the number of favorable chances, and the denominator the total number of them both favorable and unfavorable. Thus, the chance of drawing a pictured card is represented fractionally, as above, by $\frac{3}{13}$, or by the odds as 3 to 10; of a red card, as $\frac{26}{52}$, or 26 to 26, — even chance.

The *improbability* of an occurrence is denoted by the complement of the fraction which expresses its *probability;* that is, the odds are reversed. Thus, as there are six faces to a die, all of which are supposed to be equally likely to come uppermost, the probability of throwing *six* is $\frac{1}{6}$ or 1 to 5; the improbability of it is $1-\frac{1}{6}=\frac{5}{6}$, or 5 to 1. The reason of this rule is obvious; the improbability of one event must be the sum of the probabilities of all the other possible occurrences; and as the total of all the chances, which represents what is sure to happen, is unity, the sum of the probabilities of all the others is found by subtracting the probability of this one from unity. Thus, some one of the six faces *must* come uppermost; this certainty is denoted as 1. Then, as the probability of a six is $\frac{1}{6}$, the chance of some one out of the other five faces, (in other words, the *improbability* of a six,) is $1 - \frac{1}{6} = \frac{5}{6}$. As each of the five other faces has a probability of $\frac{1}{6}$, the sum of their chances, or the improbability of the remaining one, is evidently $\frac{5}{6}$.

The probability of a compound event — that is, of two independent uncertainties happening conjointly — *is ascertained by multiplying the separate chances of the two together*. Thus, the chance of throwing six with one die being $\frac{1}{6}$, and of throwing the same with another die being $\frac{1}{6}$, the chance of obtaining sixes at once with the two dice is $\frac{1}{6} \times \frac{1}{6} = \frac{1}{36}$. This rule, again, is a direct corollary from the first principle as already enounced; for as the number of possible throws with two dice is $6 \times 6 = 36$, (since each face of the one might be combined with either of the six faces of the other,) and as only one of these is favorable, the odds are evidently as 1 to 35. To take another instance: — the chance of drawing a pictured card out of a pack being $\frac{3}{13}$, and of a red card, $\frac{1}{2}$, the probability of having a red pictured card is $\frac{3}{13} \times \frac{1}{2} = \frac{3}{26}$ or $\frac{6}{52}$, as there are six red pictured cards out of the 52 in the pack.

According to this rule, the chance of drawing a red card four times in succession, the card being replaced after each trial, so that the number in the pack shall always be 52, will be $\frac{1}{2} \times \frac{1}{2} \times \frac{1}{2} \times \frac{1}{2} = \frac{1}{16}$, or only 1 to 15. But gamblers often deceive themselves in respect to the application of this rule. As it is so unlikely that a red card will turn up several times in succession, they imagine that, *after* it has thrice thus turned up, the chance of obtaining a black card at the fourth trial is much greater than it was at first.

But it is not so; if the card drawn is always immediately replaced, the probability of drawing a black card after we have drawn a red one at three, or even at a thousand, successive trials, is precisely what it was before the first experiment, — namely, $\frac{1}{2}$. The number of cards being always the same, 26 red and 26 black, the probability of obtaining a red one is always the same, whatever previous experiments may have been made with the same pack. The three experiments already tried have reduced so many uncertainties to certainties, — that is, have thrown them out of the calculation in the Doctrine of Chances, which deals only with uncertain events. *Before* any trial was made, the chance of a red card turning up four times in succession was only $\frac{1}{16}$, each of the four results being then uncertain; *after* three trials, but one event is still an uncertainty, and the probability of its occurrence is $\frac{1}{2}$. We see, then, the folly of the gambler's expectation that his luck must soon turn, because he has had a long series of ill-luck. But all his past trials having been reduced to certainties, his chance of good fortune is now precisely what it was when he began. His only chance of success, after he has had a long series of misfortunes, is to stop playing altogether; and this is also the best thing he can do, if fortune has smiled upon him.

The development of these principles must be left to the mathematician; but a further caution in respect to the application to be made of them by the gambler may be borrowed from Buffon. "If two men," he asks, "were to determine to play for their whole property, what would be the effect of this agreement? The one would only double his fortune, and the other reduce his to naught. What proportion is there between the loss and the gain? The same that there is between *all* and *nothing*. The gain of the one is but a moderate sum; the loss of the other is numerically infinite, and morally so great that the labor of his whole life may not, perhaps, suffice to restore his property." But the fascination of gambling is so great, and the habit of it, when once formed, is so incontrollable, that every one who even begins to play may be regarded as staking his whole fortune upon the issue, and thus as voluntarily subjecting himself to these tremendous odds.

The principal intellectual Causes of Error have been already indirectly considered, inasmuch as they consist in any violation of the rules and methods which have been laid down for the attainment of truth. But the moral Causes which blind our perceptions, warp our judgments, and lead us to accept illusions in the place of truths, deserve some separate notice. Most of these are modifications or consequences of self-love, or rather of that short-sighted selfishness which has more regard for present ease and enjoyment, however trifling, than for future good, however great, if the latter be attainable only by effort and self-denial. Such are prejudices, pride, undue desires, precipitancy, and sloth. All of these are faults of character rather than of intellect; yet they are more frequent sources of delusion, and more formidable obstacles to our mental progress, than can be found in the original weakness and limited range of our faculties, or in the insufficiency of the aids and incitements which nature furnishes for the pursuit of truth. We approach the study of a subject, not as prepared to accept any conclusions to which our researches might naturally lead, but with minds stuffed with preconceived opinions, which pride prevents us from relinquishing after they have been once avowed, or with a bias in favor of some startling consequences of the inquiry, the announcement of which may feed our vanity or establish our reputation. Pride also leads us astray, by inducing us to over-estimate the extent and importance of the acquisitions that we have already made, or to adopt too easily the conclusion that the investigation has reached its limit, and that we already know as much as is capable of being known. I know of no error which is more fatal to progress than the idea that there is no progress to be made,—of no opinion which is more detrimental to improvement than the belief that no improvement is possible. It is true that a low estimate of the extent of our knowledge does not amount to the Christian virtue of humility in the largest sense. It may be, it frequently is, accompanied with a very lofty opinion of the extent of our powers, or the excellence of our natural endowments. But a conceit of ability, bad as it is, is not so injurious to progress as a conceit of knowledge. The one encourages a person to study, by leading him to believe that he can grapple with any subject; the other disposes him to sit down in idleness, under the belief that he has already mastered that subject. Seneca says, *Multos potuisse ad sapientiam pervenire, nisi putassent se pervenisse,*—Many might have obtained wisdom, if they had not supposed that they had already got it.

Moderation in our personal desires, and that earnestness of inquiring purpose which leads not so much to an abnegation as to the entire forgetfulness of self, are more important elements of success in the pursuit of truth than is commonly supposed. The brilliant results of Dr. Franklin's scientific career seem attributable, in a great degree, to his generous disregard of his own fame and standing in the eyes of the public. A lively curiosity, an eye quick at observation, great sagacity in detecting the more occult relations of facts and bearings of experiments, and a mind of incessant and intense activity, were not the only means that enabled him to accomplish so much in science. His attention was not diverted from the object of investigation by any regard for what the world might think of the importance of that object, or of his own merit in obtaining it. The necessary experiments were instituted, not to convince others, but to satisfy himself. The most brilliant results at which he arrived were communicated only in private letters to a few friends, to whom he left the care of publishing them or not, as they saw fit. His theories sat loosely upon him, and he modified or abandoned them, when further observations made it necessary, without dreading the charge of inconsistency, and without shame at confessing a mistake. He was never seduced, by the accidental brilliancy or novelty of one object of inquiry, to pay more attention to it than to another, apparently of a more homely character, but really of equal interest to a philosophical mind. He studied the means of remedying smoky chimneys with as much ardor and industry as he showed in penetrating the secrets of the clouds, and robbing the thunderbolt of its terrors. He formed theories of the earth, and projects for cleaning and lighting the streets of Philadelphia, with equal zeal; and having communicated the former in a private letter to a friend, and urged upon his fellow-citizens the adoption of the latter, he dismissed both from his mind, and pursued with fresh interest a wholly different set of investigations.

The most frequent cause of failure in any pursuit is the lack of earnestness. Habit may impart a kind of mechanical facility in the performance of a given task; but there will be little vigor or energy in the work, if the feelings be not deeply interested in it, so that the result shall be awaited with eager expectation or trembling anxiety. Long-continued labor easily degenerates into mere routine; and then, even though the specific object in view should be obtained, — though a science should be learned or a livelihood got, — there will be no strain of the faculties, and consequently no development of them, — no correction of errors, and therefore no discipline of mind. This is the secret of the great force displayed, and the large results that are often accomplished, by those who are opprobriously termed "men of one idea,"— persons who have concentrated their attention upon one object, and who pursue it, regardless of everything else, with all the strength and the bitterness of fanaticism. Half an hour of strenuous exertion is worth a week of mechanical and desultory labor. Too often we dawdle over the business of life, instead of taking it up with eagerness, and prosecuting it to the end as a work of love. There is all the difference in the world between an active mind and a passive one; between earnestly hunting after truth, and only swallowing knowledge inertly, as it is poured into the memory by a teacher or a book, and just as quickly washed out again. We are made what we are, experts or dolts, much more by our acquired habits than by success or failure in the attainment of knowledge. Aim not so much to be learned, as to be able to learn; one truly wise man is worth a hundred erudite pedants. The study of Logic itself will do little to cultivate our power of reasoning, or to improve our habits of thought, except indirectly, by the effort which is necessary for the mastery of its principles, and by the endeavor to verify or correct them in the course of our subsequent researches. What we really need to attain is Logical power, and a knowledge of the science of Logic is useful so far only as it is conducive to such attainment.

Among the occasions for the use of this power, that to which the gravest responsibility is attached is the formation of our opinions. Properly speaking, we must all begin life without any opinions which we can call our own by any better right than that of passive inheritance or unconscious inoculation. We have probably imbibed most of them just as we took the measles or the whooping-cough in infancy, from accidental contact with others. We are Whig, Democrat, or Republican, conservative or radical, — we go to the Episcopal, Presbyterian, or Congregationalist church, — simply because parents and friends thought so, or did so, formerly. Now, in one respect, this is all right and just as it should be. It is fortunate, both for ourselves and the world, that we begin life with a set of provisional opinions already formed, not by us, but for us. This *vis inertiæ* of opinion, this tendency of the human mind to move in the ruts where others have preceded it, is the great conservative principle of society, all that keeps us from intellectual and social anarchy. Without it, all the wise men who have been before us would have lived in vain, and society would drift along helplessly, without keel or rudder. If we were not willing to accept opinions before we are able to form them for ourselves, — ay, and to cling to them with the fondness which early association imparts, — half of the time we should act at random, and the other half extravagantly and foolishly.

But we cannot pass through life merely as docile children; and our first duty as men — at any rate, as educated and thinking men — is to begin the great work of fashioning our own creeds in politics, religion, philosophy, and social economy. When we have attained our majority, we have become as accountable for our opinions as for our conduct. A wise man, however, might hesitate before going as far as Descartes, who urges us to begin by doubting everything; his advice is, to take up every question, as it were, *de novo*, with a determination not to accept any answer to it the correctness of which is not made out by evidence satisfactory to our own minds, and elicited by our own inquiries. A safer course, as it seems to me, is to begin, not by discarding all our previous opinions, but by examining the foundations on which they rest. There is just as much of prejudice and rashness in presuming that they are all false, as in believing, previous to inquiry, that they are all true. Do not ask, Why may it not be otherwise? but rather, Why is it so? The presumption is in favor of the received doctrines in any science, until good reasons are made to appear for doubting or denying them. But the duty of inquiry, in order to ascertain whether there are such reasons, is one which always exists, and which opens the largest and fairest field for the exercise and development of our powers of thought. Only by such exercise can we hope to perfect our knowledge of the principles of Logic, and to make that knowledge of use to ourselves and others. "We employ reason," said the Port-Royalist logicians, "as an instrument for acquiring the sciences, whereas we ought to use the sciences as a means of perfecting our reason, correctness of judgment and accuracy of thought being infinitely more valuable than all the speculative knowledge which we can obtain from the best-established sciences. Wise men, therefore, ought to engage in the study of the sciences only so far as they conduce to this end, and to make them only the training-ground, and not the field for the regular employment, of their mental powers."

THE END.

Cambridge: Stereotyped and Printed by Welch, Bigelow, & Co.

www.ingramcontent.com/pod-product-compliance
Lightning Source LLC
Chambersburg PA
CBHW022109300426
44117CB00007B/641